EXPLORER'S GUIDE

NEW MEXICO

By

NEW MEXICO

SHARON NIEDERMAN

THE COUNTRYMAN PRESS
A division of W. W. Norton & Company
Independent Publishers Since 1923

Also by Sharon Niederman:

Explorer's Guide Santa Fe & Taos

Return to Abo: A Novel of the Southwest

*A Quilt of Words: Women's Diaries, Letters & Original
Accounts of Life in the Southwest 1860–1960*

New Mexico's Tasty Traditions: Recollections, Recipes and Photos

Signs & Shrines: Spiritual Journeys Across New Mexico

*New Mexico Farm Table Cookbook: 100 Homegrown Recipes
from the Land of Enchantment*

For information about permission to reproduce selections from this book, write to
Permissions, The Countryman Press, 500 Fifth Avenue, New York, NY 10110

For information about special discounts for bulk purchases, please contact
W. W. Norton Special Sales at specialsales@wwnorton.com or 800-233-4830

Manufacturing by Versa Press
Book design by Chris Welch
Production manager: Devon Zahn

The Countryman Press
www.countrymanpress.com

A division of W. W. Norton & Company, Inc.
500 Fifth Avenue, New York, NY 10110
www.wwnorton.com

978-1-68268-190-9 (pbk.)

10 9 8 7 6 5 4 3 2 1

The Truth We Prefer

The young woman who opened a gift shop
Selling glass bead earrings, Mexican imports, replica flour sack aprons
Offering Dia de los Muertos workshops
Tells me this place was a stagecoach stop
No ghosts she knows of
But her aunt remembers stories
That doorway is narrow, watch your head
The real estate office across the street was a coffin factory, you know
The church was complete, except for the bell
So the women gave their silver
Scant history, legend perhaps, the truth we prefer
But it is true, isn't it
A hundred years ago, longer
The farmers from Alameda
And those from Los Griegos
Processed after Mass on San Lorenzo Day
And wherever they met held a fiesta, right here in this street?

—Sharon Niederman

EXPLORE WITH US!

Explorer's Guide New Mexico is broken down into sections representing different areas of the state. Because of the state's size, most of these geographic sections are sub-divided into "mini-chapters" for easy navigation. Each chapter opens with a general introduction touching on the history and highlights of the area, and then continues with information on destinations, accommodations, and restaurants that guide you to the best of New Mexico.

I focus on independent venues for two reasons. Most readers are familiar with easily found, well-advertised franchise food and lodgings. More important, independent businesses, such as mom-and-pop cafés and vintage motels, are often undiscovered and more likely to deliver an authentic New Mexican experience. While you might have some initial reluctance to try an unknown restaurant or lodging, those in these pages are carefully vetted. I have done my best to share my knowledge of the state based on more than two decades of traveling and writing about its cuisine, history, culture and customs, architecture, and natural beauty. I want to show you my favorite places and give you an honest appraisal. I have curated available choices to bring you an extraordinary travel adventure. All sampling is done anonymously and, unlike many "influencers" out there, I do not receive perks in exchange for good reviews.

We have done our best to keep the information contained in these pages as current as possible. If you find a brilliant new recommendation, send it our way.

New Mexico offers rich sense of place in its varied geography, terrain, long history, and complex cultures. Even if you have traveled here many times, there is always more to learn. May you enjoy the discovery, be transformed by it, and vow to return soon.

GUIDANCE Guidance lists such entities as chambers of commerce, visitor centers, and public land managers that you can refer to for information on the area.

GETTING THERE Getting There tells you the best routes to take and what means of transportation are available to get you there.

GETTING AROUND Getting Around lists means of public transportation or shuttles, where they are available.

MEDICAL EMERGENCY Medical Emergency lists hospitals and/or clinics. Dialing 911 is also an option at all times.

TO SEE To See lists attractions and points of interest you may want to visit, including museums, historic sites, scenic drives, and more.

TO DO To Do features key activities available in each area.

LODGING Lodging will give you ideas of where to find unique and consistently good places to stay, even in more remote areas.

WHERE TO EAT Where to Eat lists venues that serve dependably good food. There are two categories here: "Dining Out," the better restaurants, and "Eating Out," the more casual options. Please let us know if the food or service is up to the standard we expect—places do change hands and have off nights.

ENTERTAINMENT Entertainment gives suggestions on theater, music, and relaxing in the evening.

SELECTIVE SHOPPING Selective Shopping points you in the right direction for shopping, particularly for wares that are characteristic of a place.

SPECIAL EVENTS Special Events is a month-by-month compendium of the most important annual events and festivals in each community.

Please send any comments or corrections to:

Explorer's Guide Editor
The Countryman Press
A division of W. W. Norton & Company
500 Fifth Avenue
New York, NY 10110

KEY TO SYMBOLS

⚭ The wedding rings symbol appears beside facilities that frequently serve as venues for weddings and civil unions.

🍴 The special-value symbol appears next to lodgings and restaurants that combine high quality and moderate prices.

🖉 The kids-alert symbol appears next to lodgings, restaurants, activities, and shops of special appeal to youngsters.

🐾 The dog-paw symbol appears next to lodgings that accept pets (usually with a reservation and deposit) as of press time.

♿ The wheelchair symbol appears next to lodgings, restaurants, and attractions that are partially or fully handicapped accessible.

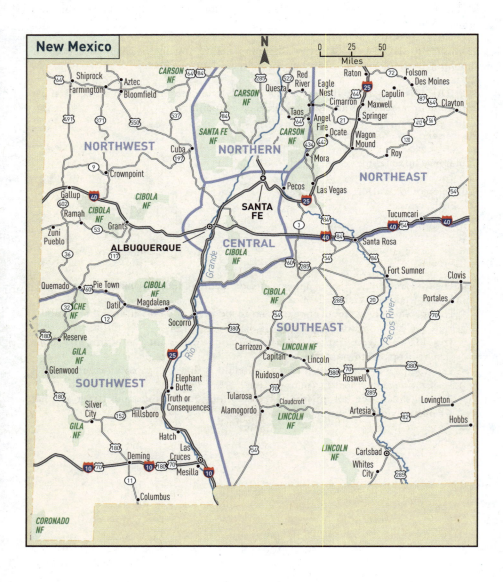

CONTENTS

MAPS

INTRODUCTION

The first time I saw New Mexico was on a road trip with a school buddy many years ago. We drove down I-25 from Boulder, where I was attending graduate school at the University of Colorado. It was nighttime when we crossed Raton Pass into northern New Mexico. I had never seen so much empty space, and the expanse made me nervous.

"Why are there no people or lights out there? What's wrong?" I asked my friend as I experienced a mild panic attack.

A native of this place, she laughed. "You mean where are all the crowds and traffic? The pollution and sirens?"

A few years ago, I was showing my well-traveled East Coast cousin around northern New Mexico. We drove from Albuquerque to Ojo Caliente Hot Springs.

She was visiting from New Jersey, the most densely populous state in the US. As we turned out of Española onto the road north, she looked at me and asked, "Where are you taking me?," with a catch in her voice. "This is the middle of nowhere!"

Now it was my turn to laugh. "No," I replied. "The middle of nowhere is the gas station in Vaughn where the wind always blows." As an interesting footnote, this cousin subsequently moved west, as soon as she retired.

To paraphrase Governor Lew Wallace, who presided over the state during the tumultuous Lincoln County War era of the 1860s, "Calculations based on experience elsewhere do not work in New Mexico." Governor Wallace, who hailed from Indiana, made that observation from his vantage point in the Palace of the Governors in Santa Fe, while writing his classic novel *Ben Hur* and attempting to bring Billy the Kid to justice.

Governor Wallace may have been moved to make his observation because New Mexico operates in its own time zone. While not exactly the land of *mañana*, it remains the land of *poco tiempe*, or "pretty soon," just as originally characterized by writer Charles L. Lummis in 1893.

New Mexico remains one place, perhaps the only place, in the United States where its oldest cultures are truly alive. They have cohabited and adapted to the impacts of outsiders—including twenty-first-century urbanization—for centuries, and they continue to practice their languages, religions, and lifeways. The nineteen Indian pueblos, each a sovereign nation with distinct language, customs, and ceremonies, Navajo and Apache nations, Hispanic villages, and ranching towns with homesteader legacies persist. Indian ruins and mission churches, the graveyards and the wealth of vernacular architecture, are no more than a drive just down the road from virtually anyplace in the state.

Speaking of roads, despite the fact that New Mexico was, and is, crisscrossed by many of the great trails across the continent—the 1800-mile north–south Camino Real de Tierra Adentro span from Mexico City to the farthest reach of New Spain, Santa Fe; the east–west Santa Fe Trail trade route from Independence, Missouri, to Santa Fe; Route 66 from Chicago to Los Angeles; and the first paved intercontinental highway, the Ocean to Ocean Highway, US 60 (each bringing goods, ideas, visitors, colonizers, and eventual residents)—somehow the state remains remote. Today, even if you're traveling on the north–south I-25 corridor, or the east–west I-40, or any of the state roads that meander through the quadrants between, traces of the old roads remain. Many of the sites named in this book will assist that process of assembling the fragments of history.

New Mexico's cuisine, festivals, arts, ancient customs, and history remain accessible, constant, and exciting. Consequently, the exotic, what one hungers for in planning a trip to a foreign land, may be experienced here by the explorer without so much as a visa.

New Mexico remains in its own time frame, with one foot planted in yesterday and the other in no hurry to get to tomorrow. Roads may not be marked as clearly as you would like. You may receive such instructions as, "Turn left at the dip, then right at the big cottonwood," so detailed maps are necessary. Your GPS may mislead you. Anyone can get lost, so bring water and don't let your gas tank go below half-full. The altitude really can cause discomfort, so be sure to adjust before hiking Wheeler Peak or the Aspen Vista Trail, stay hydrated, and remember that in addition to ibuprofen, chocolate is said to help with altitude adjustment. Naturally, dark chocolate works best. Alcohol packs a bigger punch while acclimating.

WEATHERED ADVERTISEMENTS SPEAK OF BYGONE DAYS ALONG ROUTE 66

Outsiders may not find efficiency, public transportation, speed of service, and promptly returned messages they are accustomed to. Hours posted do not always align with hours kept. New Mexico was the forty-seventh state admitted to the Union, in 1912. Awareness that everything takes longer than expected is probably a good idea to adopt to avoid elevated blood pressure. In Santa Fe, rapid employee turnover means a likelihood of encountering inexperienced service people. If you are prone to frustration in these matters, it is probably best to book a lodging that provides experienced concierge services.

Therefore, it is smart to call a destination ahead of time. Do not assume it will be open or that it even still exists. Every effort has been made to ensure the reliability of establishments, but there is no guarantee that it has not gone out of business or moved

If you love the outdoors, it is all here: Hiking, fishing, skiing, snowboarding, (when there is sufficient snow), river rafting, golfing, birding, and zip lining. The beauty of the night skies and many superb dark sky locations, the fun of discovery in ghost towns; the power inherent in the great ruins of Chaco Canyon or the Gila Cliff Dwellings; the back road adventure of a finding a café that takes pride in serving real home cooking, with homemade pie and real mashed potatoes; the freedom of driving down an open two-lane road without billboards under a wide-open sky make this journey memorable and worthwhile.

When to Come

There really is no bad time to come to New Mexico, no real "off-season." It is up to you to plan your visit to coincide with your interests, which may be skiing Taos in winter, attending Santa Fe Indian Market in summer, or soaring with the Albuquerque Balloon Fiesta in fall. You can be sure that if you are planning to come during a highly popular event, however, that lodging rates will be pricier, and advance reservation times will be longer. The advantage to a perceived "off-season" time, say, October–November in northern New Mexico, or January–February in southern New Mexico, is, of course, less competition for rooms and tables. You will have the place more to yourself. The beauty of the place is always present in any season, though, and there are always plenty of sights to see and events to attend.

A Few Interesting Facts

New Mexico remains the fifth-largest state in land area, boasting a population of 2,059,179. Most of that populace is centered in the biggest cities: Albuquerque, Rio Rancho, Santa Fe, and Las Cruces.

The State Plant is the yucca; the State Tree is the piñon; the State Gem is the turquoise; the State Tie is the bolo; the State Motto is "Crescit eundo" (It grows as it goes);

HORSE AND BUGGY RIDES AT EL RANCHO DE LAS GOLONDRINAS, A PRESERVED HISTORIC HACIENDA

offers a daily nonstop flight between the New York area and Albuquerque.

ACCESSIBILITY Please contact the **Center for Development & Disability Information in New Mexico** (800-552-8195) concerning accessibility at restaurants and lodgings, and wheelchair rentals.

BUS SERVICE **Greyhound Bus Lines** (800-231-2222; www.greyhound.com) delivers travelers to New Mexico. To travel between Albuquerque Airport and Santa Fe, contact **Sandia Shuttle Express** (505-474-5696; www.sandiashuttlecom).

REST AREAS To download a map of New Mexico rest areas, go to dot.state .nm.us/content/dam/nmdot/travel /maps/Rest_area05.pdf or www.interstate restareas.com/new-mexico/. Rest areas are maintained along I-40 and I-25, as well as US 285.

ROAD REPORTS Go to nmroads.com for the most current weather and road condition reports throughout the state.

SCENIC BYWAYS The state's twenty-five designated scenic byways, including eight of America's 126 scenic byways within the state, celebrating its diverse beauty and rich history, can be traced at www. newmexico.org/parks-and-byways. Among the most celebrated is the **Route 66 National Scenic Byway** (www.rt66 nm.org).

TRAINS New Mexico Rail Runner Express (866-795-7245; www.nmrail runner.com) commuter trains run daily between Belen and Santa Fe, stopping in downtown Albuquerque and elsewhere; and Amtrak's *Southwest Chief* makes one stop each day, both ways, between Chicago and Los Angeles, in Raton, Las Vegas, Lamy (Santa Fe), Albuquerque, and Gallup. The narrow-gauge train ride on the **Cumbres Toltec Scenic Railroad** (888-286-2737; www.cumbrestoltec.com)

between Chama and Antonito, Colorado is one of the best ways to experience the beauty and history of the land.

General Information

AREA CODES New Mexico has two area codes. Area code 505 works for Albuquerque, Santa Fe, Espanola, Gallup, and Los Alamos; 575 is for the rest of the state. You may encounter some irregularities in coverage, so if one does not work, try the other.

CELL PHONES Only hands-free devices are permitted while driving in Santa Fe, Albuquerque, and Taos. You will be ticketed for talking or texting on a mobile device while driving.

CITIES The state's largest cities are Albuquerque, estimated at nearly a million, then Las Cruces, Rio Rancho, and Santa Fe. For information on cultural and outdoor activities in Albuquerque, dial 311 or go to www.itsatrip.org/everyday. For activities in Santa Fe, go to www .santafe.org. The state capital, the oldest government seat in the United States, is Santa Fe.

CLIMATE Sunshine, sunshine, and more sunshine is what you'll find in New Mexico, with an average of 256 days of sunshine a year. Even most rainy days have at least some sunshine; plus, after it snows, the sun usually melts it off pretty quickly. That said, "If you don't like the weather, just wait a half-hour and it will change," is the standard wisdom. Whether driving or in the outdoors, be sure to be prepared for unexpected temperature drops and precipitation by dressing in layers according to the season. A perfectly sunny summer morning will likely bring an afternoon thunderstorm. Expect temperatures to vacillate by 40 degrees during the day. The state is arid to semiarid, with about 9 inches of rain per year.

Emergency: 911
To report drunk or dangerous driving (on your mobile phone): #DWI
Indian Pueblo Cultural Center: 866-855-7902; www.indianpueblo.org
Information on accessibility: www.newmexico.gov/accessibility.aspx
B&Bs: www.nmbba.org/index.php
Information about New Mexico: www.newmexico.org
Information about Santa Fe: www.santafe.org
$25 bargain pass to museums and state monuments: www.newmexicoculture.org
Fairgrounds: www.countyfairgrounds.net/newmexico
Fishing: www.wildlife.state.nm.us/recreation/fishing
Motels: www.motelguide.com
Parks: www.nmparks.com
Road conditions: 800-432-4269; www.nmroads.com
New Mexico RV campgrounds: www.rv-clubs.us/newmexico_rv_campgrounds.html
Scenic byways: www.newmexicoscenicbyways.org
Skiing: www.skinewmexico.com
State parks: 888-NMPARKS or 888-667-2757; www.nmparks.com
Wine: www.winecountrynm.com

GENERAL INFORMATION

COUNTIES New Mexico has thirty-three counties and 102 towns.

EMERGENCIES Call 911 for immediate help, or contact the **New Mexico State Police** (505-827-9300; 505-827-3476) or **Search and Rescue Resource Officer**, 4491 Cerrillos Road, Santa Fe (505-827-9228; Robert.Rodgers@state.nm.us). **Drunk Busters DWI Hotline** (877-DWI-HALT or 877-394-4258) is a toll-free hotline; #394 (or keypad letters DWI) is the convenience key for cell phones.

MAPS The *New Mexico Road & Recreation Atlas* (Benchmark Maps, $29.95) may be ordered at newmexico.mybig commerce.com.

PUBLIC LANDS New Mexico contains more than 77,766,400 acres of national lands, including thirteen national parks, two national monuments, numerous national forests, and about 18 million acres of land administered by the BLM; as well as state-owned lands, including a dozen state parks, a state recreation area, and numerous state historic sites.

SMOKING New Mexico is a smoke-free state.

SPEED LIMITS AND SEAT BELTS Seat belts are mandatory. If you are stopped and not wearing a seat belt, expect a minimum $40 fine. The speed limit on the interstates is 75 mph and lower within city limits. The speed limit on state roads is 55–60 mph. Be wary of driving through small towns, such as Cimarron and Eagle Nest, which have posted speed limits of 35 mph. Exceed posted limits and you will be ticketed.

STATISTICS With a land area of 121,599 square miles, including 234 square miles of inland water, New Mexico is the fifth-largest state. The highest point is Wheeler Peak, at 13,161 feet. Lowest point is Red Bluff Reservoir, southeast of Carlsbad, at 2,842 feet. The population of New Mexico is 2,085,538: approximately 47 percent Hispanic and 10 percent Native American.

TRAVEL INFORMATION The New Mexico Department of Tourism operates four strategically located visitor centers around the state. Here you can pick up free brochures, maps, and travel advice. They usually offer coffee, restrooms, picnic areas, and Wi-Fi. They can be found in Manuelito, Glenrio, Lordsburg, and Santa Fe. Be sure to pick up the very handy free New Mexico Vacation Guide, also available online.

Attractions

ADMISSION FEES If an admission fee is $7 or less, it's simply listed as "fee." Fees greater than $7 are spelled out. Although fees were accurate when this book went to press, keep in mind that yearly increases are likely, especially for larger attractions and theme parks.

ARCHAEOLOGY Several of North America's great ruins are located in New Mexico: cliff dwellings at Bandelier National Monument, Chaco Culture National Historical Park, Gila Cliff Dwellings National Monument, Salmon Ruins, and Aztec Ruins National Monument. Other outstanding examples of New Mexico's built cultural history are Salinas Pueblo Missions National Monument and Jemez State Monument, as well as petroglyph sites at Three Rivers Petroglyph Site, Petroglyph National Monument, and many others that provide illumination of the ancient past. Going even further back in time, evidence of earliest North American habitation may be found at the Clovis Man site at Blackwater Draw.

ART GALLERIES AND STUDIOS Certain areas of towns are known for their high concentration of art galleries, such as Canyon Road in Santa Fe, Sudderth Drive in Ruidoso, Old Town and Nob Hill neighborhoods in Albuquerque, and Yankie Street in Silver City. In addition to galleries, however, several towns, including Albuquerque, Las Cruces, and Truth or Consequences, offer monthly gallery tours. During fall and spring, artists open their studios for tours along the High Road, in Dixon, Abiquiu, Pilar, El Rito, Corrales, and Placitas, and many other places. For information the arts, please go to www.newmexico.org/art -and-culture.

ARTIST STUDIO TOURS For a list of open studio tours by date, go to www .collectorsguide.com/fa/fa103.html.

FIBER ARTS **The New Mexico Fiber Arts Trail** (www.nmfiberarts.org) will lead you to shops and galleries where you can purchase fiber, see the work of locals, and learn the arts of weaving, felting and more. Notable fiber arts resources in New Mexico include the Taos Wool Festival, Victory Alpaca Ranch, and fiber arts galleries galore in Taos and Arroyo Seco.

GAMING Numerous Las Vegas–style casinos, operated primarily by Native American tribes, exist throughout the state. Some of the better-known gaming resorts include Inn of the Mountain Gods near Ruidoso and Buffalo Thunder north of Santa Fe. While casinos are clustered around Albuquerque and Santa Fe, you can find them also along I-40, such as Route 66 Casino and Sky City Casino, as well as in Dulce. Taos Mountain Casino is the only smoke-free casino in the state. Horse racing takes place at Ruidoso Downs, which hosts the All-American Futurity, the richest quarter horse event in the country, runs on Labor Day and during the State Fair, held in early September. **Sunland Park** (newmexico.casino city.com) also has a racetrack and casino, The Downs at Albuquerque, which features a casino and horse racing, is centrally located at Expo, NM, a.k.a. the State Fairgrounds.

HOT SPRINGS Aaah. Mineral hot springs in New Mexico include Ojo Caliente Mineral Springs Resort & Spa, Ten Thousand Waves Japanese-style baths,

Faywood Hot Springs, Gila Hot Springs, Jemez Springs, and, of course, Truth or Consequences. Undeveloped hot springs may be found in the Jemez National Forest and the Taos area. Contact visitor centers listed in this guide for specific information.

SPACE HISTORY Astronomical destinations include the Very Large Array, featured in the movie *Contact*; the New Mexico Museum of Space History; and White Sands Missile Range Museum, also in Alamogordo. A reconstruction of Robert Goddard's rocket workshop is found at the Roswell Museum and Art Center. **Follow the Sun, Inc.** (505-897-2886; ftstours.com) offers tours of the Spaceport facility outside Truth or Consequences. The **New Mexico Space Trail** (www.nmspacemuseum.org/documents /SpaceTrails_map.pdf) charts 52 historic sites across the state UFOs are celebrated annually at the **Roswell UFO Festival** (575-624-7704; www.ufofestival roswell.com) held during the Fourth of July weekend.

ZOOS The state's premier zoo is located at the **Albuquerque BioPark** (505-768-2000; www.cabq.gov/culturalservices /biopark). Alamogordo is home to **Alameda Park Zoo** (575-439-4290), the Southwest's oldest zoo; and Carlsbad, to **Living Desert Zoo and Gardens State Park** (575-887-5516; www.nmparks.com).

Outdoor Activities

BALLOONING **Albuquerque International Balloon Fiesta**, attracting over 500 hot air balloons from around the world, held annually the first two weeks of October, is the state's premier event (888-422-7277 or 505-821-1000; www .balloonfiesta.com). Many other towns, including Chama, Taos, Angel Fire, Raton, and Gallup, host balloon rallies various times throughout the year.

BASEBALL Albuquerque's Triple-A baseball team, the **Isotopes** (855-360-3113; www.milb.com/index.jsp?sid=t342), a Pacific Coast minor league, play April–September baseball in the beautiful stadium is a big-time event.

BICYCLING For events, clubs, links, roads, and more, please go to www .nmcycling.org.

BIRDING With over 500 birds on New Mexico's list, the state, with its mountain to desert to wetlands ecosystems offers one of the largest counts in the United States. Especially fruitful are the Orilla Verde Trail on the Rio Grande, Bosque del Apache National Monument, Sandia Crest, and Randall Davey Audubon Center & Sanctuary, Santa Fe. Please visit www.wildlife.state.nm.us/recreation/ birding/index.htm or nm.audubon.org/ birding-trails-new-mexico for more information.

BOATING AND WATER SPORTS Visit Elephant Butte Lake, Heron Lake, Conchas Dam, Chama River, Navajo Lake, San Juan River, Cochiti Dam, rafting the Taos Box on the Rio Grande or floating the Chama.

FISHING New Mexico boasts an abundance of lake, stream, and river fishing. Holy grails of fly-fishing are the Quality Waters of the San Juan River near Farmington and the San Antonio River in the Valles Caldera National Preserve. Cimarron Canyon, the Rio Grande Gorge near Taos, and Elephant Butte Lake also offer fishing opportunities. Please visit www .wildlife.state.nm.us/ for fishing reports and license requirements.

GOLF COURSES Year-round opportunities for golfing exist here, in desert and high-altitude conditions. Please see the individual chapters for specific courses, or visit www.golfnewmexico.com.

GUIDES AND OUTFITTERS To discover outdoor adventures in New

A FEW KEY DATES IN NEW MEXICO HISTORY

1540: Francisco Coronado searches for the Seven Cities of Cibola through New Mexico.

1598: Juan de Oñate establishes the first permanent settlement at San Juan Pueblo

1680: Pueblo Revolt drives Spanish governors and Franciscan fathers out of New Mexico.

1692: Diego de Vargas's Reconquest of New Mexico

1821: Mexico gains control of New Mexico and Santa Fe Trail opens.

1846: Stephen Kearney's "Army of the West" gains occupation of New Mexico making it a territory of the United States.

1848: Treaty of Guadalupe Hidalgo expands borders of US.

1879: Railroad arrives.

1912: New Mexico becomes the 47th state.

1926: US Route 66 goes through New Mexico.

1937: US Route 66 realignment.

1945: The atom bomb is tested successfully at Trinity Site.

Mexico, visit www.newmexico.org/outdoor. Reliable and experienced guides also advertise in *New Mexico Magazine*'s annual *Vacation Guide*.

HIKING For information about hiking, go to www.explorenm.com/hikes/.

HUNTING An abundance of big game—elk, mule deer, pronghorn, moose, and more—as well as smaller game, such as sage grouse, wild turkey, rabbit, and others, draw hunters to New Mexico. Once-in-a-lifetime nonnative ibex permits are granted by lottery. Nonresident big game hunting licenses are issued by a lottery system; hunters must apply far in advance of the season. Please visit the hunting section of the **New Mexico Game and Fish Department** website (www.wildlife.state.nm.us) for license requirements.

ROCK CLIMBING For rock-climbing opportunities by region, visit www.rockclimbing.com/routes/North_America/United_States/New_Mexico/.

SNOW SPORTS With eight alpine ski areas and four Nordic parks, New Mexico offers plenty of ski adventure and family fun. Visit www.skinewmexico.com and www.newmexico.org/ski for more information. *Cross-Country Skiing in Northern New Mexico*, by Kay Matthews, remains the most thorough guide to forest and park trails.

Lodging

Lodgings described in this book are focused away from national-brand hotels and motels and more on each region's unique offerings, such as bed & breakfasts, lodges, family-owned and -operated budget motels, or some other sort of distinctive facilities.

BED & BREAKFASTS From rustic to regal, there's a B&B for every taste and occasion in New Mexico. Taos and Santa Fe have a surfeit of these lodgings, while you may need to hunt a little harder while on the road or in more remote locations. **New Mexico Bed and Breakfast Association** (505-766-5380; www.nmbba.org) is a good way to find approved and inspected lodgings throughout the state.

CAMPGROUNDS To make camping reservations at any of the state parks, please contact newmexicostateparks.reserveamerica.com/ to purchase a New Mexico Annual Camping or Day Use Pass.

RETREAT CENTERS New Mexico has many centers for retreat, contemplation, and education. Among the better-known such places are the Benedictine Monastery of Christ in the Desert and Ghost Ranch, both near Abiquiu; the Mandala Center in Des Moines; the Center for Action and Contemplation in Albuquerque; the Lama Foundation north of Taos, which hosts high-mountain solitary hermitage retreats; and Upaya Zen Center in Santa Fe. It is possible to arrange stays to accommodate your situation, from a couple of days to weeks.

RV PARKS Visit www.rv-clubs.us/new mexico_rv_campgrounds.html for a directory, by region, of New Mexico's RV parks and campgrounds.

Food and Drink

CHILE The main item on the menu is chile—never chili. Starting in late July and through September, the fragrance of roasting green chile, the fundamental ingredient in New Mexico cuisine, the fiery, spicy flavor that so many find addictive, may be enjoyed everywhere in the state, in stews, over enchiladas, and topping off cheeseburgers. Later on, when it ripens into its red stage, it is harvested and dried. Hatch calls itself the "Chile Capital of the World," and is famous for green chilies. The best of the old landrace red chile comes from Chimayo, but it is becoming harder to find.

CUISINE A fusion of Native American, Mexican, and Spanish cuisine, using such local ingredients as beans, chilies, and corn, produces an amazing variety of flavors. Such aromatics, spices, and herbs as garlic, cumin, and oregano add to the mix. In addition, waves of immigrants and pioneers have tossed their cooking heritage into the stewpot: Albuquerque abounds with Vietnamese and Thai restaurants and cafés, fine Italian

and French dining is available, and you will find plenty of western-style barbecue and Route 66–style home cooking. Santa Fe chefs produce dishes fit for the world stage, and the farm-to-table movement has everyone excited.

CULINARY EVENTS Hatch Chile Festival, Wagon Mound Bean Day, Pie Town Pie Festival, Santa Fe Wine & Chile Fiesta, Roswell's Chile & Cheese Festival, Silver City's New Mexico Tamal Festival, Rio Rancho's Pork & Brew State BBQ Championship, Southwest Chocolate and Coffee Festival, and National Fiery Foods & BBQ Show are some of the better-known feasts open to the public. During New Mexico Restaurant Week, held three weeks in late February–March, restaurants in major cities offer special bargains well worth taking advantage of.

MICROBREWERIES Contact the **New Mexico Brewers Guild** (nmbeer.com) for information on the state's two dozen independent microbreweries and taprooms. Here you can find such distinctive brews as green chile beer and Pancho Villa Stout.

RESTAURANTS This state is memorable for its cuisine. From four-star restaurants in Santa Fe to mom-and-pop cafés on back roads, to Route 66 nostalgic dining, New Mexico has a venue for every taste. Each chapter is loaded with interesting dining opportunities that have been tested by the author for value, service, and culinary skill. You won't find chain restaurants listed here. To trace the New Mexico Green Chile Cheeseburger Trail and map your adventures, go to www.newmexico.org/culinary. Check out the Margarita Trail, the Burrito Byway, and the Ale Trail.

WINERIES AND WINE-FESTIVALS As the oldest wine-producing state, New Mexico has experienced a renaissance of winemaking and now produces excellent bottles. More than forty wineries may be found scattered throughout just about every part of the state. Most offer tastings at selected times. Special events featuring wine include Memorial Day weekend's Southern New Mexico Wine Festival, Fourth of July weekend's Santa Fe Wine Festival at Ranchos de las Golondrinas, and the Las Cruces Harvest Festival. Contact www.winecountry nm.com for a complete, free map, including drive times, of New Mexico wineries.

History and Culture

CRYPTO-JEWS Jews who fled the Spanish Inquisition in 1492 looked for safety around the world. It is said that many of New Mexico's founding families, some of whom entered the region in 1598 with conquistador Juan de Oñate, and those who returned to Santa Fe 1692, were actually Spaniards of the Jewish faith, Sephardic Jews, who practiced Catholicism in public and Judaism privately. Many descendants of these families have been practicing Catholics for generations; a recent generation has discovered Jewish roots.

CULTURAL ATLAS **The Cultural Atlas of New Mexico, Mobile App** (available for free download from Google Play or iTunes) is an interactive mobile app that puts New Mexico's historic and cultural points of interest in the palm of your hand. Designed by the New Mexico Department of Cultural Affairs, the Cultural Atlas helps users to plan vacations, weekend getaways, and day trips across New Mexico utilizing simple search functions.

CULTURE PASS The **New Mexico CulturePass** is one of the great deals for visitors: For $30, it allows admission to fourteen museums and monuments. Visit or call 505-476-1125; www.newmexico culture.org. It is also possible to walk into a public library and borrow a family pass.

DINOSAURS The best places to encounter remains of or learn about dinosaurs are the Museum of Natural History and Science in Albuquerque; Mesalands Dinosaur Museum in Tucumcari; and Florence Hawley Ellis Museum of Anthropology at Ghost Ranch, where the state fossil, the Coelophysis, the "littlest dinosaur," was found. The Dinosaur Trackway at Clayton Lake State Park is the Western Hemisphere's second-richest site of prints, and the Las Cruces Museum of Nature & Science showcases recent finds from the southern part of the state.

GENEALOGY is a popular activity in New Mexico. The Garrey Carruthers State Library and Archives in Santa Fe is a center of genealogical research. The Main Library in Albuquerque, downtown at 5th and Copper, also has a fine special collections genealogy center. Get started at www.genealogybranches.com/new mexico.html.

HISTORIC MARKERS For a region-by-region guide to New Mexico's historic markers, including the program for Women's Historic Markers, please visit www.nmhistoricmarkers.org/ historicmarkers.php.

NATIVE AMERICANS Each of New Mexico's nineteen Indian Pueblos is a sovereign nation. The Navajo and the Apache also have their own reservation lands, where their legal systems and police preside. The main contact for Indian feast days and celebrations open the public is the **Indian Pueblo Cultural Center in Albuquerque** (www .indianpueblo.org/19pueblos/). Three special events showcasing Native dancing, arts, foods, and culture are the Gallup Inter-Tribal Indian Ceremonial, Taos Pueblo Pow Wow, and Gathering of Nations Pow Wow in Albuquerque. The words "Native American" and "Indian" are used interchangeably.

PUEBLO ETIQUETTE

- When visiting a pueblo, think of your visit as if you were an invited guest in someone's home.
- Inquire ahead of time about visitor's hours. Remember that some pueblos are closed to outsiders on certain days for religious activities.
- Drive slowly.
- Never bring drugs or alcoholic beverages to a pueblo.
- For your comfort, bring folding chairs to watch the dances—and do not assume folding chairs occupied by local families are available to you.
- Do not walk into or onto a kiva (a ceremonial structure sometimes, but not always, circular).
- Follow the tour leader and remember homes, kivas, and ceremonies typically are not open to visitors. However, if you are invited into someone's home to eat, it is considered impolite to refuse. It is also considered polite to eat and leave promptly so others may enter and eat.
- Do not step on or cross the plaza or area where dances are being performed—instead, walk on the perimeter.
- Applause is not appropriate at dances.
- No photography, recordings, or sketching is permitted, in general, at events open to the public. Observe each pueblo's regulations on use of cameras, tape recorders, and drawing. If you want to photograph a pueblo resident, ask permission first and offer a donation to the family. In some cases, such as at Taos Pueblo, it is possible to purchase a photography permit, so long as photography is only for personal use. Be aware that in recent years, violations of photography and video rules have threatened to restrict public attendance at ceremonial dances.
- Any publication or public use of information about pueblo activities must receive prior approval from the tribal government.
- No pets are allowed.
- Questions about ceremonies, dances, and rituals are considered rude. For complex historical reasons, Indians do not customarily share details of their culture with outsiders.
- When entering a structure, such as a church, observe the same protocols as you would in any sacred building.

LUMINARIAS Christmastime in New Mexico is made special by candles in paper bags, also known as *farolitos*. Christmas Eve luminaria walks in Albuquerque and Santa Fe are notable, as are luminaria events in Sugarite Canyon State Park and at Jemez State Monument and Coronado State Monument.

PENITENTES Organized in the early 1800s as a lay religious order and prevalent mainly in outlying small towns along the High Road between Santa Fe and Taos, in small communities and other remote locations where a priest's visits were few and far between, the Penitente Brotherhood assisted the community with life events, burials, special blessings of land and water, and other observations. They gathered—and still do—in windowless *moradas*, and they traditionally maintain secrecy. Penitentes are historically known for rigorous "penance" rituals, such as flagellation, and are especially active during Holy Week and on Good Friday, culminating in pilgrimages to the Santuario de Chimayo and Tome Hill. You may observe their large white crosses on hillsides as you drive through New Mexico.

Shopping

PLACES TO SHOP Perfectly normal citizens have been known to lose their wits—and the contents of their wallets—when shopping in Santa Fe. Save your allowance! There are too many things on Canyon Road you "must have." The Portal Program of the Palace of the Governors in Santa Fe, as well as the flea markets, will make you a shopper even if you are not normally one back at home. Also, the southern edge of Santa Fe boasts an outlet mall. Other top shopping destinations are Nob Hill and Old Town in Albuquerque, Sudderth Drive in Ruidoso, Bent Street in Taos, and arts-and-crafts festivals throughout the year.

FARMERS' MARKETS Please visit www.farmersmarketsnm.org for information on dozens of farmers' markets throughout the state, CSAs, agri-tourism, and farm-to-table programs. New Mexico loves and celebrates its farmers' markets. Outstanding examples are the Las Cruces Farmers' and Crafts Market, the Santa Fe Area Farmers' Market, and, in Albuquerque, the Downtown Farmers' Market at Robinson Park and the Los Ranchos Farmers' Market. Practically every town now has its own growers market, and more are appearing all the time.

Events

MUSIC With a sound for every taste, music festivals include the Clovis Music Festival in early September, celebrating rock and roll; Taos Solar Music Festival; Santa Fe Chamber Music Festival; Silver City Blues Festival; Santa Fe Bluegrass and Old Time Music Festival; and Albuquerque Folk Festival. In addition, the Santa Fe Opera; Cimarron's Shortgrass Music Festival; Music from Angel Fire; Taos School of Music's Summer Festival; Mariachi Spectacular; Festival Flamenco; Thirsty Ear Festival, Klezmerquerque, and the Globalquerque! world music festival, held at the National Hispanic Cultural Center in Albuquerque, are glorious.

RODEOS New Mexico State Fair, the county fairs, Colfax County Fair, Gallup Inter-Tribal Indian Ceremonial, and Maverick Rodeo on the Fourth of July in Cimarron are but a few of the events at which to enjoy a real rodeo. For a complete calendar, go to www.coyotesgame.com/rodeo.html.

ROCKHOUNDING Deming deserves the title of "Rockhounding Capital." At Rockhound State Park there, it is possible to haul 25 pounds of rocks, and Rockhound Roundup is held in Deming every mid-March.

Nature and the Outdoors

BUREAU OF LAND MANAGEMENT With a wealth of recreational and outdoors opportunities, including the Continental Divide Trail, the El Camino Real Trail, and wilderness experiences galore, contact the (BLM) Lands Public Information Access Office in New Mexico (505-954-2000). Please see www.blm.gov/nm/st/en/info/directory.html for guidelines and information.

STATE PARKS AND MONUMENTS New Mexico has thirty-five state parks. See www.emnrd.state.nm.us/prd/parktours.htm or www.stateparks.com/nm.html for more information. For a great deal, go to www.nmstatemonuments.org/ to buy an annual pass for $40 that provides a year's worth of unlimited admission to all state parks and seven historic sites.

WILDERNESS AREAS To find your wilderness escape in New Mexico's 166,658 acres of wilderness, go to www.nmwild.org/2011/maps/map-of-new-mexicos-wilderness-areas/ or www.blm.gov/nm/st/en/prog/wilderness.html.

WILDFLOWERS With New Mexico's varied ecology, from mountain to desert, wildflowers are profuse. Starting up north, in Sugarite Canyon State Park, the wildflower season progresses from wild iris to columbine, wild rose, and geranium, lupine, marsh marigold, and sunflower. The desert blooms from the Rio Grande south with the yucca blossom, cholla, and prickly pear. The Organ Mountains, Bosque del Apache, Cloudcroft area, Gila and Pecos Wilderness are good places to hunt beautiful blooms. In general, the wildflower season in New Mexico runs from February to April as the early autumn, depending on altitude. A photographic field guide of New Mexico mountain wildflowers and desert wildflowers will help you identify the flowers you see in New Mexico. *Wild Plants of the Pueblo Province*, by William Dunmire and Gail Tierney, is a book that goes beyond plant identification.

WILDLIFE Pronghorn, elk, mule deer, coyote, and wild turkey are commonly sighted on roadways in northern New Mexico. Big horn sheep, fox, and raccoon may also be seen. Yes, this is the land where the antelope roam.

WILDLIFE REFUGES Bosque del Apache National Wildlife Refuge south of Socorro is probably the best-known wildlife refuge in the state, primarily for bird-watching; however, the Maxwell National Wildlife Refuge; the Las Vegas National Wildlife Refuge; and the Bitter Lake National Wildlife Refuge, a riparian habitat in Roswell, are also prime viewing areas.

Dangers and Annoyances

Rapid temperature changes are the norm. The thermometer may vary by 40 degrees or more from day to night. Therefore, always dress in layers, and be prepared for sudden weather changes. Weather warnings should always be heeded. In summer, dry arroyos (ditches) and roads can flood very rapidly from an afternoon thunderstorm. Every year, it seems, hikers set out to climb La Luz Trail in summer and end up with hypothermia. The sun here really is stronger.

Always wear sunscreen, hat, sunglasses, and take more water than you think you will need, as well as a few energy bars, just in case. Be alert for weather changes. A snowstorm may come up suddenly just while you are planning to drive over Glorieta Pass. It's better to wait it out, even if you have to adjust your plans. And intense summer rain and hail storms can also make for hazardous driving. Dust storms in southern New Mexico can close the roads, so do pay attention to weather forecasts before setting out.

You may have heard about cases of bubonic plague and hanta virus, but unless you are handling rodent feces or have contact with infected rodents or other animals, there is no need for concern.

OPPOSITE: CORONADO STATE MONUMENT, NORTHWEST OF ALBUQUERQUE, OFFERS UNPARALLELED VISTA OF THE SANDIA MOUNTAINS

CENTRAL NEW MEXICO: RIO GRANDE COUNTRY

■

WEST OF ALBUQUERQUE

Rio Rancho, Bernalillo, Placitas, Corrales,
Jemez Springs

EAST OF ALBUQUERQUE

Belen, Moriarty, Mountainair,
Madrid, Cerrillos

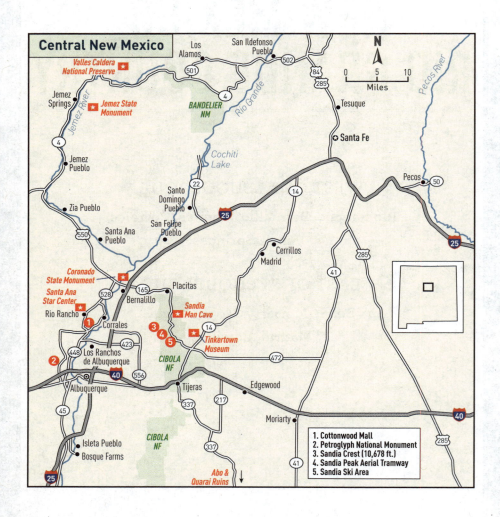

Central New Mexico

Valles Caldera National Preserve

Los Alamos

San Ildefonso Pueblo

502

501

84
285

N

0   5   10
Miles

Jemez Springs

Jemez River

Jemez State Monument

4

BANDELIER NM

Rio Grande

Tesuque

Santa Fe

Jemez Pueblo

Cochiti Lake

Zia Pueblo

Santo Domingo Pueblo

22

14

Pecos

50

Pecos River

25

Santa Ana Pueblo

550

San Felipe Pueblo

285

Cerrillos

Madrid

41

25

Coronado State Monument

Santa Ana Star Center

528

165

Placitas

Bernalillo

Sandia Man Cave

Rio Rancho

1

Corrales

423

3
4
5

14

Tinkertown Museum

2

448

Los Ranchos de Albuquerque

40

556

CIBOLA NF

472

Albuquerque

45

Tijeras

337

217

Edgewood

Moriarty

40

285

Isleta Pueblo

CIBOLA NF

337

Bosque Farms

41

25

Abo & Quarai Ruins

1. Cottonwood Mall
2. Petroglyph National Monument
3. Sandia Crest (10,678 ft.)
4. Sandia Peak Aerial Tramway
5. Sandia Ski Area

WEST AND EAST OF ALBUQUERQUE

Rio Rancho, Bernalillo, Placitas, Corrales, Jemez Springs, Belen, Moriarty, Mountainair, Madrid, Cerrillos

The Rio Grande Valley surrounding Albuquerque is rich with intricate, timeworn overlays of Spanish and Native American history. Here, the markers of earliest Spanish settlements in New Mexico coexist with Native American pueblos (villages), arts, and ceremonies. The pulsating drumbeats of Native ceremonial dances resound along with the passionate song of flamenco dancers. Here, too, the homesteading communities of the Manzano Mountains endure through seasons of drought and development, as multi-generational ranches cling to their lands and their way of life. Future Farmers of America, 4-H, county fairs and Saturday riding displays teach youngsters appreciation of their culture. Winemaking in North America dates back to the 1620s and originates in New Mexico's Sandoval County, where that practice continued in several local wineries and celebrated in numerous wine festivals throughout the state. Small farming still thrives in much of the region, with younger generations committing to organic living, while traditionalists practice the old ways, and farmers markets bursting with fresh local produce are crowded each summer, with growers proudly offering their vegetables, jams, salsas, garlic, and cheese.

This is a region fascinating for the rich cultural layers of vibrant history especially visible where trails converge. The Camino Real—the north–south colonial 1800 mile corridor of Royal Road between Mexico City and Santa Fe that follows the Rio Grande—and the original 1926 Route 66 north-south alignment as well as the post-1937 Route 66 east–west re-ordering of the roadway, have stories to tell. The traveler who takes time and pays attention may learn much by observing curving two-land roadways, architecture, roadside geography, and acequias (ditches) that channel water from the Rio Grande to flood fields of small farmsteads and native pueblos.

This is the land of the Turquoise Trail National Scenic Byway, the intriguing back road to Santa Fe that links the East Mountains to mining towns of Golden, Madrid, and Cerrillos, with turquoise so exquisite that Louis Tiffany incorporated it into his creations. To the west is the Jemez Mountain National Scenic Byway that courses through the glorious red rock country of Jemez Pueblo.

Although the Rio Grande Valley area has grown and urbanized during recent decades, values that characterize small-town life and independence, religious faith, and practices endure—sustained by generations that continue to live in the same place and follow many the same ways as did their ancestors. A few miles from the city, the area may seem like an outpost from the modern world, and it is tempting to imagine simpler times, even in the shadow of the metropolis.

The traveler will find an abundance of recreational opportunities in easy reach: snow sports, camping, golfing, hiking, fishing, and enjoyment of nature are accessible and essential to the way of life here. One need not even leave town to find in the metropolitan open spaces and Sandia foothills miles of hiking and biking trails. Distant horizons, ever-changing cloudscapes, dark skies, a winding river, and high desert mountains add up to natural beauty that fosters a respect for the planet and all its inhabitants.

The presence of a half-dozen Indian pueblos makes Bernalillo and Sandoval Counties unique. Here, ancient cultures continue to live and practice traditional ways transmitted across the generations for centuries. Visitors are welcome to attend designated feast days when tribal members offer a glimpse of their way of life. At the same time, many of these Indian tribes operate Las Vegas-style resorts offering luxurious dining, accommodations, big-name entertainment, and 24/7 gaming.

The spirit of this place is as strong as a lightning-struck cottonwood on a bosque river bank. It may be scarred, it may have broken limbs, but it has long weathered change and remains strong and deeply rooted in the *acequia* that nourishes its thick bark, profuse leaves, and multi-story branches. It has survived the severe changes brought by the seasons it has witnessed, and it endures as an essential part of the forest in which it dwells.

Mysteriously, no matter how much urbanization and gentrification may occur, the original and authentic character of New Mexico continues to assert itself. You may catch a whiff of that character in pinon woodsmoke and the flavor of homemade beans with tortillas, in the smell of rain in a sudden afternoon thunderstom and the changing light of a late winter afternoon that turns the mountains "watermelon" red. It is at once comforting and profound. Enjoy your stay, and may this place offer you a key to understanding its magic, that essence that makes it "The Land of Enchantment."

WEST OF ALBUQUERQUE

GUIDANCE Corrales Visitor Center (505-897-0502, www.visitcorrales.com), 4324 Corrales Road, Corrales. Open Mon.–Fri. 8–5.

Rio Rancho Chamber of Commerce and Visitor Center (505-892-1533; www.rrchamber.org), 4001 Southern Boulevard SE, Rio Rancho. Open Mon.–Fri. 8–5.

Rio Rancho Convention and Visitors Bureau (888-746-7262 or 505-891-7258; www.rioranchonm.org), 3001 Civic Center Circle, Rio Rancho. Open Mon.–Fri. 8–5.

Sandoval County Visitor Center (800-252-0191 or 505-867-8687; www.sandovalcounty.gov), 264 Camino del Pueblo, Bernalillo.

Walatowa Visitor Center (575-834-7235), 7413 NM 4, Jemez Pueblo. Fifty-five miles northwest of Albuquerque on US 550, north on NM 4. Open daily 9–5.

GETTING THERE Please see "Getting There" on page 55.

MEDICAL EMERGENCY **Lovelace Westside Hospital** (505-727-2000), 10501 Golf Course Road NW, Rio Rancho.

McLeod Medical Center (505-832-4434), 1108 US Rt. 66 W, Moriarty.

Durland Jean-Presbyterian Family Healthcare (505-864-5454), 609 Christopher Drive, Belen.

UNM Sandoval Regional Medical Center (505-994-7000), 3001 Broadmoor Boulevard NE, Rio Rancho.

University of New Mexico Hospital (505-272-2610), 2211 Lomas Boulevard NE, Albuquerque.

✳ To See

TOWNS **Bernalillo**. One of the first areas settled by the Spanish, this ancient pueblo site—dating to 1300 AD and perhaps earlier—is where Coronado is said to have spent the winter of 1540-41. Distinctly Catholic, Bernalillo is inhabited by faithful descendants of Spanish families with a centuries-long presence in the area. Traditions, such as the 335 year-old mid-August mysterious Matachines dances performed annually in the streets in honor of the patron saint, San Lorenzo, involve much of the village in preparation and participation. Because of its proximity to Albuquerque but well on the way to Santa Fe Bernalillo is sprucing itself up bit by bit, refurbishing its buildings even as new condos and homes appear on the edges of town. Yoga studios, cafés, galleries, and boutiques now grace the main street, whose character remains steadfastly small-town and working-class. Just beyond that main street, snug little houses with carefully tended rosebushes remain enclaves of privacy.

THE MYSTERIOUS MATACHINES DANCES HAVE BEEN PERFORMED EVERY AUGUST ON SAN LORENZO DAY FOR NEARLY 350 YEARS IN BERNALILLO

Corrales. An agricultural community settled by Hispanic, French, Basque, and Italian farmers through the nineteenth and twentieth centuries, Corrales is an exclusive village of pricey homes and elegant horses, shaded by gracious old cottonwoods. The main street is lined with galleries featuring local artists and boutiques, a winery, and a microbrewery making this pretty town worth a prowl.

Jemez Springs. A tiny, picturesque community due north of Jemez Pueblo, this village almost adjacent to Jemez Pueblo is primarily dedicated to the service of tourists, with bed & breakfasts, vintage bathhouse and hot springs, a few galleries, cafés, and a notable bar.

Placitas. A bedroom community of both Albuquerque and Santa Fe, this town is populated mainly by those who prefer to stay off the beaten track, enjoy their 360-degree views and their privacy, and who can afford to do just that.

Rio Rancho. In the 1960s, Rio Rancho was inhabited largely by coyotes and rattlers with retirement acreage staked out, as well a small population of brave retirees from the East Coast hanging in there. Growth accelerated with the arrival of Intel, and Rio Rancho has for years remained New Mexico's fastest-growing city. It boasts sophisticated medical facilities, college campuses, Cottonwood Shopping Mall, and nearly every chain store and restaurant found across America. There's no need to cross the river for shopping or entertainment unless you absolutely must. It remains the area of greatest expansion, continuing its march of sprawling development westward across the desert toward the Rio Puerco and attracts many retirees.

HISTORIC LANDMARKS, PLACES, AND SITES Coronado State Monument (505-867-5351), 485 Kuaua Road, I-25 exit 242, US 550 west 1.7 miles. Wed.–Mon. 8:30–5. Closed Tuesdays. The visitor center and small museum, designed by Santa Fe–style architect John Gaw Meem, houses the restored kiva paintings of Kuaua, circa 1300 AD, which exude a kind of sacredness and grant insight into the roots of Native American art. Walk the grounds of pueblo ruins on the 0.2-mile self-guided trail. Take in the panoramic view overlooking the Rio Grande and Sandias, especially impressive at sunset when the mountains turn watermelon red, and imagine yourself as one of the conquistadors, among the first Europeans to make contact with the New World, said to have spent the winter of 1540-41 on this spot. The shaded ramada-covered tables are perfect for a picnic anytime. But the centerpiece is the original painted kiva, accessible by ladder. $5; free to NM residents first Sun. of the month; Wed. free for seniors 65 and older. Call for RV and camping availability.

Jemez State Monument (575-829-3530), 43 miles north of Bernalillo, NM 4, 1 mile north of Jemez Springs. Open daily Wed.–Mon. 8:30–5. Closed Tuesdays. Dramatic ruins of fourteenth-century Towa pueblo and Spanish mission ruins of the church of San José de los Jémez dates to the seventeenth century. $5, age 16 and under free.

Petroglyph National Monument (505-899-0205), 6005 Unser Boulevard, NW Rio Rancho. West from Albuquerque on I-40 to exit 154, north 3 miles to Western Trail, go left and follow the signs. Open daily 8–5. Closed Thanksgiving, Christmas, and New Year's Day. From the Unser Boulevard Visitor Center, get maps to the prehistoric rock art trails on West Mesa volcanic escarpment. The monument has over 20,000 examples of indigenous rock art, including animals, birds, insects, and geometric designs, such as the spiral. This is a sacred Native American landscape. Trails are a short drive from the visitor center. Boca Negra Canyon is 2 miles north of the visitor center and has three self-guided trails. All are easy walks. Bring water, stay on trails, keep pets leashed, and beware of rattlesnakes. $1 weekdays, $2 weekends.

San Ysidro Church (505-898-1779), 5005 Corrales Road, Corrales. Call for hours. This lovingly restored 1875 village church with twin bell towers and pitched tin roof serves as a venue for community events, acoustic and chamber music concerts, lectures, and festivals. The Corrales Historic Society cares for this treasure.

Soda Dam (no phone). Two miles north of Jemez Springs on NM 4 is an inspiring and photogenic 300-foot natural dam formed by the accretion of mineral deposits.

MUSEUMS **Casa San Ysidro: Gutierrez/Minge House** (505-898-3915), 973 Old Church Road, Corrales. Open Tues.–Sat. July–August; Tues.–Sat. February–May and September–November 9:30–2:30; closed December–January. Reservations required for tours which are customarily at 10:30 AM, noon, and 1:30 PM As a branch of the Albuquerque Museum, the Gutiérrez/Minge Casa houses rare and exquisite New Mexican rugs, textiles, furniture, and art. The Ward Alan Minge family painstakingly and authentically restored this eighteenth- to nineteenth-century rancho, down to matching the original wall colors, as a labor of love. $4 adults, $3 seniors, $2 children.

DeLavy House schsinfo@sandcohist.fatcow.com, 151 Edmond Road, Bernalillo, west of Coronado State Monument and east of Santa Ana Star Casino off NM 550. Watch closely the north side of US 550 for the Sandoval County Historical Society sign. The former home of local artist Edmond DeLavy, now the home of the historical society and its archives and photo collection, this is often the site of lectures and community meetings, including the Sandoval County Historical Society.

J & R Vintage Auto Museum and Bookstore (1-888-298-1885), 3650A NM 528, a half-mile south of US 550, Rio Rancho. Open Mon.–Sat. 10–6. Closed Sundays. Founder Gab Joiner was a vintage car collector and restorer whose collection just got too big to store at home. Now his family runs the museum. The more than sixty restored classic cars and trucks on display, including Packards, Buick Roadsters, and so many more, are all for sale. There's a huge gift shop with die-cast toys, books, and memorabilia. If you don't have an auto nut in your clan, you may have to become one yourself when you see this. $6 adults, $5 seniors, $3 children ages 6–12, under age 6 free.

EAST OF ALBUQUERQUE

GUIDANCE **Belen Chamber of Commerce/Visitor Center** (505-864-8091; www.belen chamber.org), 712 Dalies Avenue, Belen.

East Mountain Chamber of Commerce (505-281-1999; www.eastmountainchamber
.com) 12129 NM 14, North Suite B, Cedar Crest.

Mountainair Chamber of Commerce (505-847-3470; www.discovermountainairnm
.com), 100 Main Street W, Mountainair.

Turquoise Trail Association (505-281-5233; www.turquoisetrail.org).

Valencia County Chamber of Commerce (505-352-3596; www.newmexico.org
/valencia-county-chamber-of-commerce), 3447 Lambros Loop, Los Lunas. Open Mon.–
Fri. 8–5.

✳ To See

TOWNS **Belen** is a town that grew up with the railroad, and it still serves as a switch-
ing station for as many as 300 Burlington Northern Santa Fe trains every day. The
main attraction here is the Belen Harvey House Museum beside the railroad tracks.

Cerrillos. Mining town, abandoned western film set, ghost town—Cerrillos melds
these identities into a place so quiet it is almost spooky, yet it has its own irresistible
allure for artists, photographers, and wanderers. The streets, where the only being you
are likely to see is a lazy dog parked in the road, seem about to reveal their secrets any
moment. For conversation, walk into Mary's Bar, where you are likely to find the locals
and old-timers. The new Cerrillos Station serves as a community center and gathering
spot with shops and spa.

Madrid. Through its incarnations as a twentieth-century coal mining town, an abandoned ghost town that was once entirely for sale, and, from the 1970s onward, a magnet
for hippies and artists who moved into the abandoned miners' homes and subsequently
turned them into pricey real estate, galleries, and cafés, Madrid makes an enjoyable
and worthwhile stop along the Turquoise Trail. The more than thirty art galleries are
lively and varied. It has always been known for its especially lovely Christmas lights.
Oscar Huber Memorial Ball Park remains as the first lighted ballpark in the state and
possibly the nation, built in 1920 for the Madrid Miners, a AA minor league team.

Moriarty. Contrary to popular legend, there is no relationship between the name
of this town and a character created by Arthur Conan Doyle, though the Sherlock
Holmes Society did gather here annually. This crossroads town, once the supply center
for Estancia Valley dry land farmers, retains its Route 66 character in its main street
architecture. It was named for Michael Moriarty, a young health-seeker from Iowa
who arrived in 1887 and found relief for his rheumatism under the sunny skies. Corn,
alfalfa, pinto beans, and pumpkins are grown nearby. The town is justly proud of its
refurbished Route 66 neon Whiting Bros. sign.

Mountainair, formerly "the pinto bean capital of the world," located along US 60, the
"slow road" or two-lane across New Mexico, is the geographic center of the state. As the
headquarters of the Salinas Pueblos National Monument, Mountainair harkens back
to its homesteading and ranching roots. New waves of artists and retirees continue to
move here and call it home. Some of New Mexico's most interesting folk art, created
by jack-of-all-trades Pop Shafter in the early twentieth century, is in the Shafter Hotel.
While the hotel is now closed, his masterwork stone embellished gate can still be seen
(pictured on page 46).

HISTORIC LANDMARKS, PLACES, AND SITES **J. W. Eaves Movie Ranch** (505-474-
3045; www.eavesmovieranch.com), 14 miles from Santa Fe via NM 14, west on NM 45,
75 Rancho Alegre Road, Santa Fe. Call for hours. If this movie set looks familiar, don't
be surprised. Many gunfights have been staged here, so you've likely seen the place

in a western or two. Daily tours, parties, and events are offered, and large groups may book staged gunfights.

Kasha-Katuwe Tent Rocks National Monument (505-761-8700), I-25 north, exit 259, follow signs to Forest Road 266. Open daily March 11–October 31, 7–7; November 1–March 10, 8–5. Gates close one hour earlier. Co-managed by BLM and Cochiti Pueblo. Hike the hoodoos, the cone-like wind-sculpted sandstone structures unique in New Mexico. These magical-looking rock formations resemble gigantic sand castles from a fantasy tale. The 2-mile Cave Loop Trail is easy, while the steep 1.5-mile Slot Canyon Trail is rated difficult. $5 per vehicle.

Mystery Rock, west of Los Lunas on NM 6 about 15 miles at the base of Mystery Mountain. One of the area's most curious "unsolved mysteries," this rock with the Ten Commandments carved into it has long been a source of intrigue. Who put it here? No one knows for sure. Stout shoes and good knees are required for the short scramble to view the rock close up.

Salinas Pueblo Missions National Monument Main Street, Mountainair. (505-847-2585). Closed Thanksgiving, Christmas, and New Year's Day. This monument is made up of three separate pueblo ruins located within a 50-mile radius on the Salt Mission Trail, with impressive ruins of Spanish mission churches built on these sites in the early seventeenth century. Once populous, these sites, located on trade routes, were abandoned over time due to severe drought. Each site has specific hours Abo, Gran Quivira and Quarai. Ranger's office in Mountainair. Free.

Sandia Peak Tramway (505-856-7325; www.sandiapeak.com), 10 Tramway Loop, NE, Albuquerque. From I-25, exit 234 at Tramway Road, follow it east 6 miles to Sandia Peak Tramway. Open Memorial Day–Labor Day 9–9, Labor Day–Memorial Day 9–8, Tues. 5–9 PM, Balloon Fiesta first two weeks in October, 9–9. Billed as "the world's longest aerial tramway," a ride, or flight as it is called, carries visitors in a dramatic ride from the desert to the crest of the mountain for 2.7 miles through four of the earth's six biozones and astounding views of the rugged mountainside, its rocky outcroppings, and canyons. At 9,600 feet, be prepared for high altitude. Atop the crest is the Four Seasons Visitor Center, open May–November, as well as restaurant and gift shop. $25 adults, $20 seniors, teens ages 13–20, and military; $15 children ages 5–12, under age 5 free.

Tome Hill (no phone). From Albuquerque, go south on NM 47; pass Peralta and Los Lunas, then left on Tome Hill Road to Tome Hill. This landform is a Camino Real landmark and Good Friday pilgrimage site. Witness New Mexico's Calvario, as marked by crosses on top of the hill. The main path to the top, the South Trail, begins at Tome Hill Park at the intersection of La Entrada—the sculpture designating the three cultures, Native, Spanish, and homesteader, who have resided here—and the Rio del Oro Loop Roads. The climb is steep and strenuous.

MUSEUMS **Belen Harvey House Museum** (505-861-0581), 104 N. 1st Street, Belen. Open Tues.–Fri.12–5; Sat. 10–5. Closed Sundays and Mondays, major holidays. Sitting beside the railroad tracks, this museum was originally a Fred Harvey Co. dining room, from 1908 to 1939. The collections relate to the history of the area and primarily to Santa Fe railroad history. Anyone interested in Fred Harvey and the history of the Harvey Girls will find this especially interesting. Free.

Los Lunas Museum of Heritage & Arts (505-352-7720), 251 Main Street SE, Los Lunas. Open Tues.–Sat. 10–5. Closed Sundays and Mondays. This recently opened museum concentrates on the heritage and families of the region, with exhibits on founding families, Civil War in New Mexico, educational exhibits for teachers, oral histories, and a Genealogy Resource Center. A rich digitalized archive. Free.

KASHA-KATUWE TENT ROCKS NATIONAL MONUMENT

Old Coal Mine Museum (505-473-0743), 2846 NM 14, Madrid. Open daily, 11–4:30 April–October. Winter hours Sat.–Sun. only. Located on 3 acres filled with vintage vehicles and other remnants of the days when this was a working coal mining town, the museum itself houses Engine 767, the most complete non-operating steam locomotive in the United States. Also on view are the coal mineshaft and original mining headquarters. Refurbished in 2012. $5 adults, $3 seniors and children.

🖉 **Tinkertown Museum** (505-281-5233; www.tinkertown.com), 121 Sandia Crest Road, Sandia Park. I-40 east, exit north at exit 175, NM 14 north 6 miles, left on NM 536. Tinkertown is 1.5 miles on your left. Open daily April 1–October 31, 9–6. There's no other museum like this. "I did all this while you were watching TV," folk artist Ross Ward said of his carving, which amounts to a 22-room collection of miniature animated scenes of Americana. Prediction: In years to come, this environmental folk artist and his work will be discovered and acclaimed as simply amazing. The book by his daughter, Tanya Ward Goodman, called *Leaving Tinkertown*, has done a great deal to spotlight this hidden gem. $3.75 adults, $3.25 seniors, $1.25 children ages 4–16, under age 4 free.

US Southwest Soaring Museum (505-832-0755; www.swsoaringmuseum.org), 918 E. Old Highway 66, Moriarty. Exit 197 from I-40, 30 miles east of Albuquerque. Open May–October Mon.–Sat. 9–4; November–April Mon.–Wed. 9–3. Antique sailplanes, hang gliders, and a history of soaring from the 1920s to the present make this an interesting stop. The collection of ninety-six model gliders in miniature is most appealing. Call for admission prices.

WHEN IN MADRID, MAKE A STOP AT THE OLD COAL MINE MUSEUM TO FIND OUT ABOUT LIFE IN BYGONE DAYS

WEST AND EAST OF ALBUQUERQUE

✳ To Do

BICYCLING **Manzano Meander** (no phone) is a 55-mile round-trip from Four Hills Shopping Center in Albuquerque over NM 333 (Route 66), 7 miles to Tijeras. At the intersection of NM 337 go right up to Cedro Canyon, the roughest part of the trip, then coast down to Chilili, an old Spanish land grant village. Be careful, though, because there isn't much in the way of shoulder along NM 337.

Straight and Easy (no phone) is a perfectly good workout on a perfectly flat road from Moriarty south on NM 41 to Estancia 17 miles, or if you are feeling strong, you can pedal all the way to Willard for another 13 miles. You'll find lots of big skies, fields, and farms along the way.

BIRDING See **Manzano Mountains State Park**, under *Green Space*.

Corrales Bosque Preserve (505-350-3955). Birding, hiking, horseback riding, and walking along a quiet and unspoiled stretch of dirt trails shaded by giant cottonwoods along the Rio Grande. Free.

BOATING **Cochiti Lake.** See "Wind Surfing."

FARMERS' MARKETS **Bernalillo Farmers' Market** (505-867-2485), 282 Camino del Pueblo, Bernalillo. Open July 6–October 26, Fri. 4–7. It's likely you will encounter growers from San Felipe Pueblo at this market.

Cedar Crest Farmers & Arts Market (505-514-6981), Mountain Christian Church, N. NM 14, Cedar Crest. Open June 27–October 15, Wed. 3–6. Get there early for the best selection.

Corrales Growers' Market (505-898-6336), next to the post office on Corrales Road, Corrales. Open April 22–October 28, Sun. 9–noon, Wed. 3–6. Sundays only September–November A bustling lively market with the highest quality, and priciest, produce. Neighbors meet up here over coffee and breakfast burritos. Out-of-this-world baked goods. Impossible to decide amongst the goodies.

FISHING **Isleta Lakes & RV Park** (505-244-8102), 13 miles south of Albuquerque on I-25, exit 215, 11000 Broadway SE. Fish peacefully from the shores of two beautiful lakes. Open daily October–March 7–5; April–September 6–7:30. Lakes stocked with channel catfish in warm weather and rainbow trout in fall and winter. There are also fifty full-service RV hookups; $37.10 per night. New Mexico fishing license not required. Limit five fish per adult. $16 age 12 and above, $9 under age 12.

Sandia Lakes Recreation Area (505-771-5190), 76 Sandia Lakes Road, Sandia Pueblo. Three lakes here are stocked with rainbow trout during the cooler months and channel catfish during the summer. One lake is strictly catch-and-release. Twenty acres of water on 56 acres of bosque forest. New Mexico fishing license is not required. 7–7; October 1–March 31, Wed.–Sun. 7–5. Closed Mondays and Tuesdays. $20, $12 children, $3 visitors, $1 child visitors.

✎ **Shady Lakes** (505-898-2568), 11033 4th Street NW, Albuquerque. Take I-25, exit Tramway Boulevard to NM 313 for 2 miles. The place known as Shady Lakes is a pleasant area with small lakes that in summer are covered with water lilies and can, for a small fee, provide every child with the opportunity to catch a fish. New Mexico fishing license is not required. As of this writing the property is for sale and it is not known if it will remain open. Mid-April–mid-August, open daily, 8–6; February weekends only 10–5; March–mid-April, 10–5. $7.95, children $5.95, visitors $3.95. Trout charge per inch $7 average cost per fish.

Zia Lake (505-867-3304), Zia Pueblo, south of San Ysidro on US 550. A tribal permit is required to fish here for bass, catfish, and trout. Gas motors are not allowed.

GOLF **Chamisa Hills Country Club** (505-896-5000), 500 Country Club Drive SE, Rio Rancho. Rio Rancho 1 and Rio Rancho 2 courses, designed by Lee Trevino, provide a total of 27 holes for all skill levels. $20–28.

Isleta Eagle Golf Club (505-869-0950), 13 miles south of Albuquerque, exit 215, 4001 NM 47 SE. Open daily. This 27-hole native desert–style course offers play around three scenic lakes and the Rio Grande. Fees for 18 holes, including cart, $50–65.

Santa Ana Golf Course (505-867-9464), 288 Prairie Star Road, Santa Ana Pueblo, is the naturally landscaped sister course of Twin Warriors. Golf around eight crystal-blue lakes, framed by three mountain ranges. $37–59.

Twin Warriors Golf Course (505-771-6155), Hyatt Tamaya Resort, 1300 Tuyuna Trail, Santa Ana Pueblo. March–October, open daily. November–February, closed Tuesdays. This is the ultimate, an 18-hole high desert championship Guy Panks–designed course where play takes place around twenty ancient cultural sites. The setting provides a truly magical experience. Rates vary by season. Please call club or book online.

HIKING **Battleship Rock**, along the Jemez Mountain Trail, is an easy 2-mile, extremely popular hike to the river, accessed at Battleship Rock turnout on NM 4, 5 miles north of Jemez Springs.

NATIVE AMERICAN PUEBLOS

For the most up-to-date information on pueblo dances and feast days, contact the **Indian Pueblo Cultural Center** (505-843-7270; www.indianpueblo.org). Christmas Eve Midnight Mass, Christmas Day, New Year's Day, King's Day (January 6), Easter, and Thanksgiving, as well as patron saints days of each pueblo, are customary times for dances to be performed, and the public is welcome.

Cochiti Pueblo (505-465-2244), population about 800, is due south of Santa Fe off I-25 and overlooks the Rio Grande. Storyteller pottery figures originated here with Cochiti potter Helen Cordero, and drums are another specialty of the pueblo. Feast day: July 14.

Isleta Pueblo (505-869-3111). From Albuquerque, I-25 south to exit 215 or take NM 47 to intersection with NM 147, go left, cross the river to the pueblo. While you can drive through the pueblo and visit the historic Church of San Augustine and buy oven bread, roasted blue corn-meal, and chile from various homes with signs offering them for sale, Isleta (which means "little island") also offers the sophisticated side of golfing, gaming, nightlife, and dining, as well as family-friendly camping and fishing facilities. Feast days: January 6, August 28, September 4.

Jemez Pueblo (575-834-7235), 7413 NM 4, Pueblo of Jemez. Go fifty-five miles northwest of Albuquerque, north to US 550 then to San Ysidro, north on NM 4. Feast days: November 12, December 12, Christmas Day, New Year's Day, January 6, Easter. See Walatowa Visitor Center, under "Guidance." For authentic dances, the opportunity to purchase fine pottery from the makers, and a warm welcome, Jemez Pueblo makes a wonderful introduction to the Native way of life.

Sandia Pueblo (505-867-3317), 12 miles north of Albuquerque off I-25. Perhaps best known for its business enterprises, this pueblo of approximately 4,000 people has entered the

Las Conchas Trail provides moderate forested hiking along the East Fork of the Jemez River Accessible and popular trail.

Red Canyon/Ox Canyon Trail, Manzano Mountains. This moderate 5.5-mile trail through Red Canyon is easily accessed. Go left in the town of Manzano along NM 337. The shady trail, good for mountain biking, too, is populated with alligator junipers and New Mexico swallowtail butterflies in summer. Another favorite area hike, very do-able.

Sandia Crest Trail, Sandia Mountains. This 27-mile trail along the top, with panoramic views, is easy to moderate. Sandia Peak provides a convenient access point. Take the tram to reach the trailhead.

10K Trail, Cedar Crest. Take NM 536, the Crest Road, to the trailhead, to access this moderate 7-mile hike along a 10,000-foot contour.

Tree Springs Trail, I-40 to NM 14 (exit 175), go north, take NM 536, the Crest Road, is one of the prettiest hikes on the east side of the Sandias, with wild primroses blooming May–June and a green, wildflower-filled landscape completely different from the desert vegetation of the west side of the mountain. It's a moderate 3-mile climb to the top, where you can connect with the Sandia Crest Trail. $3.

HORSEBACK RIDING **The Stables at Tamaya** (505-771-6180), Hyatt Regency Tamaya Resort & Spa, 1300 Tuyuna Trail, Santa Ana. A unique way to experience Pueblo back-country is with experienced native instructors and trail guides. Journey peacefully on horseback through cottonwoods along the Rio Grande and Jemez rivers on twice-daily trail rides. Over half these gentle horses are rescues. Carriage rides, pony rides,

twenty-first century with panache and now operates the grand Sandia Resort & Casino (open 24 hours) with several restaurants, including fine dining, a high-end spa, the Bien Mur Indian Market Center (where pottery and fine hand-crafted jewelry are sold), and Sandia Lakes Recreation Area. It is also the site of community events such as the annual Fiery Foods and Barbeque Festival held in early March. Feast days: January 6, June 13.

San Felipe Pueblo (505-867-3381) is known for its annual Corn Dance on May 1, a celebration that includes the sale of food, pottery, and jewelry, but perhaps better known for its Casino Hollywood, only 32 miles north of Albuquerque at exit 252 off I-25. Feast day: May 1.

Santa Ana Pueblo (505-867-3301). The ancient site of this Keresan village along the Jemez River is reserved for ceremonial functions and open to visitors only during certain annual celebrations. Today, the pueblo is known for its various enterprises, including the magnificent Hyatt Tamaya Resort & Spa and the Santa Ana Star Casino west of Bernalillo on US 550. Feast days: June 29, July 26.

Santo Domingo Pueblo (505-465-2214) holds a complex and moving Corn Dance each year on August 4. Artist Georgia O'Keeffe is quoted as saying that witnessing the Corn Dance was one of the great experiences of her life. Several hundred dancers moving rhythmically on the plaza, the sounds of their shells and bells, and the drums and singing, make this an unforgettable event. A big carnival of wares from all over (but be sure what you are buying is authentic and handmade—if the price is too good to be true, it probably isn't) and native foods makes this a fine day to be here. As of this writing, the restored Santo Domingo Trading Post is scheduled to re-open soon. Feast day: August 4.

Zia Pueblo (505-867-3304), a village of about 700 off US 550 about 15 miles west of Bernalillo, gave New Mexico its symbol, the Zia sun sign. The village was abandoned and then repopulated after the nineteenth century. Many of those who live here are superb potters and painters. Feast day: August 15.

and riding lessons are also available. Non–resort guests are welcome. Reservations required. $100 individual; $75 each in a group.

HOT SPRINGS **Jemez Hot Springs, Home of the Giggling Springs** (575-829-9175), 40 Abousleman Loop, Jemez Springs. Open Wed.–Mon., closed Tuesdays. 11–7; 11–6 winter. This serene spot across the road from the Laughing Lizard has expanded and modernized. They have also upped prices. Full day pass $100; half-day pass $75. One hour soak $25; 2 hour soak $40.

Jemez Springs Bath House (575-829-3303, 62 Jemez Springs Plaza, Jemez Springs. 10–7 daily. Owned and operated by the village of Jemez Springs. Built from 1870 to 1878, this quaint bathhouse and gift shop is fed by a rich mineralized spring and retains its Victorian sensibility. Individual private soaking tubs, massage and spa treatments available. $12 for 25-minute bathtub soak; $18 per 50 minute soak.

MOUNTAIN BIKING See **Las Huertas Canyon**, under *Green Space*, for a creek side moderate to difficult ride toward the Sandias, and **Red Canyon**, under "Hiking," in the Manzano Mountains is a favorite moderate 5.5-mile trail ride.

Also see **Turquoise Trail**, under "Scenic Drives," and East Fork of the Jemez, under "Snow Sports—Cross-Country Skiing," plus **Petroglyph National Monument** (see "Historic Landmarks, Places, and Sites") offers easy packed dirt cruises.

See **Sandia Peak Ski Area**, under "Snow Sports—Downhill Skiing." Lift open June 2–Labor Day. In summer, bring your bike up the mountain on the tram and find 30 miles of easy, moderate, and difficult trails graded like ski runs. You can ride the chairlift at the ski area to King of the Mountain, a black diamond (or difficult) trail, to Golden Eagle, marked green (or moderate), and descend King of the Mountain for a trail marked blue (or easy). Rentals are available top and bottom of the lift.

Corrales Rio Grande Bosque makes a delightful, easy, mostly level ride, or walk, for 12 miles. Follow NM 425 (Corrales Road) through Corrales; at Mockingbird Lane go left until you reach the bosque.

SCENIC DRIVES For more information on NM Scenic Byways, call 800-733-6396, ext. 24371.

Abo Pass Trail connects the Salt Missions Trail and the Camino Real for 31 miles along NM 47 and US 60. It is a journey through big open skies and the empty loneliness of the Old—and older—West, and a time to speculate how life used to be. You can imagine riding it on horseback or by wagon and appreciate the modern comforts of air-conditioning and motorized vehicles.

Corrales Road. The pretty two-lane, 6.7-mile road that winds along NM 448 through the Village of Corrales shows off the beauty of this rural community squeezed between busy Rio Rancho and Albuquerque (be sure to drive slowly, to savor the view and to avoid a ticket). Fruit orchards, horses grazing beside adobe homes, and expansive views of the Sandia Mountains speak of a less-harried time and insist you slow down, if only just to get a good look.

Jemez Mountain Trail National Scenic Byway. From Albuquerque, the length of this trail runs 163 miles. Take I-25 north to US 550, go northwest on 550 to San Ysidro, then right on NM 4. Along the way take in the Walatowa Visitor Center—where across the road and beneath the red rocks, ladies may be selling bowls of chile, Indian tacos, and oven pies—Pueblo of Jemez; Jemez Springs; Jemez State Monument; past Battleship Rock, Soda Dam, and La Cueva; past the Valle Caldera, Bandelier National Monument, and on into Los Alamos. This is a worthwhile way to see a vast amount in one day. You can loop back around to Albuquerque via Santa Fe on I-25 for a quicker return trip. Note: Fill up before you leave. There is no reliable gas station on NM 4 until you get to White Rock.

Salt Missions Trail. From Albuquerque, take I-40 east to Moriarty, south on NM 333 at Moriarty, follow NM 41, US 60, NM 513, 55, 337, and 131 for a total of 140 miles to travel the entire length of the trail and see all three ruins: Abo, Quarai, and Gran Quivira, with their Indian pueblos and 17th-century Franciscan mission churches, through the Manzano and Cibola National Forests en route. Abo is 9 miles west of Mountainair on US 60, and Quarai is 8 miles north of Mountainair on NM 55. Gran Quivira is a longer drive, 39 miles south of Mountainair on NM 55. Check at Ranger Station in Mountinair before proceeding to Gan Quivira.

Sandia Crest Scenic Byway. Take I-40 east to Tijeras exit, north on NM 14, then to Sandia Crest on NM 536 for 13.6 miles. The drive up is beautiful and green, with many marked hiking trails along the way, but once at the top of the crest, you can see 100 miles in all directions. This is a favorite destination of first-time visitors, where friends and relatives introduce them to Albuquerque. Over a half-million people drive to the 10,687-foot crest annually, and another quarter-million ride the Sandia Tramway.

Turquoise Trail National Scenic Byway is the back road between Albuquerque and Santa Fe. Take I-25 to the Cedar Crest exit, go north on NM 536, then follow NM 14 for 48 miles through mining ghost towns of Golden and Madrid, now a lively, much-gentrified arts town rather than a ghost town or hippie hangout, and Cerrillos, then on into Santa Fe. The route gets its name from local turquoise mines. The serpentine, up-and-down two-lane carries you past the Ortiz Mountains to the right, with views of the Sangre de Cristos up ahead and the Jemez Mountains to the left. Allow a good day to take your time and explore and shoot photos, perhaps have dinner in Santa Fe, then loop back down I-25 to Albuquerque.

SNOW SPORTS—CROSS-COUNTRY SKIING La Cueva (800-252-0191). Take NM 4 east for Redondo Campground, Los Griegos area, and west of La Cueva on NM 126 and Valle San Antonio Road to Upper San Antonio Canyon.

East Fork of the Jemez River is mostly level through the Santa Fe National Forest, with abundant ponderosa pine and the glorious silence of a landscape in deep winter. You'll find the trailhead 10 miles north of La Cueva. This trail is also mountain bike-friendly.

SNOW SPORTS—SLEDDING **Capulin Snow Play Area**. From eastbound Interstate 40, take Exit 175 at the Tijeras/Cedar Crest exit. Keep left and take the Cedar Crest exit to N.M. Highway 14. Drive north on N.M. 14 for approximately 6½ miles to N.M. Highway 536. Turn left onto N.M. 536. The Capulin area is approximately 8 miles up N.M. 536, about 1½ miles past the Sandia Peak Ski area. The Capulin entrance is on your right. If the gate is locked, site is closed. Other rules: no trains; only two people per tube, disc or plastic sled; no making or using jumps; no glass or alcohol; and keep pets on a leash and under control. The sledding area, located on state Highway 536, is unsupervised. It's the only designated sledding and tubing area in the Sandias. It costs $3 per vehicle to enter the Capulin area, and people can pay—cash or check only—at the pay station. Vans and buses carrying fifteen or more passengers pay only $10 per day. An annual Sandia Ranger District Amenity Pass, priced at $30, will also get you into the Capulin Snow Play Area. Passes are available during regular business hours at: Sandia Ranger Station, 11776 N.M. Highway 337 in Tijeras; Cibola supervisor's office, 2113 Osuna Road NE in Albuquerque, and REI, 1550 Mercantile Avenue NE.

SNOW SPORTS—DOWNHILL SKIING **Sandia Peak Ski Area** (505-242-9052). Take I-40 east to Cedar Crest exit 175, north on NM 14, left on NM 536 for 6 miles to ski area. Or take the Sandia Peak Ariel Tram at 30 Tramway Loop NE, Albuquerque. Open daily, depending on weather, December 16–January 6, 9–4; Wed.–Sun. and holidays January 10–March 11, 9–4. Thirty trails are serviced by four chairlifts. The area has a children's lift, some of the longest cruising terrain in the state, snow sports school, ski rental shop, and café. Skiers and snowboarders need to rent equipment at the base if taking the tram, or drive up. There are no rentals at the lift. $55 all-day lift; $65 tram and lift.

SPAS **Green Reed Spa** (505-798-3980), Sandia Resort & Casino, 30 Rainbow Road, Albuquerque. Total pampering waits in this full-service spa amid the soothing sounds of waterfalls, with body treatments that incorporate indigenous high desert botanicals. Luxe plus.

Tamaya Mist Spa & Salon (505-771-6134), Hyatt Regency Tamaya, 1300 Tuyuna Trail. Inspired by the prehistoric journey of their people, the spa offers various pathways to rejuvenation and healing through salt scrubs, herbal wraps, expert massage, and facials. Incomparable though pricey.

WIND SURFING **Cochiti Lake** (505-465-2421). Sixty miles north of Albuquerque, west of I-25 at Santo Domingo exit. Wind surfing on this no-wake lake with swimming beach, paved boat ramp, and campground is popular April–October.

WINERIES **Anasazi Fields Winery** (505-867-3062), 26 Camino de Pueblitos Road at the western edge of Placitas. Open Sundays noon–5. This winery has made a name for itself by featuring dry, not sweet, fruit wines of apricot, peach, plum, wild cherry, and New Mexico raspberry.

Corrales Winery (505-898-5165), 6275 Corrales Road, Corrales. Tasting room open Wed.–Sun. noon–5. Specializing in producing unique flavors of small-batch New Mexico wines grown from New Mexico grapes, this winery is set beside its own vineyard with knockout views of the Sandias and flocks of sandhill cranes in winter. Especially recommended is its Muscat Canelli dessert wine, but the drier reds are superb. A lovely place to spend a weekend afternoon.

Milagro Vineyards (505-898-3998), 125 Old Church Road, Corrales. Tours of vineyards and winery, as well as tasting room hours by appointment only. Call for monthly events. "Handcrafted Vine to Wine" is the slogan of this boutique winery, dedicated to making wine from grapes grown in New Mexico. Small quantities of Merlot, Zinfandel, and Chardonnay are aged in French oak.

Casa Abril Vineyards, Winery & Tasting Room (505-771-0208) 1 Camino Abril, Algodones. Thurs.–Sun. 12–5. Proud descendants of two Spanish families produce Tempranillo, Malbec, Zinfandel and Tempranillo Rose, while native roadrunners frolic in the vineyards. A delightful stop with excellent wines to offer.

❋ Green Space

Cibola National Forest and Grasslands (505-346-6803). Six developed campgrounds and 100 miles of hiking and horse trails are found, mainly in the Manzano Mountains, within an hour to a two-and-a-half-hour drive from Albuquerque, east on I-40, and south at Tijeras exit. Two of the most popular camping areas are at Tajique, and Fourth of July Canyon is famous for its flaming red fall color. Roads and campgrounds are frequently closed during winter months, so be sure to call the above number before venturing out. Free.

Fenton Lake State Park (505-829-3630), 33 miles northwest of San Ysidro via NM 4, then left at La Cueva on NM 126. Open summer 6 AM–9 PM; winter 7–7. Ponderosa pines sweep down to the shore of this picture-pretty small 28-acre lake stocked with rainbow trout. Only small rowboats and canoes are allowed. There are forty developed campsites, some with hookups. One trail that converts to an easy 2-mile cross-country ski loop in winter. Love this place! $5; $8 camping; $18 hookup.

Manzano Mountains State Park (505-847-2820). Go northwest of Mountainair on NM 55 or about an hour south of Albuquerque on I-40 east, then south at Tijeras exit., 31 NM 131. Open April 1–October 31, 7:30–sunset. Birds love this place. Take the opportunity to spot 200 species, including mountain bluebirds, hummingbirds, jays, and hawks. There is also trout fishing in Manzano Lake. Campsites. $5 per vehicle; $10–18 camping. When fire danger is high, the park is closed.

Sandia Ranger District (505-281-3304), visitor center at Sandia Crest, 11776 NM 337, Tijeras. Open 8–4:30. Closed Saturdays and Sundays and during winter. Hiking, mountain biking, cross-country skiing best accessed by driving the Crest Road, NM 536 to Sandia Crest, or taking the Sandia Peak Aerial Tram. Day use only. $3.

WILDLIFE REFUGES AND AREAS **Ladd S. Gordon Waterfowl Complex** (505-864-9187), 4 miles north of Bernardo on NM 116. Over 5,000 acres along the Rio Grande are divided into several different units where wildlife viewing, fishing, and hunting in season take place at this state managed waterfowl area.

Las Huertas Canyon (no phone). Continue on NM 165 through Placitas and up the mountain 7 miles. This narrow scenic drive up through the rugged Sandia foothills often offers the running water of Las Huertas Creek, and there are several nice places to camp and fish as well as picnic. In the evening, you have a good possibility of sighting bear. I have seen them here, so keep alert and keep food locked up unless you plan to share your picnic. They are somewhat habituated to humans. Las Huertas Canyon makes a moderate-to-difficult 15-mile mountain bike trail. Free.

Sevilleta National Wildlife Refuge (505-864-4021), 20 miles north of Socorro off I-25 at exit 169. Headquarters is located on the west side of I-25. This Chihuahuan desert ecosystem research center refuge hosts an annual open house with guided tours in October. Special educational tours may be arranged. Mon.–Fri. 7:30–4, Sat. 9–4. Closed Sundays. Tour wetlands by foot or car; hike San Lorenzo Mountain; walk three easy pristine desert trails. Family events such as butterfly counts, throughout the year. Free.

⚘ **Wildlife West Nature Park** (505-281-7655), I-40 east, exit 187, 87 E. Frontage Road, Edgewood. Open daily summer 10–6, November–mid-March noon–4 or by appointment. This is an interactive 122-acre wildlife park where rescued critters, such as coyotes, cougars, bobcats, mountain lions, and wolves, may be observed in their natural habitats. An easy walk. Camping, plus an abundance of weekend activities like music festivals, fiber and harvest festivals, and other scheduled events, including chuckwagon suppers, make this a good place for a family weekend excursion. $9, seniors $7, students $5, under age 5 free.

✳ Lodging

BED & BREAKFASTS **Blue Horse B&B** (505-771-9055; www.bluehorsebandb .com), 300 Camino de Las Huertas, Placitas. Utterly adobe, utterly Southwest, utterly situated to maximize the glorious sunsets, stars, and mesas up in Placitas, the Blue Horse promises privacy and the deep quiet that promotes deep rest in any of its three rooms. Gather around the kiva fireplace to unwind and enjoy breakfasts of muffins, waffles, and omelets. You deserve this! $115-$135.

Casa Blanca Guest House and Garden Cottage (575-829-3579), 17521 NM 4, Jemez Springs. Known for exquisite gardens, with a riverfront terrace and grandmother cottonwoods on the premises, this lodging is classically New Mexico, with thick vigas (ceiling beams) and a kiva fireplace in the guest house, which sleeps four and has a kitchenette. The cottage, where you can hear the Jemez River lull you to sleep, rents for $160 a night and sleeps two. The advantage here is that you can walk to town. $160-170.

Casa de Koshare (505-898-4500; www.casadekoshare.com), 122 Ashley Lane NW, Corrales. The *koshares* are the sacred clowns of the Indian dances, and this delightful B&B goes all the way with the Native American–Southwestern theme, with a Storyteller Suite and a Warrior Room among its four accommodations. It's a little piece of heaven here, with breakfast catered to your needs and appetite and panoramic views of the Sandia Mountains and city lights from the garden patio. Discounts are offered for extended stays. $139-199

Chocolate Turtle B&B (505-898-1800; www.chocolateturtlebb.com), 1098 W. Meadowlark Lane, Corrales. Four charming and colorful Southwest-style rooms, big picture views of the Sandias, free Wi-Fi and 24-hour complimentary snacks, plus a huge delicious breakfast served on the covered portal in season make this an appealing alternative for the business traveler simply tired of hotel living. $129-159.

Elaine's, A Bed & Breakfast (800-821-3092 or 505-281-2467; www.elainesbnb .com), 72 Snowline Road, Cedar Crest. Elaine O'Neal has been providing hospitality in the East Mountains for so long, she must be doing something right. You can be sure you will be well taken care of here in this five-room rural setting, with hot tub and handicapped access. Elaine's also offers golf packages. $109–159.

🐾 ♂ **Hacienda Vargas B&B Inn** (800-261-0006; www.haciendavargas.com), 1431 NM 313, Algodones. Saturated with history, the seven rooms here, part of a seventeenth-century hacienda, each with private entrance, compose the only bed & breakfast actually located on the Camino Real in New Mexico. Sweet dreams will be yours within the serenity of thick adobe walls, and you will be greeted in the morning with the house special, pumpkin pancakes with roasted piñon nuts. You'll be ready for a day of exploring in either Albuquerque or Santa Fe. Wedding chapel accommodates 15; packages available. Pet friendly with extra charge. $84-$159.

HOTELS, RESORTS, AND LODGES

🐾 **Elk Mountain Lodge** (575-829-3159; www.elkmountainlodge.com), 37485 NM 126, La Cueva, just west of junction of NM 4 and NM 126. If you are seeking a romantic getaway that offers convenience to hiking, cross-country skiing, and fishing in the heart of the Jemez Mountains, this four-room, comfy rustic log lodge is the place. Reviews are uniformly positive. A candlelit in-room whirlpool spa helps soothe exercised muscles, and a simple continental breakfast is included. A café and general store are just across the way. Pet-friendly. $119-$229.

♂ ♿ **Hyatt Regency Tamaya Resort & Spa** (505-867-1234; www.tamaya.hyatt .com), 1300 Tuyuna Trail, Bernalillo. Convenient to Santa Fe as well as Albuquerque, the Hyatt Tamaya works just as well as a secluded self-contained resort with the Sandias as backdrop. It has 350 rooms, many with private balconies; a fabulous spa; Twin Warriors Golf; the Rio Grande Lounge, with live entertainment; two restaurants; a knockout art collection; demonstrations of bread baking and other arts—all in an exquisite pueblo-style setting that qualifies it as a "cultural resort." You might find it worth the big bucks for the best money can buy. Golf, romance, Santa Fe day trip and spa specials and packages are available. Hypoallergenic rooms available. A top choice! Visit the website for the best deals. $.

♿ **Isleta Resort & Casino** (505-724-3800), 11000 Broadway Boulevard SE, Albuquerque; 13 miles south of Albuquerque, exit 215 to NM 47. Known for its gaming, golf, fishing, camping, dining, and entertainment, this is a great place just to come and play. There's even the Isleta Fun Connection, which has you covered on bowling, billiards, laser tag, and arcade games. The big names all headline here. Country stars who have appeared on this stage include Willie Nelson, Alan Jackson, and Randy Travis. Whatever your taste buds are craving, you can find it in one of Isleta's seven restaurants. There's always something happening here. Weekday Funcation packages are a fab deal at under $150. $219-$648.

♿ **Sandia Resort & Casino** (505-796-7500), 30 Rainbow Road NE, Albuquerque. Following a recent multimillion-dollar expansion, Sandia Resort has emerged as a super-luxe seven-story hotel. It has 228 Southwest-style spacious rooms with Ernest Thompson–designed furnishings. The four restaurants are the Council Room Steakhouse; the rooftop Bien Shur, featuring New American cuisine (overseen by well-known chef Jim White); a deli; and a buffet. The resort also boasts a fitness center, salon, upscale spa, the Green Reed, plus a championship golf course. The likes of Trisha Yearwood, the Gipsy Kings, Lyle Lovett, and Harry Connick Jr. appeared recently in the Sandia Amphitheater, and the lounge has live entertainment nightly until midnight. $211 and up.

CABINS AND CAMPING

See "State Parks" under *Green Space*, for camping.

Coronado Campground (505-980-8256), 106 Kuaua Road, Bernalillo, US 550 next to Coronado State Monument.

A VIEW OF THE SANDIA MOUNTAINS FROM THE HYATT REGENCY TAMAYA

Open year-round. Tenting March 1–October 1 only. No discounts for tents. Reservations advised for this serene twenty-seven hookup RV park, popular due to its views overlooking the bosque and the splendid northwest view of the Sandias. $18-$22.

🐾 **Trails End RV Park** (575-829-4072), 37695 NM 126, Jemez Springs. Open May 15–October 30. Weekly and monthly only, age 20 and older only, pre-approved pets okay, advanced reservations only for these ten full hookup sites (Wi-Fi included) located in old growth ponderosa pine stands close to all the outdoor recreational opportunities of the Santa Fe National Forest along the Jemez. $35. Prices reduced based on length of stay.

✳ Where to Eat

DINING OUT **Corn Maiden** (505-771-6060), Hyatt Tamaya Resort, 1300 Tuyana Trail, Santa Ana Pueblo. I-25 exit 242, US 550 to Tamaya Boulevard, 1.5 miles to the resort. D only, Wed.–Sun. 5:30–9. This, the Tamaya's upscale restaurant, presents the scrumptious, sumptuous signature rotisserie, more than anyone can possibly eat, of an assortment of gigantic skewers of meat, fish, house-made buffalo sausage, and chicken, each flavored with its own delectable marinade, including signature salad and green chile potatoes. Also serves NM Heritage locally ranched beef, red chile chocolate cheesecake, prickly pear duck breast, rabbit gnocci, buffalo carpaccio, reliance on regional ingredients, intriguing spin. Perfect place for a celebration. Expensive.

⚥ **Luna Mansion** (505-865-7333), 110 W. Main Street, Los Lunas. Open for D Tues.–Sun. 5–9, Sunday brunch 11–2. This grand 1821 historic mansion, an architectural anomaly of Southern plantation–style adobe architecture, with Ionic white columns spanning two stories, is a local institution that holds much of the area's history, with vintage family photos of Luna and Otero families. It is a favorite of ghost hunters—many report seeing a ghostly figure of a woman in the rocking chair on the landing. The second-story Spirits Lounge has happy hour 3:30–6, wine specials, open daily 3:30. Closed Sunday evenings. Serves aged prime steaks. Wed. $5.00 burgers. Thurs. $12.00 chicken fried steak or catfish. Moderate.

Prairie Star (505-867-3327), 288 Prairie Star Road, Santa Ana. D only. Open Sun.–Thurs. 5–9, Fri.–Sat. 5–10. A special-occasion restaurant with everything you could want in the way of atmosphere and service, Prairie Star is located in an elegant 1920s adobe home. Executive Chef Chris Olsen combines imaginative flavors in ways that allow the ingredients to chime together without confusion. The second-floor lounge shows off the Sandias, and the soft lighting and New Mexico art on the walls sets the stage for a special evening. Under management of the Santa Ana Pueblo, the Prairie Star's menu features upscale Southwest-based (not dominated) cuisine, including the very best game, fresh fish, bison, and Niman Ranch sirloin. Signature items: applewood-smoked bacon-wrapped pheasant, pan-seared bison tenderloin. Bring someone you want to impress here. Expensive.

EATING OUT **Banana Leaf Asian Grill** (505-892-6119), 355 NM 528 SE, Rio Rancho. Open daily. L, D. Serving what many believe is some of the finest Asian cuisine in the area, this casual family-run café has been a hit ever since it opened with its Thai, Vietnamese, and Chinese food, all freshly-made and brilliantly spiced. Go for the Thai. Curries and wraps are especially flavorful. And it has a surprisingly cool interior, considering the strip mall location. Inexpensive.

Corrales Bistro Brewery (505-897-1036), 4908 Corrales Road, Corrales. Open daily. Brunch Wed.–Sun., L, D, live entertainment nightly. Serving fare several cuts above standard brewpub food, with generous portions and reasonable

ALTHOUGH HE NEVER CALLED HIMSELF AN ARTIST, POP SHAFFER'S GATE IN MOUNTAINAIR IS REGARDED AS ONE OF NEW MEXICO'S FOLK ART TREASURES

TRY THE FAMOUS JEMEZ BURGER AT LOS OJOS RESTAURANT & SALOON IN JEMEZ SPRINGS

prices, this place is always hopping. My friends and I love it. Plus, there's a darn friendly atmosphere, with a homemade soup of the day; fresh salads; wraps and sandwiches, such as the embellished pastrami Pancho de la Plancha Greenblat; and the Tower of Power fries and burger. Put that together with a dozen New Mexico microbrews, and you've got a big winner. Kids welcome. Inexpensive.

Nachos Restaurant (505-832-5505), 904 Route 66, Moriarty. Open Mon.–Sat. 11–8. L, D. The sombreros decorating this local favorite cafe proclaim that this is a Mexican rather than a New Mexican restaurant, but red and green chilies flow freely here. Homemade food prepared from family recipes makes this a worthwhile stop. Even the chips and salsa are made in house, as are the outstanding tamales. Most popular though is the combination plate for $8.00, making this a family- and wallet-friendly cafe. Inexpensive.

Flying Star Café (505-938-4717), 10700 Corrales Road, Corrales. Open daily 6 AM–11 PM, Fri.–Sat. 6 AM–11:30 PM

Located just north of Alameda Boulevard in front of the Bosque Trail, with big fireplace in winter to cozy up to and outdoor patio, this is the perfect place to meet friends. Drop in for a late-night snack of Key lime pie, a morning latte and blueberry scone, or bowl of soup and sandwich, anytime. Homemade egg salad and chicken salad, and the grilled beef and chile sandwich are favorites. Known for burgers and fries, milk shakes, vegetarian fare. Known for locally-sourced ingredients. But the tab can add up quickly. Inexpensive.

Hannah & Nate's Market Cafe (505-898-2370), 4512 Corrales Road, Corrales. B, L daily. The place for Sunday brunch, this is a cozy spot where neighbors and family meet up regularly. It serves excellent coffee. I favor the spinach and mushroom omelet and huevos rancheros, and the heavenly hash, a pile of home fries topped with eggs and chile. Many dishes, such as the NM Eggs Benedict, feature the café's tender *carne adovada*. A wonderfully relaxing way to begin a Sunday. Inexpensive.

YOU MAY RUN INTO A MOVIE STAR OR A SALTY OLD MINER AT MARY'S BAR IN CERRILLOS

🍴 **Joe's Pasta House** (505-892-3333), 3201 Southern Boulevard SE, Rio Rancho. L, D Mon.–Sun. Baked cannelloni with homemade pasta, toothsome pesto, saltimbocca, and too much to list make Joe's a comfortable hangout for locals. $50 complete dinner for two with wine and dessert can't be beat. Best traditional East Coast-style Italian food around, with atmosphere to match. Consistently wins "Best Italian" awards. Extensive menu. Inexpensive–Moderate.

Las Ristras de Corrales (505-433-4192), 4940 Corrales Road, Corrales. One of the best. Truly a value. Taco Tuesday with live music and $1.50 chicken tacos all day, Thursday night prime rib and Colorado lamb chop three-course special for unbelievable prices, northern NM ranch-raised steaks grilled perfectly, falling off the platter, delectable grilled avocado salad, well-chosen and reasonably-priced wines, piquant Mexican food, gracious service, local farm produce on the plate and for sale. B, L, D Tues.–Sat., Sunday brunch only, closed Mondays. A favorite of my family. Inexpensive–Moderate.

Los Ojos Restaurant & Saloon (505-829-3547), NM 4, Jemez Springs. Nothing could be better than the dark, scruffy, woody interior of this classic western bar. Go for the "Famous Jemez Burger"

or, on weekend nights, Pam's prime rib special for $17.00. There are always folks shooting pool. Count on waitresses with attitude and characters with plenty of tales at the bar. This is the place to warm up with a hot bowl of green chile stew or a plate of red chile enchiladas in front of the massive rock fireplace after a day's cross-country skiing. Inexpensive.

Mary's Bar, 15A 1st Street, Cerrillos. It may look closed from the outside, but this bar is still hopping inside a 120-year-old building, which was built by the late proprietor Mary Mora's father. The businesss remains in the family. Here, you might encounter a movie star relaxing off the set, a grizzled miner, a rancher (or wannabe cowboy). And chances are always good that you'll meet up with a wandering Santa Fe artist at the bar. Inexpensive. Warning to the allergic: Cats abound.

The Merc at Placitas (505-867-8661), 221 NM 165, Homestead Village, Placitas. A well-stocked grocery store and take-out deli with homemade soups, and a local hangout selling beer, wine, and spirits. Plus the Sunday *New York Times*. The high point of the week is the 4–6:30 PM Friday wine tasting. Mon.–Sat. 9–8, Sun. 9–6. Inexpensive–Moderate.

Mine Shaft Tavern (505-473-0743), 2846 NM 14, Madrid. Open daily. L, D. Sun.–Thurs. 11:30–7:30; Fri.–Sat. 11:30–9; bar open "late." "New Mexico roadhouse cuisine" is the specialty, as are the locally sourced green chile burgers (Mad Burger #1) with hand-cut fries, homemade guac, salsa, and green chile stew. Don't forget about the barbecue brisket. Long a big-time biker hangout, the Mine Shaft was constructed in 1946 as a coal company town saloon with a 40-foot-long antique lodge pole pine bar. Fifteen beers are on tap. If you haven't been to the Mine Shaft, you haven't been to Madrid. Live entertainment on weekends, and often during the week. Inexpensive.

Perea's Restaurant & Tijuana Bar (505-898-2442), 4590 Corrales Road, Corrales. Open Mon.–Sat. 11:30–2. L only.

Some places serve great Mexican food, some serve great margaritas. This old-timey place has both. Don't be afraid to walk in. The 300-year-old building was constructed of terrones, blocks of mud cut from the riverbank. The original construction is displayed on a wall cutout inside. You can't eat history; however, you certainly can eat the classic green chile enchiladas, *carne adovada*, and, my favorite, the irresistible mildly spicy and gooey chicken enchilada casserole. Inexpensive.

Range Café (505-867-1700), 925 S. Camino del Pueblo, Bernalillo. Open daily 7:30 AM–9:30 PM Has live music on weekends. With its casual, consistent home cooking served in huge portions (meat loaf and mashed potatoes and chicken-fried steak), excellent pancakes, huevos rancheros, and over-the-top desserts (like the trademark "Death by Lemon"), it's no wonder that Range is a popular gathering spot. Although success of this flagship has spawned numerous spinoffs around town, I insist on dining at this, the mothership. Fabulous gift shop of NM products to browse while you wait. Expect a wait for Sunday breakfast. Inexpensive.

Santa Ana Café (505-771-6060), Hyatt Tamaya Resort, 1300 Tuyuna Trail, Santa Ana. Open daily 6:30 AM–9 PM, closed 2–5:30 PM. B, L, D. A fine place to enjoy a Sunday brunch or Friday evening prime rib buffet, and a place to try interesting lighter fare, such as fish and salads, with a native twist the rest of the time, competent, not adventuresome cooking. Patio dining. Moderate–Expensive.

Teofilo's Restaurante (505-865-5511), 144 Main Street, Los Lunas, across from the Luna Mansion. L, D. Closed Mondays. This simple, welcoming, restored 1912 adobe home serves some of the best, most consistent New Mexican food. The yeasted hot sopaipillas are little pillows of heaven when slathered with honey, and the red chile is superb. There's no better place for Sunday lunch, and the patio is lovely in warm weather. Who needs Santa Fe? This is the real deal. Hours change seasonally. Inexpensive.

✳ Entertainment

Sandia and Isleta Pueblos offer big-name entertainment: popular comedians, musicians, and performers, as well as those who were big "back in the day." See listings under "Hotels, Resorts, and Lodges."

Santa Ana Star Center (505-891-7300), 3001 Civic Center Circle, Rio Rancho. Find a busy schedule of sports events, car shows, concerts, ice shows, and much more at this spiffy facility.

🐾 **Wildlife West Nature Park** (505-281-87655), 87 N. Frontage Road, Edgewood. Sat. 10–6, June 30–September 1, chuckwagon barbecue feast followed by vintage western swing music on Saturday nights.

✳ Selective Shopping

Bien Mur Indian Market Center (505-821-5401), 100 Bien Mur Drive NE. I-25 exit 234 east on Tramway Road. Open Mon.–Sat. 9:30–5:30, Sun. 11–5:30. For high-quality, guaranteed-authentic Indian jewelry, rugs, pottery, baskets,

AT THE MINE SHAFT TAVERN IN MADRID, NOTHING GETS BETWEEN A MAN AND HIS DOG

and turquoise and silver jewelry, this is an excellent place to shop. You are sure to find something you simply must have at a fair price.

Cowgirl Red (505-474-0344), 2865 NM 14, Madrid. Everything essential for the cowgirl or wannabe cowgirl, especially those prize vintage boots—there's 500 pairs to tempt you, plus vintage and contemporary Native American jewelry and art. If you have time for only one shopping stop in Madrid, that's sad, but make this the place.

Johnsons of Madrid (505-471-1054), 2843 NM 14, Madrid. In a town with thirty art galleries, Johnsons remains the first and oldest, since 1973, featuring regional textiles, fiber arts, photography, and fine art.

Walatowa Visitor Center (575-834-7235). See "Guidance."

✳ Special Events

January: Belen, billing itself as the "world's largest matanza," where thousands show up for the traditional pig roast. (505-925-8910).

April: Tome, Good Friday procession to Tome Hill.

May: Memorial Day weekend, **Jemez Pueblo Red Rocks Arts & Crafts Festival** (575-834-7235).

June–July: **Music at the Ballpark** (505-471-1054), Madrid. Music festivals of all kinds held here. **Wildlife West** (505-281-7655), Edgewood. Third weekend in June, **Bluegrass Weekend**, with bands, vendors, workshops, zoo tours, chuckwagon barbecue, and western swing music. **Annual Pork and State BBQ Championship** (888-746-7262), early July, Rio Rancho.

August: **Las Fiestas de San Lorenzo** (505-867-5252), Bernalillo. Traditionally held August 9–10 to honor the town's patron saint, the fiesta features the ancient Matachines dances, performed in the streets.

September: Join **HawkWatch** in the Manzano Mountain watch site near Capilla Peak (801-484-6808; www.hawkwatch.org) for raptor counts in the Sandias—assist with the raptor count and learn about the migrating birds of prey from interpretive rangers on-site.

October: **Corrales Harvest Festival** (505-350-3955), Corrales: music, hayrides, produce, and storytelling. Also **National Pinto Bean Festival** (505-832-4087), Moriarty.

December: **Christmas in Madrid** (505-471-1054): an annual community open house and parade. **Christmas at Kuaua** (505-867-5351), Coronado State Monument, December 20, 5:30–8:30 PM, with luminarias and Pueblo and Spanish dancing. Free. **Farolito Tour** (505-829-3530), Jemez State Monument, 5–8 PM: pueblo dances and music, plus 1,500 farolitos light up ancient Giusewa Pueblo ruins. Free.

ALBUQUERQUE AND BEYOND

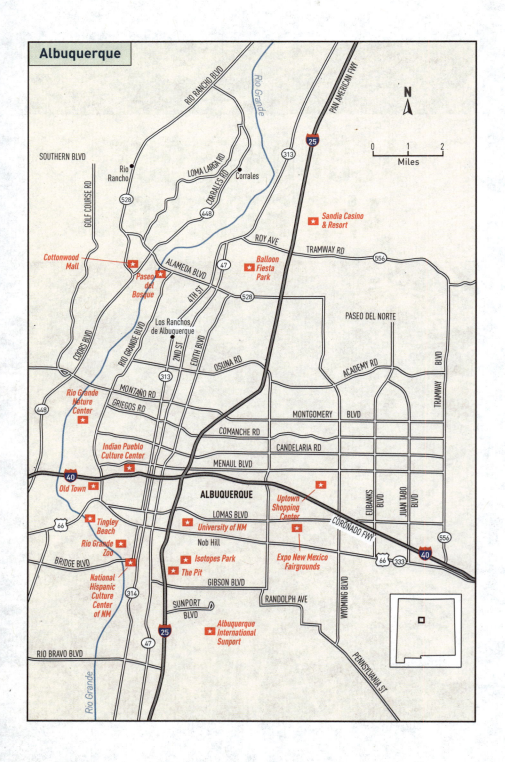

Albuquerque

SOUTHERN BLVD

Rio Rancho

Corrales

Sandia Casino & Resort

Cottonwood Mall

Balloon Fiesta Park

Paseo del Bosque

Los Ranchos de Albuquerque

PASEO DEL NORTE

Rio Grande Nature Center

MONTAÑO RD

GRIEGOS RD

MONTGOMERY BLVD

COMANCHE RD

Indian Pueblo Culture Center

CANDELARIA RD

MENAUL BLVD

Old Town

ALBUQUERQUE

Uptown Shopping Center

Tingley Beach

LOMAS BLVD

University of NM

CORONADO FWY

Rio Grande Zoo

Nob Hill

National Hispanic Culture Center of NM

Isotopes Park

The Pit

Expo New Mexico Fairgrounds

GIBSON BLVD

BRIDGE BLVD

SUNPORT BLVD

RANDOLPH AVE

Albuquerque International Sunport

RIO BRAVO BLVD

0   1   2
Miles

ROY AVE
TRAMWAY RD

ALAMEDA BLVD

4TH ST

GOLF COURSE RD

COORS BLVD

RIO GRANDE BLVD

2ND ST

EDITH BLVD

OSUNA RD

ACADEMY RD

EUBANKS BLVD

JUAN TABO BLVD

TRAMWAY BLVD

WYOMING BLVD

PENNSYLVANIA ST

LOMA LARGA RD

CORRALES RD

PAN AMERICAN FWY

Rio Grande

ALBUQUERQUE AND BEYOND

Albuquerque: The Duke City

Several years ago, something of a movement emerged to change the spelling of "Albuquerque." Inspired by a novel by beloved local author, Rudolfo Anaya, titled *Alburquerque*, the call went out to restore the original spelling. Some wanted to restore the missing *r*, so the city's name would be spelled "Alburquerque," like its Spanish forebear, the original Duke of Alburquerque who granted the first European settlers rights to the land now known as "Old Town" in 1706. Although that idea never gained real traction, there is no arguing that Albuquerque, New Mexico, counts its Spanish heritage an essential part of its identity.

There were as many as forty Indian pueblos in the province of Tiguex (t-gway) existing in the Rio Grande Valley at the time of first contact. The city was founded by a determined band of families who farmed in the Old Town area and left a legacy of an enduring Spanish identity through subsequent waves of immigration to the present.

Today's Albuquerque, which had an estimated population of 545,852 in 2017, boasts a rainbow of Italian, Greek, Chinese, Indian, Japanese, Mexican, African American, Thai, Vietnamese, and Native American communities, families, and neighborhoods. Ethnic identities continue to find expression in festivals, places of worship, restaurants, and shops that give the city much of its welcoming vitality.

Centrally located within New Mexico at the crossroads of east–west I-40 and north–south I-25, Albuquerque is fairly easy to navigate as it is divided into quadrants, with Central Avenue, or Old Route 66, dividing the city into its north and south sides. Route 66 neon lights up the night along Central, the boulevard that extends through the core of the city and where the University of New Mexico, Presbyterian Hospital, and Nob Hill, Downtown, and Old Town neighborhoods cluster. Broadway divides the city east to west. (One helpful navigational tool: The Sandia Mountains are to the east, while the volcanoes and the river are to the west.) The Rio Grande meanders the length of the city north to south, providing a 15-mile greenbelt and a much-loved running, walking, and bike path that serves as an urban park.

Albuquerque has gone through various transformations over the past 150 years. The arrival of the railroad in the 1880s brought a "New Town" commercial and population expansion to merge with the historic Old Town area settled originally in 1706. The town spread east of Carlisle Boulevard with the impetus of World War II and the post-War Atomic Era as Sandia Laboratory and Kirtland Air Force Base stimulated the numbers and diversity of the population. Then, in the 1970s, Intel Corp. arrived on the West Side, and with it a critical mass of newcomers that expanded the life of a small-town mom-and-pop business base into a magnetic relocation site for people and business. Downtown, EDO (East of Downtown), Nob Hill and the International District, all located along the Central Avenue corridor, are neighborhoods that continue to evolve and reimagine themselves as the people and businesses along this byway seek, in one way or another, to participate in an urban center that has one foot in traditions and another in a future yearning to articulate itself. Who will we become? This might be the question behind much of the city's ferment, stimulated by the arrival of the film and broadcast industries that have produced the *Breaking Bad* and *Better Call Saul* phenomena as well as successive waves of retirees and amenity migrants.

On the one hand, the city has become something of a mecca for young creatives, tech and arts-savvy, educated, and energetic young folks. Many are entrepreneurial and enterprising, and they find the diversity and openness, as well as the cultural richness of the town, to their liking. Here there is room for invention, reinvention, and growth, if one has the ability to be self-reliant and entrepreneurial. After all, Albuquerque has a tradition of small entrepreneurs, and there is a dearth of corporate headquarters. Religious and lifestyle freedom and toleration are givens, and alternative, artistic, and unconventional lifestyles coexist comfortably beside cowboy and blue-collar values. It is as if the positive side of the code of the West, particularly respect for individuality, as well as an appreciation for community, has taken hold here.

Those who seek a milder year-round climate, more reasonable housing costs, and a laid-back pace might well be attracted to Albuquerque over Phoenix, Denver, and Santa Fe. Those with resources might well maximize them here, as the New Mexico poverty rate is among the nation's highest.

The arts, theater, spoken word, and filmmaking have found a home here. There's a lively visual arts community and a variety of music scenes, too, from folk to salsa to jazz. The presence of the University of New Mexico nourishes the arts, and the push to bring filmmaking to New Mexico has drawn the talent to create an outstanding and ever-expanding theater scene.

Distinct neighborhoods well worth exploring include Nob Hill, a walking district packed with small shops and cafés east of the university; Downtown, with its movie theater and bars; the University of New Mexico, with its prototypical southwest architecture; Huning Highlands, a stronghold of Victorian homes, overlapping with EDO; and Old Town. The area most magnetic to the young and the hip is currently the gentrifying Sawmill neighborhood, close to both Old Town and Downtown. The North and South Valleys, each with their agrarian traditions, maintain their particular flavors and compounds of history, architecture, commerce, and cuisine, as well as open space, like the new Valle del Oro National Wildlife Refuge. What we think of as the North Valley actually was a group of independent farming villages until after World War II. Albuquerque has a burgeoning food consciousness, with young people committing to organic farming, bringing their produce, salsas and jams to popular farmers markets, and experimenting with food trucks and innovative cafes.

The Sawmill neighborhood, in the area of 12th Street NW and Mountain Road, and in walking distance of Old Town museums and the Harwood Arts Center, continues to gain popularity and interest that is repurposing this old neighborhood into a forward-looking area. Cafés, bakeries, and galleries keep popping up along the convenient stretch of Mountain Road between Rio Grande and 4th Street NW and marketplace developments and dwellings are green-lighted for the near future.

A walk or bicycle ride through these neighborhoods yields a feeling for the city that is impossible to obtain while driving through along the freeway, which presents a deceptive view of a city blockaded by mundane urban sprawl.

Route 66, the Mother Road, winds east to west through the city like a ribbon of neon, granting Central Avenue a nostalgic heart. From original Route 66 motels to restored historic gas stations now adapted as popular watering holes, it retains its sense as a destination for travelers and explorers, even as they mingle with the descendants of eight and twelve generations of families who continue to live in the same community. The city's latest place-making entry, the restoration of the El Vado Motel on Central Avenue across from the Biopark, is to be celebrated. While retaining the historic site widely considered to be "the purest" of Route 66 architecture, the motel has been repurposed as a delightful food and boutique court, with a splashpad for the little ones.

The city continues to interpret itself and its culture in a wider way, with the National Hispanic Cultural Center of New Mexico, the Museum of Art and History, and the New Mexico Museum of Natural History and Science; intelligent and emerging galleries of significance; and a growing diversity of shopping, dining, learning, and entertainment venues. Annual festivals, such as Globalquerque, Folk Arts, Arts and Crafts, Balloon Fiesta, Weems Arts, State Fair, and many more keep folks out and about and enjoying life.

A selection of gaming resorts nearby at Isleta, San Felipe, Santa Ana, Sandia, and Laguna Pueblo's Route 66 Casino are venues that attract top entertainment. The popularity of the Uptown outdoor shopping mall is triggering adjacent development as well as the refurbishing of Winrock Shopping Center. With 360 days of sunshine, as well as four distinct seasons, Albuquerque also appeals to those who appreciate easy access to outdoor activities.

Albuquerque has traded some of its old New Mexico edge for the influx of new people, money, ideas, shopping, and access to medicine and technology. While it continuously becomes more like everyplace else, there is something within it, perhaps the centuries of indigenous and Spanish colonial, pioneer spirit that cannot be deleted from the city's cultural memory. It is not, nor will it ever be, completely prettied up or smoothed out. It continues to be a magnet for entrepreneurs, immigrants, artists, retirees, and especially for those with hopes of making it in the West. It is retiree-friendly, with an abundance of senior centers and services, and accessible public transportation.

But the spirit of Albuquerque today is probably best expressed with the 2017 election of a new mayor and leadership that appears to be a departure from "good old boy" politics of the past—the progressive, young Tim Keller—who is filling City Hall with a bright, young, diverse staff and the city with high hopes for realizing its fullest potential.

To find out what is happening, check out www.dukecityfix.com, www.kunm.org, itsatrip.com, or look at calendars in the *Weekly Alibi* and *Venue*, the Friday entertainment section of the *Albuquerque Journal*.

GUIDANCE Albuquerque Convention & Visitors Bureau (505-842-9918), 201 1st Street NW, Suite 601, Albuquerque.

Albuquerque Hispano Chamber of Commerce (505-842-9003), 1309 4th Street SW, Albuquerque.

Greater Albuquerque Chamber of Commerce (505-764-3700), 115 Gold Avenue SW, Suite 201, Albuquerque.

Key Numbers: Dialing 311 in town brings listings of cultural happenings.

GETTING THERE *By car:* Albuquerque lies at the crossroads of I-25 and I-40.

By bus: **Greyhound Bus** (505-243-4435), 320 1st Street SW.

Grey Line and TNM&O Coaches (505-242-4998), 300 2nd Street SW.

By air: Many major airlines, including United, Southwest, Continental, and Delta, fly to the **Albuquerque International Sunport** (505-633-6155), 2200 Sunport Boulevard SE.

By train: **Amtrak** (800-872-7245 or 505-274-2372) brings passengers to Albuquerque daily from Chicago and Los Angeles. The **Alvarado Transportation Center** (505-852-9650), 1st and Central, or 320 1st Street SW, downtown is the terminal for both bus and train passengers.

GETTING AROUND ABQ Ride (311 for general information; www.cabq.gov/transit). SUN TRAN includes a public bus system known as Rapid Ride that extends through an 11-mile corridor along Central Avenue and promises to deliver you 11 minutes between each stop. Fare is $1, and it can get you most places you want to go. Rapid Ride operates 6 AM–9 PM daily, and 6 AM–3 AM during the summer. Pick up schedules at the Alvarado Transportation Center, 100 1st Street SW. Call 311 to schedule individual van pickups in advance for $2.50 fee. As of this printing, A.R.T. (Albuquerque Rapid Transit) is in the process of becoming a useful and convenient rapid transportation method, but so far is incomplete and has created quite a bit of chaos along Central Avenue. Please check with 311 for updated information. Bike Abq (www.bikeabq.org) provides bike maps. **New Mexico Rail Runner Express** (505-245-RAIL or 505-245-7245; www.nmrailrunner .com), goes south to Belen and north to Bernalillo and Santa Fe. Rates are determined by zones. Schedules vary with seasons and special events. **Albuquerque Cab** (505-883-4888) and **Uber** offer 24 hour service.

WHEN TO COME **The Albuquerque International Balloon Fiesta**, held the first two weeks of October, is the city's premier event. Just prior to Balloon Fiesta is State Fair, and the holiday season is magical, with events galore, like the delightful Twinkle Light Parade and River of Lights, and luminarias shining brightly.

MEDICAL EMERGENCY **Heart Hospital of New Mexico at Lovelace Medical Center** (505-727-1100), 504 Elm Street NE, Albuquerque.

Presbyterian Hospital (505-841-1234), 1100 Central Avenue SE, Albuquerque.

University of New Mexico Hospital (505-277-0111), 2211 Lomas Boulevard NE, Albuquerque.

Lovelace Hospital Downtown (505-727-8000), 601 Dr. Martin Luther King Jr. Avenue NE, Albuquerque

✳ To See

HISTORIC LANDMARKS, PLACES, AND SITES **Ernie Pyle Memorial Branch Library** (505-256-2065), 900 Girard SE. Open Tues.–Sat. 10–6, Wed. 11–7. Closed Sundays and Mondays. This modest little house in southeast Albuquerque, once the home of World War II correspondent and pioneer American journalist Ernie Pyle, who was killed in action, is a cozy, beloved neighborhood library with Pyle memorabilia.

Harwood Art Center (505-242-6367), 1114 7th Street NW, Albuquerque. Open Mon.–Thurs. 9–5, Fri. 9–4, first Friday of the month 6–8, and by appointment. This 1925 Methodist girls' boarding school was refurbished as a community arts center, and the Art School at Harwood now offers an impressive calendar of arts classes, yoga, and dance. With five galleries and 45 artists' studios, the place is an artists' haven, with frequent exhibitions and many shows of new work.

Old Town Albuquerque (505-243-3215), south of I-25 near Rio Grande Boulevard, or I-25 to Rio Grande Boulevard exit, then south. Or take Central Avenue W. The original site of Albuquerque, Old Town is a must-see for visitors who will enjoy museums, shops loaded with Southwestern arts and crafts, restaurants, a traditional plaza, and Southwestern architecture.

Sandia Man Cave (no phone), NM 165, 5 miles southeast of Placitas. Rumored to be a hoax dreamed up by members of the University of New Mexico Anthropology Department, this cave in the Sandia Mountains was once reputed to hold evidence of ancient man. It has, by and large, been discredited.

San Felipe de Neri Catholic Church (505-243-4628), 2005 N. Plaza Street NW, Albuquerque. Open daily. Museum open Mon.–Fri. 9–4:30, Sat. 9–5. Founded in 1706 and in almost continuous use for 300 years, this Old Town landmark maintains a strong community today. Mass is held in English and Spanish. Free.

MUSEUMS *✎* **Anderson-Abruzzo Balloon Museum** (505-768-6045), 9201 Balloon Museum Drive NE Albuquerque, Balloon Fiesta Park. Open Tues.–Sun. 9–5. Closed Mondays. Open 6–6 during Balloon Fiesta. Named for pioneering Albuquerque balloonists Maxie Anderson and Ben Abruzzo, who completed the first manned crossing of the Atlantic Ocean in 1978, this museum has exhibits that highlight the development of hot air and gas balloons in military, science, aerospace research, and for recreation. $4 adults, $3 New Mexico residents, $2 seniors, $1 children ages 4–12, under age 4 free, free 9–1 first Friday of month, excluding October.

Albuquerque Museum of Art & History (505-243-7255), 2000 Mountain Road NW, Albuquerque. Open Tues.–Sun. 9–5. Closed Mondays and city holidays. This premier city museum features art of the southwest, vintage Albuquerque, four centuries of Rio Grande Valley history, a sculpture garden, café, museum shop, and walking tours, as well as major traveling exhibitions. $4 adults, $3 New Mexico residents, $2 seniors, $1 children ages 4–12, under age 4 free. Free Sun. 9–1 and first Wed. each month.

THAT'S NOT CHIANG MAI. IT'S A BUDDHIST NEW YEAR CELEBRATION AT AN ALBUQUERQUE TEMPLE

✎ **American International Rattlesnake Museum and Gift Shop** (505-242-6569), 202 San Felipe NW, Albuquerque. Open: Summer Mon.–Sat. 10–6, Sun. 1–5; September–May Mon.–Fri. 11:30–5:30, Sat. 10–6, Sun. 1–5. In Old Town you will find the largest exhibit of rattlesnake species, art, and artifacts in the world. $5 adults, $4 students, seniors, military; $3 children.

✎ **Explora** (505-224-8300), 1701 Mountain Road NW, Albuquerque. Open Mon.–Sat. 10–6, Sun. noon–6. This is a science center where families can explore science, technology, and art through interactive activities and 250 hands-on exhibits. $8 adults, $5 seniors, $4 children ages 1–11.

516 Arts (505-242-1445), 516 Central Avenue SW, Albuquerque. This "museum-style" gallery is two floors of ambitious, adventurous, and notable national, local, and regional work. Somewhat avant-garde, it remains intelligent and accessible. Tues.–Sat. noon–5. Free.

Indian Pueblo Cultural Center (505-855-7902), 2401 12th Street NW, Albuquerque. Open daily 9–5. There is no better place to learn about New Mexico's nineteen pueblos than this museum, owned and operated by the pueblos. Exhibits showcase the history, culture, and artistic traditions of the pueblos. In addition, view exhibits of contemporary artists of painting, sculpture, and pottery. Browse the extensive gift shop that features authentic jewelry and Indian arts, plus books, music, and videos on tribal life. The Pueblo Harvest Cafe & Bakery serves Native American cuisine. Enjoy Native American dance and artist demonstrations every weekend for the price of admission. $8.40 adults, $6.40 seniors, $5.40 students and children ages 5–17, under age 5 free.

MAGNIFICENT OLD COTTONWOODS HAVE DEEP ROOTS IN THE ACEQUIAS (DITCHES) OF ALBUQUERQUE'S NORTH VALLEY

Maxwell Museum of Anthropology (505-277-4405), 500 University Boulevard NE University of New Mexico, Albuquerque. Open Tues.–Sat. 10–4. Closed Sundays and Mondays. With over 10 million items in its collection, the Maxwell is considered one of the leading anthropological museums in the United States. Free.

National Hispanic Cultural Center of New Mexico (505-246-2261), 1701 4th Street SW, Albuquerque. Open Tues.–Sun. 10–5, Sat. 12–5. Closed Mondays. This splendid facility has bloomed as a center for music, dance, theater, and exhibits of art of the contemporary Hispanic world. Community events, including Día de los Muertos, Globalquerque, Latin Dance Festival, and Cinco de Mayo, are celebrated here as well. La Fonda del Bosque is the on-site restaurant, and La Tiendita, the gift shop, has a good selection of books on related subjects. $6 adults, $5 NM residents, under age 16 free. Free first Sunday of month for NM residents.

National Museum of Nuclear Science and History (505-245-2137), 601 Eubank SE, Albuquerque. Open daily 9–5. Closed January 1, Easter, Thanksgiving, and Christmas. This museum is a resource for nuclear science, with exhibits, artifacts, and documentaries telling the story of the atomic age and its pioneers, as well as many related scientific topics. $12 adults, $10 seniors, $10 ages 6–17, free under age 5.

New Mexico Holocaust and Intolerance Museum and Study Center (505-247-0606), 616 Central Avenue SW, Albuquerque. Open Tues.–Sun. 11–3:30. Closed Mondays. The museum offers informational exhibits about genocide around the world. Admission by donation.

✎ **New Mexico Museum of Natural History and Science** (505-841-2800), 1801 Mountain Road NW, Albuquerque. Open daily 9–5. Closed Thanksgiving and Christmas. With a live volcano, huge dinosaurs, hands-on exhibits, natural history of New Mexico, a café, and an entertaining gift shop, this museum is guaranteed fun for the whole family. Starry Nights programs are given many Friday nights at the Planetarium extra charges. Lockheed Martin DynaTheater ($7–$10) shows hourly 10–5 daily. $8 adults,

NATIVE AMERICAN DANCES ARE PERFORMED ON WEEKENDS AT ALBUQUERQUE'S INDIAN PUEBLO CULTURAL CENTER

NEW MEXICO MUSEUM OF NATURAL HISTORY AND SCIENCE APPEALS TO KIDS OF ALL AGES

$7 seniors, $5 children ages 3–17, under age 3 free. Free to NM residents first Sun. of month. Free to seniors every Wed.

Rio Grande Nature Center (505-344-7240), 2901 Candelaria NW, Albuquerque. Grounds open daily 8–5, Visitor Center 10–5. This small museum (really, an expanded visitor center) provides information on the flora and fauna of the bosque, as well as blinds for viewing waterfowl. It is a major entryway to the bike and walking paths of Rio Grande Valley State Park. Educational events and festivals are held throughout the year here. $3 parking fee.

Turquoise Museum (505-247-8650), 2107 Central Avenue NW, Albuquerque. Open for guided tours only. Closed Sundays. Exhibits from sixty turquoise mines around the world, as well as the geology, mythology, and history of turquoise, plus a lapidary room and gift shop open by appointment only make this an irresistible stop. Guided tours daily 11 AM and 1 PM $10 adults, $8 seniors and ages 7–12, age 6 and under free.

Unser Racing Museum (505-341-1776), 1776 Montaño NW, Los Ranchos de Albuquerque. Open daily 10–4. Four generations of racecars, antique cars, winning pace cars, and uniforms that display the Unser family's racing accomplishments. $10 adults, $6 seniors, under age 16 free.

FOLKLÓRICO DANCES ARE PERFORMED ON OLD TOWN PLAZA DURING BALLOON FIESTA

ALBUQUERQUE'S BIO PARK

Albuquerque Biological Park (311 or 505-768-2000). Open daily 9–5, Sat. and Sun. 9–6 in summer. Closed January 1, Thanksgiving, Christmas. This complex consists of an aquarium, botanic garden, and zoo (as described below), and the Tingley Beach fishing lakes (see under "Fishing" in *To Do* and under *Green Space*). Zoo $14.50 teens and adults ages 13–64, $7.50 seniors, $6 ages 3–12. NM residents about $5 less. Aquarium/Botanic Garden tickets same price. Combo tickets, with admission to aquarium, garden, and zoo and train sold Tues.–Sun. before noon, $22 adults, $12 seniors, $8 children, age two and under, free. Significant discounts for NM residents. Tickets entitle participants to ride the Rio Line train between the aquarium and the zoo, and the Thunderbird Express, a loop around the zoo. Train does not run on Mon.

Albuquerque Aquarium (505-764-6200), 2601 Central Avenue NW, Albuquerque. Exhibits trace Rio Grande from the Rockies to the Gulf Coast, with saltwater fish, invertebrates, and habitats of the Gulf of Mexico. There is a shark tank, reef fish, and turtles. Summer concerts Thurs. nights June–August 7. See above for rates.

Rio Grande Botanic Garden (505-768-2000), 2601 Central Avenue NW, Albuquerque. Open Mon.–Fri. 9–5, Sat. and Sun. 9–6. Conservatory exhibits xeric plants of desert and Mediterranean climates, formal walled gardens, medicinal plants, Children's Fantasy Garden, Heritage Farm, and a Japanese garden. The PNM Butterfly Pavilion is open summers. Summer concerts are held Thurs. nights June–mid-August at 7 PM, and holiday light festival is open evenings during December. See above for rates.

Rio Grande Zoological Park (505-764-6200), 903 10th Street SW, Albuquerque. More than 1,000 animals are shown in their natural habitats. Those on the park's 64 acres include elephants, rhinos, giraffes, gorillas, flamingos, wolves, polar bears, big cats, seals, tigers, amphibians, and reptiles. Zoo Music Concerts June–July, Fri. at 7 PM. See above for rates.

✳ To Do

Check www.itsatrip.org for the latest sports activities in and around the city.

AMUSEMENT PARKS **Cliff's Amusement Park** (505-881-9373; www.cliffsamusement park.com), 4800 Osuna NE, Albuquerque. Roller coasters, water park, arcade, rides, and more rides: Cliff's is Albuquerque's answer to Disneyland.

BICYCLING Contact the **NM Touring Society** (president@nmts.org; www.nmts.org) for events.

The **City of Albuquerque** (311; www.cabq.gov/bike) provides maps for its many interconnecting bike paths.

Rio Grande Valley State Park has the 16-mile, practically level, Paseo del Bosque bike path through the bosque and parallel to the Rio Grande. (See *Green Space*.)

CLIMBING **Stone Age Climbing Gym** (505-341-2016), 4130 Cutler Avenue NE. Climbing school, group events, and guided climbs in the Sandias.

FARMERS' MARKETS Early July–late October Saturday mornings 7–noon.

Albuquerque Downtown Market (505-252-2959), 8th and Central SW, Robinson Park.

Albuquerque Uptown Growers' Market (505-720-7757), NE Corner Uptown Shopping Mall parking lot, Louisiana and Uptown Boulevard.

Village of Los Ranchos Growers' Market (505-890-2799), Los Ranchos City Hall, 6718 Rio Grande Boulevard NW.

Rail Yards Market, 777 1st Street SW. Repurposed historic Atchison, Topeka & Santa Fe Railyards south of Downtown in the Barelas neighborhood hosts Sunday market of baked goods, eclectic arts, homegrown produce, and all manner of curious possibilities. May–October 10–2 and at holiday time.

FISHING ✦ **Tingley Ponds.** For generations preceding the polio scare of the 1950s, Tingley Beach was a popular swimming spot for Albuquerqueans. Includes a model boat pond. Restored as a fishing area with snack bar and train service running between here and the Biopark, Tingley Ponds is a good place to walk as well as fish for stockers. Boats and bike rentals available Memorial Day–Labor Day.

GOLF **Arroyo del Oso Golf Course** (505-889-3699), 7001 Osuna Road NE. Named for the Bear Canyon Arroyo, where it is located, the sloping topography of the 27-hole course makes it best suited to intermediate-advanced players. $31.50 for 18 holes.

The Championship Golf Course at the University of New Mexico (505-277-4546), 3601 University Boulevard SE, Albuquerque. I-25 south to Rio Bravo exit, go left and continue half a mile. Open year-round, weather permitting. Soft spikes and collared shirts are required at this highly regarded 18-hole public course known as UNM South or "the Monster." It has been ranked among the Top 25 public courses and boasts rolling fairways, panoramic views of the city, and undulating greens with a three-hole beginner course and driving range. $29–39 walking/riding.

University of New Mexico North Course (505-277-4146), 2201 Tucker NE. Play a midday nine holes on mid-city greens shaded by tall trees. The perimeter of the course is also a popular walking and jogging path, adding up to 4 miles once around. Nine holes $18.

HIKING **Elena Gallegos Park** (505-452-5200), 7100 Tramway Boulevard NE. This vast mountain park offers a variety of trails, plus panoramic views of the city. Trails permit hiking, biking, and horseback riding. Prime spot for a summer evening picnic, with seven overed picnic areas. $1 per vehicle Mon.–Fri.; $2 per vehicle Sat.–Sun.

Juan Tabo Campground (505-281-3304), 10 miles northeast of Albuquerque at NM 556 and FR 333. Open year-round. 22 picnic sites. $3.

La Luz Trail (505-281-3304). The trailhead is at the end of FR 444, or access the trail from Juan Tabo Campground. This 15-mile challenging round-trip hike to Sandia Crest over switchbacks is only for the confidently in-shape. Still, it is *the* Albuquerque hike. The trail goes through four life zones and rises over 3,000 feet to an altitude of 10,500 feet with a knockout view from Sandia Crest. As they say, you can take the tram down. Some prefer to take the tram up and down. Travel well prepared for rapid weather change. Every summer, someone hikes up on a hot August afternoon in shorts and tee shirt, then gets hypothermia when temperature drops 40 degrees and a hailstorm comes in. $3 per car.

HORSEBACK RIDING **Del Sol Equestrian Center** (505-873-0888), 6715 Isleta Boulevard SW. Horse boarding and lessons.

Flying Horse School of Horsemanship (505-822-8473), 9500 Wilshire Boulevard NE. Horse boarding, riding lessons, clinics, lessons.

HORSE RACING **The Downs at Albuquerque** (505-266-5555), Expo New Mexico, 300 San Pedro NE. Open daily 10–late. Racing in season, with year-round simulcasting and slot machines providing excitement. Awesome dinner specials.

ICE SKATING ✍ **Outpost Ice Arena** (505-856-7595), 9530 Tramway Boulevard NE. Open daily. Lessons, public sessions, and group events are scheduled. Call for more information. Ages 6 and up, $7; skate rental $3.

ROLLER-SKATING ✍ **Roller King** (505-299-4494; www.rollerkingabq.com), 400 Paisano NE. Northeast corner of I-40 and Juan Tabo. Open daily. Call for specific events and hours. Ages 6 and up, $5; skate rental $3.

SKATEBOARDING ✍ **Los Altos Municipal Skate Park** (505-291-6239), 10140 Lomas, west of Eubank, east of Easterday. Open daily, sunrise–sunset. Considered "the fastest skate park in the West," Los Altos requires a helmet. Free.

SPECTATOR SPORTS **Albuquerque Isotopes Baseball Club** (505-924-2255), 1601 Avenida Cesar Chavez, at intersection of University Boulevard SE. Take I-25 to Avenida Cesar Chavez, go east. The Isotopes are a Triple-A member of the Pacific Coast League. Isotopes Stadium is a classic ballpark with an abundance of dining and treat opportunities. Take me out to the ball game! $12-24, add $2 day of game plus $1 Sat. fireworks. Go to abqisotopes.com for information.

UNM Lobos and Lady Lobos Basketball (505-925-LOBO or 505-925-5626), corner of Avenida Cesar Chavez and University Boulevard SE. Both the men's and ladies' teams play throughout the season in the Pit, or University Arena, a stadium that slopes 37 feet down toward the floor, where 18,000 fans dressed in Lobos red enjoy intimidating visiting teams and giving the Lobos their home court advantage. $12–27.

WALKING TOURS **Albuquerque Museum** (505-243-7255) offers walking tours of Old Town Tues.–Sun., 11 AM. during warmer months.

WINERIES **Anderson Valley Vineyards** (505-344-7266), 4920 Rio Grande Boulevard NW, Albuquerque. Tasting room hours Tues.–Sun. noon–5:30. One of the first contemporary vineyards in New Mexico, founded in 1973, featuring Red Chile Cabernet and Balloon Blush, as specialties.

Casa Rondeña Winery (505-344-5911), 733 Chavez Road NW, Albuquerque. Tasting room hours Mon.–Sun. noon–7. Winemaker John Calvin has created a splendid Tuscan estate in Albuquerque's North Valley to frame his award-winning creations. Lovely picnic spot.

Gruet Winery (505-821-0055), 8400 Pan American Freeway NE, Albuquerque. Proprietors are the Gruet family. Tasting room hours Mon.–Sun. 10–7. Fine sparkling wine and still wines, such as pinot noir and Chardonnay.

St. Clair Vineyards (505-243-9916), 901 Rio Grande Boulevard NW, Albuquerque. Tasting room hours Sun.–Thurs. 9–9, Fri.–Sat. 11–10. A sixth-generation winery (its original location in Deming), its Albuquerque Old Town location is a bistro with a spacious outdoor patio, fine service, and excellent food, with wines used as menu ingredients.

✳ Green Space

Rio Grande Valley State Park (505-452-5200), 2901 Candelaria NW, Albuquerque. Open daily April–October 7–9; November–March 7–7. Visitor center open daily 10–5. Closed Thanksgiving, Christmas, and New Year's Day. Two easy, approximately 1-mile trails through the center; a 3-acre observation pond with waterfowl, turtles, and dragonflies; demonstration gardens; wetlands; and interpretive nature trails make this a

CASA RONDENA WINE TASTING ROOM IN THE NORTH VALLEY

friendly place to explore the river, forest, and riparian environment. It is a migratory bird sanctuary that sponsors many events to celebrate the inhabitants. In addition, it provides access to the paved walking and bike path that extends 15 miles through the city along the bosque, or cottonwood forest. $3.

🐟 **Tingley Ponds** (505-764-6200), 1800 Tingley Drive. Open daily, sunrise to sunset. Opened during the 1930s, the city's Tingley Beach was a popular place to swim until fears engendered by the polio epidemic shut it down. In recent years, Tingley Ponds have been restored as 18 acres of ponds and wetlands that are stocked and open to public fishing. Free.

PARKS **Hyder Park.** In the beautiful southeast at the corner of Richmond and Santa Monica SE is a beloved neighborhood park with mature shade trees, benches, and a walking and running path around the circumference.

Roosevelt Park. Coal and Spruce SE. A lovely, large, unfenced off-leash dog park. Bring your own water. For a complete list of off-leash parks, go to www.abqdog.com.

Tiguex Park. 1800 Mountain Road NW. With shady old cedar trees and gently rolling paths, this Old Town green space between the Albuquerque Museum and the Museum of Natural History makes a nice respite where you can get some fresh air and sunshine and stretch your legs.

✳ Lodging

BED & BREAKFASTS, MOTELS, AND HOTELS

🦎 **Hiway House** (505-268-3971; www.hiwayhousemotel.com), 3200 Central Avenue SE, Albuquerque. If you're craving a taste of the old road, that is Old Route 66, consider this vintage remnant of what was a classic Southwest motel chain once owned by Ramada Inn founder Del Webb. You'll be in the proximity to Nob Hill, with plentiful dining and shopping choices, walking distance to the University of New Mexico, and close to the Sunport without staying in a chain airport motel. The 60 rooms are plain but serviceable. The motel is set back a bit from Central Avenue, so you'll have a bit of protection from traffic noise. Not a bad place for those seeking the character of a road trip. $75.

♂ ⚲ **Hotel Andaluz** (505-242-9090; www.hotelandaluz.com), 125 2nd Street NW, Albuquerque. A $30-million renovation of the old downtown Hilton (where Conrad Hilton brought his bride, Zsa-Zsa Gabor, for their honeymoon) created a green LEED-certified oasis. Standard rooms are smallish, bedding is grand. The rooftop Ibiza Bar offers a grand sweep of city lights and the Sandia Mountains. Best of all is the nostalgia of the Spanish-style lobby. Another delightful boutique hotel. $233.

Hotel Albuquerque at Old Town (505-843-6300; hotelabq.com), 800 Rio Grande Boulevard NW. Somewhat dated, but still stately, this is a convenient Old Town address and has a Garduno's Restaurant and bar on site. A decent business or family vacation venue. $149.

Hotel Chaco (505-246-9989; www.hotelchaco.com/2000), Bellamah Avenue NW, Albuquerque. The last word in southwest urban chic, this spiffy Old Town/Sawmill boutique hotel came on line in 2017, with a cool bar that grants splendid views of the city. The style is a gorgeous meld of Chaco Canyon Southwest theme with cutting edge

contemporary. A glass of champagne when you register. $209–299.

Hotel Blue (505-924-2400; www.thehotelblue.com), 717 Central Avenue SW, Albuquerque. An interesting place to stay Downtown, right on Route 66, Hotel Blue is a renovation of tasteful midcentury modern design with a hip ambience. The place provides unexpected attention to details and is both business and family-friendly, with a seasonal pool. Your hosts brag on their state-of-the-art mattresses and attention to guest comfort. You can walk anywhere Downtown from here, including the Convention Center and catch a bus to anywhere else you might want to go. Fresh baked cookies greet you. $70.

Hotel Parc Central (505-242-0040; hotelparqcentral.com), 806 Central SE. A 1926 Italianate hospital is restored to a deluxe urban oasis. In excellent walking distance to Downtown, this upscale boutique hotel offers seventy-four guest rooms and the Apothecary Lounge, a hot rooftop bar, the Apothecary Lounge, worth visiting on its own. $165.

♂ ⚲ **Los Poblanos Historic Inn and Organic Farm** (505-344-9297; www.lospoblanos.com), 4803 Rio Grande Boulevard NW, Albuquerque. A stay in this John Gaw Meem–designed masterpiece of classic Territorial Revival architecture overlooking 25 acres of lavender, lush old cottonwoods, a working dairy, and an organic farm gives you a sense of the expansive history of Albuquerque. The beauty of the former Simms estate has been preserved by the owners, and every detail of the property evokes its rich past. For an extra-special stay, consider the Girard Guest House, a two-room casita decorated with Mexican folk art. A variety of lodgings is available, and there is a saltwater pool. Field to fork organic breakfast (not included) is a grand affair, prepared with seasonal local produce and eggs directly from Los Poblanos Organics by James Beard Award-winning Chef Jonathan Perno. Throw in free Wi-Fi, complimentary *New*

York Times, and concierge service, and you have the premier Albuquerque lodging experience. Expect to pay upwards of $200. Creative packages. Glorious weddings.

Sarabande Bed & Breakfast (505-348-5593; www.sarabandebb.com), 5637 Rio Grande Boulevard NW, Albuquerque. For a charming North Valley retreat, you couldn't do better than Sarabande, named for the rose that grows in its courtyard. *Quiet, gracious,* and *relaxing* are all words that well apply to the mood you will find here. Lap pool open May–October. Green consciousness year-round. $174–$219.

Spy House (505-842-0223; www.albuquerquebedandbreakfasts.com/spy-house-rooms.htm), 209 High Street SE. This meticulously restored 1912 Craftsman bungalow in Huning Highlands district near downtown was once the residence of David Greenglass, brother of convicted Los Alamos Atomic Age spy Ethel Rosenberg. A gourmet breakfast is included here and at sister property, Heritage House, and in two private cottages, prepared and served by caring and knowledgeable hosts. Comfort, nostalgia, and all the conveniences expected at newer lodgings. Romantic and nostalgic, a perfect getaway even if you live here! Thoughtful packages present the city at its finest. A memorable alternative to standard lodging choices. $99–$219.

Boettger Mansion at Old Town (505-243-3639; www.bottger.com), 110 San Felipe NW, Albuquerque. Romantic, historic, serving scrumptious breakfast that includes house made sorbet over fresh fruit, with a hot tub, this B&B in the heart of Old Town has seven lovely rooms and provides intimacy and relaxation for a true getaway. An on-site wedding planner can tune you in to the Elopement Package if you wish, or here you can find a Hot Air Balloon Package for the adventurous. No better place to celebrate an anniversary or Valentine's Day. $134.

❊ Where to Eat

DINING OUT Antiquity (505-247-3545), 112 Romero Street NW. D daily, starting at 5 PM Lamb roasting on the grill greets you on entering this cozy warren of an Old Town hideaway that is charming in all seasons. Make reservations and arrive early—the specials tend to sell out. There is always a fresh fish special; fresh lobster and scallops; five delicious cuts of steak, including châteaubriand for two with béarnaise sauce; and the French onion soup is the best. Reasonable wine by the glass. All in all, a good value. Moderate.

Artichoke Cafe (505-243-0200), 424 Central Avenue SE. D nightly, L Mon.–Fri. For going on three decades, Pat and Terry Keene have set the standard for fine dining in Albuquerque. The simplest dishes here—steamed artichoke, roast chicken, and salmon of the day—are always well prepared and beautifully presented, with just the right seasoning, intriguing sauce, and side dishes. Expect classic, not adventurous. The restaurant seats 120, but feels more intimate. When excellent service is a must, the Artichoke will do the job and do it right. Moderate–Expensive.

El Pinto (505-898-1777), 10500 4th Street NW. Open Mon.–Thurs. 11–9; Fri.–Sat. 11–10; Sun. 10:30–9. When you want to impress your out-of-town guests with Mexican food that won't burn, take them to a really nice place for dinner. El Pinto, at the north end of the North Valley, is where to go and get your fix of flame-roasted Hatch green chilies. Salsa, chips, splashy margaritas on the patio, and barbecue ribs on the side go well with enchiladas and chiles rellenos. The owner speaks tequila. Moderate.

La Crêpe Michel (505-242-1251), 400 San Felipe NW. Open Tues.–Sun. L; Tues.–Sat. D 6–9. The founder holds a PhD, but more to the point, year after year she turns out authentic crêpes and quiche and classic French dishes in this enduringly romantic spot down a winding back alley in Old Town. Could not be more charming! Take a seat close to the fireplace and enjoy. Pâté and imported cheese, chicken and mushroom crêpes, *duck à l'orange*, excellent *filet de boeuf*, and then *crêpe au chocolat* or *belle Helene* for dessert. It's fun to share! It can be a bit chilly on a cold night, so bring a wrap. Reservations essential. Moderate.

Paisano's (505-298-7541), 1935 Eubank Boulevard NE. D, L Mon.–Fri. Fresh pasta, daily specials, and half-orders. Love the wild mushroom lasagna and capellini with seared scallops and the piquant house marinara. Decent house wines by the glass. Best of all, Paisano's caters to gluten-free diets (the owner is gluten-free) so delicious house-made pasta is available for special diets. "We cook like your Italian Grandma" is Paisano's motto. Good value. Moderate.

Scalo Northern Italian Grill (505-255-8781), 3500 Central SE. D daily, L Mon.–Fri., brunch Sat. and Sun., happy hour menu Mon.–Fri. 4–7. White linen sets the mood, there's crispy fresh bread to dip in flavorful olive oil, the pasta is perfectly prepared, and a nice glass of wine rounds it all out. Scalo remains, after more than 30 years, one of the city's top addresses for a business lunch or birthday celebration. A good place to meet with a good friend or someone you haven't seen in ages, as you can count on the service. The wine list has over 300 selections; there's a full bar that is a chic hangout on its own, plus there's occasional live jazz. Moderate–Expensive.

Vernon's Speakeasy (505-341-0831), 6855 4th Street NW. Open daily 4:30–9:30. D only. Vernon's is the place for relaxing with a drink and a good steak after a workweek or for celebrating an anniversary. Named one of America's Top 100 Steakhouses by Open Table, the service is impeccable, and classic American food is beautifully prepared and scrumptious. Vernon's is for serious red meat eaters only, whether you crave a slab of dry-aged prime steak or Colorado lamb chops. The sides are luscious, too, especially the "adult" mac and cheese. It's difficult to choose between the French onion soup and the lobster bisque. Recommended for a special occasion. Live music Thurs.–Sun. Bar open late. Very expensive. Vernon's also has Cafe 6855 next door, serving casual food like soups, salads, and sandwiches, open daily for lunch and weekend brunch.

Yanni's Mediterranean Bar & Gtill & Lemoni Lounge (505-268-9250), 3109 Central NE. Open Mon.–Thurs. 11–10; Fri.–Sat. 11–11; Sun. 11:30–9. Yanni's is a regular Nob Hill hangout and watering hole, as well as a power lunch spot. Greek specialties are served here, including a more than passable vegetable moussaka. Moderate.

Zacatecas (505-255-8226), 3423 Central NE. Open daily. L, D Fri., Sat., Sun. D only Tues.–Sun. Closed Mondays. Compound chef Mark Kiffin does it again, coming down from Canyon Road and finding the winning formula for Nob Hill. Authentic Mexican-style flavorful tacos and tequilas plus extensive beer selections are embraced by Duke City denizens ready to go a bit upscale from their tried-and-true New Mexican chile-slingin' mom-and-pop cafés. Real south-of-the-border flavor. Moderate.

EATING OUT **Blake's Lotaburger** (505-243-8343; www.lotaburger.com). Open daily. Hours vary by location. L, D, breakfast burritos at some loactions. Voted top green chile burger in the nation by *National Geographic Traveler*. This New Mexico fast food chain, with dozens of outlets throughout the state, serves the Lotaburger special with fries that half the town runs on. Characters in Tony Hillerman's novels pack Lotaburgers when they go out to solve mysteries. Once you try it, you will be hooked. Inexpensive.

Cheese & Coffee Café (505-242-0326), 2679 Louisiana NE; and (505-882-1226), 119 San Pasquale NW, near Old Town.

Open Mon.–Sat. L 10–3. This is the quintessential lunch stop, a deli with giant sandwiches, salads almost too big to be believed (and very fresh) and a New York–ish bustle generated by working folk and shoppers. The Old Town location is lower key, but if you're out shopping in the malls, go to the Louisiana locale. The salad trio is hard to pass up. Chicken salad is the best. Inexpensive.

Farina Pizzeria (505-243-0130), 510 Central SE. Open daily. L, D. D only Sat. and Sun. This EDO (East of Downtown) pizza café in a renovated brick building has a perfect medley of options: an intimate wine bar, excellent crispy-crust made-to-order pizzas, and fresh salads. Can get pretty crowded on Friday nights as the university crowd meets up with Downtown folk. Don't expect to conduct a private conversation unless you go for a really late lunch. Go for the *funghi* pizza with house-made sausage. Farina Alto is now in a Northeast Heights location (www.FarinaAlto.com). Inexpensive.

Frontier Restaurant (505-266-0550), 2400 Central Avenue SE. Located across Central from UNM, open daily 5 AM–1 AM, the Frontier is an Albuquerque institution. Known for fragrant cinnamon rolls, freshly squeezed orange juice, green chile–smothered huevos rancheros, and soft chicken tacos, as well as its homemade tortillas, the bustling Frontier serves as a citywide social scene and study hall in addition to restaurant. Try the Frontier burger, with hickory smoke sauce, Thousand Island dressing, and onion. Not as cheap as it used to be, however. Inexpensive.

Hartford Square (505-265-4133; orders@hartfordsq.com), 218 Gold Avenue SW. Open daily 7–4 Mon.–Fri., 8:30–2:30 Sat and Sun. B, L. Fresh, locally sourced, delicious, and healthy eat in or take out prepared dishes. Hip, urban, intelligent eatery—a place to read the *Times* or meet up for a deep conversation, a place to be comfortably alone while out. On the edge of Downtown, around the corner from the Old Albuquerque High lofts. Beer and wine, excellent coffee, irresistible pastries, heart-warming soups. Sunday brunch was made for this. A joy. Inexpensive–Moderate. Hours vary seasonally.

I Love Sushi Teppan Grill (505-883-3618), 6001 San Mateo NE, Suite F4. Open Mon.–Sat. Closed Sundays. L, D. Japanese food artists will dazzle you as they turn your dinner preparation into a performance at the grill. And you can't beat the sushi; they claim to have the freshest and best in town. Prices here are reasonable for the quality. Beer and wine, too.

Il Vicino Wood Oven Pizza and Brewery (505-266-7855), 3403 Central SE. Open daily. L, D. Open late. The dozen varieties of crispy, thin-crust pizza turned out in the wood-fired ovens here are perennially excellent, and when savored with a fresh spinach salad, one of Nob Hill's best budget dining experiences. Other locations around town. Panini and baked lasagna are also worth trying. Microbrews add to the experience. It's generally busy here and a tad rowdy, in a good way. This site is the original and still has the buzz.

🌸 **Mannie's Family Restaurant** (505-265-1669), 2900 Central Avenue SE. B, L, D 6 AM–9 PM daily, Mon.–Sun. Aside from its dependable hours, easy parking, central Nob Hill–university location, reliable Wi-Fi and menu diverse enough to please a crowd, why dine here? It could be for the reasonable prices, good service, fresh muffins, and bottomless cup of coffee. Go for the "66 Pile-Up." The place is hopping on a Sunday morning, when platters of house-made corned beef hash and eggs rule the roost. Try a Pile Up on Central & Girard with a homemade blueberry muffin! Daily specials. Inexpensive.

Monte Carlo Steak House (505-836-9886), 3916 Central SW. Open Mon.–Sat. Closed Sundays. L, D. Go here for the experience as much as the food. Enter through the liquor store, and then step down into the deep, dim hideaway replete with bar, red pleather booths, and 1970s-era kitsch—even Elvis on velvet.

Daily specials; the Thurs.–Fri. evening prime rib special is a good deal, as are steak dinners with mounds of french fries, swell Greek salads, and best baklava in town. The place is full of characters that more than slightly resemble those on *Breaking Bad*. Featured on *Diners, Drive-ins and Dives*. Moderate.

Orchid Thai Cuisine (505-265-4047), 4300 Central Avenue SE. L, D daily. The best of the lot of Thai restaurants in this part of town. I'm always happy here, and so are my friends, as we dine on pad thai and a big bowl of tom yum soup. Lunch specials. Many vegan options. Inexpensive.

Owl Cafe (505-291-4900), 800 Eubank Boulevard NE. Open Mon.–Thurs. 7–10; Fri.–Sat. 7–11. Closed Sundays. B, L, D. The city cousin of the San Antonio original, this Owl, which is quite recognizable from the highway, has a comfy 1950s vibe, with Blue Plate specials around $12 such as the famous burger and fries or spaghetti and meatballs, chicken fried steak, meatloaf, and more, with chocolate cake, shakes and sundaes. The menu lists just about every homey dish you remember from childhood. Nostalgia all the way. Inexpensive.

The Quarters BBQ (505-843-6949), 801 Yale Boulevard SE and in NE Heights. Open Mon.–Fri. 11–9. Sat. noon–9. Closed Sundays. L, D. When there is an argument about where to get the best barbecue in Albuquerque, many old-timers are likely to bet on the Quarters. It's dark and rowdy, being somewhat of a university hangout, and people bring their children here generation after generation. Lunch specials. Meats smoked to perfection, sauce with a recognizable tang. The Quarters has some of the best wine and beer selections in the area. Inexpensive.

Mr. Powdrell's Barbeque House (505-354-8086) 5209 4th Street NW. L, D Mon.-Sat. Situated in a historic home in the North Valley, this remains the oldest and best barbecue in the city. At least four generations of Powdrells execute the original century-old East Texas recipes. Generous platters of the works—hickory-smoked ribs, brisket, and hot links—for less than you can imagine. The sides are outstanding as well; they have the best onion rings in the city, as well as fabulous fried macaroni and cheese and fried mushrooms. Don't pass on the cherry cobbler. Inexpensive–Moderate.

Luigi's Ristorante & Pizzaria (505-343-0466), 6225 4th Street NW, Albuquerque. This 20 year-old neighborhood Italian restaurant has homestyle cooking, pasta prepared to order, an enormous menu, wine, beer, and a buffet with a half-dozen sauces, pizza, chicken cacciatore, sausage, meatballs, salad, minestrone, and dessert—all you can eat for under $15. Luigi and his mother make it all from scratch. Inexpensive.

Pizzeria Luca (505) 797-8086, 8850 Holly Avenue NE, Suite J, Albuquerque. The pizza flour used here is imported from Naples, the crust is crackling-crisp, the sausage is house-made, and the salads are fabulous. This place has a sophisticated yet laid-back bar to watch the game, meet a friend, or dine out on your own. Inexpensive–Moderate.

Standard Diner. B, L, D, Mon.-Sun. It's not standard, and it's not a diner, but this close to downtown establishment serves plump sandwiches, abundant salads, and scrumptious desserts. The food is not challenging, but it's prepared well and served in timely style. Satisfying. Beer and wine. Moderate.

Range Café on Rio Grande. B, L, D, Mon.–Sun. Located beside I-40, this iteration may be the ultimate Range Café. The menu, with standards of meatloaf, roast turkey with all the trimmings, and green chile chicken enchiladas, is familiar. Desserts are the speciality, so save room for coconut cream pie. And the decor is magical, with fanciful cows bursting through the wall painted to resemble a colorful surreal version of the surrounding desert. It's all in fun. Moderate.

Siam Café (505-883-7334), 5500 San Mateo NE #101. Open Mon.–Sat. 11–9.

Others come and go, but we return here for authentic Thai. Lunch specials under $10. Green curry, drunken noodles, pad thai, and hot and sour chicken soup—a family favorite of ours—are consistent and served with aplomb. Just about every dish on the menu can be ordered vegetarian. Authentic. Inexpensive.

✒ **66 Diner** (505-247-1421), 1405 Central Avenue NE. Open Mon.–Fri. 11–10; Sat. 8 AM–11 PM; Sun. 8 AM–10 PM. Perhaps the best chicken-fried steak in town, with real mashed potatoes and pie for dessert. Definitely worth the carbo-load. The Route 66 motif is so omnipresent, you long for your poodle skirt. Daily Blue Plate specials and mouthwatering pies, especially those with peanut butter. Inexpensive.

Campo B daily 7:30–11:30, D Wed.–Sun. 5–9. The latest addition to the compound of Los Poblanos Historic Inn and Organic Gardens, located in the newly-restored historic dairy barn, this is a fine place for breakfast or a light meal you want to turn into a special occasion. The name means "field," and most of what is served comes from the fields and orchards of the grand property. You can get a great eggs benedict here. Moderate.

Streetfood Asia (505-260-0088), 3422 Central Avenue SE. Mon.–Sun. L, D. Stylish, raucous, and crowded in a way that makes the scene lively (but difficult to conduct intimate conversation as you pretty much need to shout to be heard), SFA is a cool place for lunch or dinner. I adore the pan-Asian noodle dishes, satays, and wok delights as well as the chilled fruity beverages. Inexpensive.

Sushi King Sushi & Noodles (505-842-5099), 118 Central SW. Open daily. L, D. Open late Fri.–Sat. For après-cinema sushi or noodle soup, you'll love this place, with its urban feel and superb tastes. And it has beer and wine. Check other locations around town. Moderate.

Taj Mahal Cuisine of India (505-255-1994) 1430 Carlisle Boulevard NE. L, D, Mon.–Sun. Traditional Indian fare. The savory, varied lunch buffet remains one of the best deals in town. Inexpensive.

Thai Vegan (505-884-4610), 5505 Osuna Road NE and Nob Hill location at 3804 Central SE. Open daily. L, D. Elegant yet informal spot for tasty vegetarian and beyond vegetarian fare. A local favorite lunch stop. Beautiful presentation. Love the spicy eggplant with the sign. You may wish to dabble in the faux (soy) chicken, fish, and other dietary preparations, all authentically spiced. Inexpensive.

🍴 **Tomato Cafe Gourmet Italian Food Bar** (505-821-9300), 5920 Holly NE and NE Heights location on Juan Tabo Boulevard. Open daily 11–8:30. L, D. All you can eat! Yes, it is a buffet, and yes, it is a bargain. But the food doesn't taste like buffet food. There's unlimited handcrafted pizza; pasta with a choice of homemade sauces, such as roasted tomato garlic; giant meatballs; garlicky green beans; minestrone soup; fresh salad; spinach and ricotta ravioli, to name just a few items. All these and much more make this a fine place to bring teenagers with bottomless stomachs, or yourself and your honey after a workout at the gym, when you just can't stand to cook or don't have time to put a real meal on the table. You'll spend less than if you shopped and cooked. Moderate.

🍴 **Western View Diner & Steakhouse.** (505- 836-2200), 6411 Central Avenue NW, Albuquerque. B, L, D. Closed Sundays. Biscuits and gravy, homemade pie, real mashed potatoes, served with a big slice of Mother Road authenticity. The regulars sit at the counter, the waitresses know your name, and the daily specials are crazy generous. You'll feel like you're on a road trip just from eating here on the edge of town. Inexpensive.

BREWPUBS AND WINE BARS **Kelly's Brew Pub** (505-262-2739), 3222 Central Avenue SE. L, D 11–10 daily. On summer nights, it sometimes seems the entire town is sipping a brew on Kelly's Nob Hill patio, and it just may be. In other towns, a place like Kelly's might just be a college hangout, but this establishment rises above that designation. This historic building, the 1939 Jones Motor Co., was renovated to keep its Route 66 feel, and the salads and sandwiches decent. With over 20 in-house brews on tap, no wonder this place is usually jammed. Inexpensive.

Marble Brewery (505-243-2739; www .marblebrewery.com), 111 Marble Avenue NW. Definitely the place to sip suds and hang out Downtown. Food trucks are parked out front. Check the website for music and entertainment events. Also now on Santa Fe Plaza.

O'Niell's Irish Pub (505-255-6782), 4310 Central Avenue SE; another location in the NE Heights at 3301 Juan Tabo Boulevard NE. L, D, late night Mon.–Sun. Pub food taken to an art form. The fish-and-chips made of wild caught cod are especially good, as is the Caesar salad. Vegetarians can be happy here, too. Open mic, frequent live entertainment, happening patio. Half-price burgers on many a Monday. A comfortable place to meet up with a pal or hang out on your own at the bar. Incredible selection of beers on tap. Geeks who Drink is a popular event and attracts crowds on Wed. nights. Live music on Sunday nights attracts a "mature" crowd. NE Heights location, too. Inexpensive.

Zinc Wine Bar & Bistro (505-254-9462), 3009 Central Avenue NE. Open daily. L, D till 11 PM. Sunday brunch only. Wine cellar open 5 PM–1 AM nightly, closed Sundays. The chic upscale restaurant is on the main floor and mezzanine, but the real hangout is the wine bar downstairs, where you may purchase wine flights and interesting bar food. Well-mixed drinks. Feels like a place to sip a martini and be an adult. You could be in Seattle, or even Paris. Expect bistro food, seasonal, leaning towards the locavore diet. And the live entertainment is top-notch. Moderate–Expensive.

CAFÉS **Flying Star** (505-344-6714; www .flyingstarcafe.com), 4026 Rio Grande Boulevard NW. The Bernsteins started on a shoestring, and now run a tidy chain of locally owned, popular cafés all over town, each with a different style, but all featuring patios and fireplaces. The Flying Star has grown into an Albuquerque institution. The tagline, "You're never far from a Flying Star," is indeed true. The cafe's baked goods are out of sight, particularly the towering Key lime pie, carrot cake, or strawberry-rhubarb pie. Burgers and fries are good, and the daily lunch and dinner specials go quickly. The Bernsteins brag that everything is made from scratch, and you will pay a little more for that. Wi-Fi may be restricted during busy hours, and it's not always the easiest to connect. Moderate.

Café Lush (505-508-0164), 700 Tijeras Avenue NW, Albuquerque. B, L. Closed Sundays. *Better Call Saul* fans will recognize this place downtown. It's a corner café, with patio, serving upscale breakfast and excellent sandwiches with their special bacon and sprinkling of "lush dust," their secret ingredient. Attracts the downtown crowd and perfect for post-Growers' Market Saturday brunch. Inexpensive.

🚲 **Green Jeans Farmery** (505-401-1000), 3600 Cutler Avenue NE, Albuquerque. This out-of-the-way collection of colorful repurposed shipping containers is like a tiny village of restaurants, a brewpub, a gyms, street tacos, ice cream and pizza parlors that is pure fun, the way a trip to the boardwalk is fun, with plenty of people watching. A cycling destination and by all means worth a visit. Parking is tricky to wild, very crowded with little backup space. Inexpensive.

Downtown Java Joe's (505-765-1514), 906 Park SW. Open 6:30–3:30. B, L. If you hanker for a bygone era—shall we say the 1960s?—and you love good coffee and great scones and cinnamon rolls, by all means come on down to this Downtown hangout, where live folk and jazz transpire over much of the weekend. Scruffiness is encouraged; tattoos, while not required, are omnipresent, and

SEVEN FAVORITE ALBUQUERQUE MEXICAN RESTAURANTS

Barelas Coffee House (505-843-7577), 1502 4th Street SW. Open daily. B, L. Closed Sundays. Politicos and TV celebrities come here to mingle with the working folk. You never know who you'll run into. It's best known for its thick, burning red chile and delectable slow-baked *carne adovada*, but the huevos rancheros are not to be missed. For serious chile lovers and those who swear they know their chile. Try to come at off hours, or be prepared to wait in line. Then you'll have your choice of seating, including the pocket-size enclosed patio. It's a short walk to the National Hispanic Cultural Center from here. Inexpensive.

Casa de Benavidez (505-219-2287), 8032 N. 4th Street NW. With its pretty green patio, waterfall, fountains, and full bar, Casa B's is a longtime, reliable favorite of North Valley residents. HOME OF THE SOPAIPILLA BURGER, reads the marquee, but that doesn't really describe the experience. The side café, geared toward takeout, is a popular morning hangout and serves up a contender for the best chorizo breakfast burrito in town. The fajitas are among the best, too. It's a bit pricey for Mexican food, but the portions are immense. A nice place to bring the folks for dinner or a special occasion. You'll find locals unwinding here on Fri. evening with a margarita and live guitar of Maestro Hector Pimentel. Moderate.

Casa de Ruiz Church Street Café (505-247-8522), 2111 Church Street, Old Town. Open Sun.–Wed. 8–4; Thurs.–Sat. 8–8. Claiming to be located in the oldest building in Old Town, dating to the 1700s, the Church Street Café does for sure serve delicious Mexican food prepared from family recipes. If you're not in the mood for spicy red, there's sandwiches, salads as well as wine and beer. Inexpensive.

Duran's Pharmacy (505-247-4141), 1815 Central Avenue NW. Open Mon.–Tues. 9–6:30, Wed.–Sun. 9–8. Weave your way through cosmetics and household goods to the back, where you will find a line waiting for a seat at the legendary lunch counter or on the patio, or for one of the half-dozen tables, to taste the tortilla soup and what is likely the most delicious tortillas

the bagels and lox are just fine, thanks. Homemade soup and famous egg salad available daily. Inexpensive.

Michael Thomas Coffee Roasters (505-255-3330), 1111 Carlisle Avenue SE and 202 Bryn Mawr Drive SE in Nob Hill. Some folks in "the Q" prefer to drink the Fair Trade Guatemalan coffee fresh roasted in this locally owned small café. "Hand roasted coffee for a busy world" is their motto. Their off-the-beaten path spots are favorites with the "mature" set, who may sit undisturbed as a cat in a sunny corner with the *New York Times* and a mug of coffee, or lounge meditatively on the patio.

Satellite Coffee (505-899-1001), 1640 Alamdea Boulevard NW, and several other locations around the city. If you long for a quieter place to check your email, sip a latte, study, or read the paper, ease on into one of these Flying Star

siblings, where you can also grab just a little bite to eat and a comfy easy chair. A Wi-Fi hot spot, for sure. Moderate.

Zendo (505-926-1636), 413 2nd Street SW. There is an actual buzz about Zendo, one of several fine coffee cafes to pop up around Downtown in recent times. It's a buzz that invites conversation and inspiration.

BAKERIES **Le Chantilly Fine Pastries & Wedding Cake Designers** (505-293-7057), 8216 Menaul Boulevard NE. Impeccable made from scratch croissants, brioche, cheese sticks, and napoleons are the order of the day here at this classic French bakery. Now with gluten-free offerings. You'll feel secure with a hostess or host gift from here.

Golden Crown Panaderia (505-243-2424), 1103 Mountain Road NW. Home of the green chile cheese bread, this

around, hot off the grill and doused in butter. Portions are immense, so unless you are famished, be prepared to share. Inexpensive.

El Patio de Albuquerque (505-268-4245), 142 Harvard Drive SE. Open daily. B, L, D. This slightly funky beloved university area restaurant has been serving the same reliably fluffy, light sopaipillas and savory green chile chicken enchiladas (my standby and perpetual crave) for over 30 years. How pleasant to sip a cold one on the shady, well-trodden patio on a hot summer day and savor the true flavors of New Mexico. In fall, when the chile crop comes in, the green is over-the-top hot. No matter how many others come and go, this place remains a favorite. Live music Thurs.–Sun. and Sunday brunch. Breakfast served all day. With a new location serving the same great menu in the North Valley at Griegos Road and Rio Grande Boulevard NW. Inexpensive–Moderate.

Garcia's Kitchen (505-242-1199), 1736 Central SW. Open daily 7–9. B, L, D. Don't start your East Coast friends out on the red chile here. Only experienced chile eaters need apply. It takes a true chile addict to ooh and aah over the roasty green chile stew served with homemade fresh tortillas, and you can easily become addicted to the brisket tacos and the *carnitas* (marinated beef strips) breakfast. You've just gotta have it! Of the many Garcia's around town, the one on Central near Old Town, with its carnival decor, is probably the best. But we each have our favorite. Daily weekday specials are a good deal. Breakfast served all day. Open late. Inexpensive.

Mac's La Sierra Restaurant (505-836-1212), 6217 Central Avenue NW. Open daily 6–11. B, L, D. If you can find a better deal than Mac's Sat.-Sun. red enchiladas with steak fingers for $4.95, by all means go for it (but you probably won't). Between the battered Naugahyde booths, dim lighting, neighbors who've been eating here for an eternity, and waitresses always in a hurry, hoisting trays of nothing fancy but plain old reliable tasty Mexican food and steak specials, you've got yourself an authentic experience on the far end of Old Route 66. By the time you finish eating here, you'll feel like one of the gang. Inexpensive.

COME FOR THE COFFEE, STAY FOR THE COMPANY AT ZENDO, ONE OF THE MANY INDIE COFFEE HOUSES FOUND DOWNTOWN

longtime neighborhood favorite can supply your dinner party with a bread sculpture of a turtle or armadillo, or a turkey for your Thanksgiving. Empanadas, *biscochitos*, New Mexican wedding cookies, and other local favorite sweets fill the display cases. And you can lunch on the bakery's beloved "bakery-style" pizza, sandwiches, and latte at the in-house café. Featured in *Gourmet* magazine. The rustic patio is a summer night's dream come true.

Great Harvest Bread Co. (505-293-8277), 11200 Montgomery Boulevard NE. Folks drive from all over town to stock up on the hearty, whole-grain breads that Great Harvest turns out in delectable varieties. Artisan and homestyle breads and buns, as well as cookies, bars, and sweets. Different varieties baked daily. Montana stone-ground red wheat available for your own baking. Gluten-free selections available. Go to www.ghabq .com/sched.html for baking schedule.

CHOCOLATE, COFFEE, AND TEA **Figments Tea Shoppe & Gallery** (505-323-1606) 8510 Montgomery Boulevard NE. A ladies' tea shop done to perfection. Cozy, with plenty of intriguing browsing of garden decor, gift items all well-chosen. A great little spot to meet a friend.

Moons Coffee & Tea (505-271-2633), 1605 Juan Tabo Boulevard NE. Suite F. You're likely to hear about a place like Moons at your book club. Let the knowledgeable Mrs. Moon be your guide through the fine coffees, such as Jamaica Blue Mountain and Kona, the flavored coffees, and Many Moons, the house blend, as well as the dozens of varieties of exquisite teas, including chai and rare white teas. Over 100 varieties of loose teas to choose among.

New Mexico Tea Company (505-962-2137), 1131 Mountain Road NW. This tiny shop is packed with several dozen elegantly arrayed varieties of fine imported teas, the exotic and the rare, as well as New Mexico–grown organic herbals and medicinals. Shopping here is a most pleasant experience, where you can deepen your tea experience and knowledge and find excellent tea ware.

Theobroma Chocolatier (505-293-6545), 12611 Montgomery Boulevard NE. Come here when you want the good stuff, the very best quality chocolate, in interesting thematic shapes, such as footballs and chocolate heart-shaped boxes, or such flavors as chocolate-covered ginger. The dark chocolate is sinfully luscious and creamy and irresistible.

Whiting Coffee Co. (505-344-9144), 3700 Osuna Road NE. Closed Tuesdays and Sundays. It's worth a trip to this small strip mall for the finest freshly roasted coffee beans, original blends, an ample selection of loose teas, brewing devices, imported spices, chocolates, and cookies. There's always a free sample cup brewing. Where many discriminating Albuquerqueans insist on obtaining their coffee.

Trifecta Coffee Company (505-800-7081), 413 Montano Road NE. Do not be deceived by the drive-by strip mall location. Trifecta is the coffee lover's coffee shop. It happens to be my neighborhood café, but even if it wasn't, it would be worth the drive for the Americano crowned with exquisite crema. Fair trade, meticulously sourced beans roasted on the spot. Always friendly.

GROCERIES **La Montanita Co-op** (505-265-4631), 3500 Central SE. Five locations, including Gallup and Santa Fe. Pay $15 a year to join, and you support a member-run food co-op that is a small supermarket featuring organic, local, and sustainably produced edibles. The take-out deli selections can be a tad unfamiliar, but if you are vegan or vegetarian, you can't live without this place. Your membership fee entitles you to a rebate at the end of the year and specials, too. Shop here and feel good about where you're spending your money.

Natural Grocers (505-292-7300), 4420 Wyoming (also on the West Side). Formerly known as "Vitamin Cottage," this is a Colorado-based family chain that stocks the freshest organic, and for my money, most reasonably priced produce around. If you care to eat healthy, you can stock up on freshly ground flour, nuts, and spices for your kitchen, and purchase your nutritional supplements and beauty products at the same time. Well-trained, friendly consultants are on hand to assist. Like shopping in the small family-owned grocery of old. West Side location also.

Sprouts (505-821-7000), 6300 San Mateo NE. A half-dozen locations around town offer a huge assortment of fresh fruits and vegetables at reasonable prices. Bulk groceries, natural remedies and vitamins, fresh fish, plenty of prepared takeout.

TaLin Market World Food Fare (505-268-0206), 88 Louisiana Boulevard SE. The most exotic grocery shopping experience in town, with aisles dedicated to India, Thailand, China, and the Caribbean. If you can't find the ingredient you're looking for, it probably doesn't exist. The produce and fresh fish sections are also geared to cooks of Asian cuisine. The store offers bargain prices on produce and there's a café and cooking lessons. On Fri. and Sat., the pop-up dumpling shop serves the most exquisite, translucent dumplings, made while you wait, in what could be the biggest bargain in town at under $10 a plate. What more could a foodie want? Food trucks assemble here in a giant pod on Wednesdays 10–2. Ta Lin is also in Santa Fe.

Trader Joe's (505-796-0311), 8928 Holly Avenue NE (off Paseo del Pueblo Norte). Uptown location also. Albuquerque became a city the day Trader Joe's opened its doors. Snacks and nuts, prepared salads, and take-out meals; bargain wines; and variety of frozen foods make this the favorite place to have fun while spending the weekly grocery budget. Every reason to look good in the kitchen is here, and a stop is essential for party planning. Daily 9–9.

Whole Foods Market (505-856-0474), 5815 Wyoming Boulevard NE. The concept of grocery shopping as entertainment has come to Albuquerque with a glorious Whole Foods. Expensive, but the fish is delivered daily and the produce the most beautiful around. Takes a canny shopper to make a trip here make sense. Shopping in-house brands will lower your tab. Cheese and wine sections, as well as the bakery, make this a worthwhile stop. Carlisle location also.

Keller's Farm Store (505-294-1427); 2912 Eubank Boulevard NE. West side location also. Fine food emporium, long-standing, old-fashioned, packed with delicacies. The best of the best, from soup to nuts and back again.

PET GOURMET AND BOUTIQUE

🐾 **Canine Country Club and Feline Inn** (505-338-1408), 7327 4th Street NW. Also on the West Side. Both you and your beloved pet will be treated well here, whether your pup is in for grooming, boarding, or "doggie day care." You'll get a report card, too.

🐾 **Clark's Pet Emporium** (505-268-5977), 4914 Lomas Boulevard NE. This fine local pet shop has been catering to its clientele with the best in bird, fish, dog, and cat supplies for 40 years. They stock everything you could possibly need, provide personal attention, and all in a store that is definitely not a big box. You can trust this place to provide the best for your pet and there are helpful, knowledgeable salespeople about.

🐾 **Long Leash on Life** (505- 299-8800), 9800 Montgomery Boulevard NE, Suite 13, Albuquerque. Pet nutrition super-store. Specialists give nutrition consultations.

🐾 **Three Dog Bakery** (505-294-2300), 9821 Montgomery NE. Organic dog biscuits, fancy and fanciful doggie pastries and birthday cakes, doggie wear, and "Yappy Hour" make this a popular stop for large dogs and their human companions. Ask about discounts!

🐾 **Groomingdale's Pet Spa** (505-345-4455), 405 Montano Road NE. Where I take my precious Airedale terrier,

Kelsey, for pampering. She can't wait to get out of the car and receive the luxurious bath and brushing that keep her feeling pretty. Reduced rates for regular appointments. Also a NE Heights location.

WINE SHOPS **Jubilation Wine & Spirits** (505-255-4404), 3512 Lomas Boulevard NE. Not the biggest, but perhaps the best wine shop in town, with an in-depth selection that will tempt you to try a new one. The emphasis is on service. Wine tastings bring in knowledgeable instructors. Always busy.

Kelly Liquors (505-296-7815), 2226 Wyoming Boulevard NE. A huge selection of wines, beers, and liquors at discount prices makes this a good stop before a dinner party. Other locations in North Valley and Rio Rancho, eleven in all around town.

Quarters Discount Liquors (505-247-8579), 801 Yale Boulevard SE. Notice the two key words in the name: "discount" and "liquors." This place has a wide array of imported beers in stock. Other locations around town, too.

✳ Entertainment

Adobe Theater (505-898-9222), 9813 4th Street NW. A dedicated band of theater lovers produce a variety of consistently high-quality performances on this tiny out-of-the-way stage.

Albuquerque Little Theater (505-242-4750), 224 San Pasqual Avenue SW. One of the oldest ongoing community theaters in the country, the Little Theater continues to draw an audience of dedicated and loyal followers, typically to a playbill of conventional, established theater favorites, usually very well executed. They have a strong children's theater program also.

Aux Dog Theater (505-254-7716), 3011 Monte Vista Boulevard NE. This theater has not only survived, it's thrived. An intimate stage with reliably quality and

engaging productions of lesser-known and more challenging works, such as the 2017 staging of Arthur Miller's complex "After the Fall."

The Cell (505-766-9412; www.fusionabq.org), 700 1st Street NW. The FUSION Theatre Company is a top-notch provocative theater that competes well with any other form of entertainment out there. Expect that chances will be taken and boundaries will be stretched. The Cell is home to: New Mexico's only professional Equity theatre company—FUSION Theatre Company, the Screen

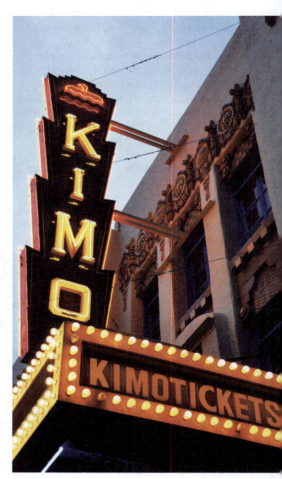

THE NAME "KIMO" MEANS "KING OF ITS KIND," AND IS FITTING FOR DOWNTOWN ALBUQUERQUE'S PUEBLO DECO THEATER

THE RAILYARDS ARE THE CITY'S NEW FAMILY-FRIENDLY WEEKEND DESTINATION THAT IS PART FLEA MARKET, PART CRAFT FAIR, PART FOOD COURT

Actors Guild "Conversations" series, the "One Night Stand Cabaret," and 150 nights of live all-ages music yearly.

Keshet Dance Co. (505-224-9808), 4121 Cutler Avenue NE, Albuquerque. Perhaps best known for "Nutcracker on the Rocks," an annual holiday performance that includes differently-abled young dancers, Keshet has inspired young dancers and their families and continues to make a huge difference in the Albuquerque community.

KiMo Theater (505-768-3522), 423 Central Avenue NW. Originally built in 1927 as a movie palace in the flamboyant Pueblo Deco style, which used Indian ornamentation on art deco, the restored landmark KiMo is worth a visit on its own or to take in a concert, film, dance, or theater production. Go upstairs to see the Von Hassler murals.

Outpost Performance Space (505-268-0044), 210 Yale Boulevard SE. This intimate space is the place to come and hear a variety of live music, including jazz, folk, world music, local acts, and touring companies, as well as spoken word. Check out the outstanding New Mexico Jazz Festival.

Popejoy Hall (505-925-5858), 302 Cornell Drive SE. University of New Mexico's Popejoy Hall, with 2,000 seats, is the city's premier stage venue for the New Mexico Symphony and big-stage road show musicals. The university offers a regular schedule of theater events, from Broadway road shows like "Lion King" to student-produced work. Emmylou Harris, Sweet Honey in the Rock, and Ralph Stanley are some of the great acts to appear on this stage. Several other smaller theater spaces are in this building as well, including Keller Hall for classical music performances, Rodey Hall for smaller theater pieces, and the Experimental Theatre.

South Broadway Cultural Center (505-848-1320), 1025 Broadway Boulevard SE. A library, exhibition space, and beautiful small theater space, the cultural center is a stage for live theater and touring world music acts.

Tricklock Theater Company (505-414-3738), 110 Gold Avenue SW. Tricklock is a solid and intelligent ensemble that performs exciting, new, and experimental work and tour internationally. They produce the annual International Theater Festival each January.

Vortex Theatre (505-247-8600), 2900 Carlisle Boulevard NE. For 35 years, the Vortex has been home to the offbeat, avant-garde, edgy theater designed to make you think.

✳ Selective Shopping

Albuquerque Flea Market (505-319-2849), 300 San Pedro NE, Expo New Mexico. Open Sat.–Sun. 7–3, weather permitting. With acres of booths to survey, you can find everything and anything, from bargains on CDs to blankets and pots and pans. They also have everything you didn't know you needed, from sets of long-handled iced-tea spoons to handmade soaps to calico cat cookie jars. However, there's lots more imported stuff from China than there used to be—it's become quite commercialized nowadays.

Dan's Boots & Saddles (505-345-2220), 6903 4th Street NW. Even real cowboys shop here, but if all you want to do is find the right pair of jeans, western shirt, boots, or hat, by all means get yourself to this store that's been selling feed and saddles since 1938. Where local farm folk rub shoulders with the North Valley horsey set.

Mariposa Gallery (505-268-6828), 3500 Central Avenue SE. The finest, most adventurous, and well made in crafts by local artisans, grace the walls and shelves of this long-established gallery, including glass, jewelry, sculpture, pottery, and ceramics, in all price ranges. If you have time for only one gallery, make this the one. The best of the best.

🐾 **The Palms Trading Co.** (505-247-8504), 1504 Lomas Boulevard NW. Stop in here, just outside Old Town, for deals on handmade Indian jewelry, antique Indian pots, and all other manner of Native American wares. You are bound to find something you want, need, and adore.

The Yarn Store at Nob Hill (505-717-1535), 120 Amherst Drive NE. Extensive assortment of fine yarns, plus everything the needle crafter needs for any project at all. Knitting lessons, too, and visiting experts. There are always a group of friendly crafters working around the table, a moveable feast of craft.

Old Town Basket & Rug Shop (505-842-8022); 301 Romero Street SW. The best selection of clothing, souvenirs, accessories, rugs, jewelry, kitchenware, makes this a very fun place to shop.

Old Town Hat Shop (505-242-4019); 205 San Felipe NW. Golly. Not only hats, but bags, accessories, plus an excellent selection of casual and outdoor women's wear. So happens they carry some of my favorites labels: Parsley & Sage, for example. I cold be happy in here at least a week.

INDEPENDENT AND USED BOOKSTORES **Bookworks** (505-344-8139), 4022 Rio Grande Boulevard NW. Specializing in children's books, service, and the latest in current events books, plus offering book signings, by national stars to local personalities, to fill the calendar. Bookworks has managed to survive the changes in the book business, and has recently opened up its space with a cool remodel. The entire North Valley loves to browse here, then meet friends for tea at the adjacent Flying Star Café. The store recently added a selection of used books, which may or may not please you.

Page One (505-294-2026), 5850 Eubank Boulevard NE. Over 40 years of independent bookselling in the NE Heights. Open mic nights, events, new and used, and good deals at www.page1book.com/coupon. Antiquarian book room book lovers dream about.

Treasure House Books & Gifts (505-242-7204); 20012 S. Plaza Street. Open 10–6 daily. Good Old Town shop to find books by local authors and books about New Mexico.

Title Wave Books (505-294-9495), 1408 Eubank Boulevard NE. Somehow, Title Wave keeps rolling along with an intelligent selection of used books that is both wide and deep. This is that rare bookstore where you will find just what you are looking for as well as the next big thing you had no idea you were interested in, until you spotted it here.

SHOPPING CENTERS

ABQ Uptown, Louisiana and Indian School NE. Albuquerque's 25,000-square-foot shopping center has become the favorite place to shop. It is designed for walking outdoors browsing upscale retailers Anthropologie, Chico's, Pottery Barn, Williams-Sonoma, the Apple Store, and many other desirable national chains. Here you have every opportunity to be fashionable and really spend some money. For a break, try the Elephant Bar, which is a fine and reasonable restaurant and bar.

Nob Hill Shopping Center, Carlisle and Central SE. Built in 1937, this vintage shopping center was the first "mall" constructed west of the Mississippi. Today, the art deco center houses an engaging variety of galleries, chic home furnishings stores, a shoe store, jewelry shops, a trendy salon, La Montanita Food Co-op, a bar, and a Scalo's restaurant. Free parking one block south of the center.

Winrock Town Center (505-883-6132); 2100 Louisiana Boulevard NE. The latest and greatest, with Nordstrom Rack and a state of the art 3-D movie theater. Newly-redesigned, with plenty of good stores.

VINTAGE AND RECYCLED

Buffalo Exchange New and Recycled Fashion (505-262-0098), 3005 Central Avenue NE. If you are stylish, trendy—or want to be either of those things—you can trade in wardrobe items you are tired of and cash in on the huge supply of both men's and women's fashions and accessories that fill the racks at Buffalo Exchange. Both styles and sizes appear geared to the university set.

My Best Friend's Closet (505-298-4099), 9450 Candelaria Road NE. An in-depth assortment of seasonally well-chosen, gently worn, generally reasonably priced apparel is available here, sold on consignment. From sportswear and sweaters to evening-wear, bargains abound.

🏵 **Assistance League Thrift Store** (505-265-0619); 5211 Lomas Boulevard NE. So many good causes supported by this place offering gently-used clothing, housewares, and furniture. The lovely retired ladies offer a pleasant attitude and help in so many ways.

✳ Special Events

Check 311 or the local paper for information on the monthly Friday evening **ARTSCrawl** (505-244-0362; www.artscrawlabq.org), when various gallery districts open their doors.

January: **Revolutions International Theater Festival** (505-414-3738), Tricklock Theater Co., 110 Gold Avenue SW.

March: **Rio Grande Arts and Crafts Festival—Spring Show** (505-292-7457), Expo New Mexico. **National Fiery Foods and BBQ Show** (505-873-8680), Sandia

TAKING HOME THE BLUE RIBBON AT THE STATE FAIR PIE CONTEST WILL ALWAYS BE A COVETED HONOR

DÍA DE LOS MUERTOS (DAY OF THE DEAD) IS CELEBRATED IN ALBUQUERQUE'S SOUTH VALLEY WITH THE MARIGOLD PARADE

Resort and Casino, I-25 and Tramway Boulevard.

April: **Gathering of Nations Powwow** (505-836-2810), NM Expo. **Albuquerque Isotopes** baseball games (505-924-BALL), Isotopes Park, 1601 Avenida Cesar Chavez SE. April–September.

May: **Cinco de Mayo Concert Celebration** (505-246-2261), National Hispanic Cultural Center, 1701 4th Street SW.

June: **Festival Flamenco Internacional de Albuquerque** (505-242-7600), 1260 Central Avenue SE. **NM Arts and Crafts Fair** (505-884-9043), **Sizzlin' Summerfest** (311) offers musical themes from a variety of cultures each Saturday night in Civic Plaza Downtown.

July: **Mariachi Spectacular de Albuquerque** (505-836-0306); Albuquerque Convention Center, www.mariachispectacular.com/

September: **New Mexico State Fair** (505-222-9700), Expo New Mexico, held for two weeks each September. Livestock, home arts, Indian and Hispanic arts, food, midway with rides. The fair celebrates all things New Mexican. **Globalquerque** (www.globalquerque.org), **National Hispanic Cultural Center**, 1701 4th Street SW, at Avenida César Chávez.

October: **Albuquerque International Balloon Fiesta** (505-821-1000), 4401 Alameda Boulevard NE, Balloon Fiesta Park, I-25 and Alameda NE. Held first two weeks of October, this is the world's largest hot-air balloon gathering, with over 500 balloons from all over the world, including special shapes, lifting off each weekend morning in mass ascensions. Balloon glows, special shapes rodeo, fireworks, gigantic midway.

November: **Día de los Muertos** (505-246-2261), National Hispanic Cultural Center, 1701 4th Street SW. **Marigold Parade** (505-314-0176, 505-433-5829), Westside Community Center, 1250 Isleta Boulevard SW. **Weems International Artfest** (505-293-6133), Expo New Mexico, 300 San Pedro NE.

December: **River of Lights** (505-768-2000), Rio Grande Botanic Garden, November 24–December 29.

OPPOSITE: ABIQUIU LAKE

NORTH CENTRAL NEW MEXICO: GEORGIA O'KEEFFE COUNTRY

■

TAOS AND THE ENCHANTED CIRCLE

Taos, Questa, Red River, Angel Fire,
Taos Ski Valley, Arroyo Seco

HIGH ROAD COUNTRY

Chimayo, Truchas, Cordova, Peñasco, Dixon

RIO CHAMA COUNTRY

Abiquiu, Española, Tierra Amarilla, Los Ojos

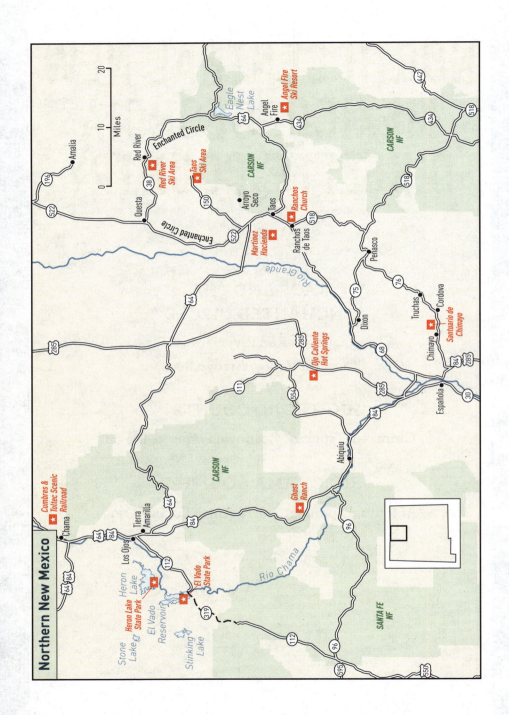

Northern New Mexico

Miles

20

10

0

Amalia

522

196

Questa

Red River

Enchanted Circle

Red River
Ski Area

38

Taos
Ski Area

150

Arroyo
Seco

Enchanted Circle

522

Eagle
Nest
Lake

64

Angel
Fire

CARSON
NF

434

Angel Fire
Ski Resort

442

CARSON
NF

518

434

518

Taos

Ranchos
Church

518

Martinez
Hacienda

Ranchos
de Taos

Rio Grande

Peñasco

518

75

76

Truchas

Cordova

Santuario de
Chimayo

64

Dixon

68

Chimayo

84 285

30

Española

285

84

Ojo Caliente
Hot Springs

285

111

554

285

84

285

Abiquiu

96

Rio Chama

Ghost
Ranch

Cumbres &
Toltec Scenic
Railroad

Chama

64 84

64
84

Tierra
Amarilla

64

84

CARSON
NF

Los Ojos

112

Heron
Lake

Stone
Lake

Heron Lake
State Park

El Vado
Reservoir

El Vado
State Park

Stinking
Lake

319

112

96

595

550

SANTA FE
NF

NORTH CENTRAL
NEW MEXICO

There is something about northern New Mexico that speaks to our deepest feelings about the state. Perhaps it is the adobe houses shaded by grandmother cotton-woods, the scent of piñon smoke, or the figures of saints hand painted on the altars of High Road mission churches, the descansos at the edge of the highway. Then there is the rush of water through an ancient *acequia*, the sight of snow on Taos Mountain, the curve of the buttress on the Ranchos Church, the rhythms of drum and rattle at an Indian dance, the wind-sculpted red rocks of Abiquiu . . .

Whatever it is, in northern New Mexico we catch our breath around every bend in the road as we wind through the Rio Grande canyon on the way up to Taos or follow the Rio Chama northward. Perhaps we learned this love by looking at the art of the Cinco Pintores and the Taos Moderns, those captivated by northern New Mexico light.

Here is where the four seasons unfurl most deliciously, from the stillness of a snow-covered landscape overlooking the Mora Valley, to the green bursting forth from Velarde apple orchards, to the busy summer season in Santa Fe, with rainbows stretching across the sky, to, as writer John Nichols titled one of his books, "the last beautiful days of autumn" in Taos.

VIGIL'S IN CHIMAYO IS A PLACE TO FIND HANDMADE NORTHERN NEW MEXICO CRAFTS

The changing seasons renew the enduring traditions, as each season brings its own: clearing the *acequias* in spring, the farmers' markets at harvest time, fly-fishing, chopping wood, and retreating to the warmth of the fire and the simple pleasure of a pot of beans and chile on the stove.

Northern New Mexico reminds us that this can be a sustainable way of life in harmony with the land, where one eats what one grows and warms oneself through the labor of one's hands. The crafts of weaving and carving are more than decorative; they are life essentials. Take away the asphalt and the television satellite dishes, and the High Road, along with many mountain villages of New Mexico, has changed very little in the past three or four centuries. Big changes to accommodate larger-scale tourism have been proposed; however, these plans are fiercely protested by local residents and have thus far come to naught. Some people consider such thinking backwards. Up here they will tell you they like things just the way they are. Anyone who thinks northern New Mexicans can be changed or informed there is a better way to go about life is in for an awakening, if not total enlightenment. Up here, people are proudly change averse, which might explain why the feeling of settled

This section of the state offers much variety: retreat at artist Georgia O'Keeffe's Ghost Ranch, visit traditional weavers at Chimayo or Los Ojos, enjoy artists' studio tours during fall at Dixon and Abiquiu, attend the Santa Fe Opera and immerse in the rich menu of cultural events in that extraordinary capital city.

To facilitate your travel and allow you to focus on the delights of each area, think of it in three geographic sections: Taos and the Enchanted Circle Country of Questa, Red River, and Angel Fire; High Road Country of Chimayo, Truchas, Cordova, Peñasco, and Dixon; and the Rio Chama Country of Española, Abiquiu, Tierra Amarilla, Los Ojos and Chama, Ojo Caliente, and El Rito. US 84/285 parallels the course of the Rio Chama north to the Colorado border.

TAOS AND THE ENCHANTED CIRCLE

Taos, Questa, Red River, Angel Fire,
Taos Ski Valley, Arroyo Seco

Warning: the beauty and magic of the Taos area may change your life. Taos Mountain is famous for doing that—as well as for bringing out the dreams and creativity you have long yearned to express. The natural splendor of this area had a huge impact on D. H. Lawrence, Millicent Rogers, Georgia O'Keeffe and Mabel Dodge Luhan, to name a few. Aldous Huxley picked up a few ideas here, and Julia Cameron wrote her seminal book, *The Artist's Way* in the shadow of Taos Mountain. Add art, history, Native American and Hispanic culture, fine dining, and outdoor activities of hiking, skiing, rafting, and fishing for the sum of a destination with four-season appeal. You are guaranteed to love this region whenever you visit—and may it be soon.

GUIDANCE **Angel Fire Convention and Visitors Bureau** (575-377-6555; www.angel firefun.com), 3365 Mountain View Boulevard, Angel Fire.

Eagle Nest Chamber of Commerce (575-377-2420; eaglenestchamber.org), 284 E. Therma Drive, Eagle Nest.

Red River Visitor Center (575-754-1708; www.redriver.org), 220 E. Main, Red River.

Taos Visitor Center (800-348-0696; www.taos.org), 1139 Paseo del Pueblo Sur, Taos.

Village of Taos Ski Valley Chamber of Commerce (800-776-1111; www.taosskivalley .com), 122 Sutton Place, Taos Ski Valley.

MEDICAL EMERGENCY **Christus St. Vincent Regional Medical Center** (505-946-3233), 455 St. Michaels Drive.

Española Hospital (505-327-0360), 1010 Spruce Street, Española.

Holy Cross Hospital (575-751-5835), 1397 Weimer Road, Taos.

Los Alamos Medical Center (505-662-2932), 3917 West Road, Los Alamos.

Taos Urgent Care (575-758-1414), 330 Paseo Del Pueblo Sur, Taos.

Railyard Urgent Care (505-501-7791), 831 St. Francis Drive, Santa Fe.

GETTING THERE From Santa Fe, go north on NM 68. It's a slow 67 miles to Taos. From Taos, take NM 522 north, about 25 minutes, to Questa and the Enchanted Circle. Also from Taos, take NM 150 to Taos Ski Valley, a half-hour drive.

✳ To See

TOWNS **Angel Fire.** A town of many second-home condominiums and rentals with a resort at the center, yet also with a small, involved community of year-round citizens. It is a good place to stay and play year-round. It was the fall meeting grounds of the Ute and took its name from the Indian "breath of spirits," later Christianized by Franciscan friars to "breath of angels." Hiking, mountain biking, cross-country skiing,

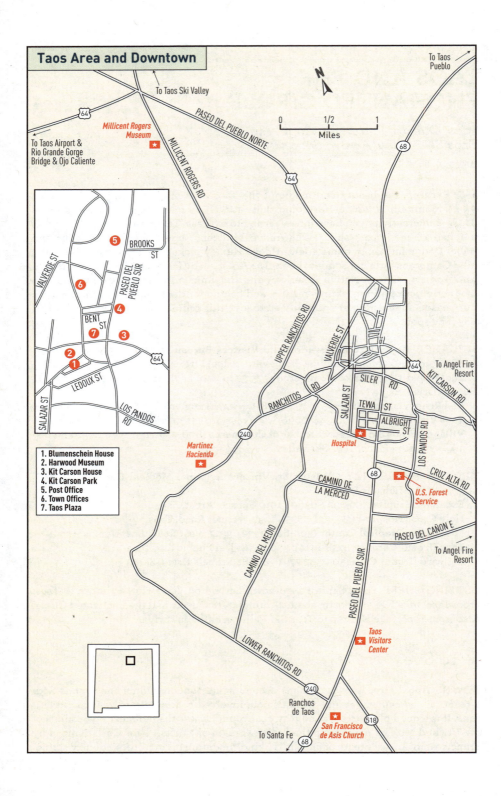

Taos Area and Downtown

To Taos Pueblo

N

To Taos Ski Valley

PASEO DEL PUEBLO NORTE

64

To Taos Airport &
Rio Grande Gorge
Bridge & Ojo Caliente

Millicent Rogers
Museum ★

MILLICENT ROGERS RD

0   1/2   1
Miles

68

64

BROOKS ST

5

VALVERDE ST

6

PASEO DEL PUEBLO SUR

4

BENT ST

7   3

2

1

64

LEDOUX ST

LOS PANDOS RD

SALAZAR ST

1. Blumenschein House
2. Harwood Museum
3. Kit Carson House
4. Kit Carson Park
5. Post Office
6. Town Offices
7. Taos Plaza

UPPER RANCHITOS RD

VALVERDE ST

64

To Angel Fire
Resort

KIT CARSON RD

SILER   RD

SALAZAR ST

TEWA   ST

RANCHITOS RD

ALBRIGHT ST

LOS PANDOS RD

Hospital ★

240

Martinez
Hacienda ★

CAMINO DE
LA MERCED

68

U.S. Forest
Service ★

CRUZ ALTA RD

CAMINO DEL MEDIO

PASEO DEL CAÑON E

To Angel Fire
Resort

PASEO DEL PUEBLO SUR

Taos
Visitors
Center ★

LOWER RANCHITOS RD

240

Ranchos
de Taos

518

San Francisco
de Asis Church ★

To Santa Fe

68

snowboarding, tubing, and zip-lining are its leading attractions, in addition to skiing. It is also home to Vietnam Veterans Memorial State Park.

Arroyo Seco. This pretty little village on the road to Taos Ski Valley has cafés, shops, and a historic church.

Questa. The drive north of Taos to Questa along NM 522 passes several interesting potential explorations, including the valley of Arroyo Hondo and Lama Mountain, where the Lama Foundation—an ecumenical retreat center founded in the 1960s, still survives. Questa was for many years primarily a mining community where molybdenum, an agent used for hardening steel, reigned, but it is now home to a combination of artists, organic growers, and multigenerational Hispanic families.

Red River. A family resort town created for fun, with a ski area, plenty of lodging, cafés, and shopping that is a pleasant four-season family escape. At 8,750 feet, it is the highest town in the state. Founded in 1892 by homesteaders; prospectors followed suit and found their way to the settlement. The Red River takes its color after rains due to the high mineral content.

Taos. The legendary town of artists and the home of the multi-storied 1,000-year-old Taos Pueblo has a magnetism and mystique like nowhere else. Established in 1615 as a northern outpost of New Spain, it was the site of the annual autumn rendezvous and trade fair of mountain men who hunted and trapped for the beaver trade. The town itself is a historical composite of three parts: Ranchos de Taos on the south, Don Fernando de Taos in the central part of town radiating out from the Plaza, and Taos Pueblo. Eventually, these three sections grew together to form a unit we think of today as Greater Taos. In addition to its arts, Taos is also known as the home of larger-than-life characters such as Kit Carson, Padre Martinez, Mabel Dodge Luhan, and D. H. and Frieda Lawrence. With close to a dozen coffee houses, several outstanding brewpubs and wine tasting rooms, diverse restaurants, film, theater, literary events, and music galore, there's an outsized cultural life to ensure no one ever gets bored.

PRAYER FLAGS WAVE OVER THE RIO GRANDE GORGE ATOP LAMA MOUNTAIN

Taos Ski Valley. Located in the old mining area of Twinings, TSV is the state's premier ski resort, internationally known for its challenging runs. Summer activities, such as concerts by Taos School of Music, are scheduled along with winter fun, including snowboarding.

HISTORIC LANDMARKS, PLACES, AND SITES **Hacienda de los Martinez** (575-758-1000), 708 Hacienda Way, off Lower Ranchitos Road, Taos. Two miles south of the plaza on NM 240 or 4 miles west of Ranchos de Taos on NM 240. Open Mon.–Sat. 10–5, Sun. noon–5; call for winter hours, likely to be closed Wednesdays, and open only until 4 PM. If you want to see what a nineteenth-century hacienda looks like, come here and experience the fortress-like restored building designed to keep out Comanche and Apache raiders. Exhibits explain trade on the Camino Real, and Spanish colonial culture of New Mexico. It is furnished authentically, with demonstrations of quilting, *colcha* embroidery, weaving, and other traditional crafts. $8 adults, $4 under age 16, under age 5 free.

Kit Carson Cemetery (no phone), Kit Carson Park. History makes strange bedfellows Stroll this historic cemetery in the center of town to find graves of Mabel Dodge Luhan, Padre Martinez, and Kit Carson within a stone's throw of one another.

Picuris Pueblo (575-587-2519), NM 75 at MM 13, Peñasco. Attractions at this tiny Pueblo on the High Road to Taos include a museum, the ancient Pot Creek Pueblo site, and historic restored church. The Pueblo is known for its golden-flecked mica pottery. The haunting Matachine dances are performed here December 24–25.

Pot Creek Cultural Site (575-587-2519). Nine miles from Taos on NM 518. Open late June–early September. Wed.–Sun. An easy 1-mile trail leads to a reconstructed pueblo that includes a ceremonial kiva. This site was inhabited by the Ancestral Pueblo people between A.D. 1100 and A.D. 1300. Many pots were found here when the Spanish arrived, hence the name. Free.

Rio Grande Del Norte National Monument (www.blm.gov/nm/st/en/fo/taos_field_office.html) is one of the nation's newest national monuments. In March 2013, President Barack Obama declared these 27 million acres of Rio Grande Rift and Taos Plateau a nationally significant landscape to be preserved permanently. Encompassing several Native American pueblos, rock art, wildlife, native grasslands, geologic features formed over 70 million years, and much more, the area is a haven for hiking, rafting, fishing, hunting, and sightseeing.

Rio Grande Gorge Bridge (no phone), at intersection of NM 68 and NM 150 (Taos Ski Valley Road), go left 17 miles on US 64. Completed in 1965, at 650 feet above the Rio Grande, this bridge is the nation's second-highest span: 2,000 feet from rim to rim across the gorge. The winding Rio Grande below and view of the Taos Plateau is a look into the deep heart of New Mexico. From this height, river rafters on the Taos Box look like tiny specks. Hang on to your hat! The wind always blows hard up here. Free.

San Francisco de Asis Church ("Ranchos Church") (575-758-2754), Ranchos de Taos. Four miles south of Taos on NM 68. Open Mon.–Sat. 9–4. This building, the most frequently painted and

MUDDING THE RANCHOS DE TAOS CHURCH IS AN ANNUAL SPRING COMMUNITY EVENT

photographed church in the United States, was built sometime between 1776 and 1813. Its massive adobe walls change appearance with the changing light. $3 to see video and Mystery Paintings in Parish Hall.

Taos Pueblo (575-758-1028), 2 miles north of Taos off NM 68. Feast days: September 29–30, San Geronimo. Open Mon.-Sat. 8–4:30. Sun. 8:30–4:30. Closed during private Pueblo events. Pueblo may be closed during February–March and August. Taos was well established long before Europe emerged from the Dark Ages, and the ancestors of today's people have been in this area for at least 1,000 years. About 150 people live on the Pueblo full-time, and about 2,000 are living on Taos Pueblo lands. This is the only living American Indian community that is both a UNESCO World Heritage Site and a National Historic Landmark. The present Pueblo has been occupied since about 1450 AD. To honor the residents' traditions, there is still no indoor plumbing or electricity at the Pueblo. The Rio Pueblo, running from the sacred Blue Lake in the Sangre de Cristo Mountains, courses through the Pueblo. The Feast of San Geronimo is a highlight of the year, as is Christmas Eve. Local artists are known for their micaceous, gold-flecked pottery, which is sold on the Pueblo. Entrance fees include a guided tour. It is appropriate to tip your guide. $16 adults. Parties of 8 or more, $14 per person.

Vietnam Veterans Memorial State Park (575-377-6900), 34 Country Road, Angel Fire. 24 miles east of Taos on US 64. Visitor center open daily 9–5. Chapel open daily, 24 hours. Established in 1971 by Dr. Victor Westphall to honor his son, David, killed in Vietnam in 1968, this is the only state park in the country dedicated as a Vietnam Veterans Memorial. The 6,000-square-foot visitor center offers informative and deeply touching videos, exhibits, and memorabilia. Architect Ted Luna designed it with the idea "such that no person entering it could leave with quite the same attitude toward peace and war." Free.

MUSEUMS **Ernest L. Blumenschein Home** (575-758-0505), 222 Ledoux Street, Taos. Mon.–Tues. 10–4; Sat. 10–4, Sun. noon–4; call for winter hours. Closed Wednesdays and Thursdays. Taos Society of Artists founders Ernest and Mary Greene Blumenschein lived and worked in this 1797 Spanish colonial adobe. Meticulously restored, the house appears much as it did in their day, with original colors and artwork brought back to life. $8 adults, $4 under age 16, under age 5 free.

Couse/Sharp Historic Site (575-751-0369; admin@couse-sharp.org), 146 Kit Carson Road, Taos. Now on public view, studios of members of Taos Society of Artists, almost exactly as they appeared when in use by the artists. Open and tours by appointment.

Harwood Museum of Art (575-758-9826), 238 Ledoux Street, Taos. Closed Mondays and Tuesdays. Open Wed.–Fri. 10–5, Sat.–Sun. noon–5. Closed holidays. Here is a treasury of Taos art, housed in an exemplary nineteenth-century Spanish-Pueblo adobe structure. Founded in 1923, the Harwood contains the work of the artists who made Taos famous: Victor Higgins, Ernest Blumenschein, Andrew Dasburg, and Patrocinio Barela, as well as that of contemporary artists, such as Larry Bell, Fritz Scholder, Anita Rodriguez, and Melissa Zink. Of special note is the Agnes Martin Gallery, where seven canvasses of the nation's most acclaimed minimalist and Taos resident for contemplation in a light-filled chamber. $10 adults, $8 seniors and students.

Kit Carson Home and Museum (575-758-4945), 113 Kit Carson Road, Taos. Open daily 11–5. Closed Thanksgiving, Christmas, New Year's, and Easter. Famed mountain man and Indian scout Kit Carson and his wife, Josefa, lived in this twelve-room adobe for a quarter-century. It is authentically furnished, and guides in period costume give tours. Next door is the Carson House Shop, an excellent showcase of Indian and folk art, jewelry, Christmas ornaments, and the work of Taos artist Valerie Graves. $5 adults, $4 seniors, $3 teens, $2 children, under age 6 free.

THE 1,000-YEAR-OLD ADOBE DWELLINGS OF TAOS PUEBLO SHINE WITH BEAUTY IN ALL SEASONS

Millicent Rogers Museum (575-758-2462; www.millicentrogers.org), 1504 Millicent Rogers Road, Taos. Four miles north of Taos off NM 522. Turn left on Millicent Rogers Road and follow the museum signs. Open daily 10–5 November–March. Closed Mondays and Easter, Thanksgiving, Christmas, New Year's. This outstanding private museum was founded in 1953 by relatives of Millicent Rogers, a model, heiress, and socialite who moved to Taos in 1947. Her love of regional architecture and Indian and Spanish colonial art, including Penitente Brotherhood artifacts, inspired an extensive collection of jewelry, textiles, basketry, pottery, and paintings. Here find one of the most important collections of black pottery by San Ildefonso Pueblo artist Maria Martinez and her family. A trip here makes a great immersion into the art of the region. $10 adults, $8 seniors, $6 students. Group rates available. Fantastic gift shop.

Taos Art Museum and Fechin House (575-758-2690), 227 Paseo del Pueblo Norte. Open summer Tues.–Sun. 10–5; winter hours Tues.–Sun. 10–4. A Russian-style adobe home designed by artist Nicolai Fechin features his woodwork, paintings, collection of Asian and Russian art, plus many fine works by members of the Taos Society of Artists. $8 adults; $7 seniors. Free every Sun. to Taos County visitors.

✳ To Do

BICYCLING **US 64 between Taos and Angel Fire.** An approximately 25-mile ride through narrow Taos Canyon (which can back up with traffic) and over 9,100-foot Palo Flechado Pass. Hairpin turns as you travel around the mountain down into Angel Fire.

CLIMBING **Mallette Park**, Red River. At the west end of town three blocks from Main Street is a granite face with six bolted routes. The wooded park also has a disc golf course.

FARMERS' MARKET **Taos Farmers' Market** (575-751-7575), on the plaza, Mid-May–late-October, Sat. 8–1. Northern New Mexico and southern Colorado growers from the San Luis Valley sell the most remarkable array of produce, baked goods, flowers, preserves, bath products, and beans.

FISHING **Costilla Creek/Valle Vidal.** Open July 1–December 31. Catch and release of the native Rio Grande cutthroat.

    Latir Lakes. It takes a moderate 4-mile hike to reach the nine glacier lakes that form the Latirs, which hold trophy cutthroats. The views and the wildflowers make it a worthwhile trek. The Latirs are the headwaters of the Rio Costilla.

    Rio Grande. The confluence of the Rio Grande and Red River near Questa and just below John Dunn Bridge in Arroyo Hondo.

    Rio Hondo. Parallels NM 150 from Arroyo Hondo up to Taos Ski Valley.

    Los Rios Anglers Fly Shop & Guide Service (575-758-2798), 126 W. Plaza Drive, Taos. The professional fly-fishing guides here are some of the best in the state. A complete fly-fishing shop offering gear, information, and year-round pack-and-float trips—including trips into the Rio Grande Gorge and isolated fishing on private lands.

    Solitary Angler (575-758-5653), 226C Paseo del Pueblo Norte, Taos. To book a guided trip on local public water or on the Solitary Angler's 11 private miles of Culebra Creek or the Cimarron Holy Water, give a call. There's also a club for serious fisher people.

    Eagle Nest Lake State Park Eagle Nest Marina (575-377-6941), 28386 NM 64, Eagle Nest, can give you information on boat rentals and activities. **Eagle Nest Lake**: This 2,400 surface acre lake offers some of the best trout and kokanee salmon fishing in the state. Seasonal recreation opportunities include boating, hiking, picnicking, and

FOLK LIFE FESTIVAL AT THE MILLICENT ROGERS MUSEUM

cross-country skiing, with opportunities to see an abundance of birds and other wild-life, including elk, dear, bears, and eagles. Set in the scenic Moreno Valley and surrounded by two of the state's highest peaks, Baldy Mountain and Wheeler Peak. At 8,300 feet in elevation, the park offers a cool retreat from the summer heat for fisherman, boaters, campers, and wildlife enthusiasts. A state of the art green visitor center features exhibits, a classroom, and expansive patio overlooking the lake, making Eagle Nest Lake an ideal location for wildlife viewing. In the winter, ice fishing and snowmobiling are popular sports when ice thickness permits. Snowmobiling is limited to the lake surface.

GHOST TOWNS **Elizabethtown**, 4 miles north of Eagle Nest on NM 38. The first incorporated town in NM in 1868, E-town, named for a founder's daughter, was a boom-and-bust gold mining settlement. The ruins of several buildings and the cemetery linger.

GOLFING **Angel Fire Golf Course** (575-377-4488), Angel Fire Resort, 10 Miller Lane, Angel Fire. At 8,600 feet, this is one of the highest and most lushly wooded regulation courses in the world. Usually open mid-May to mid-October, it's an 18-hole, par-72 course with driving range and putting greens, club and cart rentals, and a restaurant, snack bar, and bar. The clubhouse is glorious. Greens fee, including cart, for guests, $95.

    Taos Country Club (575-758-7300), 54 Golf Course Drive, Ranchos de Taos. Open year-round, weather permitting. Tee times are required and take up to a seven-day advance reservation. Open to the public, at 7,000 feet this is a forgiving desert course of 18 holes. $43–48.

HIKING **West Rim Trail** (575-758-8851). From the Plaza, north on Paseo del Pueblo Norte 4 miles. Left at signal at the intersection with US 64, west 7 miles. Cross the bridge and turn left at the rest stop immediately west of the bridge. A well-maintained bathroom and water are available. Nine miles each way—go as far as you like—are flat, easy to moderate views of clouds and mountains. Recommended as a beginning mountain biking trail. Careful in summer, snakes are common; can be dangerous for your four-footed friends.

    Williams Lake. The trailhead is above Taos Ski Valley, past the Bavarian Restaurant about 1.3 miles. The best time to go on this classic Taos hike, rated moderate, is during July–August, when the wildflowers are at their peak. Plan for 4 miles on a well-marked trail, at an altitude of 11,450 feet to Williams Lake at the base of Wheeler Peak.

    Wild Rivers and Orilla Verde Recreation Areas (www.blm.gov/nm/st/en/prog/recreation/taos/orilla_verde.html), 16 miles south of Taos off NM 68. Twenty-two miles of rim and river trails, easy to intermediate, amid rocky lava flows and following the winding path of the Rio Grande. Plenty of riparian areas with good birding and wildlife viewing.

HORSEBACK RIDING **Cieneguilla Stables** (575-751-2815), 13 miles south of Taos Visitor Center on east side of NM 68, near Pilar. Custom rides or ride to the miner's cabin Rio Grande Gorge canyon country.

    Taos Indian Horse Ranch (575-758-3212), Pinon Road off NM 150, Taos. Horseback rides, sleigh rides, cookouts, Indian storytellers, and Taos Mountain music. Reservations required. About $100 per person for a two-hour ride.

    Nancy Burch Roadrunner Tours, NM 64, Angel Fire. The ultimate "City Slicker" experience. Lessons, one-hour to all-day rides, sleigh rides, romantic wedding and engagement rides into the Carson National Forest and along the Enchanted Circle.

NATIVE CUTTHROAT TROUT ROVE THE RIO COSTILLA

MOUNTAIN BIKING For detailed information, visit the **BLM Pilar Visitor Center** (575-751-4899), 15 miles south of Taos on NM 68 or the **BLM Taos office** (575-751-4899) on Cruz Alta Road.

Rio Grande Gorge West Rim Trail, the Rio Grande Gorge Rest Area at US 64. An easy 9-mile one-way trip with great rewards. Check out the Rio Grande Gorge from the bridge south to NM 567.

Wild Rivers Recreation Area, 35 miles north of Taos on NM 378 east of Cerro. From the 6-mile Rinconada Loop Trail and the 5-mile Red River Fault Trail to the 2-mile Red River Fault Trail, this trailhead offers rides from easy to difficult. Maps are at the Wild Rivers Visitor Center or any BLM office. $3 day use.

NATURAL HOT SPRINGS **Blackrock (John Dunn) Springs** are located on the west bank of the Rio Grande just below the John Dunn Bridge. From Taos Plaza, go north on US Highway 64. Continue straight onto New Mexico 522 at the traffic signal where US Highway 64 turns left. Six miles past the intersection with US 64, just over a small bridge on the Rio Hondo, turn left onto the paved County Road B005. Drive slowly through the village of Arroyo Hondo. In 1 mile, the pavement ends. Cross another bridge and climb a short hill. Bear right in 0.1 mile and ignore the many side tracks as the main road snakes to the top of the hill before descending into the Rio Hondo Canyon. The road into the canyon is rough but passable. Cross the Rio Grande on John Dunn Bridge and continue 0.2 mile.

Manby (Stagecoach) Springs are located on the east bank of the Rio Grande. Access is from US 64, then onto a private road. From Taos, drive north on US Highway 64 to the intersection with New Mexico Highway 522. Continue straight on New Mexico Highway 522. In 5.3 miles, just before the road begins a long descent, turn left on County Road B007. Continue 2.3 miles on this gravel road, and turn left onto a very rutted dirt road. From this point, a high-clearance vehicle or mountain bike is recommended. Follow the main track, taking care to stay out of driveways along the way. After a half-mile on the rutted track, take the left fork, then the right fork in another 0.8 mile. Reach the parking area on the rim of the Rio Grande Gorge at the unmarked trailhead in another

BUFFALO THUNDER IS A STUNNING RESORT OUTSIDE SANTA FE

half-mile, 1.8 miles from County Road B007. Note that the roads to the trailhead are impassable during wet weather.

RIVER RAFTING The **Taos Box** and the **Racecourse** are two of the most popular white-water stretches on the Upper Rio Grande. If runoff is good, you can be on the river from May through July. Adrenaline is the name of the game. Be prepared for Class IV rapids.

Cottam's Rio Grande Rafting (800-322-8267; www.cottamsriogranderafting.com), 207 Paseo del Pueblo Sur, Taos.

Los Rios River Runners (575-776-8854; www.losriosriverrunners.com), P.O. Box 2734, Taos. In business more than 40 years.

SCENIC DRIVES **Enchanted Circle Scenic Byway** (877-885-3885). US 64 and NM 522 and 38. Setting out from Taos, the Enchanted Circle links the communities of Angel Fire and Eagle Nest, circling Wheeler Peak, the state's highest mountain. Return to Taos via Bobcat Pass through Red River and Questa. The best time to do the 84-mile Enchanted Circle is when the aspens are turning, usually the last weekend in September, but it's beautiful any time. The road takes you over Bobcat Pass, with its 9,820-foot summit, so named for the many bobcats that lived there. This was once all part of the Maxwell Land Grant, the largest private land holding in the Western Hemisphere during the nineteenth century.

High Road to Taos (no phone). Pick up the High Road by driving north on NM 68 out of Santa Fe through Española. Go right at NM 76 and continue on through the towns of Chimayo, Truchas, Ojo Sarco, Peñasco, and on to Taos on NM 75. Cordova is a jog to the right between Chimayo and Truchas. This is a scenic drive any time of year, during a golden fall, a green spring, or a snowy winter, but always be alert to weather reports and fast-changing weather, whatever the season. Pack a picnic, binoculars, camera, and fishing gear, and bring your hiking boots and multiple layers of outdoors wear. Each village has its historic Spanish colonial church, and each village lives much as it has for centuries, making them almost living history museums. The Sangre de Cristo Mountains offer heart-stopping views. Investigate the galleries, cafés, roadside stands, and historic churches along the way. Easily an all-day trip, particularly for shutterbugs.

River Road to Taos. From Española, continue north on NM 68 for 47 miles to Taos. The road follows the course of the Rio Grande and swoops past the green agricultural villages of Alcalde and Velarde, then Embudo, then past the landmark Ranchos Church in Ranchos de Taos. In fall, produce stands along the way are filled with the new harvest—local apples, cider, plums, pears, squash, melons, and preserves. From late May on through midsummer, you are likely to see river rafters down below. It's fun to stop at the little store and café in Pilar, a.k.a. the Pilar Yacht Club, where rafters put in. If you have time and inclination, you can turn right on NM 76 toward Dixon and take the remaining High Road to Taos through Peñasco, Ojo Sarco, and on into Taos along NM 76-75.

Wild Rivers Back Country Byway (www.newmexico.org/things-to-do/scenic -byways/wild-rivers/), 26 miles north of Taos, goes west on NM 378 off NM 522, north of Questa. This is a phenomenal 13-mile ride that parallels the Rio Grande and Red rivers along NM 378, with access to Wild Rivers Recreation Area north of Taos. Scenic overlooks above the Rio Grande Gorge into the canyon will have you in a state of wonder. You must return the same way you drove in. A word of caution: If you are thinking of hiking down to the river, be prepared for a Grand Canyon–Bright Angel Trail–style return—in other words, the hike up and back is only for those in shape, wearing good hiking boots. While it is not a difficult hike, it is extremely steep and seems to become longer with every step. And there are no mules to come rescue you.

SKIING For cross-country ski instruction and tours in the Taos area, call **Millers Crossing** (575-754-2374; 800-966-9381), 417 W. Main Street, Red River. The place to go touring near Taos is the **Enchanted Forest Cross Country Ski Area** (575-754-6112), 29 Sangre de Cristo Drive, Red River. Just east of Red River atop Bobcat Pass, it offers 30 kilometers of groomed and ungroomed trails amid 600 forested acres. Here, you'll find not only dog-friendly trails and prime ski terrain for classical, freestyle, and Telemark, but also instructors, patrols, warming huts, and rentals, plus snowshoeing and special events. $10 a day; rentals $12 a day; or $27 for three days

Angel Fire Resort (575-377-6401; 800-633-7463 information, snow report, and reservations; www.angelfireresort.com), 10 Miller Lane, Angel Fire; 22 miles east of Taos via US 64 and NM 434. With 10,677 ft. peak elevation; 2,077 ft. vertical drop; 210 in. average snowfall; snow-making over 52 percent of the area; trails: 67 downhill (31 percent beginner, 48 percent intermediate, 21 percent advanced); groomed 35-kilometer cross-country track; lifts: 5 chairlifts (2 high-speed quads, 3 doubles, 2 Sunkid Wondercarpets); $64 adults, $48 half day; $44 ages 7–12; 6 and under/70 and over free; sightseers may purchase a single lift ride to the summit for $20. Today, it is known as a family resort and a "cruiser's mountain," featuring a variety of long, well-groomed trails (the longest is 3.5 miles). Angel Fire is predominantly tailored to beginning and intermediate skiers; however, it also offers a number of outstanding expert runs, including the addition of a new expert trail called C-4. A short 15-minute hike from the top of the Southwest Flyer chairlift, C-4 will top the adventurous skier and boarder's must-hit list on any fresh powder day. Widespread snow-making guarantees 2,000 vertical feet of skiing even in the driest of years, and only in the very busiest of times does the lift line require more than a five- or ten-minute wait. Another plus is the large picnic pavilion on the mountain that can accommodate several hundred skiers at a time.

With 3,000 beds, Angel Fire has one of the largest, most affordable lodging bases in the state. The resort also boasts more major events than almost any other area— for example, the world shovel race championships, featuring the wild antics of riders careening down the mountain at more than 60 miles an hour on scoop shovels.

Angel Fire Resort has also bolstered its freestyle parks with exciting features, helping cement Angel Fire's position as snowboarding capital of the state. They have added more than a dozen high-quality freestyle rails and fun box features, including the most popular flat rails, rainbows, double-kinks, C-rails, tabletops, and a few surprises—open challenges to freestyle skiers, as well as boarders.

The Angel Fire Resort Nordic Center offers 10 kilometers of groomed classic and skate cross-country ski trails of graded levels, plus snowshoeing lanes and a family snow play hill for sledding. Lessons, equipment rental, retail, and pull-sleds are available in the full-service winter sports shop downstairs. When you're done playing outside and need to warm up, come into the Club and grab a hot chocolate and enjoy the beautiful views of the Sangre de Cristo Mountains. Snowboarding lessons are available at the ski school. Other opportunities for outdoor fun include a terrain park, zipline, tubing, polar coaster, and cross-country skiing.

Red River Ski Area (575-754-2223 information, snow report; 800-331-SNOW reservations; www.redriverskiarea.com), P.O. Box 900, Red River; 37 miles north of Taos via NM 522 and NM 38. With 10,350 ft. peak elevation; 1,600 ft. vertical drop; 214 in. average snowfall; snow-making over 85 percent of area; trails: 57 downhill (32 percent beginner, 38 percent intermediate, 30 percent advanced); cross-country available nearby at Enchanted Forest; lifts: 7 lifts (2 double chairs, 3 triple chairs, 2 surface tow); $64 adults, $49 half day; $58 teens; $49 children and seniors, over 70 and under 3 free. Red River was started in 1961 by a well-loved oilman and character named John Bolton, and its first lift consisted of used derricks and cables that Bolton imported from an oil field in Texas. Located in the northern arc of the Enchanted Circle, Red River is another family-friendly ski area, a great place to learn, with extensive snowmaking and numerous wide beginner and intermediate trails. Runs such as Kit Carson and Broadway allow plenty of room for everybody to fall down, while expert speedways like Cat Skinner and Landing Strip are enough to get anyone's adrenaline pumping. The area rents about 1,000 pairs of skis, with another 2,000 pairs available in Red River. It also hosts on-slope bars and restaurants.

"That was sick" is one of the most common phrases you'll hear out here. Red River has three terrain parks tiered for every level of expertise, and its modern park designs will keep you coming back for more. Graduate from Pot O' Gold Terrain Park, located on Gold Rush Hill, cruise into Bobcat Terrain Park, located on Bobcat Run, or head over to Hollywood Terrain Park, where your freshest tricks can be seen from the new triple chair.

Red River features a 4,500-bed lodging base less than a block from the ski area. During February's Mardi Gras in the Mountains, the whole town turns to cooking Cajun food and dresses in festive southern garb. There's a moonlight ski and snowshoe event, and Spring Break Torchlight and Fireworks show. Red River has a Kinderski school for ages four to ten and Buckaroo Child Care for ages six months to four years.

Claiming to offer the best value among Rocky Mountain ski areas, Red River caters to juniors, teens, small children, and families. There's tubing, snowboarding, and a well-respected ski school. You can enjoy excellent skiing on the 10,350-foot mountain, which rises from the middle of town toward the Old Western mining sites of the 1800s. High in the southern Rockies, skiers tackle 57 powder-covered runs. Gaining popularity is the "Moon Star Mining Camp," where the family can ski to a replica of the Moon Star Mine of the 1890s. $76.

Taos Ski Valley (575-776-2291; 800-776-1111; www.skitaos.com), P.O. Box 90, Taos Ski Valley; 18 miles northeast of Taos via US 64 and NM 150. With 12,481 ft. peak elevation; 3,281 ft. vertical drop; 300 in. average snowfall; snow-making 100 percent, beginner and intermediate; trails: 110 downhill (24 percent beginner, 25 percent intermediate,

51 percent advanced), no cross-country; lifts: 10 chairlifts (4 quad, 1 triple, 5 double), 2 surface lifts; $110 adults; $70 children 7–12.

The indefatigable founder of Taos Ski Valley, Ernie Blake, long dreamt of his own resort, spending countless hours flying his small plane over the Sangre de Cristo Mountains, scouting for the perfect site. The valley he finally located got an inauspicious start as a ski resort, with unreliable investors and near inaccessibility. But Blake persevered.

When Taos Ski Valley opened as a fledgling family ski area in 1955, a 300-foot, diesel-driven T-bar was its first lift. Taos Ski Valley has never looked back.

The tradition at Taos Ski Valley is service, and that begins with excellent engineering and design. From lift-line management to trail marking, cafeteria food, and ski school programming, the pattern is consistently high quality. Even with a record-breaking abundance of snow and people, the whole system usually works flawlessly. Exceptions are the parking lots, which because of the lay of the valley tend to be long and narrow.

Lowlanders will definitely feel the elevation here. Drink plenty of water and take frequent rests. The views across the valley and from the top of Kachina Peak (12,481 ft.) are worth a pause. The skiing is challenging, even for experts, but there are plenty of intermediate and novice slopes as well, including a few from the very top. The combination of trails called Honeysuckle, Winklereid, and Rubezahl can bring even a first-day skier down safely from the peak. If you're into pushing the envelope, you'll do no better than to bump and pump your way down such mogul-studded trails as the infamous Al's Run (under the newly installed high-speed quad on Lift 1), or to try the steep trails off the West Basin Ridge.

Amenities are provided at midstation snack bars (Phoenix and Whistlestop) and in numerous lodges and restaurants at the base. Families are efficiently accommodated, with daycare for tots ages 6 weeks and up, ski school for the kids, convenient lockers and storage baskets, and a most welcome addition: ski patrollers who actually patrol the slopes and slow traffic down in tight quarters.

SNOWMOBILING **A.A. Taos Ski Valley Wilderness Adventures** (575-751-6051).

Carson National Forest. Access from Angel Fire tour from Forest Road 76 or the Elliot Barker Trail on Palo Flechado Pass.

Red River. Greenie Peak and Midnight Meadow are north of town.

There's an exhilarating network of trails for snowmobilers through both the Santa Fe and Carson National Forests. Many of these regularly groomed mini-highways twist and turn through thick forests to high-alpine meadows where speedsters can zoom across wide-open spaces to their hearts' content. Be sure to check with district forest service offices before you choose a trail. Three of the best are Fourth of July Canyon, Old Red River Pass, and Greenie Peak in the **Questa Ranger District** (575-758-6200) near Red River. A number of businesses in Red River also provide safe, guided snowmobile tours, complete with mountaintop hot dog cookouts. And in January, the **Angel Fire Ski Area** (575-377-3055) hosts the Angel Fire Snowmobile Festival, with races, free rides, buffet dinner, and prizes.

SNOWSHOEING See **Angel Fire**, **Taos**, **Red River**, and **Enchanted Forest** ski areas for snowshoeing fun. Many trails are located in the Carson National Forest as well, which are often shared with cross-country skiers and snowmobilers.

STATE PARKS **Cimarron Canyon State Park** (575-377-6271), P.O. 28869 US Highway 64, Eagle Nest; 3 miles east of Eagle Nest via US 64. A 33,000-acre mountainous preserve with numerous wonderful trails and camping and picnic areas.

Kit Carson Memorial Park (575-758-8234), 115 Civic Plaza Drive, Taos. Offers short walks and a playground on 22 acres.

Rio Grande Gorge State Park (contact state parks number above; 16 miles southwest of Taos on NM 570). Includes shelter, barbecues, trails, drinking water, and campgrounds along the road by the river, as well as boating at Orilla Verde.

Vietnam Veterans Memorial State Park, 34 Country Club Road, Angel Fire. Established in 1968 by Dr. Victor Westphall and his wife, Jeanne, to honor their son David, killed in Vietnam in 1968.

Eagle Nest State Park (575-377-1594), 42 Marina, Eagle Nest. Located along the Enchanted Circle in the Moreno Valley, the lake here is stocked with salmon and trout. Boating, wildlife viewing, camping, it's a cool, pristine, high mountain refuge in summer, ringed by mountains.

✳ Lodging

BED & BREAKFASTS, MOTELS, AND HOTELS Air B&B and VRBO offer numerous listings in Taos.

Taos Lodging (575-751-1771), 100 Brooks Street, Taos.

Angel Fire Resort (575-377-6401), 10 Miller Lane, Angel Fire. With 157 rooms, Angel Fire Resort is by far the biggest lodging establishment in town. The decor is contemporary Southwestern, and the ski area is right outside the window. The inn has two restaurants, a lounge, and an indoor pool and hot tub. It is quite comfortable. $99–220.

American Artists Gallery House B&B (800-532-2041; aagh@newmex.com; www.taosbedandbreakfast.com), 132 Frontier Lane, Taos; 1 mile south of the Plaza. As the name implies, artists and their art are celebrated at this peaceful B&B on a secluded Taos lane. The hosts are warm and the breakfast scrumptious. The inn displays more than 300 works of art, and artists are sometimes invited to discuss their work. Kiva fireplaces and knockout views of Taos Mountain contribute to your developing love of place. With ten rooms and three very private, luxurious Jacuzzi suites in the southwestern-style complex, this B&B offers an ideal opportunity to relax and catch up on some genuine R&R. One room with partial handicapped access. $139.

The Blake at Taos Ski Valley (888-569-1756; theblake.com). Eighty-room rustic-elegant base area lodge adjacent to Lift #1, The Blake is the new face of Taos Ski Valley. A hotel where less is more, much more, where there is comfort in the use of natural materials, the display of fine local art, and sophisticated understatement rules, highlighting the light and beauty of the surroundings. There is a hush here. It is the hush of old money, or new money dressed as old, and if you have to ask the price, you probably can't afford it. On-site dining and bar. Suites with gas fireplaces, kitchenettes, and laundry facilities, and pet-friendly lodging available. $200–300 per night.

Best Western Kachina Lodge, Resort Hotel & Meeting Center (575-758-2275), 413 Paseo del Pueblo Norte, Taos; 4 blocks north of the Plaza. Learn to time travel in Taos. Just north of the city center, this Best Western is a classic roadside motel straight out of the 1950s. Don't miss the circular Kiva Coffee Shop, dominated by a bizarre hand-carved totem pole. Hot breakfast is included. All 118 guest rooms look onto a spacious courtyard with a broad lawn, tall pine trees, and a large outdoor heated swimming pool. The grounds have a country club feel. The Indian decor is laid on a bit thick, and there are even Indian dances on summer nights, but that's how they did things 40 years ago. What makes this place is that it evokes nostalgia without really trying. Close to town, homey, and the price is right. Seven rooms with partial handicapped access. $89.

Casa Benavides Historic Inn (575-758-1772; www.casabenavides.com), 137 Kit Carson Road, Taos; one block east of the Plaza. Airy, light, and colorful, this sprawling B&B boasts thirty-eight guest rooms in six different buildings on 5 downtown acres. Five of the buildings are traditional southwestern adobe, and one is a western Victorian home. The rooms are spacious and modern with all the usual southwestern accents: Navajo rugs, flagstone floors, ceiling fans, skylights, Indian pottery, and kiva fireplaces. There are even a few surprises, including deerskin drums and an authentic Indian tomahawk. Owners Tom and Barbara McCarthy are native Taoseños who've headed a number of different retail businesses in town. Return for afternoon tea to the aroma of freshly baked cookies. The big breakfasts include homemade tortillas and waffles, Mexican eggs, and homemade muffins. A short walk to the Plaza. Guests are inevitably pleased. One room with full handicapped access. $155.

Cottonwood Inn (575-776-5826; www.taos-cottonwood.com; cottonoodinn@gmail.com), HCR 74, Box 246092, State Road 230, El Prado, Taos. Located just off the route to Taos Ski Valley, Cottonwood Inn is the brainchild of two delightful and charming California refugees who are very much in love with their renovated classic and live on-site. Pueblo estate, formerly the residence of flamboyant local artist Wolfgang Pogzeba. Cottonwood Inn is now a two suite rental. With kiva fireplaces, balconies, viga ceilings, Jacuzzis, wet bars, and skylights in most rooms, all guests need to do is kick back and enjoy the spectacular views and fabulous breakfasts. Winters bring the warmth of a roaring fire, while summer is the time to enjoy the lovely gardens on 4 acres of paradise. One room with full handicapped access. Moderate–expensive.

Dreamcatcher Bed and Breakfast (575-758-0613; 888-758-0613; www.dreambb.com), 416 La Lomita, Taos;

LOVERS OF ROADSIDE MEMORABILIA WON'T WANT TO MISS THE CLASSICAL GAS OUTDOOR MUSEUM ALONG THE RIVER ROAD TO TAOS

about 1 mile southwest of the Plaza. Done up in true southwestern style, the seven cozy rooms, each with fireplace, have some unusual touches, like an aqua-colored tile floor (with radiant heat, most appreciated in winter). Big country breakfasts are served. Within walking distance of the Plaza, this casual B&B with hot tub tucked away in a country-like setting, makes for a most comfortable stay. The emphasis here is on green; much of the produce is garden fresh, grown in the garden on the premises. And there is no more delightful hostess than Prudie. She and husband John exited the corporate world for Taos, and they are now "living the dream." Two rooms with full handicapped access. $130.

✿ **El Monte Sagrado Living Resort** (575-758-3502; www.elmontesagrado.com), 317 Kit Carson Road, Taos. The phrase *green grandeur* might best describe the eco-friendly opulence of this resort. Some might find it a bit over the top. It feels like a tropical jungle transplanted to the high desert, and it is known for its claims of environmental purity and innovative recycling. The eighty-four lodgings include five casitas, each with its own private courtyard, and eight Global Suites, each with a wet bar, private courtyard, and gas-burning fireplace. The themes run from Native American to Marrakesh. You may stroll the exquisitely landscaped grounds studded with cascading waterfalls and crystal ponds. In addition to the Living Spa, with exotic body treatments you've never even heard of, this oasis offers a fabulous Aqua Center with salt-water pool, hot tub, and fitness center. The restaurant, De la Tierra, strives for elegance, while the light-filled Gardens serves a more casual breakfast and lunch. Pet friendly with fee. Three rooms with full handicapped access. $200 a night.

Hacienda Del Sol (575-758-0287; stay; www.taoshaciendadelsol.com), 109 Mabel Dodge Lane, Taos. Shaded by giant trees, this B&B was chosen by *USA Today Weekend* as one of America's ten most romantic inns. Two of the eleven guest rooms are located in the main house, a beautiful 180-year-old adobe; five are in a casita, with an additional room found in a separate casita; and three are attached to the main house. Brick floors, Saltillo tiles, and hardwood floors are found in the main building, as are Pueblo-style archways, viga-and-*latilla* ceilings, *bancos*, *nichos*, and stained-glass windows. Four rooms have their own steam bath, while the honeymoon suite has a double-sized black Jacuzzi with a skylight for stargazing. The luxuirous level of comfort provided by the hosts, who have experience as an executive chef and cruise director, is superlative. You could easily wake up here from a restful night on the most comfortable bed in the world, look out at Taos Mountain and

weep for joy, have a vision, and decide to move to Taos! Super-romantic. One room with full handicapped access. Moderate–expensive.

Hotel La Fonda de Taos (575-758-2211; www.hotellafonda.com), 108 S. Plaza, Taos; on the Plaza. If you want to be in the thick of the action, here's the place for you, directly on the Plaza. The historic 1937 La Fonda, the grande dame known for years as the gallery of D. H. Lawrence's paintings, underwent a complete renovation a while back. The art-embellished lobby is still sheltered by giant vigas, and the mezzanine, where continental breakfast is served, retains a mood of old-fashioned comfort. Many of the twenty-four beautifully redecorated rooms now have kiva fireplaces and a view of the Plaza below. To stay here is to travel back in time (without sacrificing any contemporary amenities) and experience the nostalgia of Taos's heyday, when such movie stars and celebrities as Gary Cooper, Judy Garland, and Tennessee Williams visited here. One room with full handicapped access. Moderate–expensive. (Note: As of press time, we hear Hotel La Fonda has been acquired by the local chain, Heritage Hotels, so may be in for something of a makeover.)

Inn on the Rio (575-758-7199; www.innontherio.com), 910 Kit Carson Road, Taos; 1.5 miles east of the Plaza. Brilliant flower gardens and brightly painted flowers adorn this charmingly renovated 1950s-style motor court inn with heated outdoor swimming pool and hot tub, all beautifully tended by Robert and Julie Cahalane, who will do whatever it takes to make your stay perfect. Julie is a master baker who provides fresh-baked quiche, lemon poppy-seed cake, and blueberry blue corn muffins each morning to accompany a full, hot, hearty breakfast. This vintage inn, with baths whimsically hand decorated by Taos artists, is a superb place to really kick back and relax—and a great family spot as well. Featured as a choice destination in numerous national magazines with an AAA Three Diamond rating. Four rooms with partial handicapped access. Moderate.

La Doña Luz Inn (575-758-9000; 800-758-9187; www.stayintaos.com), 114 Kit Carson Road, Taos; 0.5 block east of the Plaza. If you want to be surrounded by colorful folk art and have the Plaza right out your front door, this 200-year-old inn is the place for you. These walls contain enough history and stories to keep you intrigued during your entire visit. The five guest rooms in this centrally located—practically on the Plaza—inn are all dazzlingly different—decorated with a collection of angels from around the world or filled with authentic Indian artifacts nestled in *nichos* or displaying a Franklin stove, claw-foot tub, blacksmith's tools, or Winchester rifle. One room features hand-carved teak woodwork, Afghani rugs, a Kuwaiti chest, and a Balinese fertility goddess suspended over the queen-sized bed. Much of this amazing array comes from a trading post on the property. Rooms are located in three different buildings (including an adobe compound with its own courtyard). Four rooms have their own hot tub, and seven have whirlpools. One room with full handicapped access. Inexpensive–expensive.

La Posada de Taos (575-758-8164; 800-645-4803; laposada@laposada detaos.com), 309 Juanita Lane, Taos; 2.5 blocks west of the Plaza. Opened in 1982 with the claim to being Taos's "first B&B," this inn has an air of romantic seclusion, perhaps because it's located at the end of a quiet dirt road that may take a bit of patience to find. Or maybe it's the honeymoon suite with a skylight directly over the bed. Whatever it is, this is an especially wonderful place to stay. The house, built by a founding member of the Taos Society of Artists, is replete with kiva fireplaces and private patios. The owners have installed their personal antique collection from England, making the six-room inn a distinctive blend of Southwest style and English

country. The two styles make a harmonious blend. Limited handicapped access. Moderate–expensive.

Blue Sky Retreat at San Geronimo Lodge (575-751-3776; www.san geronimolodge.com), 1101 Witt Road, Taos; 1.4 mi. from the Plaza, east off Kit Carson Road/US 64. To immerse in the essence of Taos, and to float in Taos's only chile-shaped swimming pool, book a stay in this 1925 inn, the town's first resort. If you have the heart of a time traveler, if you yearn for old New Mexico as it was in the heyday of the Taos Society of Artists, this eighteen-room lodge is your place. Thick adobe walls and viga ceilings envelop the visitor in a sense of the past as authentic as the imagination fancies. Authentic period art and New Mexican wooden furniture contribute to the well-worn elegance; kiva fireplaces create a glow at day's end. It's off the beaten path yet, once you know the way, it's close to town, on its northern end, toward Taos Ski Valley. Situated beside an acequia, with a clear view of Taos Mountain, amidst ancient cottonwoods and lush apricot and pear trees, San Geronimo is a place to escape to, relax, and wrap up in the romance of the distinctive locale that is Taos. A labyrinth and prayer path trail, open to guests and to the public, enhance meditative moments. Dog-friendly rooms may be shared with your beloved pooch, and dietary needs are graciously honored—advance notice requested. A luscious hot breakfast, included in the price of a stay, is highlighted by fresh fruit and house-made jams, salsas, and chutneys. Specialties like blue corn–blueberry pancakes, apricot scones, and green chile strata make breakfast an event every day. No wonder guests are known to break into song when the host plays the piano! Two wheelchair-accessible rooms. Moderate–expensive.

Mabel Dodge Luhan House (575-751-9686; www .mabeldodgeluhan.com), 240 Morada Lane, Taos; 1 mile north of US 64. Set on five acres at the edge of a

MABEL DODGE LUHAN'S HOME, LOS GALLOS, IS NOW A TAOS BED & BREAKFAST

vast open tract of Taos Pueblo land, this rambling three-story, twenty-two-room adobe hacienda *is* Taos history. This is primarily because of Mabel Dodge Luhan, famous patroness of the arts who arrived in New Mexico in 1918. Let's face it, if people are still telling stories about you fifty years after you're gone, you've lived quite a life. She came at the urging of her husband at the time, artist Maurice Sterne, who was in Taos to paint Indians. Sterne eventually left, but Mabel stayed, married Taos Pueblo Indian Tony Luhan, and bought and renovated this 200-year-old structure. It quickly came to be known as the Big House, where she lived, wrote such classics as *Winter in Taos*, and entertained. Partial handicapped access. Moderate.

From the 1920s through the 1940s, the Big House was visited by artistic and literary figures, including D. H. Lawrence, Georgia O'Keeffe, Carl Jung, Aldous Huxley, and Willa Cather. After Mabel died in 1962, the property was bought by actor-producer Dennis Hopper, who lived there during the filming of *Easy Rider*. In 1977, it was bought by a group of academics as a center for seminars and study groups. It became a B&B in the early 1980s, although workshops are still held here.

The house is filled with viga-and-*latilla* ceilings, arched Pueblo-style doorways, fireplaces, and dark hardwood floors. Just to curl up in the living room is to inhale the essence of what makes Taos, well, Taos. Mabel's Bedroom Suite still contains her original bed; Tony's Bedroom opens out onto a sleeping porch; and the Solarium, accessible only by a steep, narrow staircase, is literally a room of glass (Mabel sunbathed in the nude here)—and as legend has it, D. H. Lawrence himself painted the windows to avoid seeing Mabel's supposed attempts at seduction. There are nine rooms in the main house, a cottage for two, and a guesthouse containing eight southwestern-style rooms. Breakfast, included in the room rates, is served in the spacious dining room. If you want to immerse in Taos history, sleep here.

Old Taos Guesthouse Inn (575-758-5448; www.oldtaos.com), 1028 Witt Road, Taos; 1.8 miles east of the Plaza. Nestled amid a stately grove of trees in a rural area just east of Taos, this 200-year-old adobe hacienda has plenty of rural Spanish charm—not to mention wonderful views of the nearby Sangre de Cristo range and Taos Plateau, a nature trail of its own, and a traditional *acequia* (ditch). Its nine guest rooms, with handmade aspen furniture and all sorts of thoughtful little touches, look out onto a lovely courtyard, and the century-old central living area is classically southwestern in design and decor with a red oak floor. Spa services and facials available on site. No handicapped access. Moderate.

Adobe & Pines Bed & Breakfast (575-751-0947; www.adobepines.com), 4107 Road 68, Taos. A highly acclaimed 1830s adobe where rooms have a kiva fireplace and soaking tub. Lovely gardens surround the flagstone courtyard, and there is a labyrinth to walk and meditate in that is also open to the public. Full gourmet breakfast included. Although just off the highway south of Ranchos de Taos, the place retains a serene, secluded feel. A top choice. Moderate.

El Pueblo Lodge (575-758-8700; www.elpueblolodge.com), 412 Paseo del Pueblo Norte, Taos; 0.5 mile north of the Plaza. My family, which includes an English springer spaniel and an Airedale terrier, loves staying in this convenient, unpretentious 1940s-style motel with hot tub and pool. A satisfying breakfast with many choices, including gluten-free and vegetarian, is included in the warm breakfast room. Popular with skiers. It's a perfect location—you can walk everywhere. Hot chocolate, coffee, and tea until midnight, freshly baked chocolate chip cookies when you check in, and chips and salsa at teatime make it even nicer. Moderate.

Sagebrush Inn and Suites (575-758-2254; 800-428-3626; www.sagebrushinn.com), 1508 Paseo del Pueblo Sur, Taos; 2 miles south of the Plaza. The Sagebrush has recently changed hands and the rooms have been refreshed. The posh Sagebrush has some amazing deals for you, with surprisingly reasonable rates. Opened in 1929 to cater to the trade between New York and Arizona, the Sagebrush Inn is one of Taos's oldest hotels. Built in Pueblo Revival style, the inn is a sprawling structure with ninety-seven rooms, two restaurants, a famously friendly bar, a swimming pool, and two indoor hot tubs. The decor, both Indian and Spanish, includes a rich collection of paintings by southwestern masters, along with Navajo rugs. You may want to stay in the third-floor room where Georgia O'Keeffe painted. The separate Executive Suites offer alternative family lodging, including spacious suites (sleeping up to six people each) with fireplaces. A complimentary breakfast is included in the rate. The inn is pet-friendly, with pet fee and advanced booking. Restaurant and cantina on the premises. Two rooms with partial handicapped access. Moderate.

Taos Inn (1-877-807-6427; www.taosinn.com), 125 Paseo del Pueblo Norte, Taos; 0.25 block north of the Plaza. If immersion in the colorful atmosphere of New Mexican arts, crafts, history, and legend is your cup of tea—or shot of tequila—you can do no better than to stay at the 1936 Taos Inn. You would join a guest register that includes the likes of Greta Garbo, Thornton Wilder, and D. H. Lawrence. It has National Landmark status and was thoroughly restored and modernized in the early 1980s. The lobby is both an art gallery and a people-watcher's paradise, and the Adobe Bar is fondly known as "Taos's living room," with events from Dia de los Muertos community altars to open mike and live music every night. Doc Martin's

Restaurant, winner of the Wine Spectator Award of Excellence, is popular and atmospheric. Two rooms with full handicapped access. Moderate–expensive.

Each of the forty-four guest rooms in four separate buildings at the inn is graced with a distinct personality. Most have pueblo fireplaces, Taos-style antique furniture, bathrooms with Mexican tile, handwoven Indian bedspreads, and even cable TV. Several rooms open onto a balcony overlooking the lobby, while several more open onto a quiet courtyard in the rear. You may have to choose between the character of the main inn and the updated amenities of the back properties. The inn offers specials—if you stay three nights, you get the fourth one free, for example. A swimming pool is available in warm weather, and for weary skiers, a Jacuzzi bubbles invitingly in the plant-filled greenhouse.

Touchstone Inn Spa & Gallery (575-779-1174; www.touchstoneinn.com), 110 Mabel Dodge Lane, Taos; 1 mile north of the Plaza. Located on the edge of Taos Pueblo lands, bordered by tall trees, with splendid views of Taos mountain from the two-acre grounds, Touchstone Inn is a lovingly restored historic adobe that fulfills every fantasy of Taos. Optional breakfast is vegetarian and gluten-free; artist studio space avaialble for rental. In-room Jacuzzi tubs, outdoor hot tub, lovely gardens, and historic associations with salon diva Mabel Dodge Luhan, the spa treatments more than complete an already perfect experience. Most of the nine rooms, named for artists, have fireplaces. Spa packages available. No handicapped access. Moderate–expensive.

CAMPING **Golden Eagle RV Park** (575-377-6188; 800-388-6188), 50 W. Therma Drive, off US 64 in Eagle Nest. A 531-space RV park, including twenty-nine pull-throughs, restrooms, cabins, showers, RV supplies, propane, and game room. Open year-round. $39.95 nightly.

Questa Lodge (575-586-9913), 80 Lower Embargo Road, Questa. Motel and RV park with twenty-six full-service hookups, six cabins, tent sites, laundromat, restrooms, and children's playground, pet park. Open year-round.

Road Runner RV Resort (575-754-2286), 1371 E. Main Street, Red River. Camping for 150 vehicles with 89 full hookups, laundry, showers, tennis court, restrooms, cable TV, playground, barbecue area, picnic tables, fire ring, tepees, Wi-Fi, and gazebo. $45 nightly.

Red River RV Park (575-754-6187), 100 High Cost Trail, Red River. Pet friendly, open year round, Wi-Fi, cable, full hookups, three yurts, and river fishing.

Taos Valley RV Park and Campground (575-578-4469), 120 Este Es Road, Taos. Complete commercial campground including thirty-five full hookups, seventy-five water and electric hookups, eighteen tent sites, playground, rec room, showers, phones, convenience store, and laundromat. Open year-round. $42 nightly.

See **Carson National Forest** (page 126), where you can camp virtually anywhere.

Questa Lodge (575-586-9913), 8 Lower Embargo Road, Questa. Open May–October on the Red River, only a quarter-mile off NM 522, there is a motel and RV park with twenty-six full-service hookups, five cabins, and tent sites. $32 RV site; $60–150. A 28-acre campground has it all, including almost 100 full hookups, laundry, tennis court, wildlife, and playground. $32–37.

✳ Where to Eat

DINING OUT **Lambert's of Taos** (575-758-1009), 123 Bent Street, Taos. Open daily. L, D, Sunday brunch. In addition to having what is widely considered the most complete and intriguing wine list in town, Lambert's delivers a fine meal in a relaxing atmosphere conducive to high enjoyment. This is one of those rare places that will feel like a bargain despite the considerable tab. Appetizers featuring fresh lobster, like lobster gazpacho, and other seasonally available ingredients are creative, light, and scrumptious, like the vanilla saffron poached pear salad. The house special of ancho and espresso-rubbed lamb loin with red wine demi-glace, the Harris Ranch all-natural filet mignon, and the Maple Leaf duck two ways are but a few examples of the grace and flair demonstrated here. The menu changes seasonally. Sitting at the Treehouse Lounge, open at 2:30 PM daily, is where you're likely to find the locals. Dinner over the budget? Lunch is served daily, while the Sunday brunch is legendary. Partial handicapped access; reservations recommended. Expensive–very expensive.

Love Apple (575-751-0050), 803 Paseo Del Pueblo Norte, Taos. D only. The food is quirky, the menu limited, and everything served from the tiny kitchen in this crumbling adobe former chapel is delish, starting with the cornbread all the way to the chocolate mousse. Free range and locally sourced ingredients, intriguing salad combinations, New Mexican traditional dishes made with nontraditional ingredients, all served with casual elegance by candlelight make this one romantic adventure. Some interesting deconstructed dishes. Call ahead to be sure the menu is diverse enough for your party. The steaks are scrumptious, and, for the daring, so is the wild boar. The menu changes often. Wines are excellent, and do save room for the homemade desserts, particularly whatever is chocolate. One memorable evening guaranteed. The "love apple" refers to an antique moniker of the tomato. No handicapped access; reservations strongly recommended. Expensive.

The Bavarian Ski Restaurant & Lodge (575-776-8020), 100 Kachina Road, Taos Ski Valley, Taos. Open daily during winter; call for summer hours. L, D, après ski. This is one hopping place at lunchtime during ski season. Warm and cozy as a German beer hall, it is the place to dine and unwind. You can ski to this mid-mountain European log lodge or call for a van to pick you up at Taos Ski Valley. Featuring German and European specialties such as Wiener schnitzel, bratwurst, Hungarian goulash soup, apple strudel, and beer imported from the oldest brewery in Munich. Bask in the winter sunshine on the sundeck surrounding this re-creation of an Alpine ski lodge. Handicapped access; reservations recommended. Expensive.

Martyrs Steakhouse Restaurant (575-751-3020), 146 Paseo del Pueblo Norte, Taos. Open daily. L, D. White linen, excellent beef, fancy cocktails, and elegant service fill a dining void Taos didn't know it had. Oysters, veal, local lamb, and free-range chicken are all served with otherworldly side dishes. Whether you choose the lovely patio or indoor dining room, you will enjoy fine dining here. The prime rib is especially succulent, and unless you've just been skiing all day, the serving is generous enough to share. Expensive.

Old Martina's Hall (575-758-3003), 4149 NM, Ranchos de Taos. Open daily, B, L, D, brunch. The restoration of the former Ranchos de Taos 68 roadside eyesore does not disappoint. The food is French-ish, or you might say, "American continental," creative, and exquisitely presented. Stop in for a meal or wine and *moules*. Gorgeous bar. Superb baked goods. Early bird prix-fixe three-course menu. Moderate.

Trading Post Café & Gallery Italian Restaurant (575-758-5089), 4179 NM 68, Ranchos de Taos. L–D. Closed Sundays, Christmas, and New Year's. Located in the former general store and meeting place in town; this is a place to choose on a chilly night, in front of the fireplace or at the bar, an excellent place to dine if solo. Order a glass of fine wine and peruse the extensive menu that includes salads, fish, pastas, soups, roast duck, chicken Vesuvio, paella, and a large selection of daily specials.

In warm weather, try the patio. This is the spot for casual sophistication. Moderate–expensive.

Taos Diner (575-758-2374), 908 Paseo del Pueblo Norte, Taos. Open daily. B, L. Although Taos Diner has opened a second kitchen on the south end of town, I prefer the original, quintessentially Taos-funky location for huevos rancheros with red chile, Cobb salad, local natural burgers, and general deliciousness. You can order half a salad. Much of the food is locally sourced. The red chile is good and hot. No wonder locals flock here. Check out the upscale food emporium next door for goodies for your special picnic and extra-healthy snacks. Partial handicapped access; no reservartions. Inexpensive.

Michael's Kitchen Restaurant & Bakery (575-758-4178), 304C Paseo del Pueblo Norte, Taos; 0.3 mile north of the Plaza. Open Mon.–Thurs. 7–2:30; Fri.–Sun. 7–8, closed major holidays. B, L, D. You can't avoid Michael's Kitchen while in Taos. The menu has something for everyone, the doughnuts are beloved, the red chile is just right, and parking is no problem. And the price is right, too. Don't be put off if there is a line. It moves quickly. Michael's Kitchen serves delicious hearty dishes from fried chicken to enchiladas, chosen from a tabloid-sized menu. As you walk in the door, you will notice the large display cases full of breakfast pastries, breads, pies, and other mouthwatering desserts baked fresh daily at the restaurant. Once you finish gawking at the salad-plate-sized cinnamon rolls with cream cheese icing and confetti sprinkles on top, have a seat at the counter or at a table in one of the main dining rooms and settle in for a while. Partial handicapped access; no reservations. Inexpensive.

Bearclaw Bakery & Café (575-758-1332), 228A Paseo Del Pueblo Norte, Taos; 0.3 miles north of the Plaza. Open daily 8 AM–3 PM B, L. The former pastry chef from Taos Inn has gone out on her own and is serving gorgeous baked goods, including fabulous pastries as big as actual bearclaws and specializing in gluten free cookies, coffee cakes, and other assorted goodies. The creative menu includes spins on local traditional dishes like breakfast fajitas with organic eggs and coffee and includes an alternative serving of greens for carbs, a delicious dish of lightly sautéed chard and kale. Omelets and blue corn pancakes star at breakfast; lunch starts at 11 AM and features salads, homemade soup of the day with housemade bread, bison burger, and lamb gyro. Anthony's Bearclaw Reuben is the best! Partial handicapped access; reservations. Inexpensive–moderate.

Ranchos Plaza Grill (575-758-5788), 6 St. Francis Plaza, Ranchos de Taos. Closed Mondays. B, L. Sit on the patio, in view of the most painted and photographed church in America, the old Ranchos San Francisco de Asis Church made famous by Georgia O'Keeffe and Ansel Adams. Then dig into some of the most savory red chile you'll find anywhere. The blue corn cheese enchiladas with red chile are pure New Mexico. The Ranchos Plaza Grill specializes, most appropriately, in classic New Mexico cooking, served in an ancient rambling adobe hacienda. Partial handicapped access; reservations recommended. Inexpensive.

Taos Pizza Out Back (575-758-3112), 712 Paseo del Pueblo Norte, Taos. Open daily; closed Thanksgiving, Christmas. L, D. Don't miss this funky little pizza joint slightly outside the Taos town limits. Don't be put off by its "back in the day" appearance. The undisputed local favorite pizzeria, Out Back is one of the hippest pizza parlors you've ever seen, complete with an old-fashioned gas pump in the corner and customers' crayoned works of art hanging on the walls. It specializes in "Taos-style gourmet pizza," lovingly made to order from organic Colorado wheat. Because the place is so often packed, you may want to order in advance or do take-out. Try the Florentine, with chicken, garlic, and herbs sautéed in white wine, or the portobello mushroom pie. Servings are more than generous, and they don't scrimp on the toppings. One slice will fill you up, but it's so delicious, you'll want more. The salads are fresh and generous as well. Partial handicapped access; no reservations. Moderate.

Orlando's New Mexican Café (575-751-1450), 1114 Don Juan Valdez Lane, Taos; 1.8 miles north of the Plaza on left. Open daily, closed Sundays and Christmas. L, D. If you're in the market for authentic northern New Mexico cooking without the lard, you can't do better than Orlando's. The decor of colorful Mexican folk art, in lime and hot pink, accentuated with punched tinwork, and the scrumptious desserts all contribute to a delightful experience. Try the chile bowl "with everything," or go for one of the best Frito pies in northern New Mexico. Summer dining on the patio is a joy, though it can be very crowded during peak times, so plan accordingly. No handicapped access; no reservations. Inexpensive.

Gutiz (575-758-1226), 8128 Paseo del Pueblo Norte, Taos; 1.5 miles north of the Plaza on left. Open Tues.–Sun. 8 AM–3 PM B, L. A local favorite with luscious crepes and French toast for breakfast and outstanding soups and salads at lunch. The place for a croque monsieur, paella, or specialty sandwich. A little pricey but worth it. Go for the Gutiz grilled cheese—three varieties melted together. Bonus: sinfully good chocolate truffles in exotic flavors like cardamom and green tea, sold here and here only. No handicapped access; reservations. Moderate.

Five Star Burger (575-758-8484), 1032 Paseo del Pueblo Sur, Taos. Open daily. Get your burger in bison, lamb, turkey, veggie, or the old-fashioned way, with green chile, cheese, and Harris Ranch beef. Go for the crispy sweet potato fries. A bit pricier than your chain burger, but oh so worth it. Truly satisfying and, ultimately, a reasonable place to take the

family for lunch or dinner. Money can't buy happiness, but it can buy satisfaction. At least here it can. The decor is a bit sterile and chainlike, but don't let that deter you. Inexpensive.

Elevation Coffee (575-779-6078), 1110 Paseo del Pueblo Norte, Taos. Conveniently located on the way to Taos Ski Valley, Elevation serves up creamy lattes that are a work of art.

Bent Street Deli & Cafe (575-758-5787), 120 Bent Street, Taos; in the Dunn House complex. Tasty soups, salads, and sandwiches.

Coffee Spot (575-758-8556), 900 Paseo del Pueblo Norte, Taos. Open daily 6 AM–6 PM. Small plates, breakfast and lunch all day, fine baked goods and decadent desserts, including fudge and rice krispy treats, cheesecake and pie.

El Gamal (575- 613-0311), 112 Dona Luz, Taos. A Middle Eastern café serving fresh bagels, pita sandwiches, and hummus.

Shotgun Willie's (575-754-6505), 403 W. Main Street, Red River. Homemade barbecue by the pound, hand-breaded catfish, and New Mexican cuisine hearty enough to appease any starving skier. Looking, as it does, like a small shack of a place, you might be tempted to pass Shotgun Willie's by. Don't make that mistake. This place serves by far the best barbecue (and remember, there are a lot of Texans in Red River) and the fattest breakfast burritos, and the paper plates don't hurt a bit. Inexpensive.

Taos Cow Ice Cream Scoop Shop Café & Deli (575-776-5640), 485 NM 150, Arroyo Seco. Open daily 7–6. You might think you're in a time warp here with the longhairs and Rastafarians, but we all know a good thing when we see it. If you're an ice cream lover, head up the Taos Ski Valley Road to the ice creamery that has the creamiest, most exquisite all-natural and rBGH-free ice cream you've ever tasted, in delectable seasonal flavors, such as peach and lavender, and the chocolate variations will win your heart. Freshly roasted organic Fair Trade coffee and

Wi-Fi, too. Sandwiches and soups will satisfy your lunch cravings. Inexpensive.

Tim's Stray Dog Cantina (575-776-2894), 105 Sutton Place, Taos Ski Valley. Open daily 8–9 winter, 11–9 summer. This is the place for a lively, if not rowdy, après-ski libation. Plenty of big portions of standard American fare and "famous margaritas" await. Inexpensive.

Zeb's Restaurant & Bar (575-377-6358), 3431 Mountainview Boulevard, Angel Fire. Open daily. L, D. This big pub serves up Mexican food, burgers, steaks, and salads at reasonable prices. It may remind you of your college hangout, but there's no problem feeding a hungry family after a day of skiing. It's not gourmet fare, but it's been around a long time. Inexpensive–Moderate.

✳ Entertainment

Alley Cantina (575-758-2121), 121 Teresina Lane, Taos. Said to be Taos's oldest building, the place draws crowds of tourists and locals who dance into the late hours to the live music every night. Happy hour is a bargain.

Best Western Kachina Lodge (575-758-2275), 413 Paseo del Pueblo Norte, Taos. Local bands play here weekend nights.

Bull O' The Woods Saloon (575-754-2593), 401 E. Main Street, Red River. Live music nightly at 9 PM. Dancing, too. This is *the* nightlife scene in Red River. It's a historic bar with shuffleboard, pool, and karaoke.

El Taoseno Restaurant and Lounge (575-758-4142), 819 Paseo del Pueblo Sur, Taos. If you want to mingle with the locals, hang out here on a Friday night. One of them might ask you for a turn on the big dance floor.

Eske's Brew Pub and Restaurant (575-758-1517), 106 Des Georges Place, Taos, is still the best place to relax with a microbrew, brats, and green chile stew.

Metta Theater (575-758-1104), 1470 Paseo del Pueblo Norte, Taos. Innovative, offbeat, premier, and serious theater featuring true local talent. Worth checking out.

Sagebrush Inn (575-758-2254), 1508 Paseo del Pueblo Sur, Taos. Live music most nights at 9 PM, with some of the best local country and western performers and dancing.

Taos Center for the Arts (575-758-2052; www.taoscenterforthearts.org), 133 Paseo del Pueblo Norte, Taos. The Taos Community Auditorium here is a venue for music, theater, exhibitions, film, and concerts of all varieties.

Adobe Bar, Taos Inn (505-758-2233; www.taosinn.com), 125 Paseo del Pueblo Norte, Taos. Long considered "Taos's living room," there is a huge variety of live entertainment here most nights in the Adobe Bar to accompany your margarita. (May I recommend the Baby Buddha?) Walk right in and make yourself at home. The place can get elbow-to-elbow on weekend evenings. In warmer weather, the street side patio is the place to hangout with your adult beverage.

✳ Selective Shopping

Brodsky Bookshop (575-758-9468), 226 Paseo del Pueblo Norte, Taos. An almost "legacy" intimate shop with a wide range of western and southwestern fiction and nonfiction, general interest titles, and used books—plus maps and cards. The scent of the old days wafts through. An indie bookstore of 40 years.

🖉 **Twirl Toy Store and Play Space** (575-751-1402), 225 Camino de la Placita, Taos. Those who say there are not enough activities for kids in Taos have not been to Twirl. Part playground, part activity and crafts center, and mostly just the most magical toy store–for all ages—you have ever seen, Twirl gives kids the world from their point of view.

Overland Fine Sheepskin & Leather (575-758-8820), 1405 Paseo del Pueblo Norte, Taos. Shearling coats to see you through the coldest winters, plus hats,

GAMING

In addition to serving as venues for Las Vegas–style gaming and dining, Indian-run casinos are popular venues for celebrity performers.

Buffalo Thunder Resort and Casino (505-455-5555), 30 Buffalo Thunder Trail, on US 84/285 north of Santa Fe. The newest and most exciting place to try and win your fortune.

Camel Rock Casino (800-GO-CAMEL), 17486A US 84/285, 10 minutes north of downtown Santa Fe. Run by Tesuque Pueblo, Camel Rock offers slots, blackjack, bingo, roulette, and a restaurant.

Cities of Gold Casino (505-455-3313), 10-B Cities of Gold Road, on US 84/285, 15 miles north of Santa Fe. Cities of Gold is run by Pojoaque Pueblo and has more than 700 slot machines, in addition to other games, as well as an extravagant 24-hour buffet spread, simulcasting.

Ohkay Casino (505-747-1668), 68 New Mexico 291, Ohkay Owingeh, along US 84/285, just north of Española. Operated by San Juan Pueblo, this popular casino is well known for its breakfast buffet.

Taos Mountain Casino ((575- 737-0777), 700 Veterans Highway, Taos. The only nonsmoking casino in the state, Taos Mountain offers 200 slots, restaurant, gaming tables, smoke shop—but no bingo.

🐾 **Hilton Santa Fe Buffalo Thunder** (505-455-5555), 20 Buffalo Thunder Trail, Santa Fe. Actually located out of town on US 84/285, this is the newest and most deluxe resort in the area, with a knockout art collection, revolving tower gallery, four great restaurants, lovely pool, spa, fabulous golf course, and accessible casino. The only glitch is it is difficult to pin down rates, which are highly negotiable depending on occupancy and time of week and year. Rates are a tightly held secret, and no rate sheet exists.

THE RUSTIC-ELEGANT BLAKE HOTEL IS TAOS SKI VALLEY'S NEWEST RESORT

TWIRL IS A TOY STORE WHERE KIDS CAN REALLY PLAY

slippers, mittens, and more. Imported fine Italian leathers and gorgeous beaded leather jackets. Find something fine to fit the budget—belts, gloves, slippers, wallets—or splurge on a lifetime purchase. Items sold here will never go out of style. Look for the spring sales, starting around Valentine's Day.

Steppin' Out (575-758-4487), 120 Bent Street, Taos. Two floors of fine leather goods, from shoes to belts to handbags, is the last word in style. Some high-end waterproof boots make bad weather not only endurable but a chance for chic. Also a selection of stylish clothing to flatter the world traveler.

Starr Interiors (575-758-3065), 117 Paseo Del Pueblo Norte, Taos. Step into Starr and bring home the aura of the Southwest. Known for hand-crafted Zapotec Indian weavings "to last a lifetime," this shop also features benches, tables, and *trasteros* (cabinets) hand-carved and hand-painted by Taos artisans. Oaxacan masks and more. A reliable decor source since 1974.

Columbian art. An excellent selection of books on Navajo textiles.

At Home in Taos (575-751-1486), 117 S. Plaza, Taos. Everything you didn't know you wanted but simply must have! Housewares, clever gifts, jewelry, pottery, cards, accessories in a huge space for browsing. Can be dangerously addicting and difficult to leave.

Moxie: Fair Trade & Handmade (575-758-1256), 216 Paseo del Pueblo Norte, Taos. OK, this is where I shop. Imports from Africa, Latin America, Nepal, cottons, felts, tie dyes, wearables, unusual decor, socks, hats, toys, all that is colorful and comfortable.

Wabi-Sabi (575-758-7801), 216 Paseo del Pueblo Norte, Taos. As serene as a tea ceremony. Japanese aesthetics and the goods you need to create "less is more" Zen beauty on your person or in your home.

Made in New Mexico (575-758-7709), 104 W. Plaza, Taos. The official home of real New Mexico products, this is the place, right on the Plaza, to purchase salsa, blue corn pancake mix, chokecherry syrup, foodstuffs, and any New Mexico memorabilia you want to bring home. Good for souvenirs and gifts.

Monet's Kitchen (575-758-8003), 124 Bent Street, Taos. A nicely apportioned kitchen shop with espresso makers, woks, pottery, aprons, and table linens. Some gourmet foods and coffees as well, for a complete gift basket.

Taos Cookery (575-758-5435), 113 Bent Street, Taos. Besides featuring general kitchenware, Taos Cookery also represents many local potters. Among the most eye-catching designs are the multicolored productions of Ojo Sarco Pottery, whose husband-and-wife team creates dishwasher- and microwave-safe pottery emblazed with patterns taken from the New Mexico landscape.

Artwares Contemporary Jewelry (575-758-8850), 129 N. Plaza, Taos. Known for its stylized Zuni bears, executed in precious metals and used to adorn earrings, necklaces, and pins.

There is fine lapidary work, and a mix of Native American and contemporary-style jewelry in a reasonable price range.

FX/18 (575-758-8590), 103 Bent Street, Taos. Whimsical sculptures, retro items, silver jewelry, and dining and household wares with a playful touch. The store shows the work of younger cutting-edge local jewelers, as well as locally made soaps, notecards, and gifts.

Taos Blue (575-758-3561), 101 Bent Street, Taos. Saints and angels brush halos and wings in this gift shop specializing in objects with divine inspiration—from pottery to paintings on wood to luscious hand-knit sweaters. The place to find a unique gift by a local craftsperson.

Artemesia (575-737-9800) 117 Bent Street, Taos. Definitely the place to splurge on a handwoven chenille wrap or hand-dyed silk top. It's all wearable art and fabulous, made by locals and other artists well-selected. Seriously to die for, and the quickest way to look like a knockout at the big event on your calendar.

Francesca's Clothing and Jewelry Boutique (575-776-8776), 492 NM 150, Arroyo Seco; 1018 Paseo del Pueblo Norte, Taos. Voted the favorite shop of Taos women, packed with colorful and relaxed pieces to mix and match in unusual ways. Perfect for après-ski fun. Totally geared to the Taos imagination and look, perhaps best characterized as something of a "gypsy-cowgirl-nostalgia princess."

Spotted Bear (505-758-3040), 127 Paseo del Pueblo Sur, Taos. One of the most extraordinary clothing stores anywhere, Spotted Bear is worth a pilgrimage. Women's clothing here is exotic and exquisite, from velvet animal-print scarves to amusing flowered hats. There are dresses of hand-painted silk and vintage designer outfits, as well as unique raincoats in rich materials. Choose your era, from a period look to right-now metallic and faux leopard. If you shop

CHOKULA, LOCATED JUST OFF TAOS PLAZA, IS A MUST-DO FOR CHOCOHOLICS, WITH UNFORGETTABLE HANDMADE SWEETS, MOUSSE, ICE CREAM, AND BEVERAGES

EACH PONY ON THE VENERABLE CAROUSEL KNOWN AS TIOVIVO WAS DECORATED BY A WELL-KNOWN TAOS ARTIST

Sundays and major holidays. Since Cid's opened in 1986, owners Cid and Betty Backer have made it a point to purchase the freshest, purest food available. In addition to an array of organic, locally sourced fruits and vegetables and gourmet items, Cid's offers natural soaps, herbs, vitamins, non-animal-tested cosmetics, and biodegradable cleansers. At the same time, it has a great selection of treats such as Lindt chocolates and locally made salsas. Cid's has a first-rate meat department, with bison, fresh fish, and the best cuts of lamb, beef, and pork. Those looking for sugar-free or gluten-free products will find them here. It's also the place to run into everyone you know in town and catch up on the latest. There's a salad and hot food bar where you can eat in or take out. You can sip your smoothie in the little glassed-in café space out front.

Taos Farmers Market (575-751-7575), Plaza. Runs Mid-May–late September, Saturday mornings 8 AM–12:30 PM A bonanza of local growers, bakers, bee keepers, and crafters.

Taos Market (575-758-7093), Next door to Taos Diner. Delightful potpourri of fresh organic groceries, treats, body care, herbals, local products, and much more.

Arroyo Seco Mercantile (575-776-8806), 488 NM 150, Arroyo Seco. Anyone who loves to shop will adore this 1895 general store stocked with vintage textiles, quilts, toys, gifts, books, and garden ornaments. So much fun it should be illegal!

Weaving Southwest (575- 758-0433), Arroyo Seco. Three decades of hand-dyed locally grown fine yarns and everything the weaver of knitter's heart could desire. A mecca for craftspeople. Unsurpassed color and quality.

here, it's guaranteed no one else will be wearing anything at all resembling your outfit. And you can do well on the sale racks, especially if you are short in stature.

OptiMysm (575-741-8545), 129 Kit Carson Road, Suite E, Taos. Taos' metaphysical bookstore has a lovely atmosphere and outstanding service. Go slowly along Kit Carson or you might miss it. The shop is tucked away down the alley.

Somos Bookshop (575.758.0081), 108-B Civic Plaza Drive. A bookstore to get lost in, to be inspired by, to find what you didn't know you were looking for. An old-fashioned readers' bookshop that supplies writers with the resources they need to create. Bargain prices for excellent books on every subject. A calendar of readings and book events. Browse on!

Cid's Food Market (575-758-1148), 623 Paseo del Pueblo Norte, Taos. Closed

HIGH ROAD COUNTRY

Chimayo, Truchas, Cordova, Peñasco, Dixon

Little has changed here over the centuries. Many descendants of original settlers still farm and live sustainably, getting by with bartering, wood cutting, hunting, and fishing on land granted their families by the Spanish crown. Traditional crafts of woodcarving and weaving thrive here, along with the tried-and-true way of life. Isolated in small villages within high mountain ranges, people are polite but cool to outsiders. The mission churches of Las Trampas and Chimayo are not to be missed.

GETTING THERE From Santa Fe, take US 68 north to Española. From Española, go right on NM 76 on up the High Road to Chimayo.

✳ To See

TOWNS **Chimayo.** Ten miles east of Española on NM 76. The name comes from the Tewa Indian language, from a word meaning "good flaking stone." The village, founded near here in the early days of the Spanish Reconquest in 1692, is famous as the home of El Santuario de Nuestro Señor de Esquipalas, commonly called El Santuario, known for its healing dirt, miraculous cures, and as a Good Friday pilgrimage site. The nearby shrine dedicated to Santo Nino de Atocha is also considered holy. There is a local "belief" that says Santo Nino must have his shoes replaced, as he wears them out traveling about the village at night performing good deeds. The Plaza del Cerro is the only original fortified plaza in the southwest.

Cordova. Fourteen miles east of Española on NM 76, 1 mile south of NM 76. Traditional woodcarving is the essence of this village's soul. It's what everyone does. The Cordoba style is unpainted aspen and cedar. You can walk into anyone's studio and find exquisite tree of life, Noah's ark, nativities, and *santos* for purchase.

Dixon. Twenty miles northeast of Española, 2 miles east of NM 68. Named for the town's first schoolteacher, this village on the Embudo River has an idyllic appeal. With its Victorian architecture intermixed with adobe homes, it is a cozy community of artists, old-timers, and agricultural folk, who appear to share a vision of neighborliness. There's a sweet co-op grocery store in the middle of town next to the library where you can pick-up supplies and a decent cup of coffee.

Peñasco. Two miles SE of Picuris Pueblo on NM 75. This is probably the largest village on the High Road, where you can find an ATM, a couple of cafés, and gas. Families have lived here for generations, and everyone is either related to or certainly knows everyone else. Much of the life of the town still revolves around barter and living off the land.

Truchas. Eighteen miles northeast of Española on NM 76. Known as the place where the movie *The Milagro Beanfield War*—based on the novel set in Taos by John Nichols—was filmed; it is named for the Rio de Truchas, "trout river," nearby. Set in the high Sangre de Cristos, it is the quintessential isolated High Road village, sprinkled with galleries, with an active *morada*, the home of the Penitente Brotherhood, still quite active here. Warning: Packs of dogs roam the streets.

HIGH ROAD CHURCHES

The hand-carved and painted altar screens and *santos* (saints) found in the High Road Spanish colonial churches represent some of the most striking examples of folk art, created with natural materials, found in New Mexico. A *retablo* is a two-dimensional *santo*, while a *bulto* is three-dimensional. Those who created them are known as *santeros*. Many remain anonymous or nearly so, though numerous explanatory books are available. Check the reading room of the Santa Fe Public Library to learn more.

El Santuario de Chimayo (575-351-9961), 25 miles northeast of Santa Fe on US 84/285 to Española. Turn east on NM 76. Follow signs to Chimayo. The site of this chapel, known as the "Lourdes of America" for its "healing dirt," is believed to be a healing place of indigenous people. It was built in 1813–16 by Bernardo Abeyta, who constructed the Santuario to commemorate the remarkable healing he received here. A variation of the legend says there was a crucifix taken from a church down the road that kept returning after it was replaced, and on the spot where it returned, Abeyta built the church. Pilgrims arrive with prayers for healing all year long, but on Good Friday it becomes a pilgrimage destination for thousands who walk here.

Nuestra Señora del Sagrada Rosario (no phone), Truchas. Constructed around 1805, this beautiful church is not often open. It may be appreciated from the outside, however, or perhaps you will be lucky and find it unlocked.

San Jose de Gracia de Las Trampas (no phone), NM 76, 40 miles northeast of Santa

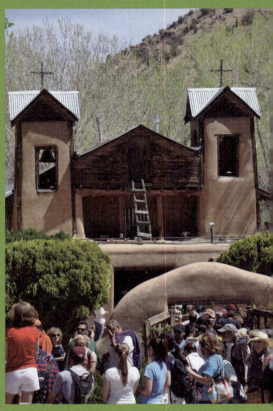

THOUSANDS OF PILGRIMS GATHER EACH GOOD FRIDAY AT EL SANTUARIO CHIMAYO

✳ To Do

BALLOONING Eske's Paradise Balloons (575-751-6098), P.O. Box 308, El Prado, offers valley and Rio Grande Gorge balloon flights year-round. Each includes an hour aloft and a champagne brunch. Ultra light flights also available. $240.

In Taos, **Pueblo Balloon Company** (575-751-9877) is available to take you aloft, offering Rio Grande Gorge flights at $250 ($220 cash).

CAMPING AND FISHING See **Carson National Forest** on page 126.

Fe. Open daily 8–5 in summer. Considered one of the most beautiful, if not the most architecturally perfect and best-preserved Spanish colonial churches in New Mexico, it was constructed between 1760 and 1780. If you arrive and find the church locked, ask at one of the gift shops on the plaza for the person who keeps the key, or call the parish number above to arrange a tour. Donations accepted.

Santa Cruz de la Cañada (505-753-3345), NM 76, Santa Cruz, 3 miles north of Española. One of the most venerable High Road churches, located in a community founded by Governor De Vargas in 1695.

ALONG THE HIGH ROAD, THE SAN JOSE DE GRACIA CHURCH IN LAS TRAMPAS IS AN OUTSTANDING EXAMPLE OF SPANISH MISSION ARCHITECTURE

Eagle Nest Marina and Mountain View Cabins (575-377-6941), NM 64, Eagle Nest. They offer fishing equipment and trips for cutthroats, rainbows, cohos, and kokanee all seasons at Eagle Nest Lake, including ice fishing in winter.

MOUNTAIN BIKING **Carson National Forest** trails off US 64 will take you all the way to Angel Fire.

Picuris Peak, access off NM 518, is an intermediate-to-difficult route with a steep grade and a great view.

Rio Chiquito, a long forest service road off NM 518 that connects with Garcia peaks, is a favorite of families and includes beaver ponds and good picnicking.

THE LOVELY BLACK MESA WINERY MAKES A WORTHWHILE STOP ON THE ROAD UP TO TAOS

WINERIES AND WINE SHOPS **Black Mesa Winery** (505-852-2820), 1502 NM 68, Velarde. Open Mon.–Sat. 11–6, Sun. noon–6. Jerry and Lynda Burd live on the road to Taos in fruit country where grapes have been cultivated for centuries. Their best known wine is probably their Black Beauty, a chocolate-flavored dessert wine, but if you prefer something less sweet, their Viognier, Antelope, and several others, especially their big reds fermented in oak barrels, are superb.

LA CHIRIPADA WINES ARE AVAILABLE IN TAOS, IF YOU'RE LOOKING FOR FINE NEW MEXICO WINE

Kokoman Fine Wines & Liquors (505-455-2219), 34 Cities of Gold Road, Pojoaque. Twelve miles north of Santa Fe. An exceptional selection of 2,500 wines, 161 tequilas, and 400 beers are sold here at competitive prices. A well-informed staff will assist you.

La Chiripada Winery (505-579-4437), 3 miles east of NM 68 at 1119-8 NM 75, Dixon. Open Mon.–Sat. 11–6, Sun. noon–6. At 6,100 feet, this is the highest commercial vineyard in the United States and the oldest ongoing winery in NM. Hearty grapes: two pinot noir hybrids, for example, ripen into intense flavor right here. A signature favorite is the Primavera, a blend of Riesling and French hybrids.

Vivác Winery (575-579-4441), 2075 NM 68, Dixon. Twenty-five miles south of Taos at the intersection of NM 75 and US 68. Open Mon.–Sat. 11–6, Sun. noon–6.

BLACK MESA WINERY TASTING ROOM

A showy place with an adobe tasting room built by the owners, colorful flower beds, colorful art, jewelry, and hand-painted chocolates. The wines are interesting, too, and the owners project themselves and their wines as "young and edgy." Their V. Series represents their highest-quality reserve blends and best varietals.

✳ Lodging

BED & BREAKFASTS **Rancho de Chi-mayo Hacienda** (505-351-2222), 297 Juan Medina Road, Chimayo; 25 miles north of Santa Fe off NM 76. A converted rural hacienda owned by the Jaramillos is your home away from home. Seven guest rooms with Spanish-Victorian flair, all with fireplaces and some with balconies. And it's right across the street from Rancho de Chimayo. $95.

🐾 **Rancho del Llano** (505-689-2347), 371 County Road 0078, Truchas. This three-bedroom guest house also offers a comfortable stall where your pony can bed down. With so much mountain and valley trail riding through piñons and meadows, with panoramic overlooks, this is a place where you can get as close as you like to nature. "A guest ranch on a high grassland at the foot of Truchas Peak." Two-night minimum. $100–150.

🐾 **Rancho Manzana Bed and Break-fast** (505-351-2227), 26 Camino de Mision; 24 miles northeast of Santa Fe off NM 76. This establishment is a working 4-acre farm known especially for lavender and apples watered by an ancient *acequia*. The lodging is a 2-foot-thick adobe dating to the eighteenth century. Gourmet full breakfasts are served outdoors under the grape arbor, weather permitting. There's a hot tub and outdoor pond for dipping, and a separate garden cottage in addition to the two guest rooms in the adobe. It doesn't get any more romantic. Weddings. Cooking school. $122.

✳ Where to Eat

DINING OUT **Rancho de Chimayo Restaurante** (505-351-4444), 300 Juan Medina Road, Chimayo. Open daily. L, D. Closed Mondays November–May.

After experiencing the beneficial effects of the "holy dirt" of the Santuario, try some of the "holy chile" served here. You will fall in love as you sip a margarita by the fireplace on a chilly winter afternoon. And if you have only one New Mexico classic restaurant to sample, do not miss this beauty, the recipient of a James Beard Culinary Heritage award. The chile is on the mild side, but that does not detract from its tastiness. This splendid adobe ranch house has been in the Jaramillo family since the 1880s. With its wooden floors, whitewashed walls, vigas, and terraced patio, you couldn't be anywhere but northern New Mexico. Flavor and service are consistent. Try the crispy nachos; the sopaipilla stuffed with beef, beans, and rice; and the Chimayo chicken, with natillas, a creamy custard for dessert. And say hello to Florence Jaramillo, the matriarch known as Mrs. J, who oversees quality control from her chair beside the kitchen. Moderate.

EATING OUT 🐌 **Sugar Nymphs Bistro** (575-587-0311), 15046 NM 75, Peñasco. Be advised to call first, as hours are not strictly adhered to. L, D daily, Sunday brunch. Locavore alert. Here's a gourmet experience where you least expect to find one. Freshly baked bread and homemade mushroom soup, pizza, and calzones made to order. Pizza served evenings only. Interesting combinations of wholesome contemporary American flavors are put together by a San Francisco–trained chef. Save room for the signature chocolate-maple-pecan pie. This tiny way off the beaten track spot has been discovered by foodies from *Gourmet* and *Sunset*. Moderate.

Sugar's BBQ & Burger (505-852-0604), 1799 NM 68, Embudo. Open Mon. and Wed.–Sun. 11–6. Closed Tuesdays. L, D. When you need a quick, tasty lunch stop, come to this unpretentious little drive-in that has a national reputation for its delectable smoked ribs and a phenomenal Sugar Burger. The sausage also

MEET AT THE VISITOR CENTER FOR A TOUR OF OFF-THE-GRID EARTHSHIPS

gets raves, as does the brisket. Hmm . . . hard to decide. Inexpensive. Hours may be uncertain.

✳ Selective Shopping

Centinela Traditional Arts (505-351-2180), Chimayo. From their shop and gallery adjacent to an old apple orchard, Irvin and Lisa Trujillo weave marvels. Wool comes from Irvin's sister's sheep, and they hand dye much of their product. Both weavers have recognition from Spanish Market as well as the Smithsonian Institute. In addition to their own rugs, table runners, shawls, vests, jackets, purses, books, and prints, they serve as a co-op for other weavers from the area. Their young daughter, Emily, recently graduated from University of New Mexico and now weaves and works in the shop as well, carrying on a multi-generational tradition.

Galeria Ortega and **Ortega's Weaving Shop** (505-351-2288), 55 Plaza del Cerro, Chimayo. Mon.–Sat. 9–5. Closed Sundays. Authentic 100 percent woolen blankets, rugs, coats, vests, and purses are handwoven here in the traditional Chimayo style. Anything you purchase here will last forever. You can watch Andrew Ortega, a seventh-generation weaver, at work in his studio.

High Road Marketplace Artists' Co-op & Gallery (505-689-2689), 1642 NM 76, Truchas. Open daily winter 10–4; summer 10–5. A must-see for lovers of local folk art. Traditional and contemporary arts and crafts by more than 70 northern New Mexico artists, mainly High Road dwellers, from whimsical sage dolls to tinwork to fine woodcarving, are found in this nonprofit community outlet.

Theresa's Art Gallery and Studio (505-753-4698), NM 76, Santa Cruz. Open daily 8–8. Local folk, Jewish, and Indian art, angels, tinwork, *retablos*, pottery, kachinas, and more make this extended family shop a worthwhile stop. The charm will make it difficult to leave.

RIO CHAMA COUNTRY

Abiquiu, Española, Tierra Amarilla, Los Ojos

I f you love the paintings of Georgia O'Keeffe, this region will have a special significance to you as it features the landscapes and wind-sculpted red rocks that inspired her iconic work. Outside of Española, known for its culture of cruising low-riders, much of the area is occupied by ranchers and villagers with a complex history of Native American and Hispanic relationships. These folks maintain strong pride in their heritage. Faith and tradition guide the way. Ghost Ranch makes a fine base for hiking and sightseeing. Weavers at Tierra Wools, who work with wool of the churro sheep, the breed originally brought by the Spanish, make Los Ojos a model of renewed sustainability.

GETTING THERE From Santa Fe, take US 68 north. Continue through Española, turn on US 84/285, and continue north.

GUIDANCE **Chama Valley Chamber of Commerce** (575-756-2306), 2372 Highway 17, Chama.

Española Valley Chamber of Commerce (505-753-2831), 1 Calle de las Españolas, Española.

✳ To See

TOWNS **Abiquiu** (ab-eh-q). Famed as the haunt and home of twentieth-century America's most famous artists, Georgia O'Keeffe, Abiquiu was founded as a Spanish land grant community and became the home of people known as *genizaros*—detribalized Indians who lost their tribal identity through warfare and captivity. Here they were Christianized and given full citizenship by the Spanish Crown. Abiquiu residents received a 16,000-acre land grant for grazing and timber. In 1829 it became the trailhead for the Old Spanish Trail linking 1,200 miles between Santa Fe and Los Angeles. Along with the beauty of its landscape, which has attracted the rich and famous, descendants of the original settlers remain proud people who continue to practice their traditions, including a contemporary revival of the Penitente brotherhood.

Española. Known as the territory of the low-riders, those who cruise the streets slowly in their elaborately altered and colorfully painted automobiles, Española is a crossroads and jumping off point to both the River Road and the High Road to Taos. According to local lore, the name means "Spanish woman," with local tradition referring to a woman who worked in a restaurant here and was known to railroad workers.

Los Ojos. A tiny community, which, during the 1960s, experienced a revival of traditional, sustainable ways through the raising of Churro sheep and the restoration of the Rio Grande weaving tradition. You'll want to visit **Tierra Wools** (575-558-7231), 91 Main Street, Los Ojos, and the weaving co-op there. You can watch the weavers and observe the hand dying of the yarn.

WEAVINGS IN THE RIO GRANDE STYLE ARE AVAILABLE AT TIERRA WOOLS IN LOS OJOS

Tierra Amarilla means "yellow earth," a name common to all the native people who lived here and used the yellow pigment for pottery. It is the county seat of Rio Arriba County. It gained notoriety in 1967 for the courthouse raid led by Reyes Lopez Tijerina.

HISTORIC LANDMARKS, PLACES, AND SITES **Dar al-Islam Mosque** (505-685-4515), 342 County Road 155, above Ghost Ranch. Built by the world's foremost adobe architect, Hassan Fathy, this mosque hosts the Annual North American Muslim Pow-Wow in June. If you choose to visit, call ahead, as access is limited.

Echo Amphitheater, 18 miles north of Abiquiu on US 84, is a remarkable natural sandstone amphitheater-shaped formation where echoes really resound. Find a few campsites here and a short, easy hiking trail.

Georgia O'Keeffe Home and Studio (505-685-4539), 12 Palvadera Drive, Abiquiu. Tours are conducted by appointment only on Tuesdays, Thursdays, and Fridays from mid-March through November, with additional tours on Wednesdays and Saturdays from June to October. All Georgia O'Keeffe tours last approximately one hour and are limited to a maximum of twelve people. Tour office is located next to Abiquiu Inn. $35. A Georgia O'Keeffe Center, where reservations may be made for tours, is scheduled to open at the Abiquiu Inn in 2018.

Ghost Ranch Education & Retreat Center (505-685-1000; 1708 US 84, www.ghostranch.org), Abiquiu. Forty miles northwest of Española on US 84. Classes and seminars in photography, writing, pottery, silversmithing, tin punching, history, health, and spirituality are offered year-round at this 21,000-acre retreat center in the heart of O'Keeffe's red rock country. Specialized historic and landscape tours are also available. Operated by the Presbyterian Church, rustic Ghost Ranch is a center of diversity. Upgraded accommodations are available, as are simple dorm spaces and camping. Intermediate hiking trails, Kitchen Mesa and Chimney Rock, traverse expansive desert landscape with clear views of forever. $5 conservation fee grants access to labyrinth, hiking trails, and museums.

Pedernal means "Flint Mountain" and is where the ancient people hunted that valuable stone. "God told me that if I painted it often enough, He would give it to me," said the painter Georgia O'Keeffe. She made the imposing peak hers, regardless of who holds the deed.

Los Brazos means "the arms" and refers primarily to the tributaries of the Rio Brazos. However, as you drive north on US 84, look to the right as you approach Chama to see striking cliffs of sheer Precambrian quartzite, popular with climbers.

Monastery of Christ in the Desert (575-613-4231; www.christdesert.org), west on US 84 past Ghost Ranch Visitor Center. Left on Forest Service Road 151. A 13-mile winding dirt road leads to monastery grounds. A Japanese monk designed the primitive rock-and-adobe church of this remote Benedictine monastery along the Chama River. In the Benedictine tradition, hospitality is offered by the community. It is possible to make a retreat here by contacting the guestmaster. You will have the opportunity to take part in the life of the monks during prayers, which focus on the Book of Psalms, and silent meals. Two-night minimum. $70–150 per night suggested donation.

Mesa Prieta (505) 852-1351); Velarde. Closed December 15–March 1. Docent-led tours through ancient rocks containing 100,000 petroglyphs. Katherine Wells donated these 149 acres to the Archaeological Conservancy for their preservation. Reservations must be made in advance. The tour—one of six routes—goes through steep and rugged territory. Children under 10 and pets not allowed. $35.

MUSEUMS **Florence Hawley Ellis Museum of Anthropology** (505-685-4333), Ghost Ranch Conference Center, Abiquiu. US 84, 35 miles northwest of Española. Open Mon.–Sat. 9–5, Sun. 1–5. Named for a pioneer anthropologist, this museum specializes in excavated materials from the Ghost Ranch Gallina digs. The Gallina culture of northern New Mexico was rooted in the people who left Mesa Verde and Chaco Canyon during a drought around 1200 AD. The adjacent ✍ **Ruth Hall Museum of Paleontology**, open Mon.–Sat. 9–5, Sun. 1–5, displays a copy of the diminutive Coelophysis dinosaur skeleton, the official state fossil.

✳ To Do

BOATING **El Vado Lake State Park** (575-588-7247), NM 112, Tierra Amarilla, has ramps, camping, and waterskiing, plus Kokanee salmon fishing waters.

Heron Lake State Park (575-588-7470), 95 Heron Lake Road, Los Ojos, is a popular sailing lake set in a ponderosa pine forest. Cross-country skiing, fishing, camping, and hiking. Because it is a restricted no-wake lake, it is ideal for canoeing and kayaking as well. During April–November, contact **Stone House Lodge Rentals** (575-588-7274) for boats and canoes, and kokanee salmon fishing waters, as well as cabins and RV hookups.

CLIMBING, SKIING, HIKING, AND PADDLING **Bumps! Ski Shop** (575-377-3146), 48 N. Angel Fire Road, Angel Fire.

Cottam's Ski Shops (575-758-2822), 207A Paseo del Pueblo Norte, Taos.

Mountain Sports Rentals (575-377-3490), 3375 NM 434, Angel Fire.

Taos Mountain Outfitters (575-758-9292), 113 N. Plaza, Taos.

Taos Mudd 'n Flood (575-751-9100); 103 Bent Street. Quality outdoor gear for all activities, with advice you can trust.

CROSS-COUNTRY SKIING Angel Fire Excursions (575-377-2799), 3329 Mountain View Boulevard, Angel Fire.

Bobcat Pass Wilderness Adventures (575-754-2769), 1670 NM 38, Red River. Horseback riding, snowmobile tours, winter fun.

Cumbres Pass, north of Chama, is a popular cross-country spot where people pull their vehicles off the road and break their own trails.

Enchanted Forest XC Ski and Snowshoe Area (575-754-6112), Bobcat Pass, Red River.

FISHING Abiquiu Lake (505-685-4433), 65 miles northwest of Santa Fe on US 84/285; turn on NM 96. Open year-round. This large, scenic reservoir behind Abiquiu Dam offers a little of everything. Kokanee salmon fishing is fine, and, if you bring your own equipment, windsurfing, waterskiing, and canoeing are all doable. RV and tent sites, too.

Canjilon Lakes (505-684-2486). From El Rito take NM 554 to NM 129 for approximately 16 miles to these gems of small lakes for some of the best trout fishing on the

THE RIO CHAMA IS THE ESSENCE OF SERENITY IN THE WANING LIGHT OF A FALL AFTERNOON

Carson National Forest. Also nearby, check out Trout Lakes and Hidden Lake. The best access to Trout Lakes is off US 84 above Tierra Amarilla; go right at Cebolla for about 2 miles. Two campgrounds available at Canjilons.

FLY-FISHING GUIDES AND OUTFITTERS **Don Wolfley** (575-588-9653), Heron Lake.
Dos Amigos Anglers (575-377-6226), 247 E. Therma, Eagle Nest.
High Country Anglers (575-376-9220), Ute Park. Orvis Guide of the Year, Doc Thompson.
Los Rios Anglers Fly Shop & Guide Service (575-758-2798), 126 W. Plaza, Taos.

HIKING **Ghost Ranch** has four popular hikes: Chimney Rock, between easy and moderate as it climbs about 600 feet, about two hours, with a stunning view of the Piedra Lumbre Basin; Box Canyon, the easiest, about 4 miles, across the arroyo in back of the main property, with a bit of rock scrambling en route; Kitchen Mesa, the most challenging at 5 miles; and the Piedra Lumbre Hike, beyond the WETLANDS sign off the main road to the left, through the bosque and over a suspension bridge crossing Canijlon Creek for a 3-mile round-trip gentle hike to the Ghost Ranch Piedre Lumbre Visitor Center. Get maps and details at the visitor office, where you must sign in. $5.

HOT SPRINGS **Ojo Caliente Mineral Springs** (505-583-2233), 50 Los Banos Drive, Ojo Caliente. Open daily. Closed Christmas. The reasons to come to Ojo Caliente are to visit the hot springs, stay at the lodge, and relax. The quality and composition of

CHIMNEY ROCK IS ONE OF SEVERAL OUTSTANDING HIKES AT GHOST RANCH

C arson National Forest (575-758-6200), 208 Cruz Alta Road, Taos. Stop in here for maps and guidance when planning a trip on this 1.5-million-acre national forest. You can find any kind of seasonal recreation you seek: snowshoeing; snowmobiling; jeeping; hiking on 330 miles of trails (which in winter become cross-country skiing trails); fishing in 400 miles of cold-water mountain streams for rainbow, brown, and Rio Grande cutthroat trout; and you can camp virtually anywhere, in a designated campground or outside one, if you prefer. The forest elevation ranges from 6,000 feet to the 13,161-foot Wheeler Peak, the state's highest. Plus, there are 86,193 acres of wilderness, limited to foot and horseback travel, including the Wheeler Peak and Latir Wilderness areas. Black bear, mountain lion, and bighorn sheep roam the old-growth forests, as do fox, deer, beaver, and smaller animals. In other words, the Carson is an outdoor paradise. Like the Gila National Forest in southwestern New Mexico, you could spend a lifetime exploring it.

El Rito Ranger District (575-581-4554)

Tres Piedras Ranger District (575-758-8678)

these geothermally heated waters is said to be comparable to the finest European spas. Ojo gets progressively more expensive as improvements are made, but it is still a bargain compared with taking the waters in Santa Fe. It is cheaper by far, and less crowded, during the week. Ask about Tues. specials, local bargain rates, sunset rates, and winter specials. A half-dozen pools of varying temperature and mineral composition are guaranteed to relax you, and there are private tubs, too, as well as mud baths in season and a new tub higher on the site. Massage is available. You can sweat out your toxins with the Milagro wrap. The wine bar is a most pleasant place to unwind. There is also a couple of interesting hikes above the springs. See *Lodging*.

RIVER RAFTING **Far Flung Adventures** (575-758-2868), El Prado.

New Mexico River Adventures (1-800-983-7756). Rafting, tubing, paddleboarding, kayaking, and canoeing.

Native Sons Adventures (575-758-9342), 207 Paseo Del Pueblo Sur, Taos.

SNOWMOBILING AND JEEPING **Bitter Creek Guest Ranch** (505-754-2587), Red River. Jeeps, snowmobiles, tours, and rentals, plus rustic cabins.

Cumbres Pass (no phone). Snowmobiles are given free rein and parking

THE GEOTHERMALLY HEATED HOT SPRINGS AT OJO CALIENTE RANK WITH THE WATERS FOUND AT THE BEST SPAS IN EUROPE

areas along NM 17 across the 64 miles of the 10,222-foot pass that borders Colorado in the Rio Grande National Forest. Be sure to travel well prepared, with maps, supplies, and water. Folks do get lost out here.

⚓ TRAIN RIDES **Cumbres and Toltec Scenic Railroad** (888-286-2737; www.cumbres toltec.com), 500 South Terrace Avenue, Chama. Open daily May 27–October 22. This narrow-gauge steam-powered railroad runs 64 miles along 10,015 Cumbres Pass between Chama and Antonito, Colorado. It was built over 125 years ago by the Denver & Rio Grande Railway to carry the products of mining and timber out of the region. The fare includes lunch at the stagecoach town of Osier, Colorado, along the route. Make reservations well in advance. Autumn color tours are especially sought after. $95.00 adults, $50.00 children and up.

✳ Green Space

PARKS **Kit Carson Memorial State Park** (575-758-8234), central Taos. This park is the site of the historic cemetery, walking paths, and a playground on its 22 acres of green space in the middle of town.

Rio Grande Gorge Recreation Area, Orilla Verde Visitor Center (575-758-8851), Picnic shelters and campgrounds along the road that runs beside the river. A stunning area where you (and your pets) do want to be wary of rattlesnakes.

✳ Lodging

BED & BREAKFASTS, MOTELS **Abiquiu Inn** (505-685-4378), 21120 US 84. Abiquiu Southwest rustic luxury in a gracious lodge with restaurant and gallery. Lectures and cultural programs related to the area can be part of your stay. $250.

Branding Iron Motel & Restaurant (575-756-2162), 1511 W. Main Street, Chama. Open May–October. This is as clean and serviceable a motel as you are likely to find. It's nothing special, but it is comfortable enough, and you will be happy to have a reservation here during railroad season. $85.

🐾 ♿ **Elkhorn Lodge and Cafe** (575-756-2105), 2663 US 84, Chama. This 50-year-old lodge on the bank of the Rio Chama has twenty-two rooms and eleven cabins. The café serves a decent breakfast and has a fine outdoor patio, and you can fish from the Rio Chama out back on Elkhorn's 10 acres. Open year-round. Pet-friendly. Even a corral for horses, llamas, and mules. Low-season prices start from $95.

Las Parras de Abiquiu Guesthouse & Vineyard (800-817-5955), 21341 US 84, Abiquiu. This casita amidst the grapevines along the Chama River has two sweet bedrooms, El Jardin and El Pedernal. Note: Breakfast is not included. $130.

Inn at Ojo. This place used to be a hostel, and it still retains that feel of informality. Local ladies come in early each morning to prepare delicious home-cooked breakfasts, but the rooms are small and lack customary amenities, like TVs. A short walk to the springs. Quiet, clean. Management was not around when we stayed here, and some people had difficulty getting into their rooms. Somewhat shabby and run-down; nonetheless, it has a certain charm. A little pricey for what you get. $129.

LODGES AND RANCHES **Cooper's El Vado Ranch** (575-588-7354), 3150 NM 12, Tierra Amarilla. On the Chama River below El Vado Lake. The state record brown trout resides in the grocery store here, which tells you something. Two-night minimum required during peak

season; three nights on holiday weekends. Ten comfortable log cabins on 100
acres make this an outdoors lover's getaway. El Vado is the put-in site for river
rafters on the Chama, which in season
gets Class II and III rapids. $122.

🛶 **Corkins Lodge** (575-588-7261),
Alamo Road, Chama. A very special
place, suitable for family reunions and
other special gatherings, with cabins
that sleep up to 12. Located in the Chama
Valley on 700 acres at the foot of the
Brazos Cliffs, there is no more beautiful
setting. Guests may fish along a private
2.5-mile stretch of the Brazos River. Half-
price specials available during the week
and off-season. $195–250.

Ojo Caliente Mineral Springs (800-
222-9162), 50 Los Banos Drive, Ojo
Caliente. Several of the older cabins
have received a renovation. Upscale
suites with a private pool are the newest
additions. You can warm yourself by
the lobby fireplace or sun yourself in a
rocker on the front porch, or make new
friends in the wine bar. And Artesian
Café serves wholesome, healthy breakfast, lunch, and dinner, with decent
salads and fresh fish on the menu. $279
(includes massage and soak) on up.

**CABINS AND CAMPING Brazos Lodge
& Rentals** (575-588-7707), 7 Sweeney
Lane, Tierra Amarilla. 15 miles southeast
of Chama in the Brazos Canyon on NM
512. Here find a no-frills, rustic lodge,
about a dozen cabins of whatever size
you need to suit your group, as well as
condos, with a minimum two-night stay.
Three-night minimum during holidays.
Pets okay. $130–250.

Rio Chama RV Park (575-756-2303),
two blocks north of depot on NM 17
toward Alamosa, Chama. Located along
the Rio Chama, this RV park with full
hookups and electric is walking distance
to downtown Chama and the railroad
depot. Open May 1 through mid-October.
RV site $30–34; tent site $14.

Sky Mountain Resort RV Park (575-
756-1100), 2743 US 84, Chama. With

unobstructed views of the Rio Chama on
10 acres are forty-six sites with full hookups. Open May 15–October 15. $34–42.

✳ Where to Eat

DINING OUT El Paragua (505-753-
8226), 603 Santa Cruz Road, Espanola, or
NM 76 just to the right of NM 68. Open
daily. L, D 11–9. This intensely Spanish
institution continues to serve consistently fine New Mexican and mes-
quite-grilled meals. If you can get past
the scrumptious *carne adovada*, chilies
rellenos, and chimichanga, there's the
garlic shrimp in butter. So thick with
locals on weekend evenings that you can
expect a wait. There's no better chips and
salsa than El Paragua's—the mark of a
fine establishment. And the natillas, a
sweet creamy custard dessert, are the
best in the land. Moderate.

EATING OUT Bode's General Store
(505-685-4422), 21196 US 84. Open
daily 6 AM–8 PM B, L. Kitchen open
10:30–3. This is no ordinary gas station.
Trader and Bode's founder Martin Bode
arrived in Abiquiu over a century ago,
and his family still operates this place, a
combination pit stop, bakery stocked
with house-baked yummies, grocery
store, hardware store, and gift shop.
Where else can you spot a monk from
Christ in the Desert Monastery buying
a shovel while you're savoring a freshly
baked cinnamon roll or Frito pie and
reading the Sunday *New York Times*?
Known for green chile cheese burgers.
This landmark is the quintessence of
local. Wine, beer, and Wi-Fi.
Inexpensive.

El Farolito (575-581-9509), 1212
Main Street, El Rito. I used to be able to
count on this place to be open Sundays,
but lately, hours have been uncertain.
Always call before taking the long drive
to confirm the café is actually open.
While they say the hours are definite,
I have found them anything but. The

BODE'S IS A LANDMARK GAS STATION, CAFÉ, AND MERCANTILE SHOP IN ABIQUIU

reason to drive to remote El Rito is to dine at this darling New Mexican eatery with eight tables and State Fair prizewinning green chile. On my top ten green chile list. Inexpensive.

El Parasol (505-753-8852), 603 Santa Cruz Road, Española. You could spot a Hollywood actress without makeup munching an out-of-sight chicken guacamole taco on one of the picnic benches at this culturally authentic taco stand, right next to the local Sikhs and low-riders. Don't miss this people-watching show. Best to phone in your order before you arrive if you don't want a long wait. Other Parasols now in Santa Fe and around, the area, but of course, the original is always best. Next door to El Paragua. Inexpensive.

Foster's Hotel, Restaurant and Saloon (575-756-2296), 393 S. Terrace Avenue, Chama. Open daily 6 AM–10

PM Winter hours may vary. B, L, D. Okay, so it's not the Ritz. It was a Harvey House serving the railroad once upon a time. The big old woodstove in the middle of the café puts out the heat, and that's just fine when the temperature is 8 below and streets are lined with 3-foot snowdrifts. Standard American and Mexican fare are offered including big steaks. Breakfast is probably the best meal. It's cozy, warm, and friendly, and you can go next door to the bar after you've eaten (or before). "Still living on Chama time," they claim, and the claim is true. Don't expect updated amentities, just a slice of real Old West history. Inexpensive.

Three Ravens Coffee House (575-588-9086), 15 NM 531, Tierra Amarilla. Good strong coffee, pastries, muffins, pannini, wraps, salads, smoothies. Who knew? Right next to the courthouse where activist Reies Tijerina made his stand in 1967 is a Wi-Fi- and espresso-endowed refuge from the road. Tasty snacks too. Call ahead for hours. Inexpensive.

✳ Entertainment

High Country Restaurant and Saloon (575-756-2384), 2289 NM 17, Chama. Order a steak and take in the live country music on weekends. You might hear a dead-ringer for Patsy Cline, who once performed at the Grand Ole Opry! This cowboy bar is the place to go for an evening in Chama.

✳ Selective Shopping

The Mystery Store: A Book Exchange and More (575-756-1059), 612 Terrace, Chama. A little bit of a whole lot: good coffee, tea, pastry, book exchange, jewelry, local crafts, pet-friendly patio. Wi-Fi free to customers.

Rising Moon Gallery & Art Center (505-685-4271), 2 County Road 187, Abiquiu. Located directly across US 84 from Bode's at the entrance to Abiquiu, this adorable gallery has handmade jewelry, tinwork, pottery, and works on paper that will make you exclaim "Charming!" again and again.

✳ Special Events

January: **Chama Chile Ski Classic & Winter Fiesta** (www.skichama.com/), XC race plus *beaucoup* fun activities.

February: **Taos Winter Wine Festival** (taos.org), last two weeks. Wine and food events, seminars, grand tastings in Taos and Taos Ski Valley

June: **Taos Solar Music Festival** (www .solarmusicfest.com), Kit Carson Park, last weekend. It rocks, with demos of sustainable energy projects as well as such bands as Los Lobos and stars as Lyle Lovett, plus the new music. **Toast of Taos** (575-758-3329), late June–early July. Golf tournament, gallery tours, wine dinners, and art auctions. **Taos School of Music Summer Chamber Music Festival** (575-776-2388), mid-June–mid-August. Tickets $20.

July: **Taos Pueblo Pow Wow** (575-737-9704) and **Fiestas de Taos** (taos .org), midmonth.

August: **Music from Angel Fire** (575-377-3233). Internationally known musicians perform classical in concerts all over northern New Mexico. $25 average,

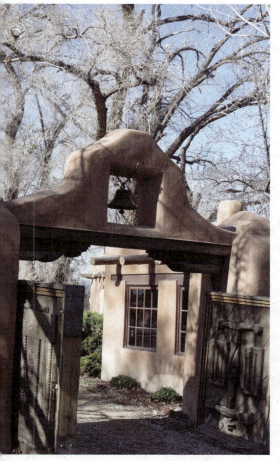

BEHIND THIS ADOBE GATE IS THE HOUSE OF TAOS MOVER-AND-SHAKER MABEL DODGE LUHAN; HER HOME IS NOW A B&B

with complimentary performances along the way.

September: **High Road Art Tour** (www.highroadnewmexico.com), last two weekends, 10–5. **San Geronimo Day** (575-737-9704), annual Taos Pueblo pole-climbing and foot race event. **Taos Fall Arts Festival** (taos.org). The **Paseo Outdoor Art Festival** (taos.org), assembly of outdoor installations.

October: **Taos Wool Festival** (www.taoswoolfestival.org), Kit Carson Memorial Park, Taos, first weekend. A celebration of the animals, textiles, fiber, and fiber enthusiasts that retains its folksy feel, even as it has grown into a huge event. **Annual Abiquiu Studio Art Tour** (www.abiquiustudiotour.org), Columbus Day Weekend.

November: **Taos Mountain Balloon Rally** (taos.org). **Dixon Studio Tour** (www.dixonarts.org), first weekend. Over fifty area artists open their studios in a grand gala of arts and crafts.

December: **Yuletide in Taos** (taos.org), all month. Farolitos, tree lighting, open studios on Ledoux Street, and lovely festivities of the season.

OPPOSITE: THE WORLD'S LARGEST COLLECTION OF FOLK ART, SANTA FE'S MUSEUM OF INTERNATIONAL FOLK ART EXHIBITS TRADITIONAL ALTARS SPECIALLY CONSTRUCTED FOR DÍA DE LOS MUERTOS (DAY OF THE DEAD)

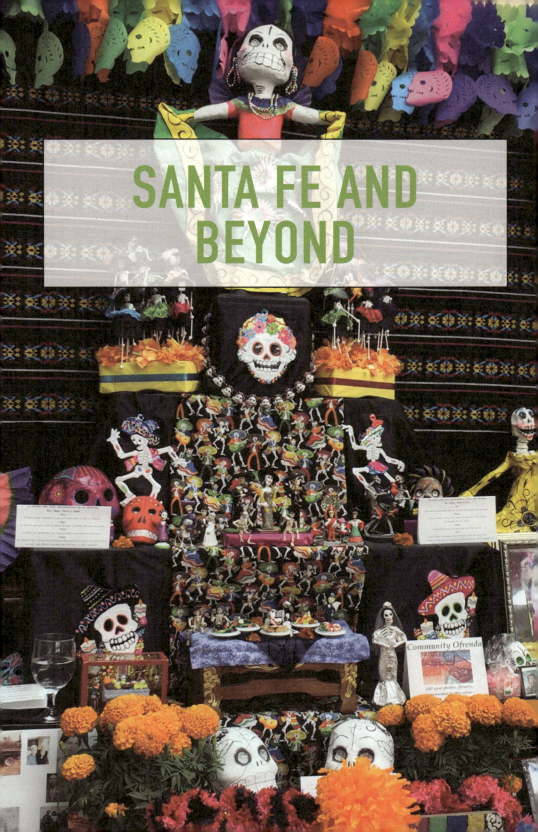

SANTA FE AND BEYOND

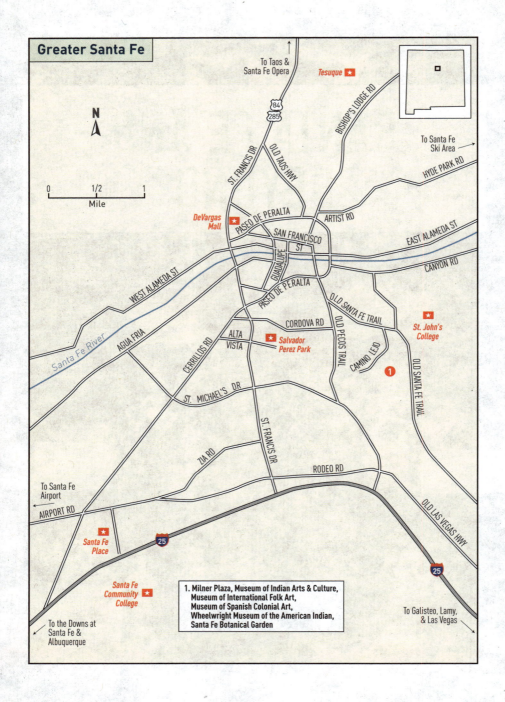

Greater Santa Fe

To Taos &
Santa Fe Opera

Tesuque ★

BISHOP'S LODGE RD

To Santa Fe
Ski Area →

HYDE PARK RD

N

0   1/2   1
Mile

84
285

ST. FRANCIS DR

OLD TAOS HWY

ARTIST RD

DeVargas
Mall ★

PASEO DE PERALTA

EAST ALAMEDA ST

SAN FRANCISCO
ST

GUADALUPE

CANYON RD

WEST ALAMEDA ST

PASEO DE PERALTA

Santa Fe River

AGUA FRIA

CORDOVA RD

OLD SANTA FE TRAIL

St. John's
College ★

CERRILLOS RD

ALTA
VISTA

Salvador
Perez Park ★

OLD PECOS TRAIL

CAMINO LEO

❶

OLD SANTA FE TRAIL

ST. MICHAEL'S DR

ST. FRANCIS DR

ZIA RD

RODEO RD

To Santa Fe
Airport

OLD LAS VEGAS HWY

AIRPORT RD

Santa Fe
Place ★

25

Santa Fe
Community
College ★

1. Milner Plaza, Museum of Indian Arts & Culture,
Museum of International Folk Art,
Museum of Spanish Colonial Art,
Wheelwright Museum of the American Indian,
Santa Fe Botanical Garden

25

To Galisteo, Lamy,
& Las Vegas

To the Downs at
Santa Fe &
Albuquerque

SANTA FE AND BEYOND

Tesuque, Los Alamos, La Cienaga, Galisteo

Santa Fe. The very sound of the name conjures visions of blazing sunsets, ancient adobe buildings, romantic patios, colorful fiestas, irresistible cuisine, and shopping beyond compare. This "City Different" is, after all, the oldest capital city in the United States, founded in 1610. This City of Holy Faith sits at the foot of the Sangre de Cristos, the Blood of Christ Mountains, at 7,000 feet. In fact, this city is so intriguing that it consistently places in the top three favorite US travel destinations. And it just keeps getting better!

What distinguishes Santa Fe from other American cities are its flat-roofed, wood-beamed adobe houses, and public buildings. This "Santa Fe Style" of architecture is called Pueblo Revival, and it is an inspired melding of Spanish, Indian, and Mexican elements. The inception of the style was embodied in one building: the Museum of Fine Arts, a 1917 structure designed by architect Isaac Hamilton Rapp that stands off the Plaza, modeled originally on San Estevan Mission at Acoma Pueblo and San Jose Church at Laguna Pueblo. This signature building style, subsequently enforced by city ordinance, was recognized by town fathers with the foresight, a century ago, to understand the city's mission was to attract tourists. The scale and the imaginative use of natural materials captures and communicates the ancient essence of this place. Because its long history is embodied in its architecture, Santa Fe retains a powerful sense of place that magnetizes visitors.

Stroll up Canyon Road and browse the galleries that endow the city with a reputation as one of the nation's top art markets, then amble over to Camino del Monte Sol and Acequia Madre, the path of the annual Christmas Eve farolito walk. These streets were made famous by artists who lived and worked in Santa Fe during the early twentieth century, and whose work still hangs in the Museum of Fine Arts and sells for six and seven figures in the better galleries. One of the best remembered artists, Will Shuster, created Zozobra, also known as "Old Man Gloom," a giant effigy that is burned at Santa Fe Fiestas every September as the season changes, in a joyous communal celebration.

And there is truth to the mystique. There is nothing like sipping a margarita on Sena Plaza when the gardens are in bloom (check out the Margarita Trail at santafe .org/Visiting_Santa_Fe/Self_Guided_Tours/Margarita_Trail/index.html) or brunching at Geronimo, or tailgating at the Santa Fe Opera, or maxing out your credit cards on Canyon Road and feeling darn pleased about it. After all, nobody back home will have anything remotely like you've found in Santa Fe to adorn your home, garden and li'l old self.

It is also true that "bargains" are not easy to come by in Santa Fe. There is no real off-season, not in a city that receives over a million visitors a year and where retail space reputedly costs more per square foot than rents on Madison Avenue in Manhattan. Finding good values and avoiding the "tourist trap" spots is the best you can hope for.

For your choice of lodging, it is necessary to make reservations well in advance, particularly if you are interested in one of the well-known annual events, such as

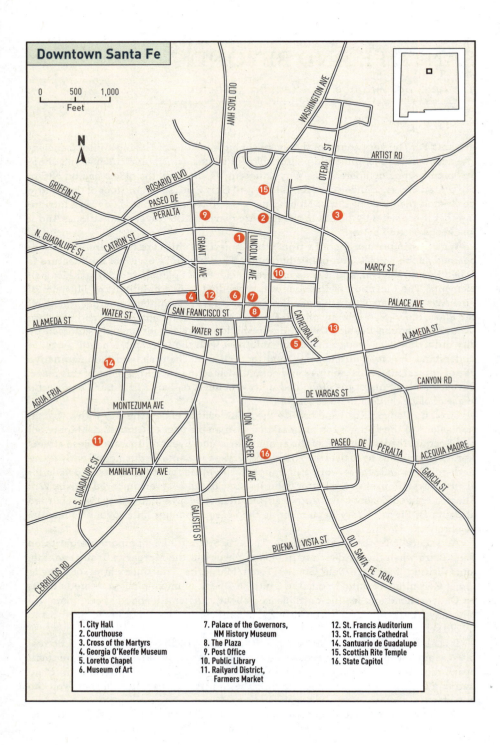

Downtown Santa Fe

0   500   1,000
Feet

N

GRIFFIN ST
ROSARIO BLVD
PASEO DE PERALTA
N. GUADALUPE ST
CATRON ST
GRANT AVE
LINCOLN AVE
OLD TAOS HWY
WASHINGTON AVE
OTERO ST
ARTIST RD
MARCY ST
PALACE AVE
SAN FRANCISCO ST
WATER ST
WATER ST
ALAMEDA ST
ALAMEDA ST
CATHEDRAL PL
CANYON RD
AGUA FRIA
DE VARGAS ST
MONTEZUMA AVE
DON GASPER AVE
S. GUADALUPE ST
MANHATTAN AVE
PASEO DE PERALTA
ACEQUIA MADRE
GARCIA ST
GALISTEO ST
BUENA VISTA ST
OLD SANTA FE TRAIL
CERRILLOS RD

1. City Hall
2. Courthouse
3. Cross of the Martyrs
4. Georgia O'Keeffe Museum
5. Loretto Chapel
6. Museum of Art
7. Palace of the Governors, NM History Museum
8. The Plaza
9. Post Office
10. Public Library
11. Railyard District, Farmers Market
12. St. Francis Auditorium
13. St. Francis Cathedral
14. Santuario de Guadalupe
15. Scottish Rite Temple
16. State Capitol

Spanish Market, Indian Market, or the International Folk Art Market. Even though Santa Fe charm has been packaged and commercialized, some say "Disney-fied," into "FantaSe," it remains an irresistible draw for even the most seasoned travelers.

It is true that if you have to ask the price of something, you probably can't afford it. No longer are there casual artists' studios on Canyon Road. Once-Bohemian Gypsy Alley is strictly high-rent and upscale these days. Artists who once might have set up shop here have likely relocated to Albuquerque, Pecos, or Truth or Consequences because they can't afford the rent. There are no shoe shops or drugstores on the plaza anymore, only expensive boutiques and galleries and upscale chain stores, and local people have been driven farther and farther from the center of town.

If you are so charmed that you dream of moving here, keep in mind that a substantial trust fund, inheritance, pension, or reliable alimony check are requirements for you to live in the style to which you would like to become accustomed. As one friend of mine is fond of saying, "You need old money to live in Santa Fe." Being a Silicon Valley billionaire might also qualify you.

On the other hand, a wealth of free entertainment and cultural events are available just about every night of the week in Santa Fe. And aside from the high ticket prices at the opera, there are many free or low-cost concerts, lectures, book signings, gallery openings, and art festivals every day of the week—almost too many to keep up. No question, culture here is juicy, and whether your penchant leans toward for a lecture by a fellow from the Santa Fe Institute or a flamenco performance on the Plaza bandstand, you will find the offerings of the highest quality.

DOZENS OF GALLERIES MAKE CANYON ROAD ONE OF THE WORLD'S FINEST ART BOULEVARDS

There is no substantial industry in Santa Fe (though rumors of a developing tech economy continue to circulate), and the biggest employers here are state government, public education, or the tourist business. As in many other places, it is who you know (or more likely, to whom you are related), not what you know, that will get you a job.

Unlike anyplace else in New Mexico, Santa Fe is a world of its own. What other small city, with a population under 70,000, has this old-world feel, this vast historic legacy, and this concentration of culture—opera, classical music, museums, galleries—as well as shopping opportunities?

Although it is located in New Mexico, Santa Fe does not think of itself as particularly Mexican. One popular tee shirt bears the slogan: New Mexico—It's Not New and it's not Mexico. Many of the longtime locals and those descended from old families identify strictly as "Spanish," and they are quite sensitive on this point. People are aware of their genealogy and its supposedly aristocratic connotations. As a cultural tip, it's helpful to be aware that established old-timers and more recent immigrants from Mexico and Central America are two entirely different cultures, even though they may both speak the a similar language, or, as I overheard two women talking in the tire shop recently, "I speak Mexican, not Spanish." The presence of recent immigrants from Mexico is obvious when you look at those cleaning the rooms, waiting on tables, and when you drive out Cerrillos Road and see all the restaurants, food carts, and businesses catering to immigrants. In truth, Santa Fe is three completely separate cities: one for the tourists, one for the struggling middle-lower middle class, and one for recent arrivals who serve the tourist economy. Cerrillos Road is a world apart from the downtown Plaza, with supermarkets, drugstores, chain stores, big box stores, and traffic crawling up and down the sprawl day and night, like in most other Western cities.

REGARDLESS OF THE SEASON, CANYON ROAD IS A LOVELY PLACE TO STROLL

The Railyard District off Guadalupe Street and Paseo de Peralta is repurposing itself as an entertainment, dining, and shopping area, anchored by the year-round Farmers' Market and awaiting the opening of the new branch of the Fine Arts Museum specializing in contemporary works. It's been reestablished long enough that several cafés have already come and gone, but there is a burgeoning gallery scene featuring, surprisingly for Santa Fe, cutting edge contemporary art.

Friday nights are the customary time for gallery openings, when in summer, especially, Canyon Road is crowded with strollers out to see what's new and to see and be seen.

To keep up or find out what's going on, check the *Santa Fe Reporter*, a weekly newspaper published on Wednesday, or *Pasatiempo*, the weekly entertainment magazine of the *Santa Fe New Mexican*, the daily paper. And do check www.santafe.com for a complete list of daily doings.

A particularly good deal is the New Mexico CulturePass, which for $30 entitles you to a visit to each of the fourteen state museums and monuments during a 12-month period. Contact www.newmexicoculture.org/index.php. The visitors information booth on the Plaza keeps up with the prices and deals.

In addition to its arts scene, Santa Fe, which has always drawn health seekers as well as quirky and eccentric people, is today a home of religious diversity, healing arts, and a great deal of spiritual searching. The town is by any measure very tolerant. Advocates for progressive causes seem to receive pretty unanimous support.

And of course, with its splendid location, it is a base for enjoying four seasons of recreation. Ski Santa Fe; the Dale Ball Trails, a 3.9 mile loop which may be accessed from town; hiking and cross-country skiing only minutes away from the Plaza are the beginning of the adventure. Appreciation for the outdoors is a way of life here.

GUIDANCE New Mexico Dept. of Tourism, Santa Fe **Welcome Center** (505-827-7336), Lamy Bldg., 491 Old Santa Fe Trail. Open daily, summer 8–7, winter 8–5.

Public Lands Information Center (505-954-2000), 301 Dinosaur Trail, Santa Fe. Open Mon.–Fri. 8:00–4:30. Information about recreation on public lands statewide, maps, camping permits, hunting, and fishing licenses.

Santa Fe Chamber of Commerce (505-988-3279), 1644 St. Michael's Drive. Open Mon.–Fri. 8–5. Business and relocation information and visitors guide

Santa Fe Convention & Visitors Bureau (505-955-6200; www.santafe.org), 201 W. Marcy Avenue. Open Mon.–Fri. 8–5.

Plaza Visitor Information Center, Plaza Galeria, 66 E. San Francisco Street, Open daily 10-6.

Santa Fe Creative Tourism and Community Gallery (505-955-6705; 505-955-6215; www.santafecreativetourism.org), 201 W. Marcy Street. An extensive listing of learning and hands-on arts, crafts, and culinary opportunities.

GETTING THERE *By car:* I-25 north or south is the most direct route into Santa Fe.

By air: The **Santa Fe Municipal Airport** (505-955-2900) is open to private aircraft and **American Eagle Airlines** (800-433-7300), which offers two nonstop daily flights between Dallas and Santa Fe and one nonstop daily flight between Los Angeles and Santa Fe. More frequent flights may be available during the summer. Flights to Denver and Phoenix are on the schedule as of this writing. Also, as of this writing, United Express flights to Santa Fe are planned.

Shuttle service is available from the Albuquerque airport, the Santa Fe airport, and the train station in Lamy about 20 miles from Santa Fe. Car rental available at airport. However, be advised if you arrive after working hours or have a flight delay, you may have difficulty finding a ride to your hotel. Transportation into town is still not the

A FEW TIPS AND CAUTIONS

- As in the rest of New Mexico, smoking in public places is not permitted.
- Pets must be leashed and picked up after.
- Talking on a handheld cell phone or texting while driving will get you a ticket. Stay off the phone! You do not want to tangle with the Santa Fe police. Do not expect them to treat you nicely, no matter who you are back home. If you get stopped for any reason, expect to be delayed, insulted, frightened, and treated like a criminal. 'Nough said! Toward that end, keep your driver's license and insurance close at hand and ready to show at all times. Be cool, patient, and humble.
- Be especially careful of your safety and your property. Be aware of your surroundings and use caution at all times. Do not ever leave anything of value in your car—no computers, no cameras, no jewelry. Be sure to lock your car, even if you'll only be gone "for a minute." Break-ins are epidemic.
- Drivers are impatient, so be ultra cautious when on the road. Wait before you step on the gas and look both ways when the light turns, as drivers frequently rocket through red lights. And you will probably be honked at for your caution. Roads are narrow, just wide enough for a burro loaded with wood, so turns can be sharp. Consult a map before you go out.
- Look both ways before you cross the street. Do not expect traffic to yield. Yes, tourists get killed here, even on the Plaza.
- While service in high-end restaurants and lodgings is generally quite good, in many establishments you may run into staff that is new or not well-trained. It's known as "turnover." However, service has improved in recent years, and you are less likely to have to deal with a show of "attitude." Nevertheless, exercise patience.
- If you spot a famous person, say Shirley MacLaine at the opera, Ali McGraw at Whole Foods, Gene Hackman at the bar, or gasp! Robert Redford at the restaurant, by all means be cool. Do not take their picture, request a selfie or an autograph. We don't do that here! These people live here, too, and we respect their right to live more or less normal lives.
- Santa Fe's history is wrapped up in its identity as a destination—as the end point of the Camino Real, the Royal Road from Mexico City, and as the end of the Santa Fe Trail, a great 19th-century trade route across the plains from Independence, Missouri. Santa Fe has never lost its appeal, despite any criticisms it has endured, and it never will. Its patina simply grows more burnished, glowing more brightly, with the years.

best. Be prepared to have some one meet you, call your own ride or rent a car, hoping rentals are open.

By train: The **Amtrak** *Southwest Chief* stops in Lamy, 18 miles south of Santa Fe. (877-444-4773). A shuttle to take you into town meets the train.

By bus: **Greyhound Lines** (505-243-4435; 800-846-0754; www.greyhound.com), 320 1st Street SW, Albuquerque. Serves Albuquerque from outside the state. Connect to Santa Fe via Rail Runner Express.

GETTING AROUND **Faust's Transportation** (505-758-3410) runs buses between Santa Fe and Taos and will pick you up and drop you off at almost any motel or hotel in Taos. The departure spot in Santa Fe is the Santa Fe Hilton, 100 Sandoval Street.

Roadrunner Shuttle and Charter (505-424-3367). Shuttle between airports and local hotels.

Sandia Shuttle Express (888-775-5696). Service between your lodging and Albuquerque airport.

Loretto Line City Tours (505-982-0092), Loretto Chapel, 207 Old Santa Fe Trail. Open daily, depending on weather. This open-air sight-seeing trolley ride covers an 8-mile loop and is a good way to get the lay of the land. The tour is approximately one and a quarter hours. $15 adults, $12 children under age 12. Call for departure time.

Santa Fe Pick-Up (505-231-2573). The Santa Fe Pick-Up shuttle service is a great way for train passengers to get around once they step off the Rail Runner Express, or others who want a fast, free way to get around downtown. Routes start and end in front of the former New Mexico Film Museum (the old Jean Cocteau Cinema) on Montezuma Avenue and run counterclockwise around downtown with stops at:

The Capitol/PERA building
The Cathedral Basilica of St. Francis of Assisi
The Main Library/City Hall
The Santa Fe Community Convention Center/Santa Fe Plaza
Eldorado/Hilton Hotel
Four stops on Canyon Road
One stop at Alameda and Paseo de Peralta

Stops are marked "Pick It Up Here." An entire route takes about 20 minutes. The shuttle drops off passengers at other places along the route if it is safe to stop there.

Santa Fe Trails (505-955-2001) provides public bus transportation around town weekdays 6:40 AM–9:50 PM, Sat. 8–8, Sun. 10–6. Pick up maps at the Public Library, 145 Washington Avenue, or City Hall, 200 Lincoln Avenue. $1 adults, $.50 seniors and children under age 17.

MEDICAL EMERGENCY **Christus St. Vincent** (505-913-3361), 1631 Hospital Drive, Santa Fe. Fast-track emergency room open daily 8 AM–midnight.

Railyard Urgent Care (505- 501-7791), 831 S Saint Francis Drive, Santa Fe. Open 8–7 daily.

❋ To See

TOWNS **Galisteo.** Twenty-two miles south of Santa Fe via I-25, US 285, and NM 41. The site of an ancient Indian dwelling, this region on the edge of the eastern plains became a land of sheepherders and later ranchers, starting life as a Spanish colonial outpost in 1614. Today, this dusty, magnificently decomposing village is home to artists, writers, healers, and the like, but its Spanish character remains predominant. It has the essence of well-worn adobe Santa Fe style.

La Cienega. Nine miles southwest of Santa Fe via I-25. The name means "the marsh." The winding streets maintain the feeling of the Hispanic agricultural village this once was—and still is. Off the beaten path, quiet, and secluded.

Los Alamos, 39 miles northwest of Santa Fe via US 84/285 and NM 502, is the secret "city on the hill" where J. Robert Oppenheimer assembled the

YOUR CHARIOT AWAITS FOR A GUIDED TOUR OF SANTA FE

distinguished, brilliant cast that produced the atomic bomb in the Manhattan Project. Today, the county has the highest concentration of PhDs than any other county in the United States, and the Los Alamos Laboratory is still the main employer around which most of the town revolves. The name means "the cottonwoods." In 1918, Ashley Pond established the Los Alamos Ranch School for boys. During the Manhattan Project era, after the school was taken over to house project scientists, Los Alamos was rumored to be a hideout for pregnant WACs. Thus secrecy was maintained. As preposterous as the cover story sounds now, at the time it was believed.

Santa Fe. The "City Different," established in 1610, has been at the heart of New Mexico history and culture for over four centuries. It is the state capital and home of the Roundhouse, where the state legislature convenes each winter, alternating between 30- and 60-day sessions. Inspiration for artists, architects, poets, writers, and anyone else who refuses to settle for an "ordinary life."

Tesuque (te-Sue-kay) is 3 miles north of Santa Fe on Bishop's Lodge Road. Named for the nearby Indian pueblo, this community dates to 1740. An exquisite village of venerable adobes and architectural gems, cottonwoods, pastoral scenes, winding roadways, and architectural masterpieces that is a quiet suburb of Santa Fe. You don't have to be rich and famous to live here, but it helps. Either that, or inherit one of these grand old places if you want to get mail delivered here.

HISTORIC PLACES, LANDMARKS, AND SITES **Canyon Road.** One of Santa Fe's oldest and most colorful streets, Canyon Road was originally an Indian trail to the mountains. In the 1920s, East Coast artists adopted it. Now the narrow, winding street is home to galleries, boutiques, and upscale restaurants. You are likely to find whatever art form interests you represented here.

Cathedral Basilica of St. Francis of Assisi (505-982-5619), 131 Cathedral Place, Santa Fe. Open daily 7–6; use the side doors. At the east end of San Francisco Street stands one of Santa Fe's most iconic and incongruous structures. Built in French-Romanesque style, it was the inspiration of Jean Baptiste Lamy, Santa Fe's first archbishop. The Hebrew inscription over the keystone is said to be a mark of Lamy's gratitude to the Jewish community for generous contributions to the cathedral's building fund.

Cristo Rey Church (505-983-8528), 1120 Canyon Road, intersection of Canyon Road and Camino Cabra. Open weekdays 8–5; call one month ahead to arrange tours; donations appreciated. An outstanding example of Spanish Colonial Mission architecture, Cristo Rey Church was designed by Santa Fe architect John Gaw Meem and built to commemorate the 400th anniversary of Coronado's arrival in the Southwest. This is one of the largest modern adobe structures in existence. The church is famous for the stone reredos (altar screen) carved by craftsmen from Mexico in 1760.

Cross of the Martyrs Walkway. Enter on Paseo de Peralta, between Otero Street and Hillside Avenue. Always open. Only a 5-minute walk from the plaza, this historic spot boasts the best view of downtown to those who brave the steep climb. A brick walkway winds up a small hill, and plaques highlight Santa Fe history. The white cross at the summit is a memorial to the twenty-one Franciscan monks killed in the 1680 Pueblo Revolt.

⚥ **El Zaguan,** 545 Canyon Road, Santa Fe. The home of Historic Santa Fe, this nineteenth-century house sits next to a Victorian garden where you can read, picnic, or enjoy the flowers. Weddings are performed here often.

Fuller Lodge. Once the dining and recreation hall for Los Alamos Ranch School, after 1943 it was taken over by the US government for the Manhattan Project. An impressive multi-story log building designed by John Gaw Meem, it is now a National Historic Landmark.

⚓ **Miraculous Staircase/Loretto Chapel Museum** (505-922-0092), 207 Old Santa Fe Trail. Open summer Mon.–Sat. 9–6, Sun. 10:30–5; winter Mon.–Sat. 9–5, Sun. 10:30–5. Closed Christmas. Loretto Chapel was begun in 1873 and designed to look like Sainte-Chapelle in Paris. Stones came from the same quarry as those for St. Francis Cathedral, and the same French and Italian stonemasons worked on both structures. The Moulys, father and son, built the chapel; however, the son died before a stairway to the choir loft could be completed. As the story goes, the sisters prayed to St. Joseph, patron saint of carpenters, for a staircase, and an unknown carpenter arrived and built them an amazing circular staircase, lacking both nails and visible means of support. Architects the world over continue to study it and marvel at the "miraculous" quality of its construction. When the job was complete, the mysterious carpenter vanished, leaving behind the impression that it may have been St. Joseph himself. A de-sanctified church that operates as a museum, this is a popular wedding spot. $3, under age 7 free.

The Plaza, center of town. Always open. Four hundred years of history speak from the Santa Fe Plaza. It was originally laid out according to the wishes of King Philip II in 1600 and is identical to Spanish Colonial plazas throughout the hemisphere. It is still one of the best people-watching spots in the city.

⚓ **Santa Fe Botanical Garden** (505-471-9103), 725 Camino Lejo. Open daily 9–5. Winter hours Tues.–Sun. 10–4 Over 20 years in the planning, the community's dream of a botanical garden has finally been realized on Museum Hill near the Museum of International Folk Art. An exquisite, well-designed retreat for strolling, picnicking, photographing, or just enjoying the blossoms and the views. Other segments of the botanic garden, found elsewhere, are located in various areas. Docent-led hikes may be requested. $7, under age 12 free.

Santuario de Guadalupe (505-983-8868), 314 S. Guadalupe Street, Santa Fe. Open Mon.–Fri. 9–4, Sat. 10–4, closed Sundays (summer). The Santuario is a Santa Fe land-mark built by Franciscan missionaries in 1776–79 with 3- to 5-foot-thick adobe walls. It is the oldest shrine in the United States dedicated to Our Lady of Guadalupe, who revealed herself in a vision to Indian worshipper Juan Diego in Mexico in 1531.

Randall Davey Audubon Center & Sanctuary (505-983-4609), 1800 Upper Canyon Road. Open summer 8 AM–dusk for garden and trails; winter hours may vary; summer house tours Fri. 2–3 PM. One of the few historic homes in Santa Fe open to the public, this center is a state office, an environmental education center, and National Audubon Society wildlife refuge. Set on 135 acres at the mouth of the Santa Fe River Canyon, it was the home of musician and artist Randall Davey. What is now the house was the original mill. An excellent bookshop is on the premises, as well as a shady picnic area (highly recommended!). $5 house tours, $2 trails, $1 children under age 12.

LORETTO CHAPEL, MODELED ON A PARIS ORIGINAL

RANDALL DAVEY AUDUBON CENTER & SANCTUARY IS A
LOVELY SPOT TO HIKE, TOUR, AND PICNIC

San Miguel Mission (505-983-3974), 401 Old Santa Fe Trail, Santa Fe. Open daily summer 9–5:30; 9–5; winter Sun. 1–4:30 year-round. Mass held at 5 PM. The oldest church in the United States, San Miguel was built around 1626. It stands in the Barrio de Analco, Santa Fe's oldest neighborhood, next door to the Oldest House, 215 E. De Vargas Street. $1, under age 6 free.

Sena Plaza, 125–137 E. Palace Avenue, Santa Fe. A separate world that resonates with the flavor of colonial Santa Fe, Sena Plaza is reached by an adobe passage from busy Palace Avenue. Now it holds private shops and a restaurant. You can stroll around and imagine the old days as you listen to the fountain, watch the birds, and enjoy the flowers and greenery.

MUSEUMS Bradbury Science Museum (505-667-4444), 1350 Central, Los Alamos. Open Tues.–Sat. 10–5, Sun.–Mon. 1–5. Photographs and documents provide in-depth education of the unfurling of "Project Y," the World War II code name for the laboratory that developed the first atomic bomb. Displays of the lab's weapons research program and models of accelerators as well as the latest research on solar, geothermal, laser, and magnetic fusion energy. A most interesting film on the history and personalities behind the Manhattan Project is screened regularly. Free.

Center for Contemporary Arts (505-982-1338), 1050 Old Pecos Trail. Open daily noon–7. Innovative, creative, challenging contemporary work shown here. The highlight is the small movie theater out back, which screens hard-to-find classic, indie, and world films. Gallery free. $8 films.

El Museo Cultural de Santa Fe (505-992-0591), 555 Camino de la Familia, Santa Fe. Open Tues.–Sat. 1–5. This museum showcases and promotes Hispanic arts, culture and heritage exhibits and contemporary and traditional artists of northern New Mexico through photography, weaving, tinwork, painting, and sculpture. Also here, find issue-oriented exhibits on such subjects as water and land use. The 200-seat theater features live performance with an emphasis on original work. Free for art, variable for performance. Also the site of a winter flea market on weekends. Located in the Railyard.

✒ **El Rancho de las Golondrinas** (575-471-2261), 344 Los Pinos Road, La Cienega. 15 miles south of Santa Fe, exit 276 off I-25 to La Cienega. Self-guided tours June–September, Wed.–Sun. 10–4. "The ranch of the swallows" has seen settlers and traders, bishops and Indian raiders in its 300-year history. It was the last stop before Santa Fe on the Camino Real. Caravans of traders, soldiers, and settlers made the six-month round-trip. The eighteenth-century house, defensive tower, water mills, blacksmith shop, and numerous farm animals are displayed best at the spring and harvest festivals, when costumed villagers portray life in Spanish colonial New Mexico. $6 adults, $4 seniors and teens, under age 12 free. Wednesdays, June through September, free for New Mexico residents. Entrance fees higher for special events.

Georgia O'Keeffe Museum (505-946-1000), 217 Johnson Street, Santa Fe. Open daily 10–5, Fri. 10–7. "In New Mexico, half your work is done for you," said the famous artist, an iconoclast in life as well as her art, of the home she adopted permanently in

SPRINGTIME IN SANTA FE PLAZA

the 1940s. Here she found the light and subject matter that built her reputation as "the most singularly original American artist before World War II." O'Keeffe's museum endeavors to show changing exhibits of the work and artists who impacted her life and art. To tour the O'Keeffe home in Abiquiu, contact the above number to arrange a tour Tues., Thurs., or Fri. at 9:30, 11, 2, or 3:30. Reservations must be made well in advance. Tours $25 adults, $20 students. Museum $13 adults, $10 seniors, under age 18 free; first Fri. of the month free to NM residents. A new Georgia O'Keeffee Welcome Center is scheduled to open at the Abiquiu Inn in Abiquiu, NM in the near future.

Los Alamos Historical Museum (505-662-6272), 1921 Juniper, Los Alamos. Adjacent to Fuller Lodge, 35 miles northwest of Santa Fe via US 285 north and NM 502 west. Open Mon.–Sat. 10–4, Sun. 1–4. Housed in a log-and-stone building originally part of the Los Alamos Ranch School, the museum imparts a concise history of the area. The exhibit "Life in the Secret City" details through vintage photographs and original accounts the story of Los Alamos during World War II. The newly acquired Beta House a short walk away gives even greater depth to this complex era. Self-guided Los Alamos walking tour available. Free.

IAIA Museum of Contemporary Native Arts (888-988-4242), 108 Cathedral Pl., Santa Fe. Mon., Wed., and Sat. 10–5. Closed Tuesdays and Sundays. Some of the best-known names in Indian art, including Allan Houser, Fritz Scholder, and T. C. Cannon, were students or teachers at Institute of American Indian Arts (IAIA), which operates the MoCNA. The museum houses a large collection of contemporary Indian art and demonstrates the vitality and innovation of these artists. Dedicated to exhibiting progressive contemporary art and its scholarship, discourse, and interpretation. $10 adults, half-price seniors and students, under age 16 free.

Museum of Indian Arts and Culture (505-476-1269), 710 Camino Lejo, Museum Hill. Open Tues.–Sun. 10–5. Closed Mondays. May-October open daily 10–5. This state museum brings together the past and present of Southwest Indian culture, including pottery, jewelry, basketry, and textile, over 50,000 artifacts assembled by the Laboratory of Anthropology. The continuing exhibit "From this Earth: Pottery of the Southwest" covers archaeological, historic, and contemporary Indian pottery. $7 New Mexico adults, $12 nonresidents, under age 17 free; First Sun. of the month free to New Mexico residents; Wed. free to New Mexico seniors with ID.

✎ **Museum of International Folk Art** (505-476-1200), 706 Camino Lejo, Museum Hill. Open November–April Tues.–Sun. 10–5; open May–October daily 10–5. Closed Thanksgiving, Christmas, Easter, and New Year's. Travel to all the continents and 100 countries through this amazing collection of folk art, including textiles, toys, masks, and clothing. The miniature Mexican village scenes delight children. The museum, established by Florence Dibell Bartlett in 1953, received the addition of Alexander Girard's collection in 1976. The Hispanic Heritage Wing, opened in 1989, showcases Spanish colonial and Hispanic folk art, emphasizing northern New Mexico. $7 NM residents; $12 non-residents; First Sun. of the month free to New Mexico residents; Wed. free to New Mexico seniors. Children under 16 free.

Museum of Spanish Colonial Art (505-982-2226), 750 Camino Lego, Museum Hill. Open Tues.–Sun. 10–5 November–April; open daily 10–5 May–October. A visit here is an excellent introduction to New Mexico history and will make any visit to Santa Fe more meaningful. An intimate museum, housed in a Pueblo Revival adobe structure created by architect John Gaw Meem, pioneer of "Santa Fe Style," it is home to the Spanish Colonial Arts Society's 3,000-piece collection, spanning 500 years. $10 adults, under age 16 free; New Mexico residents free first Sunday of month.

New Mexico History Museum (505-476-5200), 113 Lincoln Avenue. The state's newest museum; the jewel in the crown, with rich exhibitions of all aspects of New Mexico

THE ALTAR SCREEN AT EL RANCHO DE LAS GOLONDRINAS IS A FOLK ART CLASSIC

THE CATHEDRAL BASILICA OF ST. FRANCIS IS AN ESSENTIAL SANTA FE LANDMARK

history in a light-filled, spacious viewing area. Permanent Fred Harvey exhibit. Next door, the previous history museum, the **Palace of the Governors** (505-476-5100) offers permanent exhibits largely related to Spanish colonial history in the oldest continuously occupied government building (built 1610) in the United States. Open Tues.–Sun. 10–5 and Fri. 10–7 November–April; open daily 10–5 May–October. $12 nonresidents, $7 New Mexico residents, 5–7 PM. First Friday of the month free to New Mexico residents November–April; first Sunday of the month free to New Mexico residents; Wednesday free to New Mexico senior citizens.

New Mexico Museum of Art (505-476-5072), 107 W. Palace Avenue. Open Tues.–Sun. 10–5, closed Mondays May–mid-September. Open daily 10–5 and 5–7 first Friday of the month December–May. This is the 1917 Pueblo Revival building that kicked off the architectural design known as Santa Fe style. On permanent exhibition are works by early-twentieth-century New Mexico artists, such as Gustave Baumann, William Penhallow Henderson, and Jozef Bakos. The collection emphasizes twentieth-century American art, particularly by Southwestern artists. $12 nonresidents, $7 New Mexico adults, free 5–7 Friday evenings; first Sundays of the month free for New Mexico residents. Under 16 free.

Palace of the Governors (505-476-5100), 105 W. Plaza. Open Tues.–Sun. 10–5. November–April. Open daily 10–5 May–October. Admission included with admission to NM History Museum. Same ticketing policy applies. Dating to 1610, this is the oldest continuously occupied government building in the United States. While the building itself is interesting enough on its own, the artifacts inside—textiles, carvings, and ceramics—eloquently speak the history of the area.

🖉 **Santa Fe Children's Museum** (505-989-8359), 1050 Old Pecos Trail, Santa Fe. Open Wed.–Sat. 10–5, Sun. noon–5. Closed Mondays and Tuesdays. Wee Wednesdays 9–11 and Thursdays 10–6:30. Hands-on exhibits encourage children to learn by touching, moving, experimenting, and playing. Lots of ongoing interactive family programs, workshops, and performances keep things lively. $9 nonresidents, $5 chldren; $7.50 adults. Free under 17 on Thursdays 4–6:30.

GUARANTEED AND JURIED HANDMADE NATIVE AMERICAN JEWELRY FOR SALE ON THE PORTAL OF THE PALACE OF THE GOVERNORS

Site Santa Fe (505-989-1199), 1606 Paseo de Peralta, Santa Fe. Open Wed.–Thurs. 10–5, Fri. 10–7; Sat. 10–5; Sun. noon–5. Sun. noon–5. SITE Lab and lobby open Mon. and Tues. This innovative museum features contemporary art and cutting-edge exhibitions, including a challenging Biennial and works from Latin America. A recent remodel added 15,000 square feet of new exhibit space, a café, and a free experimental section. $10 adults, $5 students and seniors, free Fridays and Saturdays. 18 and under free 10–noon.

Wheelwright Museum of the American Indian (505-982-4636), 704 Camino Lejo. Open daily 10–5. Closed Thanksgiving, Christmas, New Year's. Founded by the unlikely combination of Boston heiress Mary Cabot Wheelwright and Navajo medicine man Hosteen Klah, originally for the purpose of preserving Navajo customs and ceremonies, the 1927 museum to house their collections looks completely contemporary. The Case Trading Post, modeled after early-1900s Southwestern trading posts, is a respected outlet of Navajo weaving and jewelry. Home to the Jim and Lauris Phillips collection of southwest jewelry. The site of lively discussion series. $8, free first Sat. of the month.

✎ **Meow Wolf** (505 395-6369), 1352 Rufina Circle, Santa Fe. Starting as an offbeat artists collective in 2008, Meow Wolf has grown into an international phenomenon, attracting a half-million visitors from all over the world since its inception on Rufina Circle. "Game of Thrones" author and Santa Fe resident George R. R. Martin purchased an abandoned bowling alley and turned it over to a multi-generational force of almost 200 artists who conceived and constructed the current "immersive" art experience, which combines art, technology, myth-making, and story telling. You can't come to Santa Fe and not check it out. $15.

✱ To Do

FARMERS' MARKETS **Railyard Artisan Market at the Market Pavilion** Sundays 10 AM–4 PM. The 10,000-square-foot Market Hall with year-round vending plus summer outdoor sales adjacent provides shoppers with produce fresh from the farm and local and imported handcrafted items. Hundreds of growers, however, so you have no way of knowing for sure what is organic, or for that matter, home-grown. Very pricey, and in many cases, worth it . . . but not always. Be warned: Parking is just about impossible, and you do not want a run-in with the local police.

MEET THE GROWERS AT THE SANTA FE FARMERS' MARKET

Santa Fe Farmers' Market (505-938-4098; www.santafefarmersmarket.com), 1607 Paseo de Peralta, in the Railyard. Saturdays (year-round!), fall/winter: 8 AM–1 PM, summer: 7 AM–noon); May 1–November 28, Tues. 8 AM–1 PM.

GALLERIES **Andrew Smith Gallery: Masterpieces of Photography** (505-984-1234), 122 Grant Avenue, Santa Fe. The world's leading nineteenth- and twentieth-century photo gallery. A breathtaking history of photography. You'll see familiar images and you'll also have your conceptions of documentation pushed. Ansel Adams to Annie Liebowitz, with the emphasis on Adams.

Davis Mather Folk Art Gallery (505-983-1660), 141 Lincoln Avenue, Santa Fe. One of the best collections of New Mexico animal woodcarvings and Mexican folk art resides in this small corner gallery.

Gerald Peters (505-954-5700), 1011 Paseo de Peralta, Santa Fe. This international gallery, a museum in its own right, contains classic Western and Taos Society of Artists, Los Cinco Pintores, plus contemporary realistic and minimalist work, as well as photography and sculpture.

MEOW WOLF, SANTA FE'S CUTTING-EDGE ART ENVIRONMENT LOCATED IN A REFURBISHED BOWLING ALLEY, HAS HAD INTERNATIONAL IMPACT

Nuart Gallery (505-988-3888), 670 Canyon Road, Santa Fe. You want art? This is art—deeply intriguing contemporary art of many genres that draws you in and won't let you look away. My kind of gallery.

Zamplin-Lampert Gallery (505) 982-6100, 651 Canyon Rd, Santa Fe. Perhaps the most perfect gallery of them all—intimate, beautifully arranged Santa Fe and New Mexico classic masters—of prints and paintings—with each work a commanding presence. I adore this place and its ability to nourish the soul.

Adobe Gallery (505) 955-0550, 221 Canyon Rd, Santa Fe. A must-stop for lovers and collectors of Pueblo pottery and Native painting, as well as books.

GOLF Marty Sanchez Links de Santa Fe (505-955-4400), 205 Caja Del Rio, Santa Fe. Open year-round, weather permitting, this public course offers a tremendous variety of golfing experiences, including an 18-hole championship course, driving range, and PGA-certified instructors. $48.

HIKING, CROSS-COUNTRY SKIING, SNOWSHOEING, AND MOUNTAIN BIKING

An extensive system of trails that serves hikers and mountain bikers in warmer weather becomes cross-country trails when snow falls.

Aspen Vista Trail. Easily the most popular trial in the Santa Fe area, the moderate 10-mile Aspen Vista is especially memorable in fall when the aspens are changing. It is at the top of Ski Basin Road, 13 miles from town.

Borrego Trail. A 4-mile enjoyable, slightly more challenging, but still easy round-trip hike on only a few miles beyond the Chamisa Trail. It can be crowded on the weekend.

OLD SANTA FE TRAIL LEADS THROUGH THE BARRIO DE ANALCA, SANTA FE'S OLDEST NEIGHBORHOOD

Chamisa Trail. Six miles north from the Plaza on Ski Basin Road. This is always a pleasant, as well as accessible and easy, 4.75-mile round-trip hike through rolling meadows.

Dale Ball Trails (505-955-2103). This more than 14-mile round-trip trail/bike system may be accessed conveniently in town at Canyon Road and Cerro Gordo as well as on NM 475 at Sierra del Norte. The bike trail is about 7 miles of single-track intermediate riding through the foothills of the Sangre de Cristos. The trail is generally easy but becomes more challenging as you go up the mountain. La Piedra Trail connects the Dale Ball Trail north to the Winsor Trail up near the Santa Fe Ski Basin.

Winsor Trail. The favorite of mountain bikers near and far; accessible from Ski Basin parking lot for the full thrill.

LECTURES Lannan Foundation (505-986-8160; www.lensic.com), 309 Read Street, Santa Fe. The popular Lannan "Readings & Conversations" literary series on occasional Wed. evenings September–May at the Lensic Theater brings in national and international literary stars to read and discuss issues presented in their work. Tickets go fast. $8.

Santa Fe Institute (505-984-8800), 1339 Hyde Park Road. Free, open, accessible occasional lectures by fellows and associates of the renowned Santa Fe Institute, interdisciplinary meeting ground of the world's great minds.

St. John's College (505-984-6000), 1160 Camino Cruz Blanca, Great Hall, Peterson Student Center, Santa Fe. Intriguing assortment of scholarly presentations on literature and philosophy, all free.

MUSIC AND DANCE ASPEN BALLET, FLAMENCO Santa Fe Chamber Music Festival, 208 Griffin Street, (505-982-1890; www.santafechambermusic.org). Season: July–August. One of Santa Fe's biggest draws, the festival brings in foremost composers and musicians to play classical, jazz, folk, and world music.

Santa Fe Concert Association (505-984-8759; santafeconcerts.org), 300 Paseo de Peralta. Season: September–May. Since 1931, Santa Fe's oldest music organization has been bringing outstanding musicians from all over the world to perform a repertoire of classical and modern concert music.

Santa Fe Desert Chorale (505-988-2282; www.desertchorale.org). Season: July–August and Christmas. One of the few professional choruses in the United States, the twenty-four-voice chorale performs a great many twentieth-century works, as well as major music from all periods, particularly Renaissance and Baroque.

Santa Fe Opera (800-280-4654; www.santafeopera.org). Seven miles north of Santa Fe on US 285. Season: late June or July–August. Each season of the premier summer opera festival in the United States features an ambitious repertoire that usually includes unknown or new operas as well as popular standards and a revived masterpiece. The opera's mystique is amplified by its elegant amphitheater with sunset views, and the acoustics. Bring a warm coat and blankets; temperatures plummet after dark, and you'll be out past midnight.

Santa Fe Pro Musica (800-960-6680; www.santafepromusica.com). 1405 Luisa Street. Most special are the Christmas-season Baroque ensemble concerts played on period instruments. If you can attend a performance in the Loretto Chapel, by all means go.

Santa Fe Symphony Orchestra and Chorus (505-983-3530; www.sf-symphony.org), 551 W. Cordova Road. The symphony performs various concerts at the Lensic Theater notably a popular holiday concert.

TAILGATING AT THE SANTA FE OPERA IS A FAVORITE SUMMER CULINARY EVENT

SCHOOLS AND CLASSES Santa Fe School of Cooking & Market (505-983-4511), 125 N. Guadalupe Street, Santa Fe. Want to learn how to make a great salsa or serve an entire dinner of Southwestern cuisine? This is the place to learn from well-known chefs. Hands-on and observational classes allow you to immerse in the history and culture of regional cooking. Restaurant walking tours are popular.

Las Cosas Cooking Classes (505-988-3394), 181 Paseo de Peralta, Santa Fe. Enjoy hands-on cooking classes at this abundantly-stocked kitchen shop with the latest gear and personality-plus Chef Johnny Vee, an excellent and entertaining instructor.

Santa Fe Photographic Workshops (505-983-1400), 50 Mt. Carmel Road. Workshops in all aspects of photography, taught by photographers of national and international repute, some abroad year-round. Whatever you'd ever dreamed of trying in photography, you'll find it here. Intensive workshops here are designed to move you to your next level and beyond. Free summer evening presentations by faculty are special events.

SKIING Ski Santa Fe (505-982-4429 for reservations), 16 miles northeast of Santa Fe on NM 475. Open Thanksgiving–early April. One big reason to love Santa Fe. With a base elevation of 10,350 feet and a 12,075-foot summit, this ski area is geared to appeal to every member of the family and is as fine a place to learn as it can be thrilling. Terrain Park is exceptional. It also has packages for beginners, freestyle terrain, and multiday ticket bargains. Reservations are required for the adaptive ski program for both the physically and mentally challenged (505-995-9858; www.adaptiveski.org). $78.

THEATER Santa Fe Playhouse (505-988-4262), 142 E. De Vargas Street, Santa Fe. Season: year-round. Founded in the 1920s by writer Mary Austin as the Santa Fe Community Theater, it remains the longest-running theater group in New Mexico, now at home in an intimate adobe theater in one of the city's oldest neighborhoods. A favorite each fall is the *Fiesta Melodrama*, a spoof staged the week of La Fiesta.

Adobe Rose Theatre (505-629-8688), 1213B Parkway Drive, Santa Fe. Devotees of live theater present challenging and offbeat comedy and drama. Genuine attempt at presenting authentic live theater.

WALKING TOURS Historic Walks of Santa Fe (505-986-8388), 908 E. Palace Avenue, Daily at 9:45 AM, 1:15 PM No reservations required. Professional museum docent guides specialize in the history of Santa Fe landmarks. Ghost Walks and Spirit Walks are especially popular. Santa Fe is reputedly a highly haunted city. $15, senior discounts, under age 12 free.

New Mexico Museum of Art (505-476-5072). Art walking tours of Santa Fe April–November, Mondays at 10 AM. $10, under age 18 free.

SPAS

Absolute Nirvana Spa, Tea Room, & Gardens (505-983-7942), 106 E. Faithway Street, Santa Fe. Named a hot new spa by *Condé-Nast Traveler*, this is the place to purify and calm the body and mind with a range of Asian spa rituals. Starts at $145 and up to $220 for 50 minute massage such as the Asian Fusion or the Native Reflections Ritual. Watch the website for specials.

La Posada de Santa Fe Spa Sage (505-954-9630), 330 E. Palace Avenue, Santa Fe. Santa Fe is a city with some great, great spas. This one may not be the most aesthetically posh, but it sets the standard on service. You may select the Spirit of Santa Fe treatment, which incudes a rub with blue corn meal and sage oil. Twenty percent local discount. Highly rated on Discovery Channel. Pricey, but you get what you pay for.

The Spa at Loretto (505-984-7997), 211 Old Santa Fe Trail, Santa Fe. Embracing local indigenous and Native American herbs and minerals as well as in-house crafted aromatherapy oils, this spa features exquisite facials, body wraps, couples massage, global rituals, and treatments as well as Thai massage. Consistently ranked high nationally. Pampering to the max. $125 and up.

10,000 Waves Japanese Spa and Resort (505-982-9304), 3451 Hyde Park Road, Santa Fe. Open daily 9:15–9:30. A ten-minute drive up Hyde Park Road is an exquisite Japanese bath-style spa that is a world of its own. It is considered a romantic, sensual date experience. There are public and private hot tubs and men's and women's scheduled tub hours, and patrons stroll about in fluffy white robes, sipping herbal tea. Hourly tub rates are reduced for anyone with a New Mexico driver's license and for frequent users. It is a lovely experience but can be pricey. A favorite treat for locals. Limited lodging is available in The Houses of the Moon by reservation. $42 hour basic tub rate. Massage begins at $120. Specials year round and locals get discounts.

Sunrise Springs Spa Resort (505-471-3600), 242 Los Pinos Road, La Cienega. This lovely property has re-articulated itself numerous times over the years, and now finally seems to have found its true identity. If peace is to be found, this little piece of heaven on earth south of town might just be the place. Ideal for personal or group retreat, spa services, yoga, and other modalities. Expensive.

Palace of the Governors (505-476-5100). Daily at 10:15 except Sundays. Two-hour historic walking tours conducted by the Friends of the Palace. Meet at the blue gate on Lincoln Avenue side of the Palace of the Governors. $10, under age 17 free. No tipping.

WINERIES AND TASTING ROOMS ✂ **Balagna Winery & San Ysidro Vineyards** (505-672-3678), 223 Rio Bravo Drive, White Rock. Open daily, noon–6. Sip fine wines above the clouds.

✳ Green Space

Bandelier National Monument (505-672-3861). Go 46 miles west of Santa Fe on US 285 north to Pojoaque, west on NM 502, south on NM 4. Open daily, year-round. Closed Christmas and New Year's. Summer 8–6, winter 9–5. Tucked deep into a canyon on the Pajarito Plateau is the ancestral home of Pueblo tribes that was occupied A.D. 1100–1550. You can climb among the cliff dwellings and view village ruins and ceremonial kivas. The loop trail of Frijoles Canyon ruins is an easy one-hour walk. Rangers offer "night walks" during summer. There are more rigorous hikes out here, which you can learn about at the visitor center. $10–$20.

🐾 **Frank S. Ortiz Dog Park**, 160 Camino de las Crucitas, Santa Fe, is a popular off-leash dog park where pets can run free. Acres and acres of trails with expansive mountain views make this excellent walking terrain for human companions.

Ft. Marcy Recreation Complex (505-955-2500), 490 Bishop's Lodge Road, Santa Fe. Fitness complex including pool is open Mon.–Fri. 6 AM–8:30 PM, Sat. 8–6:30, Sun. 10–6. This facility has picnic tables, tennis court, baseball field, indoor swimming pool, fitness room, a par course, and well-used walking paths. Variable fees, quite reasonable.

♂ **Hyde Memorial State Park** (505-983-7175), 740 Hyde Park Road, Santa Fe. Eight miles northeast of Santa Fe via Hyde Park Road. Open daily 8 AM–11 PM Forested with aspens and evergreens, this easily accessed park is close enough for an afternoon hike or even a long lunch-time walk. In warm weather, the almost 4-mile Hyde Park Loop Trail provides stunning views of the Sangre de Cristo Mountains, although the first third of the trail is quite steep and attention must be paid to finding the correct return path. In winter, this is a closed-in cross-country skiing, snowshoeing, and tubing area. Find the trailhead in back of the visitor center. $5 day use; $8–18 camping.

AT BANDELIER NATIONAL MONUMENT, YOU CAN CLIMB INTO AN ANCIENT CLIFF DWELLING

Santa Fe National Forest (505-438-5300), 11 Forest Lane, Santa Fe. This vast national forest, measuring 16 million acres, includes much of the most beautiful scenery in northern New Mexico. It holds four wilderness areas: Pecos, San Pedro Parks, Dome, and Chama River Canyon, and three Wild and Scenic River areas: 11 miles of the East Fork of the Jemez (great for cross-country skiing), 24.6 miles of the Rio Chama, and 20.5 miles of the Pecos River, plus over 1,000 miles of trails accessible to horses, hikers, and mountain bikes, as well as four-wheel-drive vehicles. Close to Santa Fe is the Black Canyon Campground, northeast on NM 475 and convenient to the Borrego Trail.

Valles Caldera National Preserve (866-382-5537), 40 miles northwest of Santa Fe. Continue on NM 4 past Bandelier about 15 miles. This vast, astonishing green basin—all that remains of what was once the world's largest volcano—is believed to be part of an 89,000-acre caldera, a basin formed during Pleistocene volcanic activity. Located on a 42-year-old land grant named Baca Location No. 1, it is also called the Valle Grande or Baca Location and is home to a herd of 45,000 elk. Since the area was named one of the country's newest national monuments, hiking, cross-country skiing,

THE VALLES CALDERA OFFERS HIKING, FISHING, WILDLIFE VIEWING, CROSS-COUNTRY SKIING, AND MORE

fly-fishing, mountain biking, night sky adventures, wildlife viewing, and hunting have become available for various fees on a reservations-only basis. Variable fees. $10-$20 per vehicle. As of this writing the preserve is not selling passes. They may be purchased at Bandelier. Call for information.

❋ Lodging

BED & BREAKFASTS, MOTELS, AND HOTELS ♿ **Drury Plaza Inn** (505-424-2175), 828 Paseo de Peralta, Santa Fe. Conveniently located a few blocks from the Plaza, this elegantly refurbished historic hospital building is a top choice. Service is impeccable, and guests are treated to a hot breakfast, fresh popcorn at 3 PM, hors d'ouevres enough to make a dinner from, and three drinks per night. The rooms may be a bit small, but the bedding is divine, and the service is the best in town. I speak from experience. I usually stay here when I am in town. $129.

El Rey Court (505-982-1931), 1862 Cerrillos Road, Santa Fe. This classic 1937 Route 66 motel gets high marks on several counts: convenient location, lovely landscaping, and classic Route 66 Southwest style; however, when I have stayed there, I found the antiquated heating system noisy enough to wake me at 3 AM. Many of the eighty-seven rooms have flagstone floors and exposed vigas; twenty have fireplaces. There is a heated pool and indoor and outdoor hot tubs. Perhaps the passive-solar heated rooms might deliver a peaceful night. Or just bring your earplugs. This is an in-demand place, so book early. The Lodge can accommodate reunions and workshops. Prices have been going up under the new ownership. $84–140.

♿ **La Fonda Hotel** (505-982-5511), 100 E. San Francisco Street, Santa Fe. There's been an inn of some sort on the southeast corner of the Plaza for almost 400 years. La Fonda is still the only hotel on the Plaza, and no other can match its rich past. Gone, with a controversial redesign, are the dark, old-fashioned lobby with its INDIAN DETOURS sign, the clubby bar, the check-in counter and the newsstand. All the new features are are far too light and bright for the traditionalists. But the modernists find the new arrangement much more comfortable. Remaining are the lovely La Plazuela restaurant with its colorful hand-painted glass, and the French Pastry Shop designed by Mary Elizabeth Jane Colter (designer for the Fred Harvey Hotels) which conspire to trick you into thinking you have time-traveled back into Santa Fe's past. Swimming pool, hot tubs, and spa are on-site, and La Fonda features fourteen "nontoxic" suites for environmentally sensitive guests. $119–339.

Rancho Gallina: Santa Fe Inn and Eco-Retreat (505-438-1871), 31 Bonanza Creek Road, Santa Fe. Billing itself as "the greenest place to stay in Santa Fe," here choose from five rustic rooms, enjoy a soak in a cedar hand-built hot tub, the peace and quiet of an historic ranch twenty minutes south of town off the Turquoise Trail, and farm-fresh breakfasts. $155.

♿ **Inn and Spa at Loretto** (505-988-5531), 211 Old Santa Fe Trail, Santa Fe. Built in 1975 on the site of Loretto Academy, a nineteenth-century girls' school, this inn's terraced architecture is modeled after Taos Pueblo. With 134 rooms, it includes a swimming pool, a bar with live entertainment, and a restaurant, Baleen. There is a deluxe spa on the premises, where you can reduce your stress pronto. An automatic $10-plus-tax "hotel fee" is added to each day of your bill to pay for gratuities, newspaper, Wi-Fi, and the like. Belongs to Destinations & Resorts properties. $148–261.

Inn at Vanessie (505-984-1193), 427 Water Street, Santa Fe. Formerly the Water Street Inn. This handsomely restored adobe B&B has an air of romantic intimacy. It is hidden away on a side street within strolling distance of downtown. The twelve rooms are spacious with brick floors and four-poster beds. Most have a fireplace; some have private patios with fountains. Sunset views from the upstairs balcony are splendid, and hot hors d'oeuvres are served with New Mexican wines at cocktail hour. Vanessie's piano bar—often featuring the great Doug Montgomery—is across the alley. $249.

La Posada de Santa Fe Resort & Spa (505-986-0000), 330 E. Palace Avenue, Santa Fe. A nineteenth-century mansion, built by pioneer merchant Abraham Staab, features a complex of Pueblo-style casitas and 6 acres of huge cottonwoods and fruit trees. One drawback is you have to walk outdoors from the Staab House to your room, which is not fun in nasty weather. The casitas have classic New Mexican decor: adobe fireplaces, hand-painted tiles, Indian rugs, and skylights. Guests enjoy a good-size swimming pool and lovely courtyard for drinking and dining in nice weather. The service is excellent. The "resort fee" is an additional $20–30 per day, and don't forget to tip the mandatory valet. $179.

Rosewood Inn of the Anasazi (505-988-3030), 113 Washington Avenue, Santa Fe. This striking fifty-seven-room hotel is as close to the Plaza as you can get without landing on a bench there. It is done in classic Pueblo Revival style, with viga and latilla ceilings throughout, stone floors and walls, and a beautiful flagstone waterfall. Exquisite simplicity highlights the fine local artwork. Service is tops, as are on-site business services: Staff will bring an exercise bike to your room or rent you a mountain bike. Offering the best sense of peace and privacy money can buy, this small luxury hotel continues to reign as the city's most chic address for visitors. Restaurant on-site. $195.

🍴 **Santa Fe Motel & Inn** (800-930-8002), 510 Cerrillos Road, Santa Fe. If you are looking for an attractive, affordable motel downtown, this one is set far enough off a busy intersection to have an air of seclusion. In addition to typical motel rooms, it includes ten adobe casitas with refrigerator, microwave, and patio entrance. Across the street, kitchenettes are available. Many will find this an excellent value. Plus, a complimentary full breakfast is included. $89–134. Only $89 per weeknight most of the winter, if you call in your reservation.

🍴 **Silver Saddle Motel** (505-471-7663), 2810 Cerrillos Road, Santa Fe. Vintage 1953 Route 66 motor court next door to Jackalope makes this a shopper's paradise. Absolutely reasonable with warm hospitality. Western-themed rooms are small but clean; feels like a tour back in time. Continental breakfast included. $53–65.

LODGES, INNS, AND RANCHES

🐾♿ **Inn on the Alameda** (888-984-2121), 303 E. Alameda, Santa Fe. This intimate inn across the street from the Santa Fe River feels smaller than it actually is, due perhaps to the individual private courtyards surrounding rooms. (You will pay extra for a balcony.) It has two hot tubs, exercise room, full-service bar, and comfortable sitting rooms. The morning fare is a buffet breakfast feast. $159.

CABINS AND CAMPING

Hyde Memorial State Park (505-983-7175), 740 Hyde Park Road. Open year-round. Tent sites and RV hookups available. $8–18.

Rancheros de Santa Fe Campground (505-466-3482), 736 Old Las Vegas Highway. Open March 15–October 31. Cabins, RV sites, full hookups, pool, tent sites—in short, whatever your travel style, it can be accommodated here. $27–46.

Santa Fe National Forest (505-438-5600; www.fs.usda.gov/santafe), 11 Forest Lane, Open May 15–September 30.

Two campgrounds in the Santa Fe area are Aspen Basin and Big Tesuque, each about 12 miles northeast of Santa Fe on NM 475. Both grounds offer RV sites with no hookups and tent sites. $10 and up.

Santa Fe Skies RV Park (505-473-5946; www.santafeskiesrvpark.com), 14 Browncastle Ranch. One mile off I-25 at southeast end of NM 599 on the Turquoise Trail. Open year-round. A comfortable stop for RVers with modem hookups, too, this park boasts views of four mountain ranges. $41.

✳ Where to Eat

DINING OUT **Cafe Pasqual's** (505-983-9340), 121 Don Gaspar, Santa Fe. Open daily. Closed Thanksgiving and Christmas. B, L, D. Named for the saint of the kitchen, owned and operated by Kathy Kagel, organizer of a food distribution system that feeds the hungry. Consistently on the list of "Ten Best Places to Have Breakfast in the United States"; the huge, delicious, Mexican (from Mexico) breakfast is served all day. Emphasis is on flavorful organic and natural foods. Genovese omelet with sun-dried tomatoes and pine nuts, grilled salmon burrito, toasted piñon ice cream with caramel sauce. Moderate–Expensive.

♂ **The Compound** (505-982-4353), 653 Canyon Road, Santa Fe. Chef-owner Mark Kiffin revived this Canyon Road grande dame with its Alexander Girard–designed white interior. The art of service has been perfected here. Food as entertainment on the grand scale is to be expected. The beautiful people, dressed to the nines, nibbling designer Continental dishes concocted from ingredients air-freighted in from all over the world—it is truly to die for. Sweetbreads and foie gras, grilled lamb rib eye, blue corn–dusted soft shell crabs, and liquid chocolate cake for dessert—one of the best chocolate items I have ever tasted. If you have one special splurge on your visit to Santa Fe, make your reservation here. A great place for a humble writer to pretend she has big bucks. Kiffin is a James Beard nominee and Best Chef winner. Expensive–Very Expensive.

Coyote Cafe and Cantina (505-983-1615), 132 W. Water Street, Santa Fe. The granddaddy of all nouvelle Southwestern cuisine, pioneered by anthropologist-turned-chef Mark Miller, still serves inspired dishes that blend native ingredients with sophisticated flavors. Now open year 'round the light-hearted rooftop patio serves reasonably priced simpler, but still delicious, fare, with Mexican beer, margaritas, fabulous fire-roasted salsa, Cuban sandwiches, and more. Expensive–Very Expensive, but the cantina won't bust the budget.

Eloisa (505- 982-0883), 228 E Palace Avenue, Santa Fe. L, D, Sunday brunch. Located in the Drury Hotel, 2016 James Beard-Award nominated Chef Jon Sedlar runs this comfortably contemporary and beautifully lit dining venue with a steady knowing hand, making the most of fresh ingredients with a clever Southwest flair. Love the handmade tortillas and the diver scallops, but it's all excellent. I've eaten here often and never had a disappointing meal. The bar is drop-dead gorgeous. Top choice for fine dining. Moderate–Expensive.

Geronimo Restaurant (505-982-1500), 724 Canyon Road, Santa Fe. Open daily. D only. All of Santa Fe agrees. Housed in one of the city's finest historic adobes, this restaurant is the last word in mini-malist Santa Fe elegance. The menu con-sists of American staples updated with Southwestern and other ethnic ingredi-ents. Very, Very Expensive.

Il Piatto Italian Restaurant (505-984-1091), 95 W. Marcy Street, Santa Fe. L Mon.–Sat., D Mon.–Sun. I adore this place! In its incarnation as an "Italian Farmhouse Kitchen," Il Piatto continues to delight with emphasis on local ingre-dients. Its value bargain prix fixe lunch and three-course prix fixe dinner offer great flexibility when ordering. Small plates are available. Try the pumpkin

ravioli with brown sage butter, slow roast breast of lamb, and so much more. Super-lative happy hour with half-price on appetizers, small plates, and many fine wines by the glass. Late-night dining, abundant wines by the glass. Frequently voted Santa Fe's best Italian restaurant. Moderate–Expensive.

Rio Chama Steakhouse (505-955-0765), 414 Old Santa Fe Trail, Santa Fe. Next door to a bar that is especially lively in winter when the legislature is in session. Open daily. L, D. Closed Christmas. Forget the cholesterol. Try this instead: prime dry-aged beef, succu-lent rib eyes and fillets, and Black Angus prime rib, house-made onion rings, rich creamed spinach, and shrimp cocktail. The blue cheese–green chile burgers are dripping with decadence and irresistible. Add a full bar, and you've got a real meal going. Go for the fondue. Expensive, but moderate for lunch.

La Boca (505-982-3433), 72 W. Marcy Street, Santa Fe. L, D. Modern Spanish and Mediterranean fare adored by all. Tapas. Fabulous music, no cover, the great Nacha Mendez on Sunday night. And bravo to Chef Campbell Caruso— winner of the 2013 James Beard Founda-tion Award. Moderate–Expensive.

EATING OUT **Counter Culture** (505-995-1105), 930 Baca Street, #1, Santa Fe. B, L. The hip, the pierced, the tattooed, the artistic, and even the parents of all of the above agree on the homemade fries and Asian soups of the eclectic menu served here. This little Baca Street neigh-borhood is sometimes called "the SoHo of Santa Fe" for its galleries, jewelry shops, and slightly edgy atmosphere. Inexpensive.

Cowgirl Hall of Fame Bar-B-Que (505-982-2565), 319 S. Guadalupe, Santa Fe. Open daily. B, L, D. Closed Thanksgiving and Christmas. This place is known as much, if not more, as a hopping watering hole than as a restaurant. The decor is old-time cow-girl memorabilia. The specialty is the mesquite-smoked barbecue, but beside all the meat are vegetarian chile and butternut casserole. Try the signature dessert, the Baked Potato, which is actually a chocolate sundae disguised as a spud, or just have the peach cobbler. One of the most popular, friendliest bars in town. Moderate.

🍴 **Del Charro** (505-954-0320), 101 W. Alameda, at the Inn of the Governors. Open daily 11:30 AM–midnight, slightly earlier closing on Sun. They said it couldn't be done, but at Del Charro you can find a very good, not gourmet, bargain lunch. Said lunch might be a burger, enchilada, chicken-fried steak, poblano pepper relleno, or cream of mushroom soup. Homemade potato chips, too. Give your wallet a break. Inexpensive.

Jambo Café: African Home Style Cuisine (505-473-1269), 2010 Cerrillos Road, Santa Fe. L, D Mon.–Sat. Closed Sundays. Open till 9 PM. Multiple-year winner of the Santa Fe Souper Bowl, famous for sweet potato curry soup, jerk chicken, goat and lentil stew, stuffed phyllo (recommended)—love the island spice chicken coconut peanut stew. Authentic flavors where you'd least expect to find them—in a strip mall. Inexpensive.

Maria's New Mexican Kitchen (505-983-7929), 555 W. Cordova Road, Santa Fe. Open daily. L, D. Closed Thanksgiving and Christmas. With over a half-century in the same location, Maria's is a Santa Fe classic that continues to draw crowds of all ages. You can watch the experts make fresh tortillas by hand. Sizzling fajitas, caliente green chile stew, and the classic blue corn–red chile enchiladas—you can't go wrong. Good middle-of-the-road eatery. Try ordering dinner in the bar. Moderate.

Modern General (505-930-5462), 637 Cerrillos Road, Santa Fe. Quirky upscale luncheonette kind of place. Cutting-edge book selection, kitchen and table wares, but above all else, bone broth. Get your healing, nourishing bone broth here, and while you're at it, take a quart home. Brunchy egg dishes midway between pancake and omelet. Inexpensive.

🍴 **Pantry Restaurant** (505-986-0022), 1820 Cerrillos Road, Santa Fe. Open daily. B, L, D. How about homemade

JOY! A DINNER OF ENCHILADAS AND SOPAIPILLAS IN SANTA FE

corned beef hash, freshly baked biscuits and mellow white gravy, pancakes stuffed with fruit and whipped cream, and endless cups of coffee, in a completely unpretentious spot that locals adore for good food and reasonable prices? My go-to spot for reliable, rib-sticking fare and sweet service. Sit at the counter or grab a table. Open till 9 PM. Inexpensive.

Piccolino Italian Restaurant (505-471-1480), 2890 Agua Fria Street, Santa Fe. Additional location at Agora Plaza in Eldorado. L, D daily. You may have to hunt to find it, but when you do, you will discover down-home, unpretentious, checked tablecloth local red sauce–based real Italian food. Credible pizza, calzones; very good chicken piccata and marsala. It's packed with locals who disdain the fancy-schmancy stuff and prefer value and flavor for their dining dollars. A happy place! Save room for cannoli. Inexpensive–moderate.

Plaza Cafe (505-982-1664), 54 Lincoln Avenue, Santa Fe. Open daily. B, L, D. When you're out and about and looking for a bite, this family restaurant is the place, with its black-and-white tile floor and old-timey counter service. You can count on excellent enchiladas,

sopaipillas, diner food, salads, and chicken-fried steak, all served as consistently and efficiently as they have been since 1918, making this the oldest restaurant in town. Restored to perfection after suffering a kitchen fire. Southside location, too. Inexpensive.

San Francisco St. Bar & Grill: An American Bistro (505-982-2044), southwest corner of the Plaza at San Francisco Street and Don Gaspar. Upstairs. Open daily from 11 AM L, D. Go upstairs to find a reasonably priced and well-varied menu of salads, sandwiches, and fresh fare bound to have something please any appetite. Inexpensive.

Santa Fe Bar & Grill (505-982-3033), southwest corner DeVargas Center. Open daily. L 11–5, D 5–10, Sunday brunch 11–3. Casual and warm, the place that comes to mind when you need to meet a friend for dinner or have a business lunch where you can talk. The shopping center parking lot makes it a convenient stop. Love the fish tacos with black beans, but the menu has everything from swell burgers to enchiladas and lives up to the motto, "Creative southwest cuisine." Inexpensive.

The Shed (505-982-9030), 113½ E. Palace Avenue, Santa Fe. Open Mon.–Sat. L, D. Closed Sundays. Located in an adobe dating from 1692 and tucked away in an enclosed patio, The Shed is a landmark where you can count on consistently delicious chile, ground on the premises. Perhaps the very best red chile, blue corn enchiladas. Colorful Southwestern decor adds to the fun of eating here. Selections of fish and beef are also available. Homemade hot fudge for dessert. Take a seat by a corner fireplace in winter, or on the patio on a summer night with a glass of wine, and you know you can only be in one place, the capital of the Land of Enchantment. Inexpensive–Moderate.

Tecolote Café (505-988-1362), 1616 St. Michael's Drive, Santa Fe. Justifiably famous for breakfast, Tecolote serves delicious low-cholesterol alternatives to

GO LOCAL AND GRAB A MEAL OR JUST A LUSCIOUS DECADENT DESSERT AT THE PLAZA CAFE

its heaping helping of French toast and freshly baked muffins. Inexpensive.

Tesuque Village Market (505-988-8848), junction of Bishop's Lodge Road and Tesuque Village Road, Tesuque. Open daily. B, L, D. Wood-fired pizza, organic and all-natural meats, fabulous blue corn pancakes, amazing homemade pies and decadent chocolate desserts, and boutique wine and rare tequila selections are all here at this neighborhood hangout with heated outdoor seating. Cowboys, artists, Hollywood types, and the president of the rose society are all at home here. Moderate.

Tia Sophia's (505-983-9880), 210 W. San Francisco Street, Santa Fe. Open Mon.–Sat. 7:30–2. Closed Sundays and major holidays. B, L. Located in the heart of San Francisco Street, this is an unassuming little restaurant that serves consistently authentic New Mexican meals in a family atmosphere. The breakfast burritos and huevos rancheros, with red chile with a real kick, are worth ordering, and for lunch, try one of the homemade stuffed sopaipillas. Inexpensive.

Sweetwater Harvest Café (505-795-7383), 1512 Pacheco Street, Santa Fe. B, L, D. The perfect brunch spot, if a bit out of the way. Light, fresh, nutritious offerings such as green tea smoothies, house made buckwheat granola, organic eggs, delectable pancakes. Lovely patio, bright, airy, contemporary interior, a mecca for the food conscious. Breakfast served all day. Moderate.

🖊 **Shake Foundation** (505-988-8992), 631 Cerrillos Road, Santa Fe. Santa Fe's take on an old-fashioned drive in, with delectable organic beef burgers, hand-cut fresh fries, ice cream, and of course, milk shakes, all served on picnic tables. Moderate. The little ones will love it. Inexpensive.

El Palacio (505-989-3505), 209 East Palace Avenue, Santa Fe. B, L. A dream of a cozy café, the size of a postage stamp, with reasonable prices, organic salads, homemade soups, and delish

sandwiches. One of my top go-to spots in town. Inexpensive.

Fire & Hops (505-954-1635), 222 N Guadalupe Street, Santa Fe. D Mon.–Sun. Open other times also, please check. The town's most hopping gastropub, with eleven craft beers on tap, wines by the glass, ciders, innovative small plates and flavorful house-made sausage, ice cream, and sorbet. The perfect place for a light dinner or interlude. Moderate.

COFFEE AND TEA HOUSES (Check hours before you go—they can vary.)

Chocolate Maven Bakery & Cafe (505-984-1980), 821 San Mateo, Unit C, Santa Fe. Open daily. B, L, weekend brunch. Monster chocolate croissants and unbelievable sandwiches make this one popular spot, but parking is hellacious, and you have to brave the crowds before you get to a tiny table. Solution: Go early or late. Maybe it's the lighting, but the encased pastries positively glisten with goodness. Inexpensive.

Clafoutis (505-988-1809), 333 W. Cordova Road. Open daily 7–4. Go early or go late, but go. To paraphrase *New Yorker* writer Adam Gopnik, as with the food in Paris, it is better than it needs to be. Feast on beignets, macaroons, and the best croissant in town. On the savory side of things, there's omelets, meat and cheese plates, eggs, and, of course, quiche and eggs benedict. Inexpensive.

Downtown Subscription (505-983-3085), 376 Garcia Street, Santa Fe. Good for browsing the shelves of magazines and newspapers, good for coffee, and good for hanging out on the informal patio. Inexpensive. Reserve your Sunday *NY Times* here. Inexpensive.

French Pastry Shop (505-983-6697), 100 E. San Francisco Street, Santa Fe. Just the place for a slice of quiche, fresh strawberry crêpe, a napoleon or a chocolate éclair, and a latte. So many delights, in the room designed by Fred Harvey's architect, Mary Elizabeth Jane Colter. With a croque monsieur for lunch, it is as

French as a morning on the Rive Gauche. Inexpensive.

Kakawa Chocolate House (505-982-0388), 1050 Paseo de Peralta, Santa Fe. This place specializes in preparing historic and global chocolate drinks. Want to sip the kind of chocolate Thomas Jefferson favored? Or taste the ancient brews of Mesoamerica? Expect to pay around $5 for a tiny cup of the experience. Mind-blowing house made chocolates, truffles, and brownies. A chocoholic's dream come true. Inexpensive.

Ohori's Coffee, Tea & Chocolate (505-982-9692), 505 Cerrillos Road in the Luna Center, Santa Fe. For serious coffee drinkers, please. Coffee is what it's all about here. Arabica beans are freshly roasted, and a different coffee is brewed every time the urn is emptied. The new patio is quite the spot. Roasting the best since 1984. Inexpensive.

🍵 **The New Baking Co. & Cafe** (505-557-6435), 504 W. Cordova Road, Santa Fe. Open Mon.–Sat. 6–8, Sun. 6–6. B, L, D. Read the paper; check your email on the free and reliable Wi-Fi; go for a breakfast of bacon and eggs, or the breakfast burrito special, smothered with green chile, plump and sustaining, served all day; or drool over the pastry counter. Everyone else does! As comfortable a hangout as it was in the old days. Inexpensive.

The Teahouse (505-992-0972), 821 Canyon Road, Santa Fe. The aesthetic is Zen, the tea selections are in the dozens. Lovely for Sunday brunch on the patio or a special dinner out. Even as it continues its evolution as a gourmet eatery, this place remains pure Canyon Road. Moderate.

❋ Entertainment

You can hear live music on various nights at the Santa Fe hot spots below:

Bar Alto (505-982-0883), 228 E. Palace Avenue, Santa Fe. Rooftop bar at Hotel Drury, intimate, with stunning view of the city, well-poured libations, specials, happy hour, and Cuban music Friday nights with salsa dancing as weather permits.

Agave Lounge (505-995-4530), 309 W. San Francisco Street, Santa Fe. Hip and happening lounge of the Hotel Eldorado, with popular happy hour and lively crowd, especially during ski season.

El Farol (505-983-9912), 808 Canyon Road, Santa Fe's oldest restaurant and cantina, also has nightly live entertainment in summer. Variety of world music, jazz, flamenco make this a happening night spot. Check out the newly remodeled space that is getting praise even from old-timers.

El Meson (505-983-6756), 213 Washington Avenue, Santa Fe. Come for the tapas and fine aged sherry, stay for the live jazz. A favorite weekend hangout for my friends and me. Tango on Tuesday nights.

Gig Performance Space (www.gigsantafe.com/contact.html), 1808 2nd Street, Suite H. Intimate venue for a grand variety of local and national musicians. Folk, Americana, jazz workshops, and sometimes even cameos by actor Alan Arkin.

La Café Sena Cantina (505-988-9232), 125 E. Palace Avenue, has waitstaff who belt out Broadway musical tunes, making for a delightful evening.

La Fonda's La Fiesta Lounge (505-982-5511), 100 E. San Francisco Street, is a favorite of locals and visitors, with country dancing on the intimate dance floor plus jazz and flamenco on various evenings. Margaritas and casual food.

Lensic Performing Arts Center (505-988-7050; www.lensic.com; www.ticketssantafe.org), 211 W. San Francisco Street, Santa Fe. Built originally as a grand motion picture palace, the 1930 Lensic is a fantastic creation in a faux Moorish-Renaissance style and boasts a silver chandelier from New York's Roxy in the lobby, along with the crests of Santa Fe's founding families. State-of-the-art sound equipment makes this a popular performing venue for an extraordinary variety of events, including Aspen Santa Fe Ballet, Big Screen Classics, and Live from the Met.

Maria Benitez Cabaret Theater (505-992-5800), 750 N. St. Francis Drive, Santa Fe. June–end of August. While diva Maria Benitez no longer performs, this theater features outstanding flamenco music and dance throughout the season.

Santa Fe Spirits Distillery and Tasting Room. (505-467-8892), 7505 Mallard Way, Suite I, Santa Fe. Artisan distillery that relies on local, organic fruit. You can tour the facility. The apple brandy is the super-star.

Downtown Tasting Room (505-780-5906), 308 Read Street, Santa Fe. Open daily.

Second Street Brewery (505-982-3030), 1814 2nd Street. An award-winning microbrewery, this is a relaxed pub serving fish and chips, soups, and salads, with live weekend entertainment. A second location at the Railyard is a popular entertainment venue. Aso at Railyard location. Plus taproom at 2020 Rufina Street.

Secreto Bar & Lounge at Hotel St. Francis (505-983-5700), 210 Don Gaspar Avenue, Santa Fe. Mixology supreme, featuring unique herbal concoctions. Go for the smoked sage margarita.

Staab House (505-986-0000), 330 E. Palace Avenue. The home built by Abraham Staab for his family is now a cozy night spot with live music of an evening. Nacha Mendez, diva of international Spanish song, performs most Friday nights.

Tiny's Restaurant and Lounge (505-983-1100), 10005 S. St. Francis. Open daily. Closed Sundays, except during football season. The lounge is the heart and soul of Tiny's, where you can get great *carne adovada*, chicken guacamole tacos, and *posole*. Here is where country and western meets Frank Sinatra. Live

entertainment Thurs.–Sun. and dancing on weekends. It is a time capsule that never changes.

Vanessie of Santa Fe (505-982-9966), 434 W. San Francisco Street, has a cocktail lounge atmosphere and live piano nightly, often by the legendary Doug Montgomery.

✻ Selective Shopping

Curiosa (505-988-2420), 328 S. Guadalupe Street, Santa Fe. Rarely does a new shop garner the raves this one does. All my most knowing Santa Fe friends adore this unique card and gift shop with unique collectables. Highly recommended.

On Your Feet (505-983-3900), 328 S. Guadalupe Street, Santa Fe. The best, the

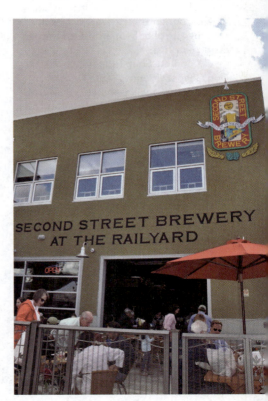

SECOND STREET BREWERY IS A RAILYARD HIGHLIGHT, WITH MICROBREWS AND LIVE MUSIC

most fashionable, and some of the most expensive—yet comfortable—shoes and accessories you will find in any city. This place has the kind of clothes you can travel the world in.

Back at the Ranch Cowboy Boots (505-989-8110), 209 E. Marcy Street, Santa Fe. You might actually go ga-ga when you look upon the fabulous selection of wild and fanciful cowboy boots. Expect to blow the budget on a lifetime purchase.

Cowboyz (505- 984-1256), 345 W. Manhattan Avenue, Santa Fe. Wow. Hundreds of pairs of used and vintage cowboy boots, flannel shirts, fringed leather jackets . . . go wild!

Design Center Santa Fe, 418 Cerrillos Road, Santa Fe. Here is some diverting browsing turf, a veritable bazaar, where you can stumble upon the unexpected piece of art, furniture, or antique that makes your entire trip worthwhile. It's also the site of offbeat ethnic and vegetarian eateries.

✎ **Doodlets Shop** (505-983-3771), 120 Don Gaspar Avenue, Santa Fe. A shop for kids of all ages. Doodlets stocks tin mermaids to chocolate sardines and all the postcards, stickers, Victoriana, and miniatures in between.

Double Take (505-989-8886), 320 Aztec Street, Santa Fe. The grandmommy of resale, Double Take is a ginormous bazaar of second-hand, vintage and western wares—clothing, household and more—that will make your brain explode. Giving away a trade secret here.

Jackalope (505-471-8539), 2820 Cerrillos Road, Santa Fe. "Folk art by the truckload" is the motto here. Whether you have a yen for handmade furniture from Mexico, chile lights, or a birdbath from the more than 2 acres of imported pottery, you will have fun shopping here. There's a patio restaurant, carousel, outdoors market, and plenty to amuse you for hours.

Jacqueline's Place (505-995-1150), 233 Canyon Road, Santa Fe. American-made

jewelry and stylish women's clothing, reasonable prices, excellent selection of contemporary looks for young girls, treasure trove of turquoise and silver. One-of-a-kind look. Why not shop here?

Keshi: The Zuni Connection (505-989-8728), 227 Don Gaspar, Santa Fe. For the best selection of guaranteed authentic Zuni fetishes, inlay and needlepoint jewelry, displayed brilliantly, with excellent advice, don't fool around, come here.

Maya (505-989-7590), 108 Galisteo Street, Santa Fe. Deliriously diverse and choice selection of timeless international imported clothing, jewelry, art, and embellishments. Don't expect a bargain, however.

Rocki Gorman (505-983-7833), 119 Old Santa Fe Trail, Santa Fe. Jewelry designer Rocki Gorman's shop is a jewel in itself. Her Southwestern-inspired one-of-a-kind pieces are irresistible, as are the Navajo broomstick velvet skirts and blouses, jackets, capes, shawls, and other accessories so beautifully arrayed in this corner shop in La Fonda. While this place may seem on the expensive side, I have found that careful shopping will yield the occasional piece that becomes a beloved wardrobe essential, at a price that even this humble writer can afford. When I pass this corner, I am always looking. I would say this fine shop has become necessary to my self-expression.

Passamenterie (505-989-1262), 115 Old Santa Fe Trail, Santa Fe. A treasure trove of colorful textiles, imported shawls to wrap yourself in, ruanas, knits, block prints—there's something for everyone. It's a place to dress as your idealized secret self—and maybe bring her out of the closet and into the world!

Palace of the Governors Portal (www.palaceofthegovernors.org/index.php), north block of the Plaza. Open daily. One of the best places in town to shop for traditional Indian jewelry is beneath the portal of the Governors' Palace. Here prices are reasonable for a huge array of juried, guaranteed authentic handmade Indian wares.

Purple Sage (505-954-0600), 110 Don Gaspar, Santa Fe. When a Santa Fe woman wants to splurge on a special-occasion outfit, she is likely to go to the Purple Sage for an ensemble in their luscious handwoven and hand-painted fabrics.

Santa Fe Flea Market (no phone), new address at Buffalo Thunder Resort, 10 miles north of Santa Fe on US 84/285. Open seasonally Fri.–Sun. 8–5. Although not the bargain-hunter's paradise this once was, the market, now operated by Tesuque Pueblo, still has a vast display of leather goods, jewelry, furniture, masks, and so much more.

Fashion Outlets of Santa Fe (505-474-4000), 8380 Cerrillos Road, 8 miles south of Santa Fe. More than 40 outlet stores with bargain prices on name brands.

Silver Sun (505-983-8743), 656 Canyon Road, Santa Fe. Offering jewelry from twenty-five turquoise mines for over thirty years, Silver Sun promises that what is sold here is the finest quality, and you will receive reliable, informed guidance. Prices are fair (not cheap), and there are sales. Look in back.

Sun Country Traders (505-982-0467), 123 E. Water Street. Specializing in Zuni beadwork, this reputable shop is well-stocked with the irresistible, the beautiful, and the well-crafted in Native jewelry, wood, pottery, and intriguing household objects, such as hand-beaded wineglasses.

Todos Santos (505-982-3855), 125 E. Palace Avenue #31, Santa Fe. Chocoholic alert. The most beautiful, imaginative artisanal chocolates, made in Santa Fe and arrayed from around the world are displayed in this jewel box of a shop in Sena Plaza. Pricey!

BOOKSTORES **Ark Books** (505-988-3709), 133 Romero Street, Santa Fe. The New Age lives and thrives here in these six rooms of books specializing in healing, world religions, magic, and mythology. Tapes/CDs, Tarot, jewelry, and incense make for a serene browse. Look for the hidden alcove with bargain books.

Collected Works Bookstore and Coffee Shop (505-988-4226), 202 Galisteo, Santa Fe. This is the city's oldest and most complete independent bookstore. Check the calendar for frequent events,

SANTERA MARIE ROMERO CASH DISPLAYS HER CARVINGS AT SPANISH MARKET

FINE CRAFTSMEN FROM ALL OVER THE WORLD ATTEND SANTA FE'S INTERNATIONAL FOLK ART MARKET

verteran bookman opens his door to an afternoon of delicious browsing, or the quest of a particular title or subject, no matter how arcane.

✳ Special Events

July: **Pancakes on the Plaza** (505-955-6200), July 4. **Spanish Market** (505-982-2226), Santa Fe Plaza, last weekend. A juried show of traditional Spanish Colonial artwork created by artists of Spanish descent. **International Folk Art Market** (505-992-7600), Milner Plaza, Museum Hill, second weekend. **Rodeo de Santa Fe** (505-471-4300), Rodeo Grounds, 3237 Rodeo Road, second weekend.

August: **Indian Market** (505-983-5220), Plaza. Weekend closest to August 19. World's largest sale of Native American arts.

September: **La Fiestas de Santa Fe** (505-471-8763) is the oldest ongoing festival (since 1712) in the United States; second weekend. **Thirsty Ear Festival** (www.thirstyearfestival.com), Eaves Movie Ranch, first weekend. **Santa Fe Wine and Chile Fiesta** (505-438-8060; www.santafewineandchile.org), last week.

November: **Winter Indian Market** (505-983-5220).

December: **Winter Spanish Market** (505-982-2226), first weekend. **Santa Fe Film Festival** (505-349-1414), emerging and established artists. Various venues. **Baumann Marionettes** (505-476-5072). Annual treat for children at St. Francis Auditorium, New Mexico Museum of Art. **Christmas at the Palace** (505-476-5100), hot cider and an old-fashioned celebration at the Palace of the Governors, midmonth. **Las Posadas** (santafe.org), midmonth, is a reenactment of a traditional holiday play around the Plaza. **Canyon Road Farolito Walk** (santafe.org), sunset–midnight, December 24.

readings and signings. This new location has a cozy fireplace and coffee bar pouring the exceptional Ikonik brew. No finer place to spend a wintry afternoon.

Garcia Street Books (505-986-0151), 376 Garcia Street, Santa Fe. With such an assortment of well-selected titles, you can't walk out without a wonderful find.

Nicholas Potter Bookseller (505-983-5434), 227 E. Palace Avenue, Santa Fe. This antiquarian Santa Fe classic has survived it all. A must-visit for book lovers. A dream of a shop.

op.cit. (505-428-0321), 157 Paseo de Peralta, Santa Fe. The indie bookstore a bibliophile can get lost in. New and used tomes, satisfying browsing.

Books of Interest (505- 984-9828), 1333 Cerrillos Road, Santa Fe. No one knows how to select and offer used books at reasonable prices like bookseller Leo Romero. In this latest incarnation, the

OPPOSITE: ENCHANTED MESA AS SEEN FROM ACOMA, SKY CITY

NORTHWEST NEW MEXICO: ANCESTRAL PUEBLO COUNTRY

■

SKY CITY COUNTRY

Acoma Pueblo, Crownpoint, Laguna Pueblo, Gallup, Grants, Ramah, Zuni Pueblo

CHACO COUNTRY

Aztec, Bloomfield, Cuba, Farmington, Shiprock

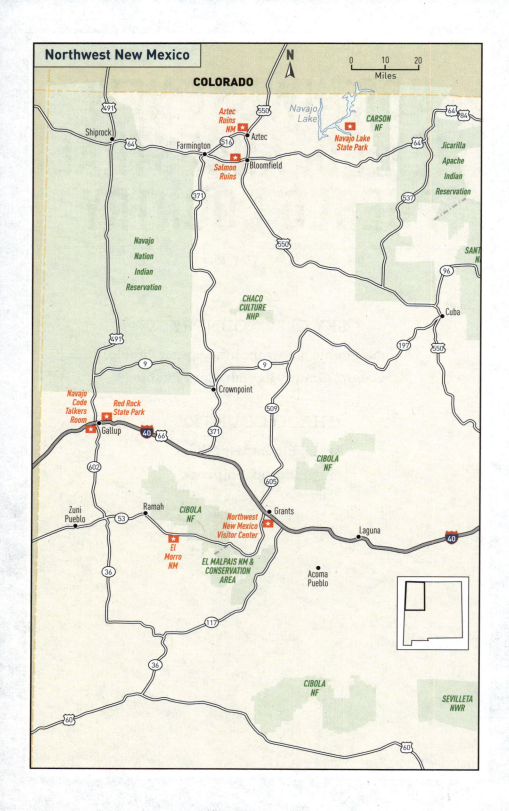

Northwest New Mexico

COLORADO

0   10   20
Miles

N

491

550

Navajo Lake

CARSON NF

64 84

491

Shiprock

64

Farmington

516

Aztec Ruins NM

Aztec

Navajo Lake State Park

64

Jicarilla Apache Indian Reservation

Salmon Ruins

Bloomfield

371

Navajo Nation Indian Reservation

550

537

SANT N

96

CHACO CULTURE NHP

Cuba

9

9

197

550

Crownpoint

509

371

Navajo Code Talkers Room

Red Rock State Park

Gallup

40 66

605

CIBOLA NF

602

Zuni Pueblo

53

Ramah

CIBOLA NF

Northwest New Mexico Visitor Center

Grants

Laguna

40

36

El Morro NM

EL MALPAIS NM & CONSERVATION AREA

Acoma Pueblo

117

36

CIBOLA NF

SEVILLETA NWR

60

60

SKY CITY COUNTRY

Acoma Pueblo, Crownpoint, Laguna Pueblo,
Gallup, Grants, Ramah, Zuni Pueblo

Making a journey to northwest New Mexico is as close as a traveler can get to the mysteries of a civilization that thrived, then vanished, long before Europeans dreamed of setting foot on this continent. The precisely made monumental structures of Chaco Canyon, the restored Great Kiva at Aztec Ruins, and the solstice marker that keeps time as well as a Swiss watch at Salmon Ruins all provoke awe in even the most worldly traveler.

The sight of these magnificent ruins raises more questions than we can answer. Was Chaco Canyon a trading or ceremonial center? A laboratory of ancient astronomy? Or the home of a priestly class? Were its arrow-straight roads, which lead to outliers throughout the Four Corners region, also related to religious traditions? How far did trading extend—to Mesoamerica, to the Andes? Did the inhabitants depart their homes because of drought, illness, or war? The best we can do is to speculate.

Long known as the Anasazi, now referred to as the Ancestral Pueblo, the people who lived here are now believed to be the forbears of contemporary New Mexico Pueblo Indians. Yet in this region one encounters, with the exceptions of Acoma, Laguna, and Zuni, not the Pueblo, but the Navajo, whose reservation extends throughout four states. For those who admire the fine weaving, silver and turquoise jewelry, and sand paintings of the Navajo, there are no better places to see these wares and shop for them than in the trading posts of Gallup and Farmington, or at the monthly Crownpoint Rug Auction.

To savvy fly-fishermen, the San Juan River outside Farmington is a holy grail, which is not to underestimate the attractions of the region for golfers, hikers, cavers, birders, and mountain bikers.

The rich, multilayered history of the exploration of the Southwest is vividly recorded on El Morro, or Inscription Rock, which bears the signs of those who passed by this water source. Petroglyphs, signatures of Spanish conquistadors, of US Calvary, of homesteaders and miners, all tell a centuries-old story. From before the time Coronado passed through in 1540 on his search for the fabled "Seven Cities of Cibola" in his quest for gold and long after, this harsh yet lush high-desert landscape—with its black lava, rich farming land, red buttes, and its resources of wood, coal uranium, natural gas, and oil—has long held out the promise of fortunes to be made.

The name "Cibola" refers to a mythic city. In medieval Europe, a popular legend told of Seven Cities of Antilia located across the Atlantic Ocean. Spanish explorers came here searching for legendary cities, in hopes of discovering the same riches of gold as they had found in the southern hemisphere, among Mayan, Aztec, and Incan cities. In 1539, explorer Cabeza de Vaca first saw Zuni, and his report fueled Coronado's quest. Zuni was believed to be the smallest of the fabled cities.

In this region you can stand at the point where four states meet, cross the Continental Divide, witness the all-night winter ceremonial of Shalako at Zuni Pueblo, and travel long stretches of the Mother Road, Old Route 66. Many of the sights and experiences that make the West the West are found here. Best of all, these experiences can be had on a personal scale. These places remain true to themselves. They are not

CHACO CANYON IS ALWAYS WORTH THE JOURNEY

overwhelmed with or by tourism, but somehow manage to absorb visitors in a comfortable fashion, still moving at their own pace. While ample selections of amenities are available, this is not an area of high-end lodges, upscale boutiques, or fine dining opportunities. Rather, it is a place to chat with old-timers in a local café, watch sunsets flame the sky, bask in the quiet of really wide open spaces, and, if you are lucky, see a mountain lion leap across the road. It is a place where adventure and discovery are still possible.

By making a giant loop, it is possible to travel through Ancestral Pueblo country without covering the same territory twice. However, this country may also be traveled conveniently in two sections: Sky City Country, linked by I-40 and anchored by Acoma Pueblo with Gallup as a base destination; and Chaco Country, linked by US 550 and anchored by Chaco Canyon with Farmington and surrounds as a base.

GUIDANCE **Sky City Travel Center** (505-552-5700), Acomita.

Gallup Convention & Visitors Bureau (505-863-3841), 103 W. Route 66, Gallup.

Gallup/McKinley Country Chamber of Commerce (575-722-2228), 106 W. Route 66, Gallup.

Grants/Cibola County Chamber of Commerce (505-287-4802), 100 N. Iron Avenue, Grants.

Laguna Pueblo (505-552-6654), 22 Capital Road, Laguna Pueblo.

New Mexico Route 66 Association (www.rt66nm.org).

Northwest New Mexico Visitor Center (505-876-2783), 1900 E. Santa Fe Avenue, off I-40 at exit 85, Grants. Open 8–5 MST, 9–6 MDT (summer). This stop is a must-do for trip planning to Chaco, El Morro, El Malpais, and all the area attractions, with an abundance of maps, books, and experience available.

Zuni Tourism (www.zunitourism.com).

GETTING THERE From Albuquerque, take I-40 west 221 miles to Gallup, passing Acoma Pueblo, Laguna Pueblo, and Grants, while following the direction of Route 66.

MEDICAL EMERGENCY **Cibola General Hospital** (505-287-4446), 1016 Roosevelt Avenue, Grants.

Rehobeth McKinley Christian Hospital (575-863-7000), 1901 Redrock Drive, Gallup.

✲ To See

TOWNS AND PUEBLOS **Acoma Pueblo, or Sky City**, is said to be the oldest continuously inhabited community in North America. Acoma people have lived here for 2,000 years. After exiting I-40 at exit 102, 65 miles west of Albuquerque, follow Indian Route 23 south to Sky City Cultural Center. Tours with native tour guides take you by bus to the top of the 357-foot-high mesa, the original village site of 300 adobe structures, and the remarkable San Esteban del Rey Mission Church. Acoma is well-known for fine pottery, which may sometimes be purchased from the makers on the pueblo tour and during feast days. Feast days and traditional observances open to the public are December 24–28, September 2, August 10, and the first or second weekend in February.

Crownpoint is situated 24 miles north of the Thoreau exit off I-40 on NM 371 and is notable for its second Fri. of the month Navajo rug auction. From here, it is about 40 rough miles farther on unpaved NM 57 to the south entrance of Chaco Canyon.

Gallup claims title as "the Indian jewelry capital of the world," with over 100 trading posts. It is the home of the annual Intertribal Ceremonial, held in late July or early August, as well as a noted Route 66 stop, and in its heyday, it was a coal mining and railroading center. The town is a gateway to the Navajo Reservation, a base for exploring Canyon de Chelley and Monument Valley, as well as a trading, shopping, medical, and educational center for the Navajo and Zuni.

ZUNI OLLA MAIDENS IN THE GALLUP INTERTRIBAL CEREMONIAL PARADE

Grants, a Route 66 stop and formerly "the uranium capital of the world" at the base of Mt. Taylor, is a good place to rest en route to Chaco Canyon and Crownpoint Rug Auction.

Laguna Pueblo. Inhabited as early as 3000 BC, this area has been occupied by Mesa Verde migrants since the 1300s. Laguna was named for a lake that no longer exists and was first mentioned in accounts of Coronado's 1540 exploration party. Old Laguna Village is now the ceremonial center of several neighboring villages. Feast days are March 19 and September 19. The stone San Jose de la Laguna Mission Church and Convento is a landmark seen from the north side of I-40 about 35 miles west of Albuquerque.

Ramah, chiefly a Mormon and Navajo town with one small museum, located along NM 53, is the home of Ramah Navajo Weavers Association, and Ramah Lake is 2.5 miles northeast of town. The Ramah Museum, open Fri. 1–4, tells the story of the town.

Zuni Pueblo, 32 miles south of Gallup on NM 53. The first Native American village encountered by Coronado on his search for the Seven Cities of Gold, it is believed Zuni was the inspiration for this conquistador legend. Shalako, the annual all-night winter ceremony held late November or early December, is noted for the dancing of the 10-foot-tall Shalakos representing guiding spirits. Today's Zuni dwellers are known for fine inlay and turquoise needlepoint jewelry, their fetishes carved of semiprecious stones, and, of course, their hand-carved kachina figures. This is the largest of the pueblos, and the people speak their own language, Zuni, unrelated to any Pueblo languages. The restored mission church, Nuestra Señora de Guadalupe de la Candelaria de Halona, originally established 1630–66, has life-size restored murals.

HISTORIC LANDMARKS, PLACES, AND SITES **Continental Divide.** Approximately 170 miles west of Albuquerque on I-40 is the pinnacle of a geological ridge that separates the nation's waterways. East of the Divide all waters flow east to the Atlantic Ocean, while those west of the Divide flow towards the Pacific.

El Morro National Monument (505-783-4226), 42 miles southeast on NM 53 from Grants. Closed Christmas and New Year's Day. Visitor center open daily October 2– DST 9–5; trails open 9–4. Check for summer hours. El Morro is also known as Inscription Rock for its 2,000 inscriptions and prehistoric petroglyphs. In 1640, Francisco Coronado wrote *Paso por aqui* (I passed by here) in the sandstone formation. It is the pool, the reliable water source beneath the huge boulder, that caused travelers to stop here throughout history. There is a paved 0.5-mile loop trail from the visitor center to Inscription Rock and a two-hour round-trip moderate hike to the mesa-top, which features thirteenth- and fourteenth-century pueblo ruins. $3, under age 16 free.

MUSEUMS **A:shiwi A:wan Museum and Heritage Center** (505-782-782-4403) www .ashiwi-museum.org), 02 E. Ojo Caliente Road, Zuni. Open Mon.–Fri. 9–5. Closed during religious ceremonies. The heritage center displays artifacts retrieved when the ancient city of Hawikku was excavated in 1920. The center is located on the site of one of Zuni's first trading posts. Tours, exhibits, and programs about the village and the environment make this a sensible place to begin a visit. Free.

Atchison, Topeka & Santa Fe Railway Depot/Gallup Cultural Center (505-863-4131), 201 E. Route 66, Gallup. Open Mon.–Fri. 10–4. This restored depot contains exhibits and a gift shop, plus the Storyteller Museum and Gallery of the Masters. Indian dances are performed nightly at 7 in summer. Free.

Navajo Code Talkers Room (505-722-2228), 106 W. Route 66, Gallup. Open Mon.– Fri. 8:30–5. During World War II, members of the Navajo Nation volunteered for a special mission. They translated intelligence documents into the Navajo language, a code that the Japanese could never break. Memorabilia and photos commemorate their contributions. Free.

New Mexico Mining Museum (505-287-4802), 100 N. Iron Avenue, Grants. Open Mon.–Sat. 9–4. Visit the world's only underground uranium mining museum, learn about rocks of the region, and ride "the cage" down an actual mineshaft. $3 adults, $2 seniors and children.

Rex Museum (505-863-1363), 300 W. Route 66, Gallup. Open Mon.–Fri. 8–3. Housed in a century-old stone building, the former home of the Rex Hotel, the museum displays memorabilia and history of this railroad and coal mining community. $12 adults, $5 children.

Sky City Cultural Center and Haak'u Museum (505-552-7861). Mesa tours are available daily on the hour May–September 8–6 (last tour 5 PM) and October–April 8–4:30. Please call ahead to confirm hours. The cultural center displays pottery, jewelry, history, and significant individuals of Acoma. Cultural center free. Tours $25 adults, $22 seniors, $17 children, $15 still camera permit.

NATURAL WONDERS **Bandera Volcano and Ice Cave** (505-783-4303), 25 miles southwest of Grants off NM 53. Open daily from 8 AM until one hour before sunset. Closed November 1–March 1. The temperature in the ice cave is 31 degrees Fahrenheit year-round, kept that way by 20-foot-thick ice on the cave floor. Bandera is the largest of twenty-nine extinct volcanoes in the region. It is a 40-minute hike to the volcano, and a 20-minute hike into the ice cave. Both are reasonably easy, but the ice cave involves some intense stair climbing. There is an old-time trading post on the premises. $12 adults and teens, 10 percent off for seniors and military, $6 ages 6–12.

La Ventana Natural Arch (www.explorenm.com/hikes/LaVentana/). Access from NM 117. *La ventana* means "the window," and that is exactly what this 165-foot-wide natural golden sandstone arch appears to be, a window onto the sky. Free.

SCENIC DRIVES **Ancient Way** (byways.org/explore/states/NM), NM 53 as it parallels the ancient trade route between Acoma and Zuni pueblos and the route originally taken by Coronado. Take exit 81 off I-40 for a 73-mile scenic drive to Zuni Pueblo that leads en route to El Morro, or Inscription Rock. En route, pass the villages of San Rafael, San Mateo, and Cebolleta.

Old Route 66. Driving east on I-40 between Albuquerque and Gallup affords many opportunities to get off the interstate and hop onto original stretches of Route 66, the Mother Road, as author John Steinbeck named it, with several Route 66 markers, such as the Rio Puerco Bridge, in evidence. The road from Chicago to Los Angeles was opened in 1926, then it was realigned in 1937 and subsequently made famous by songs and television shows that celebrated it as a road of freedom and discovery for postwar America.

Zuni Mountain Historic Auto Tour. From Santa Fe Avenue in Grants, go west to NM 53, cross I-40, and go right on Zuni Canyon Road. This tour leads 60 miles as it winds through Zuni Canyon to Agua Fria Valley to the historic town of Sawyer, and loops back to Grants via Bluewater Lake. It follows Forest Service dirt roads to trace the history of logging and railroading in Cibola National Forest with old railroad grades, town sites, and trestle remnants en route.

✴ To Do

BICYCLING For trail maps and information on area races, call 800-448-1240.

Aztec Mountain Biking and Hiking Trails (505-334-9511) includes three main trails: Aztec Trails, Mountain View Trails, and Alien Run. The system starts near the city

WILDER PLACES

Angel Peak Recreation Area (505-564-7600), 30 miles southeast of Farmington on US 550. Take the 6-mile gravel road northeast into the site. No water or services, but accessible camping and picnic areas are available, as are hiking trails and wildlife viewing. Angel Peak is a striking 40-million-year-old, 7,000-foot-high geologic formation crowning 10,000 acres of rugged wilderness in ancient seabed. Fossils and petrified wood are visible in these badlands formations. An amazing perspective on the history of the planet. This area is not recommended for RVs. Free.

Bisti Badlands/De-Na-Zin Wilderness (505-599-8900 or 505-827-4400); www.blm.gov/nm/st/en/prog/wilderness/bisti.html). Roughly 50 miles south of Farmington off NM 371, 2 miles down gravel road #7297. Remote, 42,000 acres administered by the BLM. This wind-sculpted shale and sandstone formation with its fantastic, colorful landforms might well be a journey to the moon. The best formations may be reached by hiking 2 miles east from parking area. Motorized vehicles not permitted. Primitive camping is possible, but no services. Best to visit late spring or fall. Free.

Cabezon Peak (505-761-8700; www.blm.gov/nm/st/en/prog/recreation/rio_puerco/cabezon_peak.html). Go west on US 550 onto CR 279, approximately 20 miles northwest of San Ysidro. Continue 12 miles past village of San Luis to Cabezon turnoff onto BLM Road 1114. The pavement ends just beyond San Luis. At intersection of CR 279 and BLM Road 1114, pass the ghost town of Cabezon. Follow 1114 for 2.9 miles to a dirt road that leads to a trailhead. Check road conditions before attempting this journey. *Cabezon* translates as "big head," and it is the most prominent volcanic neck in the Mt. Taylor lava fields, rising 8,000 feet above sea level. This is considered a sacred site by Pueblo and Navajo peoples. It is not recommended for children or pets. The trail, only for the fit and the adept, involves some Class 3 climbing and is accessible year-round, making it a popular climb for the well-prepared and the experienced. Caution: Rattlesnakes are active in warmer weather. Primitive recreation. Camping for 14 days or less is okay. Free.

Mount Taylor (5o5-346-3900). An 11,301-foot-high volcano visible from Albuquerque, Mount Taylor is a sacred site known as Turquoise Mountain in Navajo culture and within Cibola National Forest. The Mt. Taylor Quadrathlon is a grueling 44-mile race held every Presidents' Day weekend, starting from downtown Grants to the summit and back. The race includes biking, running, skiing, and snowshoeing. Trail 77 is a moderate 6-mile round-trip hike near the top—with phenomenal views. Go north on 1st Street in Grants to NM 547 (Lobo Canyon Road) for 13 miles, right on FR 193 for 5 miles to trailhead.

Ojito Wilderness (575-761-8700; www.blm.gov/nm/st/en/prog/wilderness/ojito.html). From Albuquerque, go north on I-25 for 16 miles, then exit on US 550 at second Bernalillo exit. Go 20 miles northwest toward Cuba on US 550. Two miles before San Ysidro, turn left onto

limits and leads to Hart Canyon, the site of the alleged 1948 UFO crash. Aztec offers almost 30 miles of trails.

BOATING See the state parks under *Green Space*.

FISHING **Ramah Lake** (no phone), 2.5 miles northeast of Ramah. Fishing, boating, and picnicking.

San Juan River/Quality Waters (505-632-2194; www.sanjuanriver.com/River Upper.htm), 26 miles northeast of Aztec off NM 173 and NM 511. Year-round fishing

Cabezon Road (CR 906), follow the left fork 10 miles to the Ojito Wilderness sign. This remote, austere, quiet place is a roadless area with no facilities, no services, and no water. The 11,000 acres are full of steep canyons and rugged cliffs to challenge experienced hikers. Horseback riding and primitive camping are allowed in this increasingly popular exploration site. You might see fossils, petroglyphs, petrified trees, and even seashells. Free.

Wild Spirit Wolf Sanctuary (505-775-3032; wildspiritwolfsanctuary.org), 378 Candy Kitchen Road, Ramah. Go 2 miles past El Morro on NM 53 (approximately 50 miles southeast of Grants), left on BIA 125 for 8 miles, right on BIA 120 for 4 miles; sanctuary on left. Open Tues.–Sun. Closed Mondays. Guided tours at 11, 12:30, 2, 3:30. Meet wolf-dogs and wolf captives born in the Zuni Mountains, as well as wolf and wolf-dog rescues. $7 adults, $6 seniors, $4 children, under age 7 free. $15 camping. $10 guided tour.

BISTI BADLANDS SUGGESTS A REMOTE MOONSCAPE

in 12 miles of open water. Sought-after trophy trout fly-fishing in the waters west of Navajo Lake Dam brings fishermen to the San Juan to catch the big ones. But those big ones swimming around your waders are wily, as they have been caught and released so many times. Enormous rainbow trout that feed well makes this one of America's top 10 trout fishing waters. A section of the river for 6 miles south of the dam flows through a magical, scenic sandstone canyon. There are four wheelchair-accessible fishing piers along the river and an easy hiking trail that runs for 1.5 miles along the north side of the San Juan River. Quality waters have special restrictions. Free.

HIKING **Pyramid Rock**, in Red Rock Park. At the summit, one can see 50 miles on a clear day. The 3-mile round-trip takes you through amazing rock formations, with a summit elevation of 7,487 feet. Church Rock Trail begins at Outlaw Trading Post parking lot, with great views of Church Rock Spires. From Gallup, go 6 miles east on Route 66/NM 118. Turn north onto NM 566 for 0.5 mile. Turn left into Red Rock Park, follow the signs. Check with the visitor center for maps.

Zuni-Acoma Trail in El Malpais National Monument traverses the Continental Divide, which stretches from Canada to the southern border of the United States. You need strong shoes to hike from cairn to cairn across the lava of this ancient trade route, a segment of an old Indian trail connecting Acoma and Zuni pueblos. Bring lots of water for this lifetime hike. It will take 5 or 6 hours and is quite strenuous, ranging from easy to moderate to difficult.

MOUNTAIN BIKING **Farmington Lake** has many trails through all types of terrain that can be accessed off the Road Apple Trail.

Farmington Trails (farmingtonnm.org/choose-your-journey/outdoor-adventures /hiking/) include **Road Apple Trail**, behind San Juan College, with sandy washes and arroyos, hilly jumps, and steep climbs; **Kinsey's Ridge**, at the end of Foothills Drive, with 6 miles of rolling hills and great views; and **Pinon Mesa**, 3 miles north of Main Street on NM 170, with a trailhead marked by a large cottonwood on the west side of the highway.

High Desert Trail System. A mountain bike trail on the high mesas northwest of Gallup has a stacked loop trail with trailheads near Gamerco and Mentmore, former coal mines. To get to Gamerco, go 2 miles north of I-40 on US 491, and left at Chino Loop traffic signal; the trailhead is on the left just after the curve. The trail heads west for 2.25 miles around the mesa top with expansive viewpoints. Or turn right at Six Flags, continuing on to Second Mesa. The third mesa is higher to the south. Challenging.

See **Zuni Mountain Historic Auto Tour** under *To See*, "Scenic Drives." Many of these old logging roads along the way are suitable for mountain biking.

SNOW SPORTS Best to check out opportunities at nearby Purgatory Resort (www .purgatoryresort.com/) and **Wolf Creek Ski Area** (wolfcreekski.com/).

WINERIES **Wines of the San Juan Tasting Room** (505-632-0879), 689 Oso Ride Route, Grants. Open Mon. and Wed.–Sat. 10–6, Sun. 2–6. Closed Tuesdays. Find this rustic tasting room 6 miles below Navajo Lake State Park on NM 511 at Turley. The San Juan region is the ideal microclimate to produce these rich, fruity wines.

✳ Lodging

BED & BREAKFASTS, INNS, AND MOTELS ♿ **Cimarron Rose, Zuni Mountain Bed & Breakfast** (800-856-5776; www.cimarronrose.com), 689 Oso Ridge Road, 30 miles southwest of Grants on NM 53. To preserve your solitude and privacy, breakfast is delivered to your room. Local artists display their wares for sale in this "green" retreat located on the Great Divide. A Zuni Mountain Inn. Each of the three rooms has its own bath. $195–210.

El Rancho Hotel (505-863-9311), 1000 E. Route 66, Gallup. One block south of I-40 at exit 22. With twenty-four rooms, each named for a movie star, and the mezzanine decorated with black-and-white photos of all the stars that stayed here while shooting movies, this 1937 hotel is the epitome of Hollywood gone western nostalgia. The hot pink neon beckons you to stop, and the pool, lounge, and quite decent restaurant serving breakfast, lunch, and dinner make this the top choice for a Gallup stay. Most of the rooms are on the small side; you can stay, however, for a not unreasonable price, in the Presidential Suite (a.k.a. the Ronald Reagan Room). The open lobby with curving wooden staircases on either side, decorated in Navajo rugs and rustic western furnishings, with a floor-to-ceiling stone fireplace, is one of the most welcoming sights along the road. $75–120.

The Inn at Halona (505-782-4547; www.halona.com), 23 Pie Mesa Road, Zuni. Located in the middle Zuni Pueblo in the historic 1940 home of trader Bernard J. Vanden Wagen and operated by his granddaughter, Elaine, this eight-room bed & breakfast imparts a sense of a faraway adventure, in comfort. Several of the rooms are graced with comfortably furnished private patios. Breakfast is included. $85.

RANCHES AND LODGES **Apache Canyon Ranch B&B Country Inn** (505-377-7925), 4 Canyon Drive, Laguna. Bordered by Indian lands, not far from Old Route 66, the ranch's views and the peace and quiet are unmatched. It's somewhat surprising to find an upscale lodging all the way out here, but there you are. The inn sits on several acres, and the main quarters has rooms and courtyards, a grand parlor for tea, a six-hole putting green, and a guest cottage with a whirlpool tub and kiva fireplace. Of course, the breakfast is gourmet quality, and dinner, should you choose to remain on the premises rather than zip over to the Route 66 Casino, may be prepared on request. $99–$250.

 Z Lazy B Mountain Retreat (888-488-5600), Fort Wingate. Open year-round, weather permitting. The descendant of the original homesteaders on this land now lives here with her husband, and together they raise horses in this somewhat desolate and wild Zuni Mountain area that was formerly a busy logging territory. There are five comfortably and completely furnished log cabins, nothing shabby here, each sleeping eight to ten people, each with kitchen, bath, lounging, and private areas, and guests may choose to have the staff cook for them or prepare their own meals. A hearty meat and potatoes freshly cooked breakfast is included, at any rate. The lodge is also known for horseback riding, offering trail, pony, and wagon rides May–October. And they will cook all meals for you, on request. $120 night double occupancy, $15 each extra person.

CABINS AND CAMPING **El Morro RV Park & Cabins & Ancient Way Café** (505-783-4612), 4018 NM 53, Ramah. Open year-round. Just down the way from El Morro National Monument are cozy cabins in the pines at the base of San Lorenzo Mesa with sleeping accommodations for four, and full hookup RV sites in a pet-friendly place with free Wi-Fi. The friendly café serves home-cooked breakfast, lunch, and dinner and is a gathering place where locals mingle with visitors for plenty of storytelling. The food is healthy, delicious, and sometimes gourmet. Perfection! $84–$99 cabin; $15 tent site.

❋ Where to Eat

DINING OUT **Don Diego's Restaurant and Lounge** (505-722-5517), 801 W. Route 66, Gallup. Open Mon.–Sat. 8–9. Closed Sundays. B, L, D. Nightlife, such as it is, may be found here, along with pretty tasty New Mexican food and good hot red chile. Inexpensive.

EATING OUT **Eagle Cafe** (505-863-2233), 220 W. Route 66, Gallup. Open Mon.–Sat. 9–5. Closed Sundays. B, L, D. You can still hear the trains rolling in on the tracks across Old 66. Now a for-real Mexican restaurant. Inexpensive.

 Earl's Family Restaurant (505-863-4201), 1400 E. Route 66, Gallup.

Open daily. B, L, D. Rightly called "Gallup's living room," this is the place to eat reasonably priced green-chile-smothered enchiladas, but if you're not accustomed to the local cuisine, plenty of real mashed potatoes and gravy are served with popular daily specials of fried chicken and meat loaf. Shop while you eat, as vendors circulate showing off their wares. If you don't care to be bothered, you can get a sign indicating so from the management. If you have time for only one meal in Gallup, by all means eat at this 40-year-old family restaurant. Inexpensive.

🍴 **Virgie's Restaurant & Lounge** (505-863-4845), 2720 W. Route 66, Gallup. Closed Sundays. Open Mon.–Sat. 7 AM–9 PM. B, L, D. In the glow of Virgie's neon, feast on enchiladas in true Old 66 splendor. Virgie's is at least as much a roadside institution as it is a restaurant serving steaks and Mexican food.

Virgie's beef stew and the chico steak smothered in green chile and cheese are favorites. Or go for the crème de la crème, the crispy chicken taquitos. This fine family restaurant started serving its homemade pie around 1960. Love Virgie's! Inexpensive.

Ancient Way Cafe (505-783-4612), 4018 Ice Cave Road/Highway 53, El Morro. Open daily 9–5 daily. B, L, D. Exceptional food where you least expect to find it in this wonderful roadside cafe. Varied menu of healthy options, dinner specials. Salads, omelets, barbecue, pan-fried trout, creative entrees. Inexpensive.

✳ Entertainment

Summer Theater Series in Lions Wilderness Amphitheater (877-599-1148; www.fmtn.org/sandstone). June 20–August 2. Repertory Theater under the stars in a

VIRGIE'S RESTAURANT & LOUNGE SERVES SOME OF THE MOST AUTHENTIC AND FLAVORFUL NEW MEXICAN FOOD IN THE STATE

natural golden sandstone arena. A most pleasant venue for light and family-oriented productions. $10 adults, $7 seniors, $5 children.

Totah Theater (505-327-4145), 315 W. Main, Farmington. A renovated 1948 movie house downtown. The facility books performances by local theater groups, such as Theatre Ensemble and traveling performers. Movies, music, smorgasbord of events.

✳ Selective Shopping

Old School Gallery (505-369-4047), 53 NM 46. Open Thurs.–Sun. 11–5. An enterprise of the El Morro Area Arts Council, here you can find current exhibits and work of local artists in diverse media for sale. Lectures, workshops, cook-offs, tarot classes, yoga, Zumba, and special events and celebrations also go on at this gallery. A busy schedule. Call for exact directions and schedule of events.

Richardson's Trading Co. (505-722-4762), 222 W. Route 66, Gallup. Open Mon.–Sat. 9–5. The selection of the best turquoise, coral, and silver Navajo and Zuni jewelry; Navajo rugs; sand paintings; pottery; and old pawn fills every nook and cranny of this creaky trading post established in 1913. As much a museum as a store. The staff is patient and knowledgeable, and Richardson's is as reliable a place (with fair prices) to make a purchase as you can find. There are treasures here at all price levels. Be prepared to take your time—it's difficult to choose!

RICHARDSON'S TRADING POST HOSTS NAVAJO WEAVING DEMONSTRATIONS

Perry Nunn Trading Company (505-863-5249), 1710 S. 2nd Street, Gallup. Fabulous array of native work arranged by artist. Price range to accommodate all budgets. Reliable. Full disclosure: I collect silver work by Alex Sanchez here. The store itself is a work of art.

Tanner's Indian Arts (5905-863-6017), 237 W. Coal Street. By appointment only. Fourth generation trader is a must-stop of serious collectors and those who would aspire to become so.

CHACO COUNTRY

Aztec, Bloomfield, Cuba, Farmington, Shiprock

Two activities dominate this region: visiting monumental ancient ruins and trying to land the big trout on the San Juan River. If your senses are truly open, you might catch a faint drum beat or a whiff of fry bread on the wind. There is a sense of being in uncharted territory, almost at the end of the world, which is highlighted in places like no other such as the Bisti Badlands or the area around Shiprock. The place is haunting and unforgettable.

GUIDANCE **Aztec Chamber of Commerce & Tourist Center** (505-334-9551; www .aztecchamber.com), 201 W. Chaco, Aztec.

Bloomfield Chamber of Commerce (505-632-0880; www.bloomfieldchamber.info/ index.php/event-calendar), 224 W. Broadway Avenue, Bloomfield.

Cuba Area Chamber of Commerce (575-289-3514), 14 Martinez Drive, Cuba.

Farmington Convention and Visitors Bureau (505-326-7602; www.farmingtonnm .org), 3041 E. Main Street, Farmington.

Navajo Nation Tourism (928-810-8501; www.discovernavajo.com), P.O. Box 663, Window Rock, Arizona.

Northwest New Mexico Visitor Center (505-876-2783), 1900 E. Santa Fe, Grants. Open daily 9–6 MDT, 8–5 MST.

MEDICAL EMERGENCY San Juan Regional Medical Center (505-609-2000), 801 W. Maple Street, Farmington.

GETTING THERE From Albuquerque, go 180 miles northwest on I-25 north to Bernalillo, then US 550 to Bloomfield, then US 64 to Farmington. Along the way pass Cuba, the road to Chaco Canyon, Bloomfield, and the Salmon Ruins.

✳ To See

TOWNS AND PUEBLOS **Aztec** is 14 miles northeast of Farmington on US 550. Supporting the early belief that the nearby Ancestral Pueblo ruins were of Aztec origin, the town's founders in 1890 named their village for them. Aztec maintains a sense of civic pride in its homesteading past. Main Street Historic District is charming and well preserved, as are the Victorian residences, which form the core of the town.

Bloomfield. Located on the San Juan River at the junction of US 550 and US 64, 11 miles east of Farmington, this oil and gas center is a convenient place to make a quick stop for gas and groceries.

Cuba is 102 miles southeast of Farmington on US 550. This little town was not named for the Caribbean country by veterans of the Spanish-American War, as is sometimes said. Rather, the name refers to a geographical feature and means "sink," or "draw" in Spanish. Several cafés and gas stations cater to travelers. The ranger station on the south end of town offers permits and information about hiking, camping, cross-country skiing, and fishing in the nearby Santa Fe National Forest (505-289-0338; P.O. Box 130, Cuba).

Farmington is 180 miles northwest of Albuquerque on US 550. Totah, "among the rivers," is the Navajo name for this gateway city where three rivers—the Animas, La Plata, and San Juan—come together. But English-speaking settlers named it for its fine agricultural produce, recognizing it as a "farming-town." The economy has gone boom and bust with the oil, gas, and uranium industries for the past 60 years, and today there are two Farmingtons—the preserved and downtown, with its trading posts, cafés, and antiques shops, and the "parallel universe" of strip malls and shopping centers. In addition to making a good base for exploring the area, Farmington serves as the entertainment, shopping, and recreational center of the region, with summer theater, museums, an aquatic center, number-one-rated municipal golf course, and plenty of family activities.

Shiprock is 29 miles west of Farmington on US 64. Taking its name from its unforgettable landmark, the imposing "rock with wings," Shiprock is mainly a center of Navajo tribal business and services. The annual Northern Navajo Fair, held each fall, is an exceptional gathering of rugs, rodeo, and tradition.

MUSEUMS ✦ **Aztec Museum and Pioneer Village** (505-334-9829), 125 N. Main Avenue, Aztec. Open April–September 10–5; October–May 10–4. Closed Sundays. Here, find a wealth of pioneer Americana, plus oilfield, military, and farm equipment exhibits. $3 adults, $1 children ages 12–17, age 11 and under free.

✦& **E-3 Children's Museum & Science Center** (505-599-1425), 302 N. Orchard, Farmington. Open Tues.–Sat. noon–5. Closed Mondays. The kids will love the hands-on, science-related, and exploration exhibits found here. Free.

Farmington Museum & Gateway Center (505-599-1174), 3041 E. Main, Farmington. Open Mon.–Sat. 8–5. Closed Sundays. Maps and trip planning; exhibits related to the history of the West and the Farmington area. Free.

✦& **Riverside Nature Center** (505-599-1422), off Browning Parkway in Animas Park, Farmington. Open Tues.–Sat. 10–6. Tuesday morning bird-watching. Wetlands! Wildlife viewing; butterfly walks; hands-on exhibits of tracks, bones and seeds; xeriscape gardens; herb garden; history walks; and stargazing. Free.

NATURAL WONDERS **Four Corners Monument** (928-871-6647; www.navajonation parks.org), 30 miles northwest of Shiprock off US 64 and US 160, Teec Nos Pas. Open daily October–May 7–5, June–September 7–7. Erected in 1912, the Four Corners Monument is the only place in the United States where four states intersect: Arizona, New Mexico, Utah, and Colorado. You will find an Indian marketplace with handmade crafts as well. $5.

Shiprock Pinnacle (no phone; www.discovernavajo.com), 10 miles southwest of Shiprock off US 491. This signature western landmark, a mass of igneous rock flanked by walls of solidified lava, was given its apt name by early area settlers. Known to the Navajo as "rock with wings," this volcanic rock formation rises 1,700 feet above the desert floor. Because it is a sacred site to the Dine, or Navajo, only viewing is permitted. There is no access.

✳ To Do

GOLF **Pinon Hills** (505-326-6066), 2101 Sunrise Parkway, Farmington. Open year-round, weather permitting. This Ken Dye–designed course is rated by a Golf Digest

SHIPROCK, THE "ROCK WITH WINGS," IS A NAVAJO SACRED SITE

readers' poll as "America's best golf bargain . . . with large terraced greens, sculptured serpentine fairways and challenging sand bunkers. #1 municipal golf course in the nation." Special rates are available for those who live within a hundred-mile radius. $35–49.

SWIMMING 🏊 **Farmington Aquatic Center** (505-999-1067), 1151 Sullivan, Farmington. Call for hours. This is a full-fledged 150-foot Olympic pool, open year-round, with a 150-foot double loop water slide. Rates vary; $2.50 lap swims.

✳ Green Space

Bluewater Lake State Park (505-876-2391), 30 Bluewater State Park Road, Prewitt, is a lovely oasis of rolling hills encircling a 7-mile lake stocked with trout and catfish year-round. Boating, wildlife watching, camping, and hiking are popular pastimes here, as well as ice fishing, waterskiing, swimming, and hiking. $6 day use; $10–18 camping.

 Navajo Lake State Park (505-632-2278; www.nmstateparks.com or www.emnrd .state.nm.us/nmparks), 1448 NM 511 #1, Navajo Dam, 45 miles east of Farmington on NM 511. Boat slips, fishing and boating supplies, and houseboat and ski boat rentals supplement this year-round boating opportunity on the 15,590-surface-acre lake. In addition, find three recreation areas with fishing and camping, and directly below the dam is the famous San Juan River fishing area. Here see blue herons, bald and golden eagles, red-tailed hawks, a variety of ducks, and Canada geese. Altogether, there are 150 miles of shoreline fed by the San Juan, Pine, and Piedra rivers. Accessible. Seasonal closures. $5 day use; $8–14 camping.

 Red Rock State Park (505-722-3839), 7 miles east of Gallup, exit 31 north of I-40, off NM 118. A surprisingly interesting, tucked-away area of history may be found here in the Heritage Canyon display at the visitor center. High, wind-sculpted red sandstone formations frame this 640-acre park that is the site of the Gallup Intertribal Ceremonial on three sides. From the parking area, a hiking trails lead to views of Pyramid Rock and the spires of Church Rock. There's a welcome mat out for horses at the Horse Park. $6 day use; $10–18 camping.

River Corridor (505-326-7602) within Riverside Park, is 5 miles of multipurpose trails accessed off Browning Parkway south of Animas River, and at Scott Avenue and San Juan Boulevard, behind the motels; **Woodland Trails**, found here, make excellent jogging and bicycling paths, with picnic areas with grills along the way.

✐ **Riverside Park** (505-326-7602), on the Animas River outside Farmington at US 550 and NM 574, 500 S. Light Plant Road, Aztec. There's excellent bird-watching year-round with wintering bald eagles fishing the Animas River, one of the last undimmed rivers in the West, and historical and wildlife interpretative signs lend depth to the experience.

WILDLIFE REFUGES **B-Square Ranch** (505-325-4275), 3901 Bloomfield Highway, 1 mile east of Farmington on US 64. Go right. The 12,000-acre Bolack Ranch is a private wildlife preserve, an experimental farm, and a working farm and ranch. Two museums feature farm machinery, wildlife, and generating equipment. Tours by appointment.

✱ Lodging

BED & BREAKFASTS, INNS, AND MOTELS **Casa Blanca Inn & Suites** (505-327-6503; casablancanm.com, 505 E. La Plata Street, Farmington. This gracious, red-tiled Mediterranean-style home high on a bluff in town is the ideal spot for either the visitor or business traveler. It's quiet the way rich people might be quiet, and the gardens are superb. When you taste the rich breakfasts of crêpes Benedict, Belgian waffles with fresh raspberry sauce, or orange almond French toast, you might wish you could stay longer. And long term rentals are available. A tasteful base for your Four Corners explorations. $139–269.

Kokopelli's Cave Bed & Breakfast (505-326-2461), 5800 Hogan Avenue, Farmington. Stay in a plush-carpeted, man-made cave inspired by the Cliff Dwellings at nearby Mesa Verde. Carved into 65-million-year-old sandstone, this single lodging is located 70 feet below the surface on a west-facing vertical cliff face granting you a 360-degree view of the Four Corners' outstanding geologic features. The bedroom balcony overlooks

La Plata River Valley 250 feet below. What a sunset! Imagine, a waterfall-filled hot tub. Meals are not served, but the refrigerator is stocked and dinner may be catered. This is an experience that can highlight your cocktail party talk for years to come! $269.

Silver River Adobe Inn B&B (800-382-9251 or 505-325-8219; www.silveradobe.com), 3151 W. Main Street, Farmington. Rustic yet elegant, the B&B perches on a sandstone cliff looking over the confluence of the San Juan and the La Plata rivers. There's a nature reserve with hiking paths, so good birding and grandmother cottonwoods are part of your stay. Enjoy the library and salon-style breakfast. You couldn't ask for a more serene getaway. The three rooms each have a private bath and entrance. In-house massage available. $115–175.

CABINS AND CAMPING 🐾 **Abe's Motel & Fly Shop** (505-632-2194), 1791 NM #173, Navajo Dam. Open daily year-round, 7–7. Abe's, a landmark since 1958, is the fisherman's mecca on the San Juan. Over time, the fly shop has added RV parking and full hookups, a restaurant and lounge, grocery store, gas station, and

ANCIENT RUINS

Aztec Ruins National Monument (575-334-6174, ext. 230; www.nps/gov/azru), 84 CR 2900, Aztec. Ruins Road, 0.75 mile north of NM 516. Open Memorial Day–Labor Day 8–6; remainder of year 8–5. Closed Thanksgiving, Christmas, New Year's Day. These dwellings, dating to 900 AD and abandoned by 1300 AD, were inhabited as a Chaco outlier for 200 years. The inhabitants were related to the Mesa Verde as well as Chacoan peoples. A 700-yard paved trail winds through the West Ruin, passing through several rooms with intact original roofs. The centerpiece is the reconstructed Great Kiva, the only one in the United States. $5 adults, under age 15 free (good for seven days).

Chaco Culture National Historical Park (505-786-7014, ext. 221; www.nps.gov/chcu), Nageezi. The best access is off US 550 from the north at Nageezi, via County Road 7900. Or take Thoreau exit off I-40 for 25 miles to Crownpoint; 3 miles farther, turn east on Indian Highway 9. Continue to Pueblo Pintado. Go north on NM 46 to CR 7900/7950 to reach the visitor center. Visitor center open daily 8–5. Closed major holidays. Park open daily 7 AM–sunset. Four-wheel drive is a necessity in difficult weather conditions. A word of caution: Call the ranger number above if in doubt. Both dirt roads are slow, rutted, and dangerously slippery when wet or icy. That said, a visit to this ancient trade and ceremonial center that linked over 100 communities in the Four Corners area is a must. There are no services, but there is a campground, and it is possible to make the moderate hike to the top of mesas where the entire complex of ruins that were deserted by 1300 may be viewed. A 9-mile self-guided paved road offers a tour of five major ruins, including massive great houses with hundreds of rooms. The Chacoan culture is believed to be the predecessor of today's Pueblo Indians. While formerly known as "Anasazi," the preferred term is "Ancestral Pueblo."

Just a few of the mysteries involve how these ancient people created their remarkable astronomical alignments, their masonry buildings, and their arrow-straight outliers—as the roads visible from the air leading to related settlements throughout the Four Corners region are known. Was this a dwelling place, or a spiritual congregational hall, or trade center? We still do not know. $20 per vehicle (good for seven days); $10 per individual (good seven days); $15 camping.

boat storage facilities. Most rooms have two double beds and kitchenette, but it is easier to bring your own utensils. The motel rooms feel more like rustic cabins, but they are clean and within walking distance of the river. El Pescador Restaurant, which serves Mexican and American food, frees you from cooking. The fly shop is the place for all your needs on the river, and it's where you can book guided tours with Born 'n Raised on the San Juan. Pets allowed. Motel $59–79; RV $18.95.

Cottonwood–Navajo Lake State Park Pine Site and Main Campground. See *Green Space*.

Ruins Road RV Park (505-334-3160), 312 Ruins Road, Aztec. This completely pleasant campground quite close to the Aztec Ruins and the Animas River offers remote tent sites as well as fifty-three RV hookups. You will do well here. $10 tent; $25 hookup for two.

✳ Where to Eat

EATING OUT **Boon's Family Thai BBQ** (505-325-5556), 321 W. Main Street, Farmington. Open daily. L, D. Craving authentic green curry? Believe it or not, you will be impressed by this pad thai. Full Thai menu. Inexpensive.

Dad's Diner (505-564-2516), 4395 Largo Street, Farmington. Open daily. B, L, D. A local, family-run place that

Salmon Ruins/Heritage Park, Archaeological Research Center and Library (505-632-2013; www.salmonruins.com), 10 miles east of Farmington on US 64. Open Mon.–Fri. 8–5, Sat. 9–5, Sun. noon–5. Closed major holidays. An eleventh-century pueblo built in Chacoan style, plus pioneer homestead. Ancestral Puebloan pottery, jewelry, tools, and hunting equipment are on display. Customized tours with professional archaeologists available. $4 adults, $3 seniors, $1 children ages 6–16.

AZTEC RUINS NATIONAL MONUMENT

serves decent milk shakes and French dip sandwiches. It looks just like a real, old-time gleaming silver diner. It is a fun place to hang out, and all you "diner experience" enthusiasts won't be disappointed. Breakfast served all day. Inexpensive.

Hiway Grill (505-334-6533), 401 NE Aztec Boulevard, Aztec. Open Mon.–Sat. B, L, D. Closed Sundays. Cute 1950s–'60s cruising theme for a restaurant and bar serving American fare of burgers, salads, and the like. The food is a standard, nothing adventurous, and a bit bland—don't expect anything but iceberg lettuce in your salad. Homemade soup. Reasonable family dining option. Live entertainment in the bar. Inexpensive.

St. Clair Winery & Bistro (505-325-0711), 5150 E. Main Street, Farmington. French country cooking, delightful wines, live jazz Thurs.–Sat. A casual, upscale dining spot was just the ticket for Farmington. Moderate.

Spare Rib BBQ Company (505-325-4800), 1700 E. Main Street, Farmington. Open Tues.–Sat. L, D. Closed Mondays. Order at the counter delicious hickory-smoked beef, ribs, sausage, chicken, homemade coleslaw, and cobbler. It's all served on picnic tables covered in red-checked cloths. You can be happy here. Very happy. Inexpensive.

Three Rivers Brewery Block (505-324-0187), 101 E. Main, Farmington. Open Mon.–Sat. L, D. Closed Sundays. A

ABE'S FLY SHOP IS A MUST-DO WHEN FISHING THE SAN JUAN RIVER

friendly family hangout serving micro-brews, homemade sodas, with a huge menu, kid's menu, and play area. Located in a 1912 building that housed the first newspaper in town. The original restaurant has expanded to the entire block and includes a tap room, game room, and pizzeria. Investigate which atmosphere you prefer before you are seated. Plenty of good cooking goes on here, resulting in soups and big salads, and you can't go wrong with the burger that made the brewery famous. It's a great place to cool off with a root beer float, made with house root beer, and the Friday night specials, such as crab boil, are a good deal. Inexpensive.

✳ Special Events

Monthly: **Crownpoint Rug Auction** (505-786-2130), newcrownpointrugauction@gmail.com. P.O. Box 454, Crownpoint. Purchase Navajo rugs directly from the makers.

March: **The Aztec UFO Conference** (505-334-7657; www.aztecufo.com) is held annually to investigate the reported UFO crash in Hart Canyon, 12 miles

outside Aztec, and is hosted by Friends of the Aztec Public Library.

June: **Aztec Fiesta Days** (www.aztecchamber.org). During the first weekend in June, this "All-American City" bids summer welcome with a parade, crafts, a carnival, and the burning of Old Man Gloom.

August: **Connie Mack World Series** (conniemackworldseries@gmail.com), Rickett's Park, Farmington. August 4–11. Teams from the United States and Puerto Rico play in front of pro scouts and college officials at this world amateur baseball event. **Gallup Intertribal Ceremonial** (505-863-3896; gallupceremonial.net). Parade down Old Route 66, Gallup; Red Rock State Park All-Indian Rodeo; indoor and outdoor marketplace; contest powwow; ceremonial Indian dances; native foods. An enormous "gathering of nations" dating back over 80 years—not to be missed!

September: **Totah Festival Indian Market & Powwow** (505-599-1173), Farmington Civic Center, 200 W. Arrington. First weekend. Annual American Indian fine arts show, rug auction, and powwow.

October: **Northern Navajo Nation Shiprock Navajo Fair** (505-368-4305), Shiprock Fairgrounds, Shiprock. Parade, fair, arts, crafts, rodeo, powwow, traditional food, song and dance, "the oldest and most traditional" Navajo fair.

December: **San Juan College Luminarias** (505-326-3311), San Juan College, 4601 College Boulevard, Farmington. December 1, sunset. The campus is illuminated with 50,000 luminarias for the largest nonprofit display in New Mexico. **Navajo Nativity** (505-326-7602), 2102 W. Main, Farmington. December 23, 6–8 PM. This living nativity with native Navajo costumes and live animals is presented by children at the Four Corners Home for Children.

OPPOSITE: LOCAL TROUBADOURS PERFORM ON SATURDAY MORNING AT THE LAS CRUCES FARMERS AND CRAFT MARKET

SOUTHWEST NEW MEXICO: GHOST TOWN COUNTRY

■

CAMINO COUNTRY

Socorro, Truth or Consequences, Elephant Butte, Hatch, Las Cruces, Mesilla

OLD HIGHWAY 60 COUNTRY

Magdalena, Datil, Pie Town, Quemado

GHOST TOWN COUNTRY

Hillsboro, Glenwood, Reserve, Columbus, Silver City, Deming

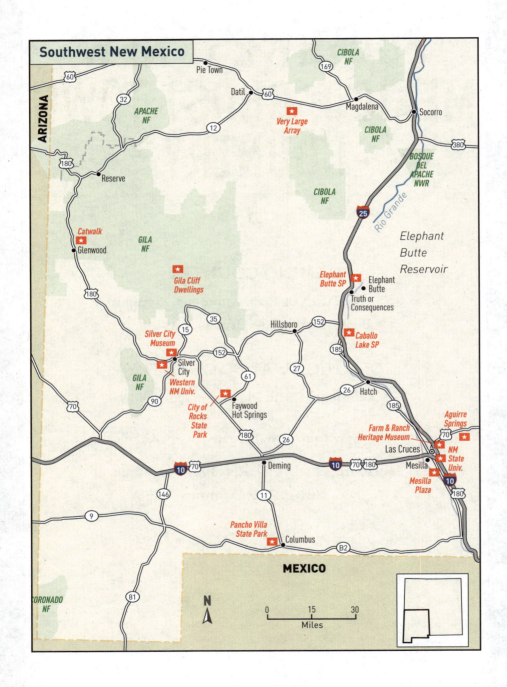

Southwest New Mexico

ARIZONA

MEXICO

Pie Town
Datil
Magdalena
Socorro
CIBOLA NF
169

APACHE NF
60
32
12
180
Reserve

Very Large Array
CIBOLA NF
CIBOLA NF
BOSQUE DEL APACHE NWR
380
25
Rio Grande

Catwalk
Glenwood
GILA NF

Gila Cliff Dwellings
180

Elephant Butte Reservoir

Elephant Butte SP
Elephant Butte
Truth or Consequences
152
185
Caballo Lake SP

Silver City Museum
15
35
Hillsboro
27
Silver City
GILA NF
152
61
Western NM Univ.
City of Rocks State Park
Faywood Hot Springs
26
Hatch
185

70
90
180
26

Aguirre Springs
70
Farm & Ranch Heritage Museum
Las Cruces
NM State Univ.
Mesilla
10
70
Deming
10
70
180
Mesilla Plaza
10
180

146
11
9
81

Pancho Villa State Park
Columbus
B2

N

0   15   30
Miles

CORONADO NF

SOUTHWEST NEW MEXICO

Driving on I-25, in only a few hours the New Mexico landscape transforms from the ponderosa pine mountain forests and piñon-juniper covered hillsides of northern New Mexico into the creosote landscape south of Albuquerque. Here, on the northern edge of the Chihuahuan Desert, the hot, dry climate creates a different ecology, where the scarcity of water is a fact of life that historically has determined where and how people live and travel. The desert is culturally different as well.

The rural way of life is the predominant mode, and agriculture and ranching are the economic mainstays. Grapes, chile, alfalfa, and cotton grow abundantly in this river valley, where farmers depend on water released from Elephant Butte Dam and cattle and horses graze in open fields. Drought, and the historic dought cycle, impacts everyone who lives here.

There is less sense of urgency among people, who seem to make more time for visiting, baking, and caring for each other and their place. A different sense of time—a proudly mañana attitude—prevails in the small towns off the superhighway. Here folks either accept life and have made peace with it, or they are resigned to its limitations. Things are never done in a "New York minute." Life moves slowly, people run late, and phone calls may not be returned in what is, in the big city, considered a timely manner.

As this area is geographically closer to Mexico, the influence of that country south of the border—its language, food, religion, and strong family ties—is visible. Some believe the border itself is an artificial line drawn through the ancient kingdom of "Atzlan," and that the southern region of New Mexico and northern Mexico spiritually and culturally, as well as geographically, belong together as one country. Border walls notwithstanding, the belief that someday, inevitably, this region will re-emerge as a totality, is alive.

Immigration issues are visible. You will see, and be required to pass through, Border Patrol stations along the way. There is no way to travel through this area without experiencing these inspections (and the emotions they may provoke) but they usually just consist of a quick look at you and your vehicle by an agent as you drive through the station—past an armed guard, multiple cameras, and ferocious-looking dogs. Of course, since the presidential campaign and election of 2016, all border issues, including drugs, immigration, and deportation, are hot buttons. If this makes you at all nervous or worried, do not travel here. However, I travel through southern New Mexico regularly, and I have neither experienced any problems.

The past is well preserved in the hot, dry New Mexican desert. That goes for the 400-year-old trail markings of the Camino Real, the Royal Road, still visible from the air. It once took oxcarts 3 years to make that round-trip between Mexico City and Santa Fe. This is the path taken by the conquistadors, by Juan de Oñate, in 1598, and it is the same path the Spanish followed when they fled to El Paso in 1680 following the Pueblo Revolt. It is the road Don Diego de Vargas took when he returned with his followers at the Reconquest 12 years later and retook Santa Fe for the Spanish crown.

Like much of the rest of the state, southwest New Mexico includes a vast area that can be thought of in distinct regions, shaped by location and resources, and the history that resulted from the uses people made of those features. Each of them, depending on your personal pace, can be at least seen in a good long weekend. These three regions are the Camino Real Country, the Old Highway 60 Country, and the Ghost Town Country.

This region includes towns accessible from I-25 from Socorro, Truth or Consequences, Elephant Butte, Las Cruces, and its next-door neighbor, Mesilla. It flows in more or less a straight line north to south, following the path of the ancient road along the river. Where it diverged from the river into the Journada de Muerto, the "dead man's journey," is a waterless stretch that tested the survival skills of those who dared cross it.

Old US Highway 60, often referred to as a link in the Ocean-to-Ocean Highway, the first paved transcontinental road, begun in 1912. It bisects southern New Mexico and remains the slow road from east to west, a two-lane with a 65 mph speed limit and no billboards, chain restaurants, or chain motels. Get on Highway 60, which still follows its original alignment through New Mexico, south of Socorro and travel to the Arizona border in a half-day passing through Magdalena, the old cattle railhead; seeing Kelly, the mining town up above it; on to Datil; Pie Town, with its remains of a twentieth-century homesteading community; the Very Large Array radio telescope installation, and Quemado; then on to Springerville, Arizona.

Let it be known that residents of Catron County, along old US 60, object to two things in particular: environmentalists and the Mexican gray wolf that they are trying to bring back. This is an area of staunch independent thinkers, with strong Old West roots, and outsiders with non-local opinions and a partiality to endangered species are neither favored nor tolerated. Conceal and carry is the rule here. Enough said.

It is possible, with any show of polite curiosity, to connect with the old-timers who still live along the road, who run the mom-and-pop shops, cafés, and motels. They have long memories and don't mind sharing their stories. There is not much going on, and days are fairly alike, so you yourself may provide the break in routine that is needed at the moment. This is where history still lives. With curiosity and a camera, you can experience the Old West—its reality, not its Hollywood glorification. People are often willing to share information about historical characters, the legends of their place, their families, the best places to fish, and those landmarks that aren't in the books—but where someone once lived, or where someone was once killed, or where a treasure is supposedly buried. They know what ghosts haunt which buildings.

People out here are generally as friendly as their sharp ability to judge character instantly allows. If they feel you are a decent person, they will literally give you the shirt off their back and the story of their lives. They will extend trust and invite you home to see their family photo albums. The locals you encounter can be much better sources of information about a place than the initial pointers you will receive at the visitor center. This may be true for travelers in general, and it is especially true in rural New Mexico, where kindness is the currency. Those who have migrated from other places, in general, prefer their privacy. A surprising number of artists manage to survive out here by running Internet businesses.

Traveling west over NM 152 through the Black Range to Silver City, pass by Hillsboro and Kingston. Much of this area has gold, silver, and copper mining in its past. Some towns, like Silver City, where mining has recently resumed, have reinvented themselves as tourist towns with service economies. Others, like Winston, Chloride, and Kingston, have faded into true, adobe-returning-to-the-earth, splintered wood ghost town status. If you treasure the silence, the ruins of former banks and jailhouses, and the spirit of place that evokes the past more eloquently than any history book, you will find plenty to intrigue you in Ghost Town Country.

Much of the country is still pretty wild, and it was among the last part of the United States to be taken from the Indians. This is the territory of Geronimo, Mangus

NO, PANCHO VILLA NEVER SLEPT HERE

Colorado, the great woman warrior, Lozen, and other great Apache warriors, who fought hard for their homeland against the encroachment of the Americans. The vanished ancestors, the Mimbres, who made distinctive black-on-white pottery, and the people who built the Gila Cliff dwellings left no written record but much to be amazed at. They settled in the hospitable river country.

This is also the part of the world that inspired the first national wilderness area, named for the naturalist Aldo Leopold, who was inspired to push for the establishment of the Gila National Forest.

Another character who occupies a great deal of psychic space, Pancho Villa, made his foray over the border into the United States at Columbus, where old-timers continue to hold on to their versions of the raid. General Black Jack Pershing gave chase in the first armored tanks to roll through Mexico, but he never managed to catch up with Villa. Pershing then went on to command the US forces in Europe during World War I.

There is a sense in much of this place that life can still be hard. Folks' survival depends as much on their ability to trust as it does on their ability to read the rain clouds, and there's not much that escapes them.

If you like your history real, you crave immersion in the stuff of legends, and you don't mind the taste of grit or standing out in the wind, you will find much to appeal to you in southern New Mexico.

For convenience's sake, *Green Space* for all of southwest New Mexico is listed toward the end of the chapter, and all *Medical Emergency* information for the area is given at the beginning.

CAMINO COUNTRY

Socorro, Truth or Consequences, Elephant Butte, Hatch, Las Cruces, Mesilla

Big skies and wide open spaces define this area, as do the green chile fields of Hatch and the "six flags" that have flown over Mesilla Plaza. History is everywhere, in the faded advertisements painted on the sides of brick buildings, the thick adobe walls, and the WPA-era buildings. There is no forgetting that this is an area linked by roads—yesterday's Camino Real, today's I-25. You will find a variety of experiences—starting with Bosque del Apache National Wildlife Refuge, to bustling Las Cruces, growing with amenities migrants and retirees, and the traditional small farming villages south of Mesilla. However, no matter how many Santa Fe and Albuquerque artists flee to quiet Truth or Consequences to open galleries and boutiques, and despite the arrival of Spaceport America, change comes slowly. Refreshingly, Camino Country refuses to join the modern world completely.

GUIDANCE **Elephant Butte Chamber of Commerce** (575-744-4708), 700 NM 195, Elephant Butte. Open Mon.–Sat. 10–2.

Greater Las Cruces Chamber of Commerce (575-524-1968), 505 S. Main Street, Las Cruces.

Hatch Valley Chamber of Commerce (575-267-5050), 210 W. Hall Street, Hatch.

J. Paul Taylor Visitor Center (575-524-3262 ext. 117), 2231 Avenida de Mesilla, Mesilla.

Las Cruces Convention and Visitors Bureau (575-541-2444), 211 N. Water Street, Las Cruces.

Socorro County Chamber of Commerce (575-835-0424), 101 Plaza, Socorro.

Socorro Heritage and Visitor Center (575-835-8927), 217 Fisher Avenue, Socorro.

Truth or Consequences/Sierra County Chamber of Commerce (575-894-3536), 207 S. Foch, Truth or Consequences.

GETTING THERE Take I-25 south out of Albuquerque. Taking this road south to Las Cruces, you'll find all the towns and attractions listed in Camino Real Country en route. To reach US Highway 60 country, take I-25 to exit 127 south to Socorro, then go west on US 60. To reach Ghost Town Country, take I-25 south to exit 63 onto NM 152.

MEDICAL EMERGENCY **Gila Regional Medical Center** (575-538-4000), 1313 E. 32nd Street, Silver City.

Memorial Medical Center (575-522-8641), 2450 S. Telshor Boulevard, Las Cruces.

Mountain View Regional Medical Center (575-556-7600), 4311 E. Lohman Avenue, Las Cruces.

Sierra Vista Hospital (575-894-2111), 800 E. 9th Avenue, Truth or Consequences.

Socorro General Hospital (575-835-8343), 1202 Highway 60 West, Socorro.

✱ To See

TOWNS **Elephant Butte** is 79 miles south of Socorro on I-25. With the construction of Elephant Butte Dam in 1912–16, a recreational area was born that today is home to marinas, vacationers, and year-rounders who enjoy the 40-mile lake and the 200 miles of shoreline that make it one of New Mexico's most popular state parks. If you look carefully—you may have to tilt your head or squint a bit—and use your imagination, you will see the silhouette of an elephant in a prominent butte.

Hatch is 34 miles south of Truth or Consequences on I-25. This agricultural town is known for three things: chile, chile, and chile! This is the home of the famous "Hatch chile," New Mexico's leading export and favorite food. Whether you favor red or green, this is the place to pull off the highway (I-25 at exit 41) and buy some. The best time to come here is August–October, when you can smell the aroma of roasting chilies and see the ripe red ones drying on rooftops and in strings, also known as ristras, all over town.

Las Cruces is 223 miles south of Albuquerque on I-25. The unofficial capital of southern New Mexico, this growing university city near the border has been discovered by retirees and others seeking to relocate and reinvent themselves, and is now a bona fide boomtown. It is home of New Mexico State University, and Aggies football and basketball are promoted and followed with fervent enthusiasm. With its climate, medical facilities, university, and a feeling of small-town well being and family friendliness, Las Cruces' attractions continue to grow.

Mesilla. One mile south of Las Cruces on University Boulevard. With Rio Grande *acequias* running through it, a historic plaza over which the flags of six nations have flown, and venerable adobe homes on streets wide enough for a burro cart loaded with wood, this sister city and next-door neighbor to the south of Las Cruces is the archetype of a historic village. The little town has plenty of galleries, cafés, and boutiques arrayed around the plaza, and it is fun to walk or jog along the ditch banks. The name "Mesilla" means "little table" and refers to the geographic spot where the town is located in the Mesilla Valley of the Rio Grande, a rich agricultural area where chile, cotton, onions, cotton, and pecans flourish. To the south along NM 28 are a string of wineries.

WELCOME TO HATCH, CHILE CAPITAL OF THE WORLD

Socorro, 72 miles south of Albuquerque on I-25, received its name from conquistador Juan de Oñate in 1598 because he and his party were given much help and aid there by the native Piros. Today it is the home of a fine college, New Mexico Institute of Mining and Technology, a legacy from the days when it was the center of a rich mining district.

Truth or Consequences is 79 miles south of Socorro on I-25. When television host Ralph Edwards made the offer to bestow the name of his program, *Truth or Consequences*, to the American city that would change its name to that of the show, the little New Mexico town of Hot Springs jumped at the opportunity and became the town of Truth or Consequences, New Mexico. True to his word, Ralph Edwards returned every year for over 50 years to lead the parade in the annual May festival. From time to time it seems the town is experiencing something of a renewal, with the arrival of artists and artistically and community-minded folks from Albuquerque and Santa Fe looking for a less expensive place to live and express themselves, but its basic blue collar character does not change. New Age–tinged paths of healing follow in the footsteps of the older healing traditions of the place. The main street is now dotted with boutiques, cafés, and a Black Cat bookstore as a result of the younger population's influence. The town sits on a 110-degree hot spring aquifer and bills itself as the "Hot Springs Capital of the World," with many spa establishments. It also claims to be the most affordable spa town in the country.

HISTORIC LANDMARKS, PLACES, AND SITES **Elfego Baca Monument** (no phone), Henry's Corner, N. Main Street, Reserve, commemorates a legendary lawman known for his solo David-and-Goliath 3-day standoff against hundreds of invaders.

Fort Craig National Historic Site (575-835-0412), 32 miles south of Socorro, I-25 exit 124, 901 NM 85. A remote station on the Rio Grande, Fort Craig, commissioned

DUTCH OVEN COOKING IS STILL THE FAVORITE WAY TO FEED COWBOYS

1854–85, was a base for US Army campaigns against Native Americans and Confederates during the Civil War. **Fort Selden State Monument** (575-647-9585), 1233 Fort Selden Road, Radium Springs. I-25 exit 19. Twelve miles north of Las Cruces. Open Wed–Mon. 8:30–5. Closed Tuesdays. The second Sat. of every month brings a living history program, plus Dutch oven cooking most Saturdays. The fort is so quiet now, the visitor would never imagine the activity it saw during the Civil War and the days of the Indian Wars. Perhaps its most famous resident was Captain Arthur MacArthur, its commanding officer in 1884, and his son, Douglas MacArthur, who became supreme commander of the Allied forces in the Pacific during World War II. $3 adults, children free; free Wed. New Mexico seniors, free Sun. New Mexico residents.

SATURDAY MORNING AT LAS CRUCES MUSEUM OF NATURE & SCIENCE IS MULTIGENERATIONAL FUN

MUSEUMS **Branigan Cultural Center** (575-541-2154), 501 N. Main Street. Exhibits and activities related to local and regional history. Free

Geronimo Springs Museum (575-894-6600), 211 Main Street, Truth or Consequences. Open Mon.–Sat. 9–5. Closed Sundays. Located beside Las Palomas Plaza, where Native Americans came to bathe in the hot springs, the museum has exhibits of each of Sierra County's cultures, from prehistoric times to the present day. Here get a good historical overview, from mastodon and mammoth skulls to the Apache room; Hispanic Heritage Room, with a diorama of the Jornada del Muerto; to the exceptional pottery room; and best of all, the Ralph Edwards Room, with memorabilia on the Annual Fiesta. $3 adults, $1.50 students ages 6–18, under age 6 free, $7.50 families.

Spaceport America Visitor Center (844-727-7223), 301 S. Foch Street, Truth or Consequences. This same building now houses the T or C Sierra County Visitor Center. Brand new. Artfully curated. Space capsule, space history, information on touring Spaceport America, located 35 miles SE of Truth or Consequences. The Spaceport is a pioneer in developing—and may eventually provide a base for—the commercial exploration of space.

Las Cruces Museum of Fine Arts and Culture (575-541-2137), 491 N. Main Street, Las Cruces. Traveling exhibits, art with a New Mexico focus. Free.

Mineral Museum (575-835-5420), 801 Leroy Place, southeast corner of Canyon Road and Olive Lane, on the New Mexico Tech campus, Socorro. Open Mon.–Fri. 8–5, Sat. and Sun. 10–3. Nicknamed "Coronado's Treasure Chest," this museum has an amazing display of gold, silver, fossils, mining artifacts, and precious gems, as well as top-quality mineral specimens found all over New Mexico. So worth a visit! Free.

_&_ **Museum of Nature & Science** (575-522-3120), 700 S. Telshor Boulevard, Las Cruces. An entirely delightful and user-friendly new museum designed to appeal to all ages, specializing in geography and natural history of the area. Free.

_&_ _&_ **New Mexico Farm & Ranch Heritage Museum** (575-522-4100), 4100 Dripping Springs Road, Las Cruces. Take the university exit 1 off I-25 and travel east, toward the Organ Mountains. Open Mon.–Sat. 9–5, Sun. noon–5. This impressive ranch-style museum maintains exhibits on agriculture in the West, and the best may be seen outside the galleries at daily blacksmithing demonstrations; the barns of sheep, cattle, and other animals; the Antique Equipment Park; and regular demonstrations of dowsing, milking, weaving, and quilting. There is ample vehicle access. The Green Bridge, New Mexico's second-oldest highway bridge, was moved here from the Rio Hondo and installed over Tortugas Arroyo. You'll also find exhibits of local photography and art. $5 adults, $4 seniors, $3 children ages 5–17, age 3 and under free.

NMSU Center for the Arts (800-840-9227), University Boulevard, Las Cruces. The home of NMSU arts programs is a big wow of a sophisticated building that includes the jewel of the Medoff Theater. Quality live theater productions found here.

✳ To Do

BIRDING **Bosque del Apache National Wildlife Refuge** (575-835-1828), 1001 NM 1, San Antonio, 9 miles south on I-25 to exit 139, east 0.25 mile on US 380 to flashing light at San Antonio, turn right onto NM 1, continue south 9 miles to visitor center. Visitor center open Mon.–Fri. 7:30–4, Sat. and Sun. 8–4:30. Tour Loop 1 hour before sunset to 1 hour after sunset. This premier winter day trip involves a drive to the bosque for the fly-in of thousands of cranes and geese at sunset. Winter is also the best time to spot bald eagles. Mid-November–mid-February is the peak time for viewing these migrants. Many varieties of birds winter here along the Rio Grande Flyway. Every season offers birding opportunities: summer is the time to see nesting songbirds, waders, shorebirds, and ducks; spring and fall warblers and flycatchers show up. Bicycling is encouraged as a way of experiencing the bosque, and many bike paths have been upgraded and made accessible. Bring your bike for miles of level cycling along the ditches, lakes, and wet-lands, and don't forget the binoculars. Fifteen-mile auto tour loop. $5 per vehicle.

Mesilla Valley Bosque State Park (575-405-9876), 5000 Calle del Norte, between Mesilla Dam and NM 538, is a day-use park state park on the banks of the southern Rio Grande, with a visitor center and interpretive programs highlighting birds and wildlife of the bosque, as well as beautiful trails for walking, jogging, and biking. $5 per vehicle.

Organ Mountains-Desert Peaks National Monument (575-525-4300), 571 Walton Boulevard, Las Cruces. 500,000 acres contained within the monument area. A federal designation made in 2014 to protect the area's history, culture, and scientific resources, while benefiting the local economy and maintaining recreational activities such as hiking, biking, and so much more. The area is rich with petroglyphs and a photographer's dream come true in the Chihuahuan desert landscape, with peaks rising 9,000 feet. The Dripping Springs Trail leads to an old hotel and is five miles round trip. Take plenty of water.

CANOEING AND KAYAKING **Leasburg Dam State Park** (575-524-4068), 15 miles north of Las Cruces on I-25 or NM 185. March–mid-October, enjoy canoeing and kayaking on the Rio Grande. $5 per vehicle day use.

CLIMBING Box Canyon (no phone), I-25 exit 147 at Socorro, go west on US 60 for 6.8 miles, immediately after bridge go east. Second left is gravel road to parking area. This is a favorite red rock climbing and rappelling area west of Socorro.

FARMERS' MARKETS Las Cruces Farmers & Crafts Market (575-201-3853), 125 No. Main Street, Downtown Mall, Las Cruces. Open-year round Wed. and Sat. 8 AM–12:30 PM. Several blocks of fresh produce and clever crafts, jewelry, handmade jams, soaps, and things you can't possibly find anywhere else make this one of the best farmers' markets. Plus, some of the best coffee you'll find anywhere, custom brewed by "Beck," and crafts galore: jewelry, glass, ceramics, textiles, woodwork, photography. I found a cast-iron jalapeño roaster here. Named #1 American Farmers Market by American Farmland Trust.

Socorro Farmers' Market (575-312-1730), 101 Socorro Plaza. July–October, Tues. 5 PM–7 PM, Sat. 8 AM–sellout. Fresh corn, watermelons, eggs, and all the glorious produce of the season sold in a neighborly, festive market.

GOLF New Mexico State University Golf Course (575-646-3219), 3000 Herb Wimberly Drive, Las Cruces. Framed by the rugged Organ Mountains and the Mesilla Valley, the course challenges all skill levels by combining desert and traditional golf on this 18-hole course that is home to the Aggies' golf team. Very reasonable.

Red Hawk Golf Club (575-520-4949), 7520 Red Hawk Golf Road. The newest, and many say, the best, golfing in southern New Mexico is here on this 200 acre links-style course. Reasonable.

HIKING Dripping Springs Natural Area (575-522-1219), 10 miles east of Las Cruces. From exit 1 on I-25, take Dripping Springs Road to the end. At the base of the rugged

OLD TIME MUSICIANS PERFORM FREQUENTLY AT FARM & RANCH HERITAGE MUSEUM EVENTS

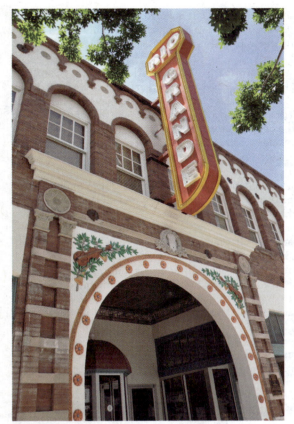

THE RESTORED RIO GRANDE THEATER IS A BUSY DOWNTOWN VENUE

Organ Mountains, this is the favorite hiking area of Las Cruces, with a 4.5-mile moderate-difficult hike. $3.

See also **Aguirre Springs**, under "Mountain Biking."

HOT SPRINGS Truth or Consequences (575-894-6673). The dozen natural hot mineral springs in the downtown Historic District are geothermally heated with temperatures between 95 and 112 degrees Fahrenheit. With a dozen public bathhouses, ranging from funky to deluxe, mostly built in the 1920s, many nicely updated, you have quite a choice of how you will experience getting into hot water here. Some have large tiled tubs, some have pebble-bottomed pools, and most have healing services such as massage, facials, aromatherapy, and hot rock treatments.

MOUNTAIN BIKING Aguirre Springs National Recreation Area (575-525-4300), 1800 Marquis Street, Organ, 22 miles east of Las Cruces on I-70. Mountain biking and camping, with a variety of trails that are part of the National Recreation Trail System. $3.

PARKS Chihuahuan Desert Nature Park (575-524-3334), 56501 N. Jornada Road, Las Cruces, east of Las Cruces on I-70, Mesa Grande exit to Jornada Road. Tues.–Sat. 7–5. Closed Sundays and Mondays. A 960-acre park with a 1.5-mile walking trail that has plant identification is a sweet education on the diverse ecosystems of the Chihuahuan Desert. Free.

WINERIES Blue Teal Winery (877-669-4637), 1710 Avenida de Mesilla, Las Cruces. Mon.–Sat. 11–6, Sun. noon–6. Hand-painted wine bottles and exhibits of local artists accompany tastings of award-winning reds

La Vina (575-882-7632), 4201 S. NM 28. Twenty miles south of Las Cruces. Open Thurs.–Tues. noon–5. What a serene drive it is down south to the oldest winery in the state, which hosts the oldest wine festival every October and a jazz festival in April.

Luna Rosso Winery & Pizzeria (575-526-2484), 1321 Avenida de Mesilla, Las Cruces. Light and bright family eatery with gelato, decent pizza, pasta dishes. Wines sold here are created here. My family enjoys dining here when we are in town.

Vintage Wines (575-523-9463), 2461 Calle de Principal, Mesilla. How is this for happiness: cozy wine bar, 50 wines by the glass, tapas, chocolates, cigars, jazz, Latin jazz, flamenco guitar, live music Fri. and Sat. and Wi-Fi, too.

✳ Lodging

BED & BREAKFASTS, MOTELS, AND INNS **Blackstone Lodge** (575-894-0894), 410 Austin Street, Truth or Consequences. Consistently voted #1 lodging in Truth or Consequences, the Blackstone's serene rooms, each styled for a period TV series (*Twilight Zone, Golden Girls*) contain private tubs. Unlike many of the remodeled old motor court lodgings in town, Blackstone feels clean and fresh. Affordable luxury. $95–135.

🐾 **Elephant Butte Inn** (575-744-5431), 401 NM 195, Elephant Butte. I-25, exit 83. From here, enjoy views of the lake and desert, spot wildlife, have a drink in the Ivory Tusk Tavern, perhaps a massage at the Ivory Spa, and hike to Elephant Butte Lake. Heated outdoor pool. Pet-friendly, handicapped accessible. A deluxe continental breakfast is included. Golf and spa packages. Very pleasant. $85.

♂ **Josephina's Old Gate** (575-613-4820), 2261 Calle de Guadalupe, Mesilla. Café, wine bar, and small luxury lodging a block from Mesilla Plaza. The big four-poster bed and secluded quarters make it ideal for honeymoon or anniversary. A place to inspire dreams or be transported to another era, long before email or even the horseless carriage came along, before the invention of the wristwatch.

🐾 **Riverbend Hot Springs** (575-894-7625), 100 Austin, Truth or Consequences. Three outdoor soaking pools and one rock pool overlooking the Rio Grande, facing Turtleback Mountain, for $12 per person per hour. Open daily 8–7. Mineral soaks used to be free with lodging, but if you are only staying the night, you must pay your way, at a discounted rate. Prices have gone up, as the place has gained popularity, is gradually

ORGAN MOUNTAINS, LAS CRUCES

shedding its old hippie ambience, and new pools, with greater temperature variations, have been added. Also, if you are looking for some peaceful time, you may prefer to reserve a private tub $15–$45. Pet-friendly. $102–$274. RV spaces $60 per night.

Sierra Grande Lodge and Spa (877-288-7637), 501 McAdoo Street, Truth or Consequences. The town's most upscale address, a restored 1929 lodge with deluxe rooms featuring sunken tubs and well-chosen art, with complimentary outdoor tubs as well as public facilities with massage and reflexology. Spa packages may be reserved in advance. This lodge was purchased by Ted Turner, who runs expeditions in the area. $175.

CABINS AND CAMPING **Caballo Lake RV Park** (575-743-0502), Caballo. Exit 59 off I-25, north 1 mile on NM 187 to Mile Marker 22. Quiet, Wi-Fi, enjoyable fishing and birding, walking distance to the Caballo Lake beach, tours of remote ghost towns, and prospecting and gold panning are in easy reach here in this desert campground. $15 plus electric hookup.

Hacienda RV Resort (575-528-5800), 740 Stern Drive, Las Cruces. This is the life! Complimentary breakfast bar, concierge service, large patio, and hydrotherapy pool, plus Wi-Fi. Spacious, top-of-the-line sites, cable TV. $30–42.

❋ Where to Eat

DINING OUT **Double Eagle Restaurant** (575-523-4999), 2355 Calle de Guadalupe, Mesilla Plaza. Daily 11 AM–10 PM. Within the oldest building on the plaza—and the most haunted; photos of the ghosts are on the walls—is the most elegant dining in the area in full Victorian splendor, though to be precise, a fantasy of Victorian splendor. Go for the opulent Sunday brunch (the Double Eagle claims the finest buffet in the Southwest, and we

won't argue about it!). But you can't miss either with the well-aged steaks, made in the only dedicated beef aging room in the state; fine wine from the extensive wine list; or just order a margarita at the long, ornate mirrored bar. The Double Eagle's flown off with a *Wine Spectator* Award of Excellence, and we have truly enjoyed our splurges here. Service is quite fine. Expensive.

La Posta De Mesilla (575-524-3524), 2410 Calle de San Albino, Mesilla Plaza. Mon.–Thurs. Sun. 8–9, Fri.–Sat. 8–9:30. For a tourist restaurant, this place does a respectable job of keeping up with a

LA POSTA, POPULAR WITH LOCALS AND VISITORS, ON MESILLA PLAZA

crowd that include plenty of locals. In fact, it serves one of my favorite chilies rellenos plates, southern New Mexico style, lightly sautéed in egg batter, not breaded, so the taste and texture of the chilies sing forth. Located in the old Butterfield Stage Building, the place is saturated in historic Southwest atmosphere. They boast of the largest tequila selection in the Southwest, and of course, the best margaritas. I especially like the one made with cucumber and jalapeno. The "ghost" was created by a pranksters' hoax. If you must wait, you can shop for salsa or commune with the parrot. Moderate.

Los Arcos Steak & Lobster House (575-894-6200), 1400 N. Date Street, Truth or Consequences. Sun.–Thurs. 5–9 PM; Fri.–Sat. 5–10:30 PM. This well-established, grown-up, scotch-and-steak sort of place is good for a splurge or a quiet conversation. A place with classic—think 1970s—restaurant atmosphere, where service is as important, or more so, than the food, which is usually very good. No need to break the budget. Early-bird specials are a good deal, and Los Arcos serves a respectable green chile cheeseburger, fun to munch in the bar. Solid wine list and well-stocked bar. Genuine cocktail lounge. Moderate–Expensive.

Pacific Grill (575-894-7687), 800 N. Date Street, Truth or Consequences. L, D. Closed Mondays and Wednesdays. I usually end up having a meal here when I am in Truth or Consequences, and I love to spend winter weekends soaking in the hot springs. Freshest salad bar in town, unique homemade soups and desserts, fine curry, diverse, mixed Asian menu, care given to preparation and service. Moderate.

St. Clair Winery & Bistro (575-524-2408), 1720 Avenida de Mesilla, Mesilla. Open daily. L, D. This lively spot immediately became a favorite for locals. Outdoor patio, live jazz Thurs.–Sat. Delightful New Mexico wine selection. Lovely addition to Southern New Mexico dining scene, featuring French country

BOBBY OLGUIN'S BUCKHORN BURGER IN SAN ANTONIO BEATS BOBBY FLAY'S

cooking. It's not all enchiladas and beans here, folks.

EATING OUT **Andele Restaurant** (575-526-9631), 1950 Calle del Norte. Open daily. B, L, D. The fresh salsa bar is the attraction here. Alas, Andele's may have gotten too big. It used to be spectacular, now it is just down a notch. Stay away from the chicken, as it is generally over-cooked and dry. The Dog House, across the street, serves the same food, with a bar and a rollicking patio. Inexpensive.

Arrey Cafe (575-267-4436), Arrey. Daily 8–8. Is it the local beans and chile of this weathered homespun spot in the road, where chile growers are chowing down on the good stuff that makes this place such a find, or is it merely that it is so out of the way on a dusty deserted street that it could be the restaurant version of *The Last Picture Show* that makes it special? Drive up the back road, NM 185, north of Hatch and find out. Lots of food for the money. Inexpensive.

The Bean of Mesilla (575-527-5155), 2011 Avenida de Mesilla, Mesilla. Open Mon.–Fri. 6:30–9, Sat. 7–9, Sun. 7–5. B, L, D. How pleasant it is to sip the fresh, strong coffee at a table on the sunny patio, munch a freshly baked chocolate croissant, and leaf through the Sunday paper. This no-frills café has Wi-Fi, and you can catch performances of local musicians Thurs.–Sat. The Bean is a top-notch hangout or meetup café, always full of friends visiting, cyclists, and seems to be the place for people with things to say. You will always feel welcomed and at home here. I never miss it when I am in town. Inexpensive.

Buckhorn Tavern (575-835-4423), 68 US 380, San Antonio. Closed Sundays. L, D. Located just across the street from the Owl Cafe; the decision about where to dine is a real dilemma. However, the green chile burgers here are among the best. Fabulous fries, too. You'd better be hungry or prepare to split yours. Since the chef-owner Bobby Olguin won his smackdown with Bobby Flay, this place has been a pilgrimage site. Sit at the bar if it's too crowded. Inexpensive.

Café de Mesilla: A Coffee Shop with Breakfast, Lunch and Gifts (575-524-0000), 2190 Avenida de Mesilla, Mesilla. Mon.–Sun. 8–4. Closed Tuesdays. B, L. Sometimes open evenings. The essence of a charming café housed in an ancient adobe. Lovely service. Coffees, ice cream, treats. Inexpensive.

Bosa Donuts (575-526-3388), 190 Avenida de Mesilla, Las Cruces. B, L. Why is everyone in town lined up at this hole-in-the-wall on Saturday morning? These tender donuts are a way of life in Las Cruces. In addition, after you select your dozen, you can grab a humdinger of a breakfast burrito and really get charged up for the day. Inexpensive.

Caliche's (575-674-5066), 590 S. Valley Drive, Las Cruces. Open daily. Good news—the frozen custard is still the best. Where else can you get a green chile pecan sundae? With a hot dog. If you can ever tear yourself away from the custard, try the mango Desert Ice to cool off. Free doggy cones! Inexpensive.

Carmen's Kitchen (575-894-0006), 1806 S. Broadway, Truth or Consequences. B, L, D Mon.–Fri.; Sat. B, L only. Closed Sundays. My husband's favorite red chile, excellent breakfast spot, now open till 8 PM with generous dinner specials several times a week. Like eating in Grandma's kitchen. Carmen hand-selects her chile from Hatch, and she does not compromise. Inexpensive.

Chope's Bar & Cafe (575-233-3420), 16145 S. NM 28, La Mesa. Open Tues.–Sat. 11 AM–2 PM and 5:30–8:30 PM. Closed Sundays and Mondays. Why are people standing in line out here in La Mesa, 12 miles south of Las Cruces, at lunchtime? If you guessed because the food served in this humble outpost is worth the long drive, you'd be right. There's a good chance there was a Chope's before you were born, way back in 1940, and it is still in the founder's Benavidez family. It had a well-deserved reputation as a political hangout in the early days, and you can see several generations of families enjoying the red chile enchiladas and beef tacos together. Inexpensive.

🍴 **Dick's Cafe** (575-524-1360), 2305 S. Valley Drive, Las Cruces. Open daily 7 AM–8 PM. The college crowd mixes with bikers, truckers, and city employees to make this a classic casual stop with the locals. The chile cheeseburger is substantial and all-day sustaining and the fries are homemade. I love to wake up to the breakfast burrito doused in red, and the coffee has guts. There's a bit of turnover in the staff, and sometimes the service can be a little ditzy, but who cares? Relax, have another cup of coffee, and read the paper, like the rest

CHOPE'S HAS BEEN SERVING LA MESA SINCE BEFORE YOU WERE BORN

of the locals. I was introduced to Dick's by a graduate of NMSU who confessed she got through school on this place's burgers, homemade fries, and delicious beans. Warning: The green chile is really hot. Inexpensive.

🍴 **Frank and Lupe's El Sombrero** (575-835-3945), 210 Mesquite, Socorro. Open daily. L, D. Enjoy a wine margarita or imported beer with your fajitas or chicken mole enchiladas. A friendly, long-established family-oriented local favorite. The pleasant patio is enclosed. Inexpensive.

International Delights Cafe (575-647-5956), 1245 El Paseo Road, Las Cruces. B, L, D. Mon.–Sun. Open till 11 PM during the week; midnight weekends. In the far corner of a strip mall, find this chic yet comfortably worn treasure trove of pastries, Middle Eastern food—shish kebab, couscous, early morning bagel and lox, and fine Turkish coffee. Imported groceries, too! Inexpensive.

🍴 **La Nueva Casita** (575-523-5434), 195 N. Mesquite Street, Las Cruces. B, L, D Mon.–Sat. B, L Sun. The last time I visited the Las Cruces' historic Mesquite District, I saw two ancient ladies wheeling an aged Pomeranian in a baby carriage. I also followed a fire truck crew into La Nueva Casita, and I was not disappointed. This has become a favorite Mexican restaurant. This family café been around for 70 years, so it must be doing something right. Best chilies rellenos! Best green chile! Four stars! A find and a bargain. Inexpensive.

Nellie's Cafe (575-524-9982), 1226 W. Hadley Avenue, Las Cruces. Open Tues.–Sat. 8–2. Nellie's is one of those local institutions that helped the city establish and keep its reputation. The minimalist, fluorescent-linoleum aesthetic only highlights the main attraction: the seriously delicious and seriously hot Mexican food. It's all good!

Nellie's started out as a burrito wagon in 1962. Inexpensive.

Owl Bar & Cafe (575-835-9946), 77 US 38, San Antonio. Open Mon.–Sat. 8 AM–9 PM. Closed Sundays. Home of the world-famous green chile cheeseburger, the Owl began when Manhattan Project scientists first came to the area to test the bomb on the nearby Trinity Site. The Owl is a New Mexico institution. The only thing to do is slide into a booth and order that burger with the homemade fries. Chocolate cake for dessert, always. Inexpensive.

Passion Pie Cafe (575-894-0008), 406 Main Street, Truth or Consequences. B, L. Vegetarian and vegan, light and bright Wi-Fi, out-of-this-world scones and pastries, lunch specials of quiche, homemade soup, and more—what's not to love? Inexpensive.

Pepper Pot (575-267-3822), 207 W. Hall Street, Hatch. B, L, D. Have a nice sit-down lunch, with tablecloths on the tables, where everyone seems to know one another, and you might even run into someone you graduated from college with, and order a big combination plate. Red or green, you can't lose. But this is green country, amigo. Inexpensive.

Si Señor Restaurant (575-527-0817), 1551 E. Amador Avenue, Las Cruces. L, D Mon.–Sun. So many good Mexican restaurants, so little time. I inevitably feel that way in Las Cruces. I believe I've tried them all, and Si Señor still scores high, with its welcoming selection of fresh chips and four salsas, keen service, and fair prices. Love the location for a post–mall shopping trip lunch; lunch

YOU CAN GET JUST ABOUT ANYTHING YOU WANT AT SPARKY'S RESTAURANT IN HATCH, INCLUDING GREEN CHILE LEMONADE

ART TO TICKLE THE IMAGINATION IS DISPLAYED IN THIS DOWNTOWN SILVER CITY GALLERY

specials are a particularly good deal. Inexpensive.

Socorro Springs Restaurant (575-838-0650), 1012 N. California Street, Socorro. Open daily. L, D. This pleasant local brewpub serves good pizza, calzones, salads, and sandwiches. Its menu has enough variety to please everyone in a relaxed atmosphere. Former New Mexico Tech grads started with a little place on the plaza, and it was so popular, it grew into a main street attraction. Inexpensive–Moderate.

Sparky's Burgers, Barbeque and Espresso (575-267-4222), 115 Franklin Street, Hatch. L, D Thurs.–Mon. Closed Tuesdays and Wednesdays. One of NM's destination cafés. Famous green chile cheeseburgers that won top honors at State Fair, fabulous coffee, decent barbecue—Sparky's has it all! Worth it for the funky decor, much of it discarded cultural icons, such as Big Boy

and the Colonel. Live music weekends. Inexpensive.

Zeffiro Pizzeria Napoletana (575-525-6757), 136 S. Water Street, Las Cruces. L, D Mon.–Sat. Closed Sundays. So much more than pizza. Excellent pasta, bread, and wine. All is fresh and delicious. A downtown bistro at which to meet friends or enjoy a casual postramble dinner Fri. evening. Give Olive Garden a break in favor of this local family-run establishment. Sibling pizza place near University. Inexpensive–Moderate.

✳ Entertainment

Capitol Bar (575-835-1193), 110 Plaza, Socorro. This 1896 watering hole presents live entertainment on the weekends. With its bulletholes in the ceiling, shadows of jail cell bars, and having survived Prohibition, "the Cap" is still the place to go in Socorro.

A DOORWAY IN HILLSBORO PRESENTS A HAUNTED QUALITY

Fountain Theater & Mesilla Valley Film Society (575-524-8287), 2469 Calle de Guadalupe, half a block south of Mesilla Plaza. The nightly screenings at 7:30 PM, as well as the Sunday matinees, can keep you current with what's hot in cinema. Run by the Mesilla Valley Film Society. This is virtually the only place south of Albuquerque where you can catch independent, foreign, and alternative films.

Manzanares St. Coffeehouse (575-838-0809), 110 Manzanares Avenue, Socorro. 7–6 daily. Lively hangout, perfect for a road trip coffee and pastry stop and a stroll around the plaza; or, you could be lucky, as I was one Sunday afternoon, to drop in on a women's knitting circle and Irish fiddle music.

New Mexico Tech Performing Arts Series (575-835-5688), Macey Center, 1 Olive Laqne, NM Tech, Socorro. September–May. Macy Center. Live and

THE FEEL OF OLD MEXICO REMAINS IN MESILLA PLAZA AT DAYBREAK

symphonic and world music, dance, performance, and film brighten the nights in southern New Mexico.

✱ Selective Shopping

Black Cat Books and Coffee (575-894-7070), 128 N. Broadway Street, Truth or Consequences. Fri.–Mon., 8–5. Help! I can't get out of this place. Between the captivating and intelligent used book selection, the house-roasted organic coffee, the Sunday *New York Times*, and the neighborliness of the folks sitting around formica tables, gabbing. Owned and operated by a bookseller who knows her business and loves books. Inexpensive.

Del Sol International Shops (575-524-1418), 2322 Calle Principal, Mesilla. This Mesilla Plaza import shop is a treasure trove of lucky finds, in the way of wearables, household art, jewelry, and decor. Casual, imports, natural fabrics, plenty of rayon and cotton for Southwest comfort, denim and hats, belts and jackets to accessorize, with good prices and sales on styles that don't go out of style makes this an enjoyable place to shop.

Hatch Chile Express (800-292-4494), 622 N. Franklin, Hatch. Surprise your favorite chilehead with a gift from this well-stocked kitschy bazaar of chile-themed kitchenware, foodstuffs, and gifts, from a red chile spoon rest to chile-print boxers and ties. Jo Lytle, proprietor, holds the Guinness World Records title for raising a 13.5-inch Big Jim chile.

Moon Goddess (575-740-2341), 415 Broadway, Truth or Consequences. Imagination rules at this boutique of fanciful feminine, upcycled vintage goods, from textiles to lacy underthings, cards, and irresistible glittery gewgaws. Magical like nowhere else. The shop is a work of art. Hours uncertain.

Rio Abajo Antiques (575-835-2872), 1783 Main Street, San Antonio, one block south of Owl Bar. Open Sun.–Wed. 10–4,

MERRIMENT ABOUNDS AT LAS CRUCES RENAISSANCE ARTSFAIRE

June–July by appointment. A complete surprise en route to Bosque del Apache is this tiny shop packed with to-die-for classic silver and -turquoise jewelry, maps, regional artifacts, religious items, books, postcards, and just about anything else worth collecting. The shop is a work of art to warm the heart of any pack rat.

Mesilla Valley Store (575-524-1003), 2350 Calle de Principal, Mesilla. Mesilla Plaza has long needed a purveyor of the authentic agricultural products of this region, products such as pecans, jams, jellies, barbecue sauce, honey and all the flavors that make the cuisine here distinctive. A delightful shop, offering many seasonal gifts.

✱ Special Events

Monthly: **Truth or Consequences Art Hop,** (575-740-6180), second Saturday, 6–9 PM, Downtown. **Las Cruces First Friday Art Ramble**, 5–8 PM, Downtown.

COLORFUL SILVER CITY STOREFRONTS ARE DOWNRIGHT IRRESISTIBLE TO PASSERSBY

February: **Festival of the Cranes** (575-835-1828), Bosque del Apache National Wildlife Refuge.

March: **Cowboy Days** (575-521-2444), NM Farm & Ranch Heritage Museum.

April: **La Vina Wine Festival** (575-882-7632), 4201 NM 28, La Union.

May: **Truth or Consequences Fiesta** (Ralph Edwards Day) (575-894-6673), Truth or Consequences. **Southern New Mexico Wine Festival** (www.nmwine.com), Southern New Mexico Fairgrounds, west of Las Cruces (575-636-2199).

September: **Hatch Valley Chile Festival** (575-635-1582) www.hatchchilefest.com), Labor Day Weekend.

November: **Renaissance Artsfaire** (575-523-6403), Young Park, Las Cruces. **El Día de los Muertos** (575-647-4767; calaveracoalition@q.com), Mesilla. **International Mariachi Conference** (575-525-1735) www.lascrucesmariachi.org), Las Cruces.

OLD HIGHWAY 60 COUNTRY

Magdalena, Datil, Pie Town, Quemado

Along Old US Highway 60, nicknamed the "Pieway," you can find, in addition to fine homemade pie, sources of fascination from the rural end of the spectrum—cowboy country and wide open spaces—to the high-tech end, personified by the Very Large Array radiotelescope. In a sense, this slow road, without chain stores or billboards, is a microcosm of New Mexico. The new and the old find the place big enough and accommodating enough to coexist and go their own distinct ways.

GUIDANCE **Magdalena Chamber of Commerce** (866-854-3310; www.magdalena-nm .com), P.O. Box 281, Magdalena 87825.

✱ To See

TOWNS **Datil**, 35 miles west of Magdalena on US 60, was named for the nearby Datil Mountains. The name translates to "date" (perhaps a wild fruit that grew here). There's not too much to see here, but the Eagle Guest Ranch has been a convenient pit stop for travelers since folks first took to the road in automobiles. Gas, food, and lodging available.

Magdalena is 27 miles west of Socorro on US 60. Supposedly the face of Mary Magdalene is visible on the mountainside at the eastern edge of town. The truth is, this was the cattle shipping railhead of the "Hoof Highway," or the "Beefsteak Trail," where cowboys rounded up and drove cattle in from ranches 125 miles west to Arizona and across the Plains of San Augustin and shipped them out on the railroad. The second weekend in July is "Old Timers' Day," when the old storytellers return and the Queen, who must be over 70, is celebrated on a float in the parade.

Pie Town is 21 miles northwest of Datil on US 60. This twentieth-century homesteader town baked its way out of the Depression by selling homemade pies to cowboys. Pies are still baked here, with a couple of cafés open, with irregular hours, at what is largely a wide place in the road. Do get there early in the day if you want pie, because things tend to shut down by 3 PM Closed much of the winter.

Quemado is 43 miles west of Pie Town on US 60. Last chance! You're only 33 miles from the Arizona border here, so if you're heading west, you might think of gassing up and stopping for some home cooking in a local café before leaving. The name of the town means "burned" in Spanish, but no one is really certain how or why this name was given to the place.

HISTORIC LANDMARKS, PLACES, AND SITES **Lightning Field** (505-898-3335), Quemado. An installation of 400 polished steel poles by American sculptor Walter De Maria that catches the changing light, and the lightning, of New Mexico's isolated high desert. You will be brought to the location, 45 miles outside Quemado, and permitted to stay overnight one night in a rustic cabin that sleeps six. You may be bunking with strangers. Call for prices.

Very Large Array (575-835-7000), 50 miles west of Socorro on US 60. Visitor center open 8:30 AM–sunset. Closed major holidays. Did you see *Contact*, starring Jodie Foster? If so, you will recognize the twenty-seven giant dish antennas of the VLA, a.k.a. the National Radio Astronomy Observatory, on the barren Plains of San Augustin between Magdelena and Datil. The visitor center shows a video and has exhibits explaining the VLA telescope and radio astronomy. An easy self-guided walking tour goes to the base of one of the antennas. Guided tours first Sat. each month 11 AM–3 PM Free.

VERY LARGE ARRAY RADIO TELESCOPE ON THE PLAINS OF SAN AUGUSTIN

✳ To Do

CAMPING Datil Well Campground (575-835-0412), US 60 at Datil, south 1 mile on NM 12. One mile moderate hiking trails through piñon-juniper and ponderosa pine at this site of one of fifteen wells that supplied water along the 1880s cattle driveway between Magdalena and Springerville, Arizona. Twenty-two campsites; firewood provided. $5 camping.

FISHING Quemado Lake Recreation Area (575-773-4678). From Quemado, west on US 60 for 0.5 mile, south on NM 32 for 16 miles to NM 103. Quiet and truly unspoiled, here are 800 acres of ponderosa pine that border a 131-acre man-made trout lake with three-season fishing. The area is regulated by the Quemado Ranger District of the Gila National Forest and contains seven campgrounds, two ADA fishing piers, and 7 miles of hiking trails. The Quemado Lake Overlook Trail is a moderate 1.5-mile hike one-way with about a 1,000-foot elevation gain and is quite a photogenic trail with birding opportunities. Several easy-moderate hikes crisscross the area.

✳ Lodging

BED & BREAKFASTS, MOTELS Rancho Magdalena Bed & Breakfast (575-517-0644), 10965 US 60, Magdalena. Located on the historic cattle driveway. Hunting and guide services are also available here. Providing rustic elegance, peace and quiet, and biscuits and coffee delivered to your room each morning. A getaway for those in need of deep R & R. $115.

Western Motel and RV Park (575-854-3135), 404 1st Street, Magdalena, offers three kinds of accommodations, including its 1956 knotty pine motel, or if you prefer, a Victorian room in old "Grandma Butter's" adobe home that served as a maternity hospital during the 1920s. Fourteen RV sites. $65.

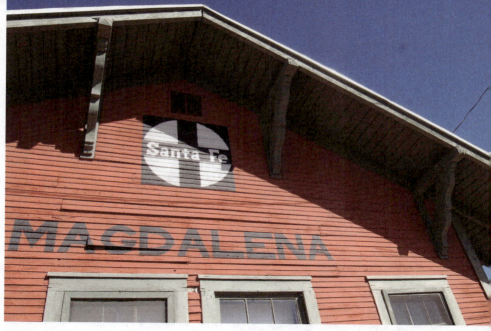

MAGDALENA, TRAIL'S END

✳ Where to Eat

EATING OUT **Eagle Guest Ranch** (575-772-5612), US 60 and NM 12, Datil. This roadhouse began as a gas station and grocery shop and dates back to the early twentieth century. It is still in the family. Steaks and burgers are the order of the day, and the Mexican food served Friday only will heat your bones. Expect to rub elbows with dusty cowboys and well-armed hunters. Inexpensive.

Pie-O-Neer Café (575-772-2711), US "Pieway" 60, Pie Town. Open Fri.–Mon. 10–3. Eat homemade pie on the Continental Divide. You have your choice of a dozen varieties; coconut cream is a big fave. Kathy Knapp bakes and feeds the wood stove as well as happy customers, who come from several countries. Homemade lunch as well. It's worth the trip! Try the new pie bar! But do call for hours before you go. Inexpensive.

KATHY KNAPP HAS BEEN DELIVERING LEGENDARY PIES IN PIE TOWN FOR ALMOST TWO DECADES

PIE-O-NEER CAFÉ, PIE TOWN

✳ Entertainment

London Frontier Theatre Company (575-854-2519; www.londonfrontiertheatre.com), 502 Main at 4th Street, Magdalena. Open select weekends March–December. With over a dozen seasons under its belt, and now housed in its historic WPA theater, the London Frontier Company regularly receives enthusiastic notices from all who experience it. The season centers on original ensemble plays related to the West and its history, with the Christmas offering in December as a highlight. $5 adults, $3 children.

✳ Selective Shopping

Blue Canyon Gallery (575-854-2953), 602 1st Street, Magdalena.

Elvires Rock Shop & Saw Shop (575-854-2324), E. Highway 60, Magdalena.
Route 60 Trading Post and Gallery (575-854-3560), 400 1st Street, Magdalena. Authentic jewelry made by Navajo living in nearby Alamo is sold here, along with cowboy art. You'll also find information on US Highway 60 here.

✳ Special Events

May: **Magdalena Festival Arts & Crafts Sale and Studio Tour** (575-854-2261), Magdalena. Also held in fall.
July: **Magdalena Old Timers' Reunion** (575-835-8927), Magdalena.
September: **Pie Festival** (www.pie-o-neer.com), Pie Town.
December: **Christmas Theater program** (575-854-2519), Frontier Theatre, Magdalena.

GHOST TOWN COUNTRY

*Hillsboro, Glenwood, Reserve, Columbus,
Silver City, Deming*

GUIDANCE **Columbus Chamber of Commerce** (575-343-0147), 401 E. Jesus Carreon Avenue, Columbus.

Deming-Luna County Chamber of Commerce (575-546-2674), 800 E. Pine, Deming.

Glenwood Area Chamber of Commerce (575-539-2711), P.O. Box 183, Glenwood.

Silver City Chamber of Commerce (575-538-3785), 201 N. Hudson Street, Silver City.

✴ To See

TOWNS **Columbus** is 32 miles south of Deming on NM 11. Not quite deserted enough to be classified as a true ghost town, Columbus receives plenty of visitors curious about Pancho Villa's March 9, 1916, border raid, as well as those touring Pancho Villa State Park. It is only 3 miles north of the Mexican border crossing at Palomas.

Deming, 61 miles west of Las Cruces on I-10, is convenient to both City of Rocks State Park and Rockhound State Park, and the town bills itself as "Rockhound's Paradise." The big annual event is the annual Rockhound Roundup held in March. It is another small town you will generally spend time in because you are on your way to somewhere else, unless you are one of the many "snowbirds" who regularly winter here. There are over thirty restaurants, many of them chains, to serve the population. It has ample motel accommodations and low overhead, but there isn't much to do in the town itself, aside from touring the very worthwhile, recently remodeled Deming Luna Mimbres Museum.

Glenwood. Sixty miles northwest of Silver City on US 180. Driving into Glenwood on a sun-dappled autumn day is like coasting into a lovely little piece of paradise, or a film set from the 1940s. It is a pleasant stop for gas and a visit to any of the cafés you might happen to find open—usually one is.

Hillsboro. Once the center of gold mining activity, Hillsboro, 17 miles on NM 152 from the I-25 exit, was well on its way to becoming a true ghost town when it was discovered by a few urbanites who moved in and fixed up the old houses or built new ones to look just like the old ones. It's a pretty place with a decent café, and it really is the gateway to the Black Range. Cowboys drew from a hat for the honor of naming it.

Mogollon. A former silver and gold mining town in the Mogollon Mountains, now with a scattering of cafés, antiques shops, and several well-weathered, photogenic wooden buildings. Still, a ghost town at heart. Silver Creek runs through the town.

Reserve is 36 miles north of Glenwood via US 180 and NM 12. Welcome to cowboy country, ma'am. A couple of bars, a gas station, and, if absolutely necessary, a motel, can provide for your immediate needs. This is not the place to share your feelings with strangers. A retreat to your motel room with a good book is the best advice.

NOTHING MUCH HAS CHANGED IN MOGOLLON FOR A CENTURY OR SO

Silver City. Seventy-two slow miles across Emory Pass west of exit 63 off I-25, Silver City makes an excellent base for exploring the Gila Cliff Dwellings, attending any of the many annual area festivals, and enjoying the birdlife and wildlife, and it is a good enough stop on its own, with two museums, plenty of galleries, and some restaurants that will not disappoint you, plus an historic downtown. Founded in 1870 and named for the rich silver deposits west of town, its period architecture is well preserved.

HISTORIC LANDMARKS, PLACES, AND SITES **Gila Cliff Dwellings National Monument** (575-536-2250), 44 miles north of Silver City on NM, trails open 9–5, visitor center 8–4:30; last visitor allowed into monument at 4 PM. Closed Christmas and New Year's Day. Contact the visitor center for information on guided tours. A short drive from the visitor center along the West Fork of the Gila River, a 1-mile loop trail leads through the dwellings, natural caves that were made into 40 rooms with stone quarried by these indigenous people. They were farmers who raised squash, corn, and beans on the mesa tops and along the river. We know them by these dwellings and for their exquisite black-and-white pottery. We do not know why they abandoned their homes and can only speculate that they may have joined other pueblos. They were the home of the Mogollon people who lived here from the 1280s until the early 1300s. The trail is steep in places, as there is a 180-foot elevation gain. For camping information, inquire at the visitor center. $10 per family, $5 per individual.

Pancho Villa State Park (575-531-2711), 400 W. NM 9, 135 miles south of Deming via NM 11, Columbus. Open daily. Visitor center daily 9–5. This is the only US park named for a foreign invader! Here you can tour an extensive desert botanic garden; see the ruins of Camp Furlong, site of the attack; and view a display of early-twentieth-century military equipment. Birding is excellent, and camping is available. The 7,000-square-foot exhibit hall showcases vehicles from the 1916 raid on Columbus in which eighteen Americans were killed. This spot marks the site of the only ground invasion of American soil since 1812. The visitor center is housed in the 1902 Customs Service Building, and it is where you can learn from historic photos and exhibits all about Francisco "Pancho" Villa's attack, though many locals continue to tell their own versions of the event, if you show a bit of curiosity. $5 day use; $18 camping.

MUSEUMS **Black Range Museum** (575-895-3321), NM 152, Hillsboro. Closed January and February. Call for hours. This was once the home of British-born madam Sadie Orchard, the archetypal lady of the night with a heart of gold. She served the town during epidemics and donated to good causes. Now her home tells the story of the early days of Sierra County, with an emphasis on mining. Donation.

GILA CLIFF DWELLINGS. REMOTE AND WORTH THE TRIP

A DELIGHTFUL COLLECTION OF ANTIQUE DOLLS AND DOLLHOUSES IS ON DISPLAY AT THE DEMING LUNA MIMBRES MUSEUM

Columbus Historical Society Museum (575-531-2414), corner of NM 9 and NM 11, Columbus. Winter hours September–April 10–4, Summer hours May–August 10–1, Sat.–Sun. 10–4. A restored 1902 Southern Pacific Railroad depot is the repository of collections on Columbus history, the Villa raid, and the railroad. Free.

✎ **Deming Luna Mimbres Museum** (575-531-), 301 S. Silver, Deming. Open Mon.–Sat. 9–4. Closed Thanksgiving and Christmas. Americana lovers, this is your new favorite place. Visit the Quilt Room; the Doll Room, with over 600 antique dolls; the ladies' fashion room; the military room, with mementos of the Pancho Villa raid; and the Indian Kiva, with outstanding Mimbres pottery and native basketry. This newly remodeled

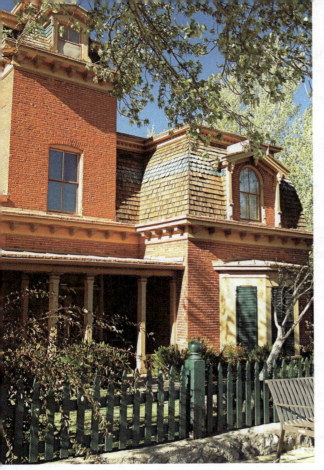

SILVER CITY MUSEUM

1916 armory has 25,000 feet of exhibit space and a motorized chairlift. Contributions welcome. Free.

Percha Bank Museum and Gallery (575-895-5652), 119B Main Street, Kingston. Open Sat. and Sun. 10–4 or by appointment. Hard as it is to believe, in 1890 this ghost town, population 30, was New Mexico's largest city, with 7,000 people. This museum offers an education on those days. This building is the only one remaining intact from the old days. Donation.

Silver City Museum (575-538-5921), 312 W. Broadway, Silver City. Open Tues.–Fri. 9–4:30, Sat. and Sun. 10–4. Closed Mondays. Open Memorial Day, Labor Day, and July 4. The museum, a brick Mansard-Italianate style home built by prospector Harry Ailman in 1880, showcases exhibits on local history. This is one of the most beloved and best-curated and maintained local history museums in the Southwest. $5.

Western New Mexico University Museum (575-538-6386), Fleming Hall, 1000 W. College, Silver City. Open Mon.–Sat. This hidden treasure of a museum houses the largest collection of prehistoric Mimbres black-on-white pottery in the nation. It will leave you breathless. Also on exhibit are Casas Grande pottery, mining artifacts, and prehistoric tools and jewelry. Open according to the university's schedule. Collection located in Watts Hall while Fleming Hall renovation underway. Call for hours. Free.

WILDER PLACES **Catwalk**, (575-539-2481), Glenwood. Take US 180 from Silver City to Glenwood; go right at NM 174 for 5 miles. Originally constructed by miners in 1889, this high walkway and suspension bridge leads to a waterfall through narrow Whitewater Canyon and over the Whitewater River in the Gila National Forest. You can easily imagine the ancient people who lived here, as well as Geronimo and Butch Cassidy hiding out here. The sycamore trees and rock walls make this place special any time of year, though especially in fall. The Catwalk follows the path of a pipeline built in the 1890s to deliver water to the mining town of Graham. The trail itself is easy and maintained the first half-mile; beyond that is very rough going—not recommended. Picnic tables, grills. Free. Please check on status and carry water if you go.

SCENIC DRIVES

Geronimo Trail Scenic Byway (575-894-1968), 301 S. Foch, Truth or Consequences, is the site of the trail's interpretive and visitor center. Open Mon.–Sat. 9–5. The geology, flora and fauna, history, and events of the area are available here. Travel a loop starting from Truth or Consequences up the Mimbres across steep, winding Emory Pass of the Black Range, passing through geological and cultural eons, and certainly, traveling in Geronimo's footsteps. The trail loops back at San Lorenzo on NM 152. This is an all-day trip at 220 miles, and you might want to overnight in Kingston.

Gila Cliff Dwellings/ Trail of the Mountain Spirits Scenic Byway (575-536-9461). Take NM 15 north from Silver City into the Gila National Forest to the Cliff Dwellings for 110 miles, through Pinos Altos, Lake Roberts, the Mimbres River, and the Santa Rita open pit copper mine to the Cliff Dwellings. Allow plenty of time, as the road is slow and there is much to see.

Lake Valley Back Country Byway (575-894-1968). Go east from Deming to Truth or Consequences via Hillsboro. Take NM 1521 and 27 for 47 miles. Slow going and well worth the trip. You'll see ghost towns and unparalleled views of the mountains south of Truth or Consequences.

NM 185 Back Road. Go north from Las Cruces or Dona Ana to San Antonio through pecan groves and chile fields for a view of the wilder side of the Rio Grande you can't get any other way. You can avoid the interstate all the way along this scenic two-lane. Glorious!

✱ To Do

FARMERS' MARKETS **Silver City Farmers' Market** (silvercityfarmersmarket@gmail .com), 1400 US 180 E., Silver City. Open May–October, Saturdays 8:30–noon. Holiday markets also.

CLIMBING THE CATWALK

GILA NATIONAL FOREST

Measuring over 3.3 million acres—the nation's sixth-largest national forest—the vast Gila is incomparable in its diversity and the opportunities it offers for outdoor recreation (3005 E. Camino del Bosque, Silver City; 575-388-8201. Ranger office open Mon.–Fri. 8–4:30). Its varied terrain ranges from high desert at 4,200 feet to rugged mountain and canyon lands at 10,900, and four of the six life zones of planet Earth are found here. Your best bet is to contact the number above to plan your trip around your specific interests. The forest, named for the Spanish corruption of a Yuma Indian word meaning "running water that is salty," is accessible from many of the small towns in southwest New Mexico, including Quemado, Glenwood, and Reserve. Whether your interests include birding, hiking, camping—which is mostly primitive, but does include RV hookups—ATV-ing, fishing, rafting, mountain biking—it is all here, at all levels of challenge. Nearly 400 species of birds make this their home or nesting area. The forest includes the Gila Wilderness and the Aldo Leopold Wilderness, the nation's first, founded in 1924. A section of the Continental Divide Trail lies within the forest. You could spend a week here, a summer, or a lifetime.

FISHING Lake Roberts (575-536-9929), US 180 north from Deming to City of Rocks turnoff. Continue on NM 61, then NM 35 for 66 miles to the intersection of NM 15 and NM 35. Or take NM 35 north from Silver City. Open year-round. This sweet trout fishing lake, which appears like a surprise on the side of the road in the Gila National Forest, has three campgrounds. $7 camping.

GOLF Rio Mimbres Country Club and Golf Course (575-546-3023), Deming. Eighteen-hole public golf course, east end of Deming with views of Cookes Peak and the Floridas, with pleasant lakes and paths. Inexpensive.

Silver City Golf Course (575-538-5041), 9 Golf Course Drive, NM 90 west from downtown, left on Ridge Road. Open year-round, weather permitting. A challenging 18-hole championship public course with high desert vistas, natural vistas, and mild weather. Inexpensive.

HORSEBACK RIDING WolfHorse Outfitters (575-534-1379), 125 Arenas Valley Road, Arenas Valley. Within the Gila National Forest, create a

CITY OF ROCKS STATE PARK RESEMBLES STONEHENGE IN ITS OWN WAY

horseback adventure with this Native American guide service. Rides through the wilderness, lodge to lodge, to the ruins, and in the moonlight. Half day $90; Full day ride $110, 6 hours, includes lunch.

HOT SPRINGS **Faywood Hot Springs Resort** (575-536-9663; www.faywood.com), next to City of Rocks State Park at 165 NM 61, halfway between Silver City and Deming. Open daily 10–10. Despite rumors Fayewood has closed or been sold to the mine, it is alive and well. There are over a dozen shaded, outdoor, natural, geothermal mineral water soaking pools, some public, some private, and some for overnight guests, who may use the public pools all night. "Limp in, leap out" is the motto here. Cabins, RV, and tent sites are available. $13 per adult per day; $25 per hour private tub.

PARKS **Big Ditch Park**, behind Bullard Street, Silver City. The flood of 1895 roared through Silver City with 12-foot-high waters, leaving behind a ditch 35 feet below street level. The subsequent flood of 1903 lowered the "Big Ditch" 20 feet more. It is now a pleasant town park for strolling and picnicking, directly behind downtown.

WINERIES **St. Clair Vineyards** (575-546-1179), 1325 De Baca Road, Deming. I-10 west from Las Cruces about 60 miles. Open Mon.–Sat. 9–6, Sun. noon–5. No appointments are needed for the tours offered Sat. and Sun. Grapes grown in the vineyards right here produce lovely Cabernet, Chardonnay, and Zinfandel. St. Clair also operates restaurants and tasting rooms in Albuquerque's Old Town, Las Cruces, and Farmington.

SAILING ALONG AT ELEPHANT BUTTE LAKE STATE PARK

GHOST TOWNS

Bayard Historical Mining District (575-537-3327). Now owned by the Phelps Dodge Mining Co., the six underground shafts with head frames of this once-busy mining district, which produced more gold, silver, copper, lead, zinc, iron, manganese, and molybdenum than all the other mining districts in New Mexico combined, may be toured by automobile. This area is popular with mountain bikers, horseback riders, and birders. The Buffalo Soldiers, the African American unit of the Ninth Cavalry, was stationed here 1866–99. Get tour information at the Bayard City Hall.

Chloride (575-894-1968), Main Street, Chloride. California retirees Don and Dona Edmund were inspired to purchase the entire town of Chloride, and they have, through the saintly labor of their own hands, been restoring it building by building. The general store has become the Pioneer Store Museum, open daily 8–5. Open for tours. All the original stock is still in place. You have to really want to come here, and it is an effort to reach this place, but you won't soon forget it, either.

Kelly. While the rumor is that Monsieur Gustave Eiffel, of Eiffel Tower fame, constructed the mining head frame here, it turns out to be a colorful story only. Once a booming mining town of 3,000 located 2 miles north of Magdalena where zinc, copper, then silver were mined, Kelly is a ghost town made for exploring. Artists come here to retrieve materials, and care must be taken, as not all the old buildings or mine shafts are well protected. However, even if you don't actually see the ghosts said to roam here, you can certainly feel their presence.

Kingston. Nine miles west of Hillsboro on NM 152. The home base of Sadie Orchard, the British madam with a heart of gold who made her fortune here, Kingston was a rip-snorting place with dozens of brothels and saloons and banks during the silver mining heyday. Hard to believe now, but it was once home to 7,000. Today, the population is just thirty. The old Victorio Hotel and Percha Bank still stand. Now it is quiet, picturesque, and the home of one delightful Black Range Lodge (see *Lodging*), and where javalinas roam Percha Creek.

Mogollon (mo-go-yone). Two hours north of Silver City on US 180, right on NM 159 between Glenwood and Alma. Calling all hard-core explorers: what is termed New Mexico's most remote ghost town, and, I must say, one of its most haunting, is accessible only by a 9-mile road that climbs 2,080 feet via switchbacks, without guardrails. The last 5 miles become a one-lane road. Founded in 1895, this gold rush boomtown was the state's leading mining district by 1915. While accommodations and attractions (aside from exploring and photographing on your own) come and go, at last moment before press time, the **Silver Creek Inn** (866-276-4882) was a functioning bed & breakfast. Do check road conditions carefully before you go.

✳ Green Space

Elephant Butte State Park, Caballo Lake State Park, and Percha Dam lie like three separate but neighboring versions of a similar geography, all fed by the Rio Grande, arrayed from north to south.

Caballo Lake State Park (575-743-3942), 16 miles south of Truth or Consequences at exit 59 off I-25. Named for the wild horses descended from the horses brought here in the 1540s by the Spanish, at Caballo find a recreation area and lake against the background of the Caballo Mountains just south of Elephant Butte, and it is much, much quieter, with excellent bass and walleye fishing. The champion striper from Caballo Lake weighed 51 pounds. There is plenty of camping available here. This is

Pinos Altos. Six miles north of Silver City on NM 15, this town sits directly on the Continental Divide. The Old West lives on here in a mining town where the Hearst Mine supplied the gold for the Hearst Castle. It is fun to photograph the splintering, wooden buildings, some housing the occasional gallery or ice-cream parlor, at sunset in their splendid decay; perhaps spot an elk wandering across the road; and order a steak at the Buckhorn Saloon.

San Antonio. Fourteen miles south of Socorro at the junction of NM 1 and US 380 off I-25 exit 139 east, San Antonio is known as the hometown of hotelier Conrad Hilton, whose father ran a boardinghouse here. It is also the gateway to Bosque del Apache National Wildlife Refuge and on the main road east to Lincoln and Billy the Kid country. Today, it is the home of two famous burger houses: the Owl Cafe and the Buckhorn.

Shakespeare (575-542-9034), 2.5 miles southwest of Lordsburg. I-10 from Lordsburg at Main Street exit 22, go south and follow the signs. Guided tours available. Shakespeare, which bills itself as "the West's most authentic ghost town," and was named for the mining company that held silver claims, was a stagecoach and mining town in its day, and here you can see the assay office, old mail station, saloon, general store, and much more. Open second weekend of the month and by appointment. $4 per person. Please call ahead.

Winston (no phone) is so close to Chloride that the two towns are generally visited on the same trip. Both towns are at the base of the Black Range.

WHIMSICAL SILVER CITY DOORWAY

just about your best bet to see migrating bald and golden eagles. We have spotted a few during the winter, and about 50 are known to reside in the area. $5 day use; $10–18 camping.

City of Rocks State Park (575-536-2800), US 80 24 miles from Deming west toward Silver City, then 4 miles northwest on NM 61. Open daily 7 AM–9 PM. With the feel of a natural Stonehenge, this state park is an astounding array of pillars of 34.9-million-year-old wind-sculpted volcanic ashes, some up to 40 feet tall. Paths run between the rock columns like the streets of a "city." There's an astronomy observatory and starry-night programs. This could be the state's premier dark-skies opportunity. $5 day use; $10–18 camping.

Elephant Butte Lake State Park (575-744-5923), I-25 exit 83, 5 miles north of Truth or Consequences. Open daily, 24 hours a day. It is huge, with 200 miles of shoreline and hundreds of campsites. This is a place for watersports of all kinds: wind surfing, fishing, and waterskiing, in addition to fishing, birding, and rock hounding. Elephant Butte Lake is the largest body of water in New Mexico, and it is well known for trophy fish, including striper, bass, and walleye. There are no elephants, only the eroded core of a volcano in the middle of the lake that somehow reminded someone of an elephant. The park hosts close to 1.7 million visitors annually. Be forewarned, Memorial Day, Fourth of July, and Labor Day can draw between 80,000 and 100,000 visitors. The US Bureau of Reclamation built the dam from 1912 to 1916, primarily for irrigation purposes; the reservoir capacity is 2.2 million acre feet. Boats and Jet Skis are available for rental at the two marinas. Public tours of the power plant are available. $5 day use; $8–14 camping. Houseboat, pontoon, ski boat rentals (505-744-5567).

Percha Dam State Park (575-743-3942). Just south of Caballo Dam. Known for its handicapped-accessible playground and spectacular birding, this park, with its huge cottonwoods, usually remains quiet, as it is still somewhat undiscovered. There are no developed hiking trails, only paths to the river, and walking along the dirt roads is a fine way to go. $5 day use; $10–18 camping.

Rockhound State Park/Spring Canyon (575-546-6182). From Deming, go south 5 miles on NM 11, then east on NM 141 for 9 miles. Open daily 7:30 AM–sunset. Set on the western slope of the Little Florida Mountains, the visitor center here has displays pertaining to the geology and history of the area. Known as a rockhounder's paradise; every visitor is permitted to take 150 pounds of rocks home. There are good pickings in jasper and perlite, and you can find some geodes or thunder eggs, as they are known. $5 day use; $10–18 camping.

✳ Lodging

BED & BREAKFASTS, MOTELS, AND INNS 🐾 **Black Range Lodge** (575-895-5652; www.blackrangelodge.com), 119

THE RUSTIC BLACK RANGE LODGE

THE REMODELED ART DECO MURRAY HOTEL IN SILVER CITY SHOWS OFF ITS INVITING LOBBY

Main Street, Kingston. When Catherine Wanek drove out from Los Angeles on her honeymoon, she spotted this old mining hotel, fell in love with it, and decided to buy it on the spot. Since that fortuitous day, this rather dark, out-of-the English countryside lodge has turned into a merry B&B. Massive stone walls and log-beamed ceilings date to 1940, but the original building dates to the 1880s, when it was built to house miners and cavalry. Despite improvements in the seven guest rooms, the original character of the place has not been tinkered with. Cyclists and tourists from all over the world are drawn here to enjoy the informality of the buffet breakfast with homemade bread, waffles, and house-grown jams and fruit. It has the feeling of a hostel, with shared claw foot tubs. The luxury guest house has a jetted hot tub and complete kitchen and wraparound deck. The Percha Creek House has five bedrooms, kitchen, dining, living room, and large deck. Catherine has become an expert and author on straw bale construction, and there are several straw bale buildings on the premises, including an all-natural meeting room that occasionally hosts live music, talks, films, and special events. $104–$181.

☀ **Casitas de Gila Guesthouses** (575-535-4455), Turkey Creek Road, Gila. Five private guest houses in perfect Southwest style and comfort are perched on a ledge overlooking Bear Creek and the Gila Wilderness. Privacy and peace and quiet are what you can expect here. The gallery displays a good selection of folk art, icons, and jewelry. Bring your binoculars to spot the bighorn sheep across the river. Ample continental breakfast is served. Also, bring your own food to cook in fully equipped kitchens. Wi-Fi, too, but no TV. Great stargazing, though. This spot frequently makes the list of "most romantic spots in New Mexico." $170. Prices decrease the longer you stay. Pet fee $10.

Gallery 400 Inn & Art Gallery (575-313-7015), 400 N. Arizona, Silver City. A downtown lodging located in an art gallery. Or an art gallery tucked away in an historic lodging? No matter.

NOTHING BEATS CURLING UP BY THE FIRE AT BEAR MOUNTAIN LODGE IN SILVER CITY

Urbane, comfortable, casual place to stay with an atmosphere that will be instantly recognizable to world travelers and visitors from metro areas. Light continental breakfast, coffee and tea bar. $90–95.

Inn on Broadway (575-388-5485), 64 Petersen Drive, Silver City. Three guest rooms and a Garden Suite conjure the glories of this 1883 merchant's home with marble fireplaces and hand-carved imports from Germany. There's a shady front veranda in this grand home. $125–$140.

Murray Hotel (575-956-9400), 200 W. Broadway Street, Silver City. Retro five-story streamline art deco hotel in the heart of Silver City's Historic Downtown Arts & Cultural District is refurbished and open for business. Another of this town's magnetic attractions. $84–$104.

Palace Hotel (575-388-1811), 106 W. Broadway, Silver City. Every town has a grand old hotel, and the 1900 Palace is Silver City's. Although rather more diminutive than grand, it is where to stay

if you collect historic hotel experiences. The eighteen rooms are small, and, facing directly on a busy street corner, it is not the quietest place in the world. The healthy continental breakfast will get you going. But it is comfortable, it has been restored, and if you are not expecting the Holiday Inn and don't mind carrying your luggage up and down a couple of flights of stairs, all will be well. The skylit upstairs lobby is perfect for hanging out, writing postcards, and visiting. And all of downtown is in walking distance. $58–$94.

RANCHES AND LODGES 🐾 **Bear Mountain Lodge** (575-538-2538), 60 Bear Mountain Ranch Road, Silver City. I am quite partial to Bear Mountain Lodge; in fact, it would have to be on my choice of top three places in NM to spend a week relaxing, regardless of the season. This eleven-room, spacious vintage 1928 lodge is a birder's dream come true, especially during hummingbird season in July–August, when numerous

varieties descend on Silver City. Gallery and café. Pet-friendly. $160–$265.

CABINS AND CAMPING **Bear Creek Motel and Cabins** (575-388-4501), 4845 NM 15, Pinos Altos. Bordering Bear Creek at the gateway to the Gila National Forest find 15 comfortable furnished cabins with porches and balconies among the tall pines. Pet friendly. $119–$159.

Continental Divide RV Park (575-388-3005), 4774 NM 15, 6 miles north of Silver City on NM 15, Pinos Altos. Smack in the middle of an apple orchard with views of the Gila National Forest, this site accommodates thirty-two RVs. Cabins and tent sites available, too. Please call for rates.

Gila Hot Springs Ranch (575-536-9314), 3778 NM 15, Mimbres. Enjoy a real kick-back time in a motel-like room; bring your RV or camp by the river. Natural hot pools and jetted tub, horseback riding, and fishing make this a real vacation. $80.

Lake Roberts Cabins & General Store (575-536-9929), Mimbres. The cabins are fully furnished with kitchens or kitchenettes, so you can catch it and cook it. $88.

✳ Where to Eat

DINING OUT **Buckhorn Saloon & Opera House** (575-538-9911), 32 Main Street, NM 15, Pinos Altos. Open daily 6–10 PM, D only. Saloon opens at 3 PM. Closed Sundays. Live music sometimes. This 1860s establishment is a necessary New Mexico experience. The Old West saturates the foot-and-a-half-thick adobe walls, and the Buckhorn radiates romance in its dimmed lights. In fact, this place may have invented "character." Dine in Victorian elegance—or belly up to the Old West bar. You're guaranteed to meet memorable characters at the bar, if that is your choice. The steaks are excellent, prepared perfectly, and served with fresh baked sourdough bread and

THE BUCKHORN SALOON IN PINOS ALTOS HAS AN EXPANDED MENU AND LIVE MUSIC ON WEEKENDS

THE ADOBE DELI IN DEMING IS A FOOD NETWORK STAR

all the trimmings, including house-made dressings for your salad. Love that filet mignon! Steak is not the only item on the menu, however. There is a variety of dishes to please any palate. Reservations are a very good idea, especially on weekends. Weekend entertainment as well. Moderate–Expensive.

🕯 **Diane's Restaurant and Bakery** (575-388-1255), 510 N. Bullard Street, Silver City. L Tues.–Sun. 11–2, brunch Saturdays and Sundays. 9–2, D Tues.–Sat. 5:30–9. No matter how many times you eat at this lovely downtown bistro, the food and service are impeccable. Fish, chicken, steak, and more light, harmonious, sophisticated fare, thoughtfully prepared, with just the right spicing and saucing, at a reasonable price—what more could you ask? Try the roast Asian duck with sweet sesame glaze, juicy meat loaf with garlic mashers, or pesto pasta. Diane's son Bodhi is busy in the kitchen, a happy chef. Fine dining with

family-sized portions. You can relax in the Parlor. Moderate–Expensive.

EATING OUT 🕯 **Adobe Deli Steakhouse** (575-546-0361), 3970 Lewis Flats Road SE, Deming. L, D Mon.–Sun. If you watch any food TV, you've probably encountered this place, as notable for the old barn/mounted heads decor as for the food. They serve as perfect a sandwich as you can find in these parts, with freshly baked bread and generous stacks of tasty meats. The signature onion soup is truly yummy, and the steaks are worth the drive. At the bar, you'll not only see the Wild West characters—here you become one. Oxygen Bar upstairs. Inexpensive–Moderate.

🕯 **Jalisco Cafe** (575-388-2060), 103 S. Bullard Street, Silver City. L, D. Open Mon.–Sat., Closed Sundays. When I first ate here about 20 years ago, there were lace curtains on the windows of a one-room establishment. When Silver

City rancher friends brought me here recently, the place had expanded to three colorful rooms of folks enjoying the hot fluffy sopaipillas, green chile chicken enchiladas, and zippy salsa on the warm, house-made chips. Consistently tasty. Inexpensive.

La Fonda (575-546-0465), 601 E. Pine Street, Deming. Enjoy the fresh warm chips, deliciously spicy salsa, fluffy sopaipillas, and delicious enchiladas at this very friendly and welcoming local spot. Inexpensive.

Millie's Bake House (575-597-2253), 600 N. Bullard Street, Silver City. Out of the kitchen come soups, salads, sandwiches, and baked goods, oh my, all with the taste of homemade. Death by Chocolate is a big favorite. Inexpensive.

Shevek's Casuals Italian Restorante (575-597-6469); 619 N. Bullard Street, Silver City. L, D Tues.–Sat. 11:30–8:30. Closed Sundays and Mondays. Mediterranean flavors in Silver City? From the world traveled longtime Silver City gifted chef Shevek, certainly. Delicious Italian food, authentic and healthy. Trouble is, you want to order everything on the menu. A delight, but with rather low-rent surroundings. Don't be put off. Inexpensive.

Vicki's Eatery (575-388-5430), 315 N. Texas, Silver City. Open Mon.–Sun., B, L. Perfect little café with super omelets, just the place to chow down, conveniently located in an historic brick building in the heart of town. Stylish, spacious, light, with homey food, good value. A local favorite. Inexpensive.

✱ Selective Shopping

Gila Hike & Bike (575-388-3222), 103 E. College, Silver City. This is the place to come when preparing a bike trip of any kind, to get equipment, service, maps, and rentals.

Seedboat Gallery (575-534-1136), 214 W. Yankie Street, Silver City. Ever walk into a place and feel like you could take home anything and be happy? The guiding hand of exquisite sophisticated taste is apparent when you walk in the door. Art off and on the wall, jewelry, sculpture, mixed media, ceramics. (As of this writing, the gallery is for sale.)

Silver City Trading Company's Antiques Mall (575-388-8989), 205 W. Broadway. The largest collection of vintage vinyl you'll find outside of a major metropolitan area, plus western memorabilia, jewelry, furniture, textiles. Easy to get lost. You may not land on the *Antiques Road Show* after a visit here, but you'll feel like you could!

Southwest Women's Fiber Arts Collective/Common Thread (575-538-5733), 107 Broadway, Silver City. This grassroots cottage industry markets the work of fiber artists in the rural Southwest. On the Fiber Arts Trail.

Yankie Street Artist Studios (575-538-3333), 103 W. Yankie, Silver City. Various local artists display their pottery and paintings here.

✱ Special Events.

March: **Rockhound Roundup** (575-544-9019), Southwestern New Mexico Fairgrounds, 4750 Raymond Reed Boulevard, Deming. Second weekend.

May: **Tour of the Gila Bike Race** (575-590-2612), 103 E. College, Silver City, first week. This event is billed as America's most popular five-day stage race. **Southern New Mexico Wine Festival** (575-522-1232), Southern New Mexico State Fairgrounds. Live entertainment and sampling of New Mexico wines. Last weekend: **Silver City Blues Festival** (575-538-2505).

July: **Magdalena Old Timers' Reunion**, weekend after Fourth of July. Cattle drive, parade, rodeo, barbecue, fiddlers' contest, and a good time is had by all (575-854-3310).

August: ✐ **Great American Deming Duck Race** (575-567-1469), 202 S. Diamond, Deming. Fourth weekend. Has it come to this? It sure has. **Silver City Clay Festival** (575-538-2505).

September: **Hatch Valley Chile Festival** (www.hatchchilefest.com /events.php) Labor Day Weekend, despite its popularity and longevity, retains its down-home authenticity with food and craft booths, live music, and, of course, lots of freshly roasted chile to sample and buy. **Pickamania** (575-895-5652), Black Range Lodge, Kingston.

November: **Festival of the Cranes** (575-835-2077; www.festivalofthecranes .com), Bosque del Apache National Wildlife Refuge, mid-November. Workshops, tours, special birding events. **Día de los Muertos** (Day of the Dead) (calaveracoalition@q.com), Mesilla Plaza, Mesilla.

First weekend. Following the Mexican custom of building altars and feasting on the graves of departed family members, Mesilla Plaza is now filled with altars and craft booths at this time, and the custom has been revived here during the past 10 years to include a procession to the cemetery.

Renaissance Artsfaire (575-523-6403), Young Park, Las Cruces. Second weekend. Joust on, all ye lords and ladies, knights and maidens, in costume, please.

December: **Tamal** y Mas Fiesta (scgreenchamber@gmail.com), Silver City. Most towns and many state parks and monuments have luminaria tours during the month. Please check individual listings.

SOUTHEAST NEW MEXICO: BILLY THE KID COUNTRY

BILLY'S STOMPING GROUNDS
Capitan, Fort Sumner, Lincoln, Carrizozo, Tularosa, Alamogordo, Ruidoso, Roswell, Cloudcroft, Clovis

CAVERN COUNTRY
Carlsbad, White's City

OIL PATCH COUNTRY
Artesia, Hobbs, Lovington, Portales

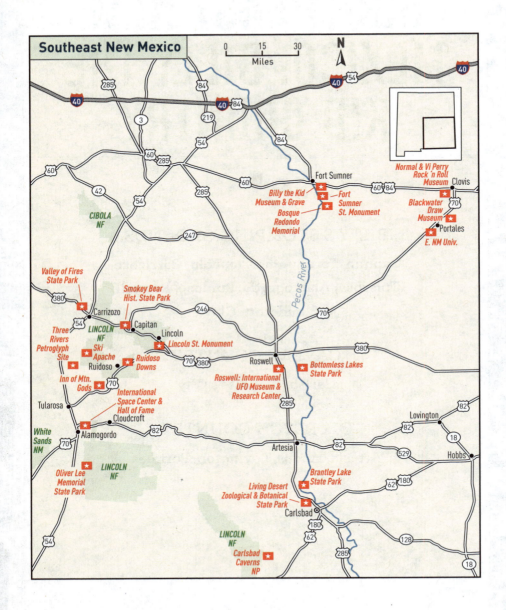

Southeast New Mexico

0 15 30
Miles

N

Fort Sumner

Normal & Vi Perry
Rock 'n Roll
Museum

Clovis

Billy the Kid
Museum & Grave

Fort
Sumner
St. Monument

Blackwater
Draw
Museum

Bosque
Redondo
Memorial

Portales

E. NM Univ.

CIBOLA
NF

Pecos River

Valley of Fires
State Park

Smokey Bear
Hist. State Park

Carrizozo

LINCOLN
NF

Capitan

Lincoln

Three
Rivers
Petroglyph
Site

Ski
Apache

Ruidoso
Downs

Lincoln St. Monument

Roswell

Bottomless Lakes
State Park

Ruidoso

Inn of Mtn.
Gods

International
Space Center &
Hall of Fame

Roswell: International
UFO Museum &
Research Center

Tularosa

Lovington

White
Sands
NM

Cloudcroft

Alamogordo

Artesia

Hobbs

Oliver Lee
Memorial
State Park

LINCOLN
NF

Brantley Lake
State Park

Living Desert
Zoological & Botanical
State Park

Carlsbad

LINCOLN
NF

Carlsbad
Caverns
NP

SOUTHEAST NEW MEXICO

L ike a hidden canyon where exposed walls reveal the earth's turbulent formation, southeast New Mexico tells the tumultuous story of the West's natural and social history. In this accessible region, it is possible to experience within a few days the history of the West, from prehistoric petroglyphs of Three Rivers to one of the West's most notorious battles, the Lincoln County War, starring William H. Bonney, a.k.a. Billy the Kid. In addition, southeast New Mexico displays the beginnings of the Atomic Age at the Trinity Site and the visual record of space travel at the New Mexico Museum of Space History in Alamogordo. Along the way are enduring legends and unsolved mysteries, agricultural festivals, and Apache ceremonials, all highlighted by eye-popping natural beauty.

Entering southeast New Mexico off I-25 south of Socorro and heading east, the visitor traverses the Valley of Fires State Park, a glistening black rock landscape, known as *malpais* (badlands), created by a lava flow as recently as 1,000 to 1,500 years ago. The landscape is relieved by the 10-foot-high yucca stalks. Critters living on the black lava flows have evolved to blend in, just as creatures that dwell in the White Sands, such as the earless lizard, have adapted white color schemes.

A user-friendly, well-maintained road system links towns and sites efficiently while granting the traveler continuous access to the area's varied natural beauty. Getting on and off the more traveled highways onto two-lane and scenic byways is easy.

As in other areas of New Mexico, it is always wise to be aware of rapid changes in weather, particularly afternoon thunderstorms that may cause flash floods. Temperatures may vary by as much as 40 degrees from day to night, so it is advisable to dress in layers and travel with warm jackets and rainwear, even if the sun is shining and the thermometer reads 80 when you set out. Good hiking boots or sturdy walking shoes are essential. Sunscreen, ample water, and a solid spare tire with proper installation tools are a must.

In this region, the mysterious vastness of the White Sands National Monument and the World Heritage Site of Carlsbad Caverns, with its fantastic crystal formations, coexists with the stomping grounds of the West's most notorious outlaw, Billy the Kid. Vibrant Apache initiation ceremonials such as kenalda,

THE SOUND OF RUNNING WATER IS EVERYWHERE, AS IT FLOWS THROUGH HAND-DUG ACEQUIAS (DITCHES) IN HISTORIC TULAROSA

ANOTHER THEFT OF BILLY THE KID'S GRAVESTONE IN FORT SUMNER SEEMS UNLIKELY

the young woman's coming of age ceremony, still take place in Mescalero, and the hundred year-old *acequias* (irrigation ditches) hand dug by pioneers, still flow with water from 12,000-foot snow-capped Sierra Blanca through the streets of Tularosa's historic district.

Memories are long here, and it is possible to run into Lincoln County old-timers who grew up hearing versions of the Lincoln County War and its participants that never appeared in history books. To many natives, Billy the Kid is regarded as more of a likeable Robin Hood than a violent thug. Questions about "the Kid" still evoke passionate debate: Did he really kill one man for each of his 21 years? Or was he simply doing what was just, at least according to the "law west of the Pecos," avenging the honor of his comrades, resulting in no more than three murders by his own hand?

The disappearance of attorney Albert Fountain and his son Henry in the White Sands more than a century ago, to this day New Mexico's leading "unsolved mystery," still evokes strong opinions about "who done it" among locals. And somewhere out there, supposedly, is a cache of Spanish gold waiting to be discovered.

In addition, southeast New Mexico beckons with family fun, with downhill skiing at Ski Apache, ice skating, cross-country skiing, and tubing in Cloudcroft, picnicking and "sledding" the dunes at White Sands National Monument, and camping, fishing, and hiking in the Lincoln National Forest. Other highlights include Smokey Bear Historical Park in Capitan and Alamogordo's Kid's Kingdom with the Toy Train Depot and the Southwest's first zoo, as well as the comprehensive New Mexico Museum of Space History. Warm-weather bat flights out of Carlsbad Caverns are another family favorite.

The forested Mescalero Apache Reservation, home of the elegant yet comfortable Inn of the Mountain Gods, with its Las Vegas–style casino, champion golf course, upscale dining and terrific buffet, is but a fraction of the land formerly occupied by this nomadic tribe of hunters and warriors. Today, efforts are under way to preserve, record, and teach the Apache language and cultures.

For those intrigued by the phenomenon of UFOs, Roswell is the capital of speculation about extraterrestrial life, and Fourth of July weekend is the great gathering of thousands magnetized by UFOs, many in costume.

As the area is large, when navigating or planning your tour, it may be best to think of it in three separate, broadly defined areas: Billy's Stomping Grounds, Cavern Country, and Oil Patch Country. Descriptions of each follow.

The *Green Space* listing is found near the end of the chapter, before the *Special Events* calendar.

Whether or not you believe in UFOs, and whether or not you believe Sheriff Pat Garrett really shot and killed Billy the Kid in cold blood one night in 1881 at Pete Maxwell's ranch, and that Billy actually is the individual interred in Fort Sumner, one thing is sure: in southeast New Mexico you will encounter both the grand beauty and great legends of the American West.

BILLY'S STOMPING GROUNDS

Capitan, Fort Sumner, Lincoln, Carrizozo, Tularosa, Alamogordo, Ruidoso, Roswell, Cloudcroft, Clovis

Where else can you time-travel between such wildly varied eras as the Old West of Billy the Kid and the Roswell crash of 1947? Between attractions, you have a lot of space, which you will need as there are so many interesting sights and so much information to absorb. It is hot and dry year-round, with few exceptions, such as the historic district known as the "49 blocks" of Tularosa. The mountains of Mescalero, Ruidoso, and Cloudcroft also provide a refreshing break from the desert. Rich in history and natural marvels, this part of New Mexico is an essential tour for the dedicated roadmeister.

GUIDANCE **Alamogordo Chamber of Commerce** (575-437-6120; www.alamogordo .com), 1301 N. White Sands Boulevard, Alamogordo.

Capitan Chamber of Commerce (575-354-2273; www.villageofcapitan.com; www .smokeybearpark.com), 443 W. Smokey Bear Boulevard, Capitan.

Carrizozo Chamber of Commerce (575-648-2732; www.townofcarrizozo.org), P.O. Box 567, 401 8th Street, Carrizozo.

Cloudcroft Chamber of Commerce (575-682-2733; www.coolcloudcroft.com), 1001 James Canyon Highway, Cloudcroft.

Clovis/Curry County Chamber of Commerce (575-763-3435; www.clovisnm.org), 105 E. Grand Street, Clovis.

Fort Sumner/DeBaca County Chamber of Commerce (575-355-7705; www.ftsumner chamber.com), 707 N. 4th Street, Fort Sumner.

Roswell Chamber of Commerce (575-623-5695; www.roswellnm.com), 131 W. 2nd Street, Roswell.

Roswell Convention & Visitors Bureau (575-624-7704), 912 N. Main, Roswell.

Ruidoso Valley Chamber of Commerce/Visitor Center (575-257-7395; www.ruidoso now.com), 720 Sudderth Drive, Ruidoso.

GETTING THERE To get to southeast New Mexico, take US 380 east off I-25 at San Antonio, 13 miles south of Socorro. Continue east on US 380 through Carrizozo to Capitan and Lincoln and on to the Hondo Valley to Roswell; or south on US 54/70 past Three Rivers into Tularosa, Alamogordo, and White Sands. From Tularosa, follow US 70 north to Mescalero, Ruidoso, and San Patricio, then east to Roswell. From Roswell, go south on US 285 through Artesia to Carlsbad.

MEDICAL EMERGENCY **De Baca Family Practice Clinic** (575-355-2414), 546 N. 10th Street, Fort Sumner.

Eastern New Mexico Medical Center (575-622-2259), 405 W. Country Club Road, Roswell.

Gerald Champion Regional Medical Center (575-439-6100), 2669 N. Scenic Drive, Alamogordo.

Lincoln County Medical Center (575-257-8200), 211 Sudderth Drive, Ruidoso.

Presbyterian Healthcare Services Carrizozo Healthcare Center (575-648-2317), 710 Avenue E, Carrizozo.

Sacramento Mountain Medical Center (Presbyterian Medical Services) (575-682-2542), 74 James Canyon Highway, Cloudcroft.

✲ To See

TOWNS **Alamogordo** lies at the junction of US 54/70 and US 82. The home of Holloman Air Force Base and one of the region's larger towns at pop. 30,000, with a variety of restaurants, chain motels, and a shopping mall, Alamogordo makes a good overnight stop or a base for exploring White Sands. Here find New Mexico International Space Museum, IMAX Theater, and children's activities, as well as the Flickinger Center for the Performing Arts.

PLAY "FIND THE BURRO" IN THE CROSSROADS TOWN OF CARRIZOZO, WHICH HAS SPROUTED A FEW INTERESTING GALLERIES AND CAFÉS

Capitan, where US 380 meets NM 246 and NM 48, makes an attractive lunch stop where kids will love the Smokey Bear Restaurant, either before or after a tour of the Smokey Bear Historical Park.

Carrizozo, at the junction of US 380 and US 54, at the gateway to the Valley of Fires State Park, has a homegrown art scene and cafés worth checking out. A drive around the streets surrounding downtown reveals a growing number of updated homes. The "Burro Trail" reveals colorful sculptures perched on rooftops and peering around corners.

Cloudcroft. Twenty-six miles east of Alamogordo on US 82, is high in the Sacramento Mountains at 9,100 feet. Originally founded as a railroad town, early on it became a cool vacation escape for El Pasoans. With its superb Lodge at Cloudcroft, unique shops, and galleries on Burro Street, a plethora of B&Bs and other accommodations, tiny Cloudcroft is the perfect base for hiking the Lincoln National Forest and enjoying winter snow sports or a cool getaway in the summer.

Clovis, 67 miles east of Fort Sumner on US 60, named for the French king who converted to Christianity, has roots deep in railroading and agriculture. It is today a superb place for antiquing and for appreciating Pueblo Deco architecture and rock-and-roll history. The home of Cannon Air Force Base, Clovis has ample modern amenities, shopping malls, and motels.

Fort Sumner, 41 miles southeast of Santa Rosa on US 84, holds the legendary gravesite of Billy the Kid. The pleasant little town, which feels as if it has stepped back in time, also has museums and shopping opportunities for Kid souvenirs and memorabilia. Fort Sumner State Monument, where Navajo and Apache people were confined during the 1860s following the Long March from their destroyed homelands in Canyon de Chelly, with the Bosque Redondo Memorial to that epoch sited here.

Lincoln, 46 miles southeast of Carrizozo on US 380, is the quiet, well-preserved site of the Lincoln County War, essentially a rivalry between mercantile factions that indelibly marked New Mexico and western history. Step into that history here at the Lincoln County Courthouse, where Billy the Kid slipped through handcuffs to make his daring escape, and learn the entire story, which is well documented at the Lincoln State Monument museum.

Roswell, at the crossroads of US 285, US 70, and US 380, a major stop on the Goodnight-Loving and Chisum cattle trails of the Old West, has reinvented itself several times. After losing Walker Air Force Base in 1967, the town diversified into a thriving hub of business, education, and tourism. Dairies replaced many cattle operations, and the old downtown is filled with UFO museums and shops marketing UFO-themed curiosities and trinkets. Best of all, the Roswell Museum exhibits a must-see collection of Southwestern artists, in particular Roswell native Peter Hurd and his wife, Henriette Wyeth, whose landscapes and portraits of their Hondo Valley neighbors are seldom seen elsewhere.

IF ONLY THE FORTIFIED WALLS OF LINCOLN'S TORREON COULD SPEAK

Ruidoso, 32 miles northeast of Tularosa on US 70, famous for Ruidoso Downs, home of the country's richest Quarter horse race, and a bustling community filled with shops, restaurants, and condominiums. In addition to tourists, the town, whose name translates to "noisy water," for the stream, which runs through town, attracts retirees and vacation homeowners. There's plenty to do here, with abundant golfing, arts activities, hiking, shopping, horseback riding, and fishing opportunities.

Tularosa, at the junction of US 54 and US 70, is as charming an oasis as exists in New Mexico. Giant pomegranates, poplars, and sycamores sink deep roots into the ditch banks that run throughout the historic district. This district, known as "the 49," was the original town site established by nineteenth-century pioneers who moved here from Mesilla after their farmlands were flooded. Following the Civil War, Union soldiers of the California Column settled here, married local women, and built homes, many of which have been restored. The variety of vernacular architecture is well worth a stroll. Tularosa has a few eateries but lacks lodgings.

THE MONUMENT AT BOSQUE REDONDO COMMEMORATES THE LONG WALK OF THE NAVAJO PEOPLE

GHOST TOWNS **White Oaks.** Three miles north of Carrizozo on US 54, 9 miles east on NM 349. A full-fledged ghost town, these quiet remains of an 1880s gold mining boomtown have a historic cemetery, a School House Museum and Miners Museum that are catch as catch can for being open, and the No Scum Allowed Saloon, the place most likely to be open, with a shuttle that runs to Carrizozo. The town has been for some time experiencing a slow-motion revival, with artists occupying the old houses.

HISTORIC LANDMARKS, PLACES, AND SITES ✐ **Alameda Park Zoo** (575-439-4290), 1321 N. White Sands Boulevard, Alamogordo. Open daily 9–5. Closed Christmas and New Year's Day. Established in 1898, this is the oldest zoo in the Southwest, with 300 animals of ninety species. $2.50 adults and children over age 12, $1.50 seniors, children under age 12, under age 2 free.

Blackdom (no phone), 18 miles south of Roswell, 8 miles west of Dexter. This all-black homesteading town founded in 1911 by 20 families was led by Francis Marion Boyer, who walked from Georgia to New Mexico, hoping to establish a self-sustaining community. Blackdom was abandoned in the 1920s. Very little remains on the site. Free.

Bosque Redondo Memorial at Fort Sumner State Monument (575-355-2573), 3 miles east of Fort Sumner, NM 60/84, 3.5 miles south on Billy the Kid Road. Open Wed.–Sun. 8:30–4:30. Closed Mondays and Tuesdays and major holidays. This moving memorial commemorates and honors Navajo and Apache forced from their homelands in 1864 in the "Long March." Cultural and historic programs are presented throughout the year. A museum designed by Navajo architect David Sloan and an interpretive trail cast light on this tragic period in US history. $3 adults, children age 16 and under free, Sunday free to New Mexico residents with ID, Wednesday free to New Mexico seniors with ID.

Fort Stanton Historic Site (575-354-0341; www.museumofnewmexico.org). 104 Kit Carson Road, Fort Stanton. East on US 380 from Capitan, right on NM 220. Open daily

10–4. Established in 1855, abandoned during the Civil War, and reoccupied after the Civil War by Kit Carson, this was the base of the Buffalo Soldiers of the Ninth Cavalry. After it was decommissioned in 1896, it served as a TB hospital, later on, it was an internment camp for World War II German POWs and Japanese. A Merchant Marine cemetery is on the site. Living history programs during the summer months. The big annual event is Fort Stanton Live, the second Saturday in July, with Civil War re-enactments, lectures, and food trucks. Admission by donation.

Goodnight Loving Trail (no phone). Originally spanning 2,000 miles between Texas and Wyoming, this cattle trail was blazed in 1866 by Charles Goodnight and Oliver Loving. The New Mexico portion follows the Pecos River to Fort Sumner.

✐ **Smokey Bear Historical Park** (575-354-2748), 118 Smokey Bear Boulevard, Capitan. Open daily 9–4:30. Closed Thanksgiving, Christmas, and New Year's Day. Opened in 1979 in honor of the bear cub found with burned paws after a disastrous 1950 forest fire in the Capitan Mountains, which became the symbol of forest fire prevention. After living at the National Zoo in Washington, DC, Smokey was returned to his home and buried here. Presentations and exhibits on ecology, forest health, and fire prevention, plus a playground, picnic area, and the original Capitan train depot highlight the park. Smokey Bear Days are held the first weekend in May. $5 per vehicle.

Three Rivers Petroglyph National Recreation Site (575-585-3457), 28 miles south of Carrizozo off US 54. East 5 miles from US 54 at Three Rivers on County Road B30; 455 Three Rivers Road. Open daily April–October 8–7, October–April 8–5. Closed Christmas. The mystery of this place is best perceived during the fall, when you are most likely to have it to yourself. The half-mile gently inclining trail contains outstanding examples of 21,000 petroglyphs, or rock carvings, carved by the vanished Mogollon people 1,000 years ago. Another short trail leads to a partially excavated prehistoric village. Caution: Stay on the path as rattlesnakes really do live here—beware. $5 per vehicle.

ROCK ART IS EVERYWHERE AT THE THREE RIVERS PETROGLYPH SITE

LITTLE ONES LOVE THE TOY TRAIN DEPOT AND TRAINRIDE IN ALAMOGORDO

🚂 **Toy Train Depot** (575-437-2855), 1991 N. White Sands Boulevard, Alamogordo. Open Wed.–Thurs. 12–5; Fri.–Sat. 10–5; Sun. 2–5. Closed Mondays and Tuesdays. Closed Christmas and New Year's Day. Ride the toy train 2.5 miles around Alameda Park (departures every 30 minutes) and visit the century-old depot with a gift and model train shop. More than 1,200 miles of model train track and toy trains on display, plus historic railroad artifacts to intrigue train buffs. Adjacent Kid's Kingdom Park is a great place for children to play and let off steam. Admission $5; train rides $5. Bargain rate is $8 for both museum and train ride. Age 3 and under free.

Trinity Site (505-319-6448), 12 miles east of San Antonio on US 380, 5 miles south through Stallion Range Center. Open at Stallion Gate first Saturday April and October only, 8–2. At the north end of White Sands Missile Range is ground zero, where the first atomic bomb was detonated on July 16, 1945. Free.

Tularosa Basin Museum of History (575-434-4438), 1301 N. White Sands Boulevard, Alamogordo. The joys of the local on display here, right next to the visitor center, plus research center and photo archive. Mon.–Sat., 10–4. Free.

MUSEUMS 🚂 **Billy the Kid Museum** (575-355-2380), 1435 E. Sumner Avenue, Fort Sumner. Open May 15–September daily 8:30–5, October–May 15 Mon.–Sat. 8:30–5, closed Sundays. Learn about the Old West, including views of a variety of Billy the Kid memorabilia. $5 adults, $4 seniors age 62+, $3 children ages 7–15, under age 6 free.

Carrizozo Heritage Museum (575-937-6555), 103 12th Street, Carrizozo. March–November, Thurs.–Sun., 10–2. Nice gift shop. major holidays. Emphasis here is on the town's railroad history and local ranching. Free.

🚂 **Hubbard Museum of the American West** (575-378-4142; www.hubbard museum.org), 26301 Highway 70 W. Ruidoso Downs. Thurs.–Mon. 9–5. Closed Thanksgiving and Christmas. An affiliate of the Smithsonian Institution. Collection of over 10,000 western items. Exhibits of western and cowboy artifacts, saddles, wagons, Pony Express rig, Kid's Corral, and the Anne C. Stradling collection of antiques, horse equipment, and memorabilia. Includes the Racehorse Hall of Fame, with exhibits dedicated to Triple Crown Champions, All American Futurity winners, women in racing, as well as

THE SITE OF THE FIRST ATOM BOMB DETONATION IS OPEN TO THE PUBLIC TWICE A YEAR

memorabilia from world champions. $7 adults, $5 seniors and military, $2 children ages 6–16, under age 6 free.

✏ **International UFO Museum & Research Center** (575-625-9495), 114 N. Main Street, Roswell. Open daily 9–5. Closed Thanksgiving, Christmas, and New Year's Day. Expanded hours during Roswell UFO Festival, first week of July. Find in this vast warehouse-like space the Roswell Incident Timeline, eyewitness testimonies, photographs, maps, and newspaper and radio reports that endeavor to give a complete account of the purported UFO incident that occurred here in July 1947. This center also contains the largest and most comprehensive collection of UFO-related information in the world, as well as records of those who have experienced sightings, abductions, or actual contact. $5 adults, $3 military and seniors, $2 children ages 5–15, age 4 and under free.

Lincoln State Monument (575-653-4025), 12 miles east of Capitan on US 380, Lincoln. Open daily 9–5. Old Lincoln Town's main street—actually, its only street—is lined with eleven buildings of stone and adobe that make up this National Historic Landmark. Here history seems very close at hand, because this site looks as it did during the heyday of Billy the Kid and Pat Garrett, and just as it did when the Lincoln County War raged during 1878–1881. The Old Lincoln County Courthouse Museum gives some context, with information on Hispanic settlers, Buffalo soldiers, major players in the Lincoln County War, and the politics of the time. $5, under age 16 free. Sun. free to New Mexico residents, Wed. free to New Mexico seniors.

✏ **New Mexico Museum of Space History** (575-437-2840). 3198 NM 2001, Alamogordo. Open daily 9–5. Closed Thanksgiving and Christmas. Five stories of space history include artifacts, models, and exhibits celebrating space voyage. The Stapp Air and Space Park displays actual rockets; the International Space Hall of Fame and the Tombaugh Education Center as well as the New Horizons Dome Theater and Planetarium, the first of its kind in the world to create a total immersion experience

THE FIGURE OF SUSAN MCSWEEN RECALLS THE LINCOLN COUNTY WAR

intriguing to children and adults. $7 adults, $5 seniors and military, $4 children ages 4–12, under age 4 free.

Roswell Museum and Art Center (575-624-6744), 100 W. 11th Street, Roswell. Open Tues.–Sat. 9–5; Sun., holidays 1–5. Closed Thanksgiving, Christmas, and New Year's Day. The term "regional" in no way diminishes the fine exhibits of contemporary and classic artists of the West shown here. Permanent exhibits of native Peter Hurd and wife Henriette Wyeth are staggering, while works of such renowned artists as Fritz Scholder and Georgia O'Keeffe appear regularly. The Goddard Rocket Museum is included. Free.

Robert H. Goddard Planetarium (575-624-6744), 912 N. Main, Roswell. The planetarium has science exhibits, including Goddard's rockets as well as star

AIRCRAFT AND SPACE EXPLORATION ENTHUSIASTS WILL RAVE OVER THE ALAMOGORDO NEW MEXICO MUSEUM OF SPACE HISTORY DEDICATED TO THEIR PASSION

shows and hands on exhibits to foster understanding of space phenomena. Call for changing schedule of full dome planetarium shows and hours. Has recently undergone a complete renovation and shows are spectacular! $5, $3 children 4–15 and seniors and Roswell residents.

NATURAL WONDERS **Sierra Blanca.** At just under 12,000 feet, this imposing mountain is a snow-capped beacon throughout most of southeast New Mexico.

White Sands National Monument (575-479-6124 www.nps.gov/whsa), 19955 US 70, 15 miles west of Alamogordo on US 70. Closed Christmas Day. Open daily Memorial Day–September 2, 7 AM–9 PM; winter hours 7 AM–sunset. Dunes Drive is 17 paved miles of the 300 miles of pure white gypsum dunes. This place's vastness and beauty make it seem like a moonscape here on Earth. You can get out of the car, hike, and play in the dunes. Reservations required for monthly Full Moon Nights and accompanying programs. The gift shop is vast, and the bookstore has a rich selection of Southwest and nature reading. $5 per person over age 15; under age 15 free. Ticket good for seven days.

SCENIC DRIVES **Billy the Kid National Scenic Byway** (575-378-5318; www.billybyway .com). Follows NM 48; NM 220; US 70/380 for 84.2 miles. The Billy the Kid National Scenic Byway Visitor Center, next to the Hubbard Museum of the American West in Ruidoso Downs, is the best place to orient the trip and make the most of it with maps and brochures. The byway links Ruidoso, Lincoln, Fort Stanton, and the pleasant green Hondo Valley. The entire area was Billy's stomping ground.

WINERIES **Arena Blanca Winery** (800-368-3081), 7320 US 54 Expressway, Alamogordo, 6 miles north of Alamogordo on US 54. In combination with McGinn's Country Store at the Pistachio Tree Ranch, Arena Blanca offers free wine tastings plus free pistachio samples. Located on a 111-acre pistachio orchard.

Tularosa Vineyards (575-585-2260), 2 miles north of Tularosa on US 54 at 23 Coyote Canyon. Tasting room open Mon.–Sat. 9–5. Sun. noon–5. Taste award-winning wines made from grapes specially acclimated to New Mexico. This winery specializes in premium reds and highly drinkable whites and blushes. Tours by appointment. Please call ahead if you plan to visit.

✳ To Do

BICYCLING AND WALKING **Spring River Recreation Trail** (575-624-6700), Spring River Park, 1101 W. 4th Street, Roswell, offers 5.5 miles of paved, gentle, and scenic hiking and biking.

BIRDING See the state parks under *Green Space*.

BOATING See the state parks under *Green Space*.

FISHING **Bonito Lake.** Take a left off NM 48 onto NM 37, 1.5 miles to "Y," then left to Bonito Dam to a man-made lake. Well stocked during fishing season, with easy to moderate hiking trails and camping areas. Free.

    Lake Van is 15 miles southeast of Roswell on NM 256/NM 2, in the hamlet of Dexter. Cool, pleasant Lake Van has lazy fishing, some camping, and swimming, or just picnicking. Free.

    Rio Peñasco (505-687-3352), 37 miles east of Cloudcroft on US 82 is the southernmost spring creek in United States.

GOLF **Clovis Municipal Golf Course** (575-769-7871), 1200 N. Norris Street, Clovis. Nine-hole public course. Very affordable.

    Desert Lakes Golf Course (575-437-0290), south end of Alamogordo on US 54. Open year-round. This is an attractive suburban municipal course in the Sacramento foothills with elevated greens and water hazards. Very affordable.

    Inn of the Mountain Gods (800-446-2963), Carrizo Canyon Road, Mescalero. Elegant eighteen-hole public course. $40–135.

    The Links at Sierra Blanca (575-258-5330), 105 Sierra Blanca Drive, Ruidoso Downs. Open year-round, weather permitting. This challenging, highly rated 18-hole spikeless Scottish-style course was designed by PGA Seniors Tour player Jim Colbert. $35–80.

    The Lodge at Cloudcroft (575-682-2089), 1 Corona Place, Cloudcroft. Open April 1–October. High-altitude, mountain bluegrass fairways, and Scottish rules of play make a memorable nine holes. $28–$34.

HIKING **Dog Canyon National Recreational Trail** (575-437-8284), Oliver Lee Memorial State Park. A 5.5-mile strenuous hike, with panoramic views of Tularosa Basin, Lincoln National Forest, and White Sands, was an ancient Native American Trail. The trail rises about 3,100 feet. Bring water and hiking stick. $6.

WHITE SANDS, A MAGICAL PLACE ANY TIME OF YEAR

Sacramento Rim National Recreation Trail, south of Cloudcroft. Follows rim of Sacramento Mountains 14 miles. Moderate hike. Sprawling views of Tularosa Basin 5,000 feet below.

Cloud Climbing Trestle Trails (Cloud-Climbing Rail Trail) (575-682-2551). The Rails-to-Trails Association has created all levels of hiking paths out of the overgrown railroad beds out of use since trains last toted logs out of the Sacramento Mountains in 1947.

HORSE RACING Ruidoso Downs Race Track (575-378-4431), 2 miles north of Ruidoso on US 70. Open Memorial Day–Labor Day. This track has the reputation as top Quarter horse racetrack in United States, and the richest Quarter horse race, the All American Futurity, where instant millionaires are made, runs Labor Day Weekend. Casino open daily.

HORSEBACK RIDING Chippeway Riding Stables (575-682-2565), 602 Cox Canyon Highway, Cloudcroft. Call for prices and hours.

ICE SKATING James Sewell Ice Rink (575-682-4585), 751 James Canyon Highway, Cloudcroft. Open daily during the season, weather permitting. Skate rentals, and later on warm up with hot cocoa by the inside fireplace.

MOUNTAIN BIKING Rim Trail (575-682-1229), Cloudcroft. Access this steep, difficult 13.5-mile trail, T105, which parallels Sunspot Scenic Byway part of the way for views of the Tularosa Basin. Visit Altitudes, the local mountain bike shop, for detailed trail maps and to explore the possibilities.

SNOW SPORTS Ski Apache (575-464-3600), 6 miles north of Ruidoso on NM 48. Left on Ski Run Road. Owned and operated by the Mescalero Apache Tribe on the Lincoln National Forest; the stated goal is to "provide the best ski experience for all ages and abilities." Both skiers and snowboarders of all levels find terrain variety on fifty-five trails served by eleven lifts. Lines are rare; elevations between 9,600 and 11,500 feet provide abundant snow that makes for a 180-inch annual average. Children's programs, rentals, and lessons. Moderate.

🖉 **Ski Cloudcroft** (575-682-2333), 19201/2 US 82, Cloudcroft. With 21 trails at all levels, three lifts, tubing, snowboarding, and a ski school on 68 acres at 9,000 feet, this tiny area could be just right for the whole family. $20–45.

🖉 **Triple M Snowplay Area** (575-682-2205), south of Cloudcroft on Sunspot Scenic Highway. Snowmobile rentals, tubing with a lift.

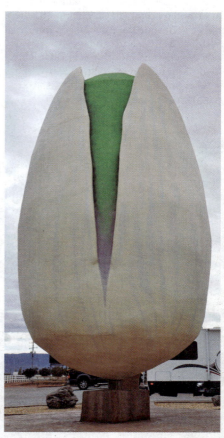

WORLD'S LARGEST PISTACHIO, AT MCGINN'S PISTACHIOLAND IN ALAMOGORDO, IS ONE FANTASTIC PHOTO OP

✳ Lodging

BED & BREAKFASTS, INNS, AND
MOTELS **Fite Ranch B&B** (575-838-0958; www.fiteranchbedandbreakfast.com), 7.5 miles east of San Antonio exit off I-25 on US 380. The Fite Ranch B&B is located on a working ranch that has been in existence since the 1930s. In 2002, ranchers Dewey and Linda Brown purchased it from original owner Evelyn Fite and the place is now run with love and care by their family. A home-cooked full and filling breakfast is served every day. The B&B is furnished with antique western decor with a touch of the Southwest. Each of the five lodgings includes at least one bedroom, a kitchen, a personal living area, and a private bath. The ranch borders the Bosque del Apache National Wildlife Refuge and is a favorite of birders. Weekly and monthly rates available. Two-night minimum. $125.

🐾 ♿ **Smokey Bear Motel** (575-354-2253), 316 Smokey Bear Boulevard, Capitan. The convenient Smokey Bear Motel has been operating here for 40 years in this, the final resting place of the original Smokey Bear. The clean, comfortable ersatz-rustic motel has some rooms that include refrigerator and microwave. The Smokey Bear Restaurant, with vintage photos of Smokey, on the premises serves hearty breakfast, lunch, and dinner, with such specials as chicken-fried steak and beef stew seven days a week. The motel is located 13 miles from Ski Apache. RV parking, too. No pets, unfortunately. $60.

🐾 **Wortley Hotel** (575-653-4300), US 380. Lincoln. Open year-round. So much fun! "No Guests Gunned Down in Over 100 Years" is the motto here in this 1874 creaky adobe building formerly owned by Sheriff Pat Garrett. Western rusticity and a total immersion in the Wild West that was Lincoln County. History comes alive and lives on here. Delicious, cooked to order complimentary gourmet breakfast included. Dietary preferences honored. $120. (If you can't stay the night,

THE LODGE AT CLOUDCROFT IS A FAVORITE SMALL INN, WITH AN EXCELLENT RESTAURANT AND GOLF COURSE

at least try to sit down for a meal. Taco Tuesday is popular with the locals and these tacos have been proclaimed "Best in the Southwest" by many publications. B, L Thurs.–Sun.)

LODGES AND RANCHES **Burnt Well Guest Ranch** (575-347-2668; www.burnt wellguestranch.com), 399 Chesser Road, Roswell. Thirty-five miles southwest of Roswell. Call for exact directions. If you're looking for a "ranch vacation," this may be the place. This hacienda-style inn with Old West rustic decor has only two rooms. Three generations of the Chesser family live on the property and run a working cattle and sheep ranch. The hacienda includes an inviting covered porch, and a great room with a checkerboard table, hobbyhorse, and piano. Guests have access to a kitchenette and laundry facilities. Capacity is 10 people with some bunk beds. Guests are invited to join in the daily workings of the ranch, including cattle drives. Dutch oven suppers fixed from ranch-raised meats, old-time storytelling, and riding the range to your heart's content are all part of the deal. $320 per person per day adults, three-night minimum.

Hurd–La Rinconada Gallery and Guest Homes (575-653-4331), 105 La Rinconada Lane, San Patricio. Twenty miles east of Ruidoso on US 70 at Mile Marker 281. The exquisite gallery and five guest homes are located on the historic and splendid Sentinel Ranch, home of the first family of American art, the Hurd-Wyeth family. Stay in the Helenita, for example, named for family friend Helen Hayes. Located among quiet rolling hills near the Rio Ruidoso River, the original ranch-hand quarters on Sentinel Ranch have become utterly romantic guest houses with modern conveniences. They are filled with antiques and designer furnishings and art created by the Hurd-Wyeth family. Each of the houses has a private patio. On the southeast corner of the family polo field is an impressive gallery of original works by members of the Hurd-Wyeth family. Rates are based on the number of people in your party, ranging from $150 for two to $350 for six; two-night minimum. Additional fees for single-night stay. Weddings!

Inn of the Mountain Gods Resort and Casino (575-764-7059), 287 Carrizo Canyon Road, Mescalero. Four miles south of Ruidoso on NM 48. The 273-room, stunning, exciting Inn of the Mountain Gods Resort and Casino is set in the picturesque Sacramento Mountains next to shimmering Lake Mescalero. Recreational activities include the Inn of the Mountain Gods Resort Championship Golf Course, a fully equipped workout facility, indoor pool, fishing, horseback riding, and sport clay shooting. Ski Apache is approximately 45 miles away. Las Vegas–style casino gaming at the resort offers everything from penny slots to high roller games. Dining options include steak-and-seafood fine dining at Wendell's, casual barbecue meals including breakfast at Apache Summit BBQ Co., the superior Gathering of Nations Buffet, and burgers, sandwiches, and beer at the casual Big Game Sports Bar and Grill. No need to leave the resort, once you check in. Some great deals to be had here folks. Rooms are gorgeous, spacious, and light. Rates vary dramatically, depending on weeknight versus weekend and time of year. $70–279.

✺ **The Lodge Resort and Spa at Cloudcroft** (800-395-6343), 601 Corona Place, Cloudcroft. The Lodge Resort & Spa is located in Cloudcroft at 9,000 feet elevation in the Sacramento Mountains, surrounded by the Lincoln National Forest. The resort offers fifty-nine rooms and suites. The original resort was destroyed by fire, and the current property is said to be haunted by characters from its past, in particular a wronged maid named Rebecca. Every New Mexico governor has slept in the elegant Governor's Suite. Amenities include a heated outdoor pool, year-round sauna and outdoor hot tub, fitness room, nine-hole traditional Scottish format golf course, and hiking trails. A variety of treatments are available at the Spirit of the Mountain Spa. Rebecca's, named after the resident ghost, serves breakfast, lunch, and dinner, plus an elaborate Sunday brunch. Rebecca's Lounge, which was once owned by Al Capone, serves drinks throughout the day as well as light lunch fare. The Lodge has had several famous guests: Judy Garland, Clark Gable, and Pancho Villa. If you climb to the top of the bell tower, you can see where Clark Gable inscribed his name. In the 1930s, the resort was managed by Conrad Hilton, who was born and raised in San Antonio, New Mexico. According to reports, Hilton was familiar with The Lodge and wanted to be closer to his family while his hotel chain took off. Words cannot do this delightful and beautifully well-managed place justice. It is simply divine, one of my favorite New Mexico escapes, where you can truly make the world go away. Sit by the fire and you'll agree. My highest recommendation, whether for romance, celebration, or relaxation. It is especially lovely at Christmastime and Valentine's Day. Murder Mystery weekends are a hoot. Great deals Wed.–Sun. starting at $98. Average $164.

CABINS AND CAMPING For camping, see the state parks listed under *Green Space*.

Cabins at Cloudcroft (575-682-2396), 1000 Coyote Avenue, Cloudcroft. The sixteen delightful cabins at Cloudcroft are open year-round in the aspens and pines, yet still within village limits. Cabins include full kitchens, baths, and firewood, and a coin-operated laundry is on the premises. Guests may choose between a wood-burning stove or a fireplace. Propane grills and picnic areas are available during the summer months. Two night minimum; one-night stay negotiable. Small pets allowed. $109–129.

Story Book Cabins (888-257-2115 or 575-257-2115), 410 Main Road, Ruidoso. Located amid the tall pines of Ruidoso's Upper Canyon along the "noisy" Ruidoso River, these "upscale rustic" cabins feature hot tubs, Jacuzzis, fully equipped kitchens, fireplaces, grills, private porches, and patios, as well as cable TV and DVD. The knotty-pine cabins have between one and six bedrooms. Secluded, yet close to in-town dining, galleries, and shops. Two night minimum. $134.

THE HURD FAMILY RANCH IN SAN PATRICIO IS NOW A LOVELY GUEST RANCH

THE MESCALERO APACHE–OWNED INN OF THE MOUNTAIN GODS IS THE LAST WORD IN LAS VEGAS–STYLE LODGING

✳ Where to Eat

DINING OUT Can't Stop Smokin' BBQ (575-630-0000), 418 Mechem Drive, Ruidoso. Open Tues.–Sun. 10–7. L, D, delivery. Wow! Head over here when the big barbecue craving hits. The slow-smoked brisket, ribs, and chicken are fall-off-the-fork tender, and the place can be a tad rowdy and a lot of fun. The "secret spice" mixture is MSG- and preservative-free. Really, really, really yummy. Inexpensive.

🐾 **Gathering of Nations Buffet** (800-545-9011), Inn of the Mountain Gods Resort and Casino, Mescalero. Open daily. B 7–10; L 11–3:30; D Sat. 4:30–10, Sun.–Thurs. 4:30–9. This is quite possibly the best, biggest, tastiest, freshest of the casino buffets. Watch out for holiday specialties, prime rib, seafood extravaganza and crab leg nights. The food, plus the warmly lit atmosphere, make it a favorite. Prices still under $15 for dinner make this a bargain. Inexpensive.

Martin's Capitol Cafe (575-208-5161), 110 W. 4th Street, Roswell. Mon.–Sat. 6 AM–8:30 PM. B, L, D. Martin's has been downtown so long, it must be doing something right—and it is! Absolutely authentic, tasty New Mexican red and green chile, just hot enough to be serious, served in a warm, Mexican-style dining room. Martin's has been discovered so is usually busy. Try for the off-hours. Inexpensive.

Old Road Restaurant (575-464-4674), 692 Old Road, Mescalero. Open daily 9–9. Guaranteed some of the most delicious New Mexican food you will ever put in your mouth. Go for the red combination, or just the red enchiladas. Chef-owner Henry Prelo Jr. makes his chilies rellenos fresh every morning. A comfortable log cabin atmosphere with local art and stellar service. A favorite with the motorcycle set. Inexpensive.

Rebecca's (575-682-3131), The Lodge, 1 Corona Place, Cloudcroft. B, L, or a very special dinner. Classic fine dining. Try châteaubriand for two, served and sliced before your eyes with an elegance fit for Queen Victoria. Famous for its deluxe Sunday brunch buffet and panoramic view of the Tularosa Valley from the Conservatory. The finest restaurant in the area. When you've really got something to celebrate. Moderate–Expensive.

Rockin' BZ Burgers (575-434-2375), 3005 N. White Sands Boulevard, Alamogordo. L, D Mon.–Sun. Only one reason—and it's a swell one—to come to this formica-sterile café near the mall: the State Fair Championship–winning green chile cheeseburgers served here. They're stuffed with grilled onions, topped with Hatch green chile and Wisconsin Cheddar—delish! Inexpensive.

Smokey Bear Restaurant (575-354-2253), 310 Smokey Bear Boulevard, Capitan. See Smokey Bear Motel listing. Inexpensive.

Tinnie Mercantile Store & Deli (575-622-2031), 412 W. 2nd Street, Roswell. 10–5:30 Mon.–Sat.; closed Sundays. Ladies who lunch and business folk alike come to dine on the awesome fresh salads and sandwiches. No better lunch spot in town, and if you have to wait, the shop stocks many lovely gifts, from stationary to jewelry. Inexpensive.

🍴 **Village Buttery** (575-257-9251), 2701 Sudderth Drive, Ruidoso. Voted Lincoln County's "Best Lunch" many times. Yes, there are plenty of ladies dining here, but the food goes way beyond "ladies lunch" fare. If you have only one lunch to eat in Ruidoso, you'd be wise to head here. Three house-made soups every day, delicious overstuffed sandwiches, daily affordable comfort food specials like pot roast, roast turkey, sour cream enchiladas, plus a display case of luscious desserts. Dine outside on the deck in sunny weather. Inexpensive.

Wendell's Steak & Seafood Restaurant (575-464-7842), Inn of the Mountain Gods Casino & Resort, Mescalero. Open D only Mon.–Thurs. 5–9; B, L, Fri.–Sat. 8–2, D 5–9; Sunday brunch 11–2, D 5–9. Steaks galore, with a $66 Kobe-style filet mignon in truffle sauce headlining the menu, plus pan-seared fresh halibut, New Mexico elk tenderloin in apple brandy reduction, and other delights. Expensive. The café adjacent Wendell's Lounge serves soup, burgers, sandwiches, and salads daily 11–10. Inexpensive.

Yum Yum Donut Shop (575-585-2529), 460 Central Avenue, Tularosa. It is worth going out of your way to stop at this tiny, modest-looking café that is so much more than a doughnut shop. Although you won't want to pass up a fresh daily "wildcat paw" or maple doughnut, do not, repeat, do not miss the brisket burrito with green chile. Mrs. Abeyta, who has lunch here every day, says the brisket is so tender she can "take her teeth out to eat it." 5 AM–3 PM, but can have erratic hours, so call first. Inexpensive.

Twin Cronnies Drive-In, (575-763-5463), 709 Commerce Way, Clovis. The last working cronnie machine in existence, so they say. What is a cronnie? It is a mini-hotdog cooked by circulating over a gas flame grill. Daily specials, like fried catfish Fridays. Many diner treats: cherry coke, lime rickey, all the stuff so bad for you from the good old days. A must-do for nostalgia hunters.

Foxy Drive-In, (575-763-7995), 720 W. 7th Street, Clovis. Don't ever, ever tell your cardiologist you went here. Everything is fried. Deep fried. Said to be the place where Buddy Holly, Roy Orbison, Waylon Jennings, and other musicians who recorded with Norman Petty at the 7th Street Studios hung out between sets. Inexpensive.

✳ Entertainment

Flickinger Center for the Performing Arts (575-437-2202), 1110 New York Avenue, Alamogordo. "The Flick" is a remodeled venue for a lively season of music, theater, and dance entertainment the family can enjoy together.

Le Cave at Le Bistro (575-257-0132), 2800 Sudderth Drive, Ruidoso. This is a special place for a glass of wine of an evening. A venue for live music.

Ruidoso Downs Race Track and Casino (575-378-4431), 26225 US 70 E, 2 miles north of Ruidoso on US 70. Open Memorial Day–Labor Day. Summer country music stars.

Sacred Grounds Coffee and Tea House (575-257-2273; www .sacredgroundscoffee.net), 2825 Sudderth Drive, Ruidoso. Sunday night movie; Friday night open mic. Winter hours: B, L Sun.–Thurs.; B, L, D. Fri.–Sat. Freshly baked goodies, quiche, wraps, light meals. Serving an expanded B, L, D menu during the summer, open 7:30 AM–9 PM, with daily happy hour 4–6, featuring local wine and NM beer. Fair Trade coffee, vegan, and gluten free dishes.

Spencer Theater for the Performing Arts (575-336-4800), 108 Spencer Drive, Alto. Presenting a full season of outstanding theater, dance, and music September–May. Headliners have included Moscow Festival Ballet, violinist Natalie MacMaster, and Mel Tormé.

The theater itself, with Dale Chihuly glass decor, is worth seeing.

✳ Selective Shopping

Burro Street, Cloudcroft. Find here a worthwhile row of local craft shops, boutiques, antiques stores, galleries. You can stuff a teddy bear or get a gelato, have a beer in an Old West bar or find yoga attire.

Heart of the Desert: Eagle Ranch Pistachio Groves (575-434-0035), 7288 US 54 Expressway, Alamogordo. Open Mon.–Sat. 8–6, Sun. 9–6. Hop on a free tour of these family-run pistachio groves, munch red and green chile–flavored nuts, shop for New Mexico gifts, and splurge on homemade pistachio ice cream.

Sudderth Street, Ruidoso's premier shopping street. The place to find stylish household decor, western wear, women's clothing—at Rebekah's and Michelle's, featuring American-made SW-style clothing—and lunch and a cold one.

CAVERN COUNTRY
Carlsbad, White's City

What's great here are the caverns. That's the reason to come. Carlsbad Caverns are one of three World Heritage Sites in New Mexico, the others being Taos Pueblo and Chaco Canyon. You can easily spend days exploring the underground formations, sure to instill a sense of wonder in anyone who views them. It can be very hot in the summer, but it's always cool in the caverns. Bat flights and the water slide at White's City make this an excellent family vacation spot.

GUIDANCE Carlsbad Chamber of Commerce/Convention and Visitors Bureau (575-887-6516; www.carlsbadchamber.com), 302 S. Canal, Carlsbad.

White's City (575-785-2291; www.whitescity.com), 6 Carlsbad Caverns Highway, White's City.

MEDICAL EMERGENCY Carlsbad Medical Center (575-887-4100), 2430 W. Pierce Street, Carlsbad.

Lea Regional Medical Center (575-492-5251), 5419 N. Lovington Highway, Hobbs.

❋ To See

TOWNS Carlsbad, at the junction of US 285 and US 62/180, while known for its underground caverns, has made the most of its location on the Pecos River with its annual "Christmas on the Pecos" boat rides to see the lights along the banks. Make time for a visit to the Living Desert Zoological and Botanical State Park north of the city off US 285, a showcase of flora and fauna native to the Chihuahuan Desert. Also along the Pecos, stroll 2.5 miles of winding pathways. Boating, fishing, swimming, and waterskiing are all available here.

White's City, 13 miles south of Carlsbad on US 62/180, White's City is at the entrance to Carlsbad Caverns National Park. Named for Jim White, the discoverer of Carlsbad Caverns. Numerous motels, RV park, dining, water park just outside Carlsbad Caverns National Park.

HISTORIC LANDMARKS, PLACES, AND SITES ✐ **Living Desert Zoo and Gardens State Park** (575-887-5516; www.nmparks.com), 1504 Miehls Drive, Carlsbad, northwest end of town, off US 285. Open daily summer 8–8, winter 9–5. Closed Christmas. This marvelous indoor/outdoor attraction highlights native plants and animals of the Chihuahuan Desert. An easy 1.3-mile trail leads through desert habitat. Another is the greenhouse packed with succulents and cacti. Over 40 species of critters, including mountain lion, endangered Mexican gray wolf, bobcat, javelina, and bear, call this zoo home. $5 per vehicle.

NATURAL WONDERS Carlsbad Caverns National Park (575-785-2232), 727 Carlsbad Cavern Highway, Carlsbad. Memorial Day weekend–Labor Day weekend daily 8–5, last entry into cave 3:30 PM. Cave tours begin 8:30 AM. Labor Day–Memorial Day weekend 8–5, last entry into cave 2 PM. Cave tours begin 8:30 AM. The "Eighth Wonder of the World," with a year-round temperature of 56 degrees Fahrenheit that is constant throughout this phenomenal underground display of stalactites and stalagmites that were formed drop by drop over millions of years. Over 100 limestone caves predate the dinosaurs. An elevator is available for those who prefer to ride the 750-foot descent. Ranger-guided tours available for the Hall of the White Giant, Spider Cave, and others for $8.50–$20. Pet kennels are available, and portions are wheelchair accessible. The park also has over 50 miles of primitive backcountry hiking, with trailheads located along park roads. $12 adults, $3 children, under age 15 free. Good for three days.

Scenic Byways **Guadalupe Back Country Scenic Byway** (575-234-9572). NM 137/ US 285, 30 miles. Twelve miles north of Carlsbad or 23 miles south of Artesia, enter at junction of NM 137 and US 285 near Brantley Lake State Park. Travel 30 miles to the southwest for dramatic views of the East Guadalupe Escarpment along a winding road with waterfalls, rugged limestone hills, and canyons. There are many possibilities for discovery here, with jeep trails and opportunities for hiking, caving, and mountain biking. Driving south on the byway, you encounter a sign that directs you to Sitting Bull Falls Recreation Area (open year-round, 8:30 AM to sunset, $5 per vehicle). The road descends 8 miles through winding canyons on the way to the falls. The recreation area is for day use only; stone picnic shelters with grills are available. A paved path leads from the picnic shelters to the falls; a dirt path leads up to the top of the mesa. Two hundred million years ago, in the Permian period, this area was an inland sea. Sitting Bull Falls is a small remnant of the water from this ancient time. The falls are the result of water flowing from a spring located in the canyon above. From the observation point at the end of the paved path, a 200-foot-high wall of tufa looms in front of you. It extends up the canyon for three-quarters of a mile. The creation of this lightweight, porous rock from calcium carbonate precipitating out of the water has taken hundreds of thousands of years. When plants die and fall into the water, a chemical reaction occurs and fossils are formed. This process is still ongoing at the bottom of the falls.

OIL PATCH COUNTRY
Artesia, Hobbs, Lovington, Portales

This is the land that oil built. Aside from ranching, the fossil fuel business is what keeps folks in beans here. Artesia displays a strong sense of itself as a community with civic roots and pride.

GUIDANCE **Artesia Chamber of Commerce** (575-746-2744; www.artesiachamber.com), 107 N. 1st Street, Artesia.

Hobbs Chamber of Commerce (575-397-3202; www.hobbschamber.org), 400 N. Marland Boulevard, Hobbs.

Portales/Roosevelt County Chamber of Commerce (575-356-8541; www.portales .com), 100 S. Avenue A, Portales.

MEDICAL EMERGENCY **Artesia General Hospital** (575-748-3333), 702 N. 13th Street, Artesia.

✽ To See

TOWNS **Artesia** is located on US 285, midway between Roswell and Carlsbad. This little town built on oil refining has a restored railroad station and an excellent small museum showcasing local history.

Hobbs, 63 miles northeast of Carlsbad on US 62/180, lies just across the Texas state line. Plenty of parks and swimming pools; fishing in Maddox Lake and Green Meadows Lake; and RV hookups, camping, and fishing in Harry McAdams Park make this friendly town a convenient stop.

Lovington, 44 miles east of Artesia on US 82, is the site of the Western Heritage Museum and Lea County Cowboy Hall of Fame, housed in a historic hotel building. With homesteading roots, the town boomed from oil and remains a center of an agricultural and ranching economy. Chaparral Park offers lake fishing.

Portales, 18 miles south of Clovis on US 70, is famous for its peanut industry. It is also the site of Eastern New Mexico University, and north of town on US 70 is the Blackwater Draw Museum, where artifacts representing the oldest habitations in North America are displayed. Also nearby is the Blackwater Draw site, where the Clovis points were unearthed in 1928, along with remains of ancient bison and mammoth.

MUSEUMS **Artesia Historical Museum & Art Center** (575-748-2390), 505 W. Richardson Avenue, Artesia. Open Tues.–Fri. 9–noon and 1–5, Sat. 1–5. Closed Sundays, Mondays, and major holidays. Exhibits of regional material culture and social history in a 1920's cobblestone-façade home. Free.

⌀ **Blackwater Draw National Historic Landmark & Museum** (museum 575-562-2202; www.bwdarchaeology2enmu.edu). 1500 S. Avenue K, Portales. Museum open daily. Site: Closed November–March. Memorial Day–Labor Day Mon.–Sat. 9–5, Sun. 9–5. Closed Mondays. Site open Memorial Day—Labor Day 9–5 daily; April–May,

Bat Flights, Carlsbad Caverns National Park (575-785-2232), (575-236-1374 for info on ranger talk), 727 Carlsbad Caverns Highway, Carlsbad, sundown, mid-April–late October. Witness an awesome living swarm of thousands of bats as they leave the caverns. Amphitheater seating is available. Free.

Dalley Windmill Museum (505-356-8541), US 70 and Lime Street in Roosevelt County Fairgrounds, Portales. Call for hours. Begun in 1981 when Bill Dalley obtained a Standard-brand windmill, this collection includes eighty-five restored, working windmills from around the world, each with a unique story, now preserved. Free.

Norman and Vi Petty Rock and Roll Museum (575-763-3435; www.pettymuseum.com), 105 E. Grand Avenue, Clovis. Open daily Mon.–Fri. 8–5. Closed 12–1 PM and Saturdays and Sundays. $5. Also, check out the Norman Petty 7th Street Studio (1313 W. 7th Street, Clovis). Tours by appointment call 575-356-6422 by reservation and two weeks advance notice only. See the original 1950s recording studio where Petty produced the "Clovis sound" back in the day that made stars of Buddy Holly, Roy Orbison, and the Fireballs on the Nor-Va-Jak label. It is unchanged from those days, and the studio is in perfect condition. A must-do for rock 'n roll aficianados.

September–October 9–5 weekends only. May be closed major holidays. Museum is 5 miles east of Portales on US 70. Site is 5 miles north of Portales on NM 467. This museum displays and explains the finds made at Blackwater Draw, recognized since 1929 as one of the most significant archaeological sites in North America due to 13,000-year-old remains of Clovis Man's era. In addition to the finely carved "fluted" stone points of Clovis Man, other weapons and tools, as well as the remains of ancient bison, mammoth, and other creatures of the Late Pleistocene era, were found preserved here. $3 adults, $2 seniors $1 children ages 6–13 and students with ID, age 5 and under free. Fourth Sun. every month free.

✎ **Western Heritage Museum & Lea County Cowboy Hall of Fame** (575-492-2678; www.nmjc.edu), 1 Thunderbird Circle, Hobbs. Closed major holidays. Open Tues.–Sat. 10–5. Sun. 1–5. Located on the campus of New Mexico Junior College, this museum features exhibits of ranchers and rodeo performers while sharing history from the perspective of Indians, homesteaders, buffalo hunters, and soldiers. $5 adults, $3 seniors and students, children ages 6–18; under age 5 free.

✳ To Do

BICYCLING AND WALKING **Pecos Beach Park & River Walk** (575-887-1191; www.cityofcarlsbadnm.com/parksrecreation), Carlsbad. Seven and a half miles of paved bike trails and walkways along the Pecos River are a pleasant way to explore the area. Three covered picnic shelters, too.

HIKING **Rattlesnake Canyon;** (575-785-2232) Carlsbad Caverns National Park. Features a 670-foot descent into the canyon on an easy 2.2-mile hike. If there has been precipitation, wild flowers are stunning in spring. Excellent cacti displays. Trailhead #9 on Desert Loop Drive.

MOUNTAIN BIKING **Cueva Escarpment Mountain Bike Trail** (575-887-6516), Carlsbad. Three miles of single-track riding at Bottomless Lakes State Park.

WILDER PLACES

Hondo Iris Farm and Gallery (575-653-4062), US 70 and Mile Marker 284, Hondo. Open Tues.–Fri. 10–5. Closed Sundays and Mondays. Perhaps not exactly wilder, but definitely off the beaten path, this exquisite display of hundreds of varieties of iris, a botanical garden of sorts, is at its height during mid–late May. Exquisite picnic site, outstanding gallery of imported clothing and home fashions, and Alice Seely's affordable, fine original silver jewelry. Magical! Free. Weddings.

Lake Lucero (1-877-444-6777; www.nps.gov/whsa/planyourvisit/lake-lucero-tours.htm), White Sands National Monument. January–April and November–December monthly, three-hour guided tour of the dry lake that is the source of the White Sands. Advance reservations necessary, group size limited. Drive 18 miles and hike 0.75 mile to Lake Lucero. $8, $4 children 15 and older.

Mescalero Apache Reservation (575-464-7777), 16 miles east of Tularosa on US 70. A magnificent forested place deep in the Sierra Blanca mountains, recognized in 1874 as the Mescalero homeland, it is home to 3,100 Native Americans. Famed for its fierce warriors, the tribe is now known for its tradition of Kenalda, the Apache Maidens' Puberty Rites, with dances of the Mountain Gods, celebrated in annual July 4 festivities at Inn of the Mountain Gods, Ski Apache, and St. Joseph Mission. Murals depict the history of the people. You can find fishing in Eagle Creek Lakes, which also offer camping, and Mescalero Lake, as well as horseback riding, and the fabulous Inn of the Mountain Gods Resort, with Las Vegas–style gambling.

Slaughter Canyon Cave (877-444-6777; www.nps.gov/cave/planyourvisit/slaughter_canyon_cave_tour.htm), Carlsbad Caverns National Park, Carlsbad. Check for hours tours are offered. Strictly for the adventurous, this challenging six-hour tour explores an undeveloped cave 23 miles from the visitor center. Here find unearthly beauty deep within the earth, with formations not seen elsewhere. Meet at Visitor Center. $15 adults, $7.50 children. Children under 6 not allowed.

❋ Green Space

RIVERS AND LAKES **Bottomless Lakes State Park** (575-624-6058), 14 miles southeast of Roswell via US 30 and NM 409, 545A Bottomless Lakes Road, Roswell. Open year-round, daily, 7 AM–9 PM. Hang out among eight small lakes bordered by high red bluffs with walking trails, plus pleasant swimming, fishing, and rental paddleboats. Non-motorized boats OK. $5 per vehicle day use; $10–18 camping.

Brantley Lake (575-457-2384), 16.5 miles northeast of Carlsbad via US 285 and County Road 30; 33 East Brantley Lake Road, Carlsbad. Find here boating, waterskiing, and fishing, with lakeside camping on 3,800-acre Brantley Lake. Excellent birding. $5 per vehicle day use; $18 camping.

Oasis State Park (575-356-5331), 6.5 miles north of Portales via NM 467. 1891 Oasis Road, Portales. Truly an oasis in the high plains, with tall cottonwoods and a fishing pond stocked with catfish and trout. Plenty of wildlife and over 80 species of birds to spot. There's camping, easy hiking, and a playground. $5 per vehicle day use; $14 camping.

Sumner Lake State Park (575-355-2541), 32 Lakeview Lane, Sumner Lake. Calling all water sports lovers: powerboats, canoes, sailboats, and windsurfers abound here. This park makes a great camping base to explore nearby Billy the Kid sites, with sites for large RVs to simple tenting alongside the lake. Gently rolling juniper-covered hillsides frame the rocky shoreline. $5 per vehicle day use; $14 camping.

✏ **White's City Water Park** (575-785-2291), at Carlsbad Caverns National Park. Open seasonally. Two two ample pools, two spas, and two 150-foot water slides. Admission included for resort guests.

MOUNTAINS AND DESERTS **Lincoln National Forest** (575-434-7200), 3463 Las Palomas Road, Alamogordo. A million acres of hiking, backpacking, trail riding, camping. A 20-mile drive goes through terrain from desert, hills, and valleys filled with orchards to high mountain meadows and peaks covered in tall evergreens. A haven for alpine sports in winter, with good cross-country skiing through the Sacramento Mountains near Cloudcroft. Many camping facilities are located within a 4-mile radius of Cloudcroft, accessible by Highways 82, 130, 244, and 6563 in the **Sacramento Ranger District.** Contact listed number or drop by the office for maps and permits. Near Carlsbad, the **Guadalupe Ranger District** of the forest includes 285,000 acres and Sitting Bull Falls Recreation Area, open October–March 8–5 and April–September 8–6, with a 150-foot waterfall. $5 per vehicle.

Oliver Lee Memorial State Park (575-437-8284), 12 miles south of Alamogordo via US 54 at the western base of the Sacramento Mountains. Open year-round. Tour Oliver Lee's restored ranch headquarters and picnic, plus camping at one of 44 developed sites. $5 per vehicle day use; $18 camping.

Valley of Fires State Park (575-648-2241), 5 miles west of Carrizozo on US 380. The park is 426 acres, with picnic and camping areas and a playground. The nature trail has a 0.75-mile wheelchair-accessible portion. The entire Malpais, or badlands, of the lava flow covers 125 square miles. Here are archetypal, dramatic landscapes photographers will exalt in. $5 per vehicle; $18 camping.

WILDLIFE REFUGES **Bitter Lake National Wildlife Refuge** (575-623-5695), Roswell. North on US 285, east on Pine Lodge Road, 9 miles to headquarters. Open daily year-round, dawn to dusk. This Pecos River wetlands is home to over one hundred species of dragonflies and damselflies, one of the best places to see these species in the US, and 357 bird species visit or live here, plus some endangered species. Several short, easy hikes feature native plants and butterflies. Eight-mile auto tour is an excellent way to spot wildlife. Bike riding is available on the 8-mile gravel drive of the paved 4-mile round-trip trail; hiking, horseback riding. Quite a bit of hunting goes on here as well. The best viewings are available a half-hour before sunrise to a half-hour after sunset. One of my very favorite New Mexico places. Free.

❋ Lodging and Dining

No Whiner Diner (575-234-2815), 1801 S. Canal Street, Carlsbad. L, D Mon.–Fri. Closed Saturdays and Sundays. Old-fashioned all-American home cooking in small-town diner style—generous portions of real food—meat loaf, chicken-fried steak—prepared and served very nicely. Prime rib specials Thurs.–Fri. Emphasis on homemade and fresh. Mom and Pop all the way. Inexpensive.

Trinity Hotel (575-234-9891), 201 S. Canal Street, Carlsbad. Skillfully renovated downtown 1892 bank building with seven rooms provides an interesting alternative to chain motel lodging. In a word: class. Restaurant, coffee bar, wine tasting. However, a bit pricey, for Carlsbad, and the rate does not include breakfast. $169–$239.

Adobe Rose (575) 748-3082; 1614 N. 13th Street, Artesia. Five rooms plus a classy restaurant, with chef Chloe Winters, NM Chef of the Year, on the premises serving a creative seasonal menu. Gorgeous food. Beer and wine, live music on the patio in warm weather. $109.

✳ Special Events

April: **Trinity Site Tour** (575-678-1134).

May: 🔥 **Smokey Bear Days** (575-354-2748), Smokey Bear Historical Park, Capitan, first weekend, with parade, crafts marketplace, chainsaw carving, music.

June: **Mountain Park Cherry Festival** (highrollsfestivals.com), High Rolls, midmonth. **Old Fort Days** (575-355-7705), Fort Sumner, midmonth. Storytelling and book signing featuring Navajo literature.

July: **Roswell UFO Festival** (575-914-8018), Roswell, first week in July. **Fourth of July Celebration** (575-464-4494), Mescalero; Apache Maidens Puberty Rites, powwow, rodeo. **Smokey Bear Stampede** (info@smokeybearstampede.com), Capitan, Fourth of July week; more contestants than any other US amateur rodeo. **Art Loop Tour** (www.artloopstudiotour.org/), Lincoln County, first weekend. Tour of diverse artists' studios for some of the most original jewelry, pottery, fiber art, and fine art to be seen anywhere. **Bluegrass Festival** (bluegrassfestivalguide.com), Weed.

August: **Lincoln County Fair** (lincolncountynm.gov), Smokey Bear Historical Park, Capitan, second week. **Old Lincoln Days, Billy the Kid Pageant** (575-653-4372), **Lincoln Pony Express Race**, Capitan Gap to White Oaks. **Lea County Fair and Rodeo** (575-396-8686), largest county fair in state. **Art and Wine in the Cool Pines**, Cloudcroft (575-682-2733; coolcloudcroft.com/art-wine-in-the-pines/), **Alto Artists Studio Tour** (www.altoartistsstudiotour.com).

September: **Chile and Cheese Festival** (575-914-8018), Roswell. **All American Futurity** (575-378-4431), Ruidoso Downs, the world's richest quarter-horse race. **Clovis Music Festival** (575-763-3435), Clovis. Rock and roll like back in the day.

October: **Lincoln County Cowboy Symposium** (575-378-4140), Glencoe. Second weekend in October. Chuckwagon cook-off, cowboy poetry, swing dancing, western art, crafts, cowboy gear, rodeo, roping for kids, country music concert. **Christmas on the Pecos** (575-628-0952). November 23–December 31. Closed Christmas Eve. Twelve departures nightly view; over one hundred homes decorated with holiday lights along the banks of the Pecos River.

December: **Christmas Eve Luminarias** (575-257-2002), Historic Lincoln. **Santa Land** (575-682-2733), Zenith Park, Cloudcroft. Santa and Mrs. Claus arrive with candy and cookies, hot cider, and holiday music.

NORTHEAST NEW MEXICO: SANTA FE TRAIL COUNTRY

SANTA FE TRAIL REGION

Capulin, Cimarron, Clayton, Des Moines,
Eagle Nest, Folsom, Raton, Roy, Springer,
Wagon Mound, Mosquero

LAND GRANT COUNTRY

Las Vegas, Maxwell, Mora, Ocate, Pecos

ROUTE 66 COUNTRY

Santa Rosa, Tucumcari

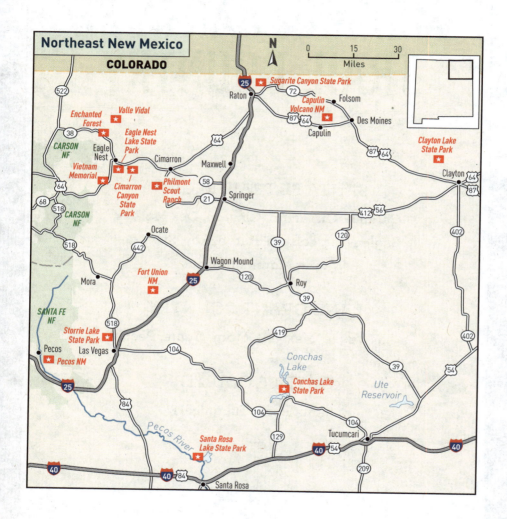

Northeast New Mexico

N

0   15   30
Miles

COLORADO

522

I-25   Sugarite Canyon State Park
Raton   72   Capulin   Folsom
Enchanted   Valle Vidal   Volcano NM
Forest   87   64   Des Moines
38   Eagle Nest   Capulin
CARSON   Lake State   64   87   64
NF   Park   Cimarron   Clayton Lake
Eagle   Maxwell   State Park
Nest
Vietnam   64   Clayton   64
Memorial   Philmont   58   87
64   Cimarron   Scout   Springer
Canyon   Ranch   21
68   State   412   56
518   Park
CARSON   Ocate   120
NF   442   39   402
518   Wagon Mound
Fort Union   120
Mora   NM   I-25   Roy
39
SANTA FE
NF   518   419   402
Storrie Lake   Las Vegas   39   54
Pecos   State Park   104
Pecos NM   Conchas
Lake   Ute
Conchas Lake   Reservoir
I-25   State Park   39
84   104   54
104   Tucumcari
Pecos River   129
Santa Rosa   I-40   54
Lake State Park   129   209
I-40   84   Santa Rosa   I-40

NORTHEAST NEW MEXICO

Northeast New Mexico is an explorer's delight as much as for what it lacks as what it offers. If you like clear turquoise skies and 360-degree views; back roads beckoning onward to the horizon; miles of fields and meadows with few people, billboards, or sign of human habitation save an occasional tumbledown, abandoned homesteader's cabin; wildflowers galore . . . or just a place so big it can make you feel small, this could become your new favorite region. Encounters with antelope, elk, deer, wild turkey, and, occasionally, bear and bobcat are part of the journey, and at night, spangled pitch dark skies unfurl to dazzle the stargazer. Best of all, the outdoors is easily accessible, right up the road—just about any road.

Still, the visitor is not without familiar diversions. In Clayton, you can see a movie in the 1916 restored Luna Theater with its vintage neon winking moon sign. You may feel as if you've found the best "last picture show." You can see first-rate live theater at the century-plus jewel box Shuler Theater in Raton and hear great live classical music at Music from Angel Fire. You can also find festivals of cowboy poetry, mountain men, and vintage vehicles.

In the great northeast, you can also be the only person hiking a trail for miles; fish for trout in transparent mountain streams, with enough quiet to really hear that stream babbling; and experience a wonderland of butterflies, wildflowers, and birds at Sugarite Canyon State Park; or stop the car for a herd of elk crossing the road in Cimarron Canyon. And you might even be able to arrange a selfie with a real live buffalo or get photo-bombed by a bald eagle on the wing.

This place will take you in and wrap you in its natural warmth and lack of pretension.

Here you can follow the heart line of western history—the Santa Fe Trail, where wagon ruts still trace the path westward, and the place is changed so little it is easy to imagine the sights and sounds of the pioneer experience.

And if you enjoy odd, funky little out-of-the-way museums where history has not yet been gift-wrapped, and where the volunteer at the front desk knows everyone in town, you will be in heaven.

Still, despite the similarities of people, customs, and economies, the place is so big and diverse, it's best to think of it by breaking it into three main geographic areas: the Santa Fe Trail Region of the northeast corner, where the small towns of northeast New Mexico—Clayton, Raton, Cimarron, and Springer share a common history of ranching, railroading, and mining; Land Grant Country, with Las Vegas as the central and largest town; and Route 66 Country veering off I-40 to the east.

The population of northeast New Mexico is a mixture of descendants who immigrated to work the mines—from Italy, the Slavic countries, Greece, and Mexico; the descendants of homesteaders; ranchers and ranching families; those who count as their ancestors the original Spanish settlers; and those who somehow found their way here by way of escape from the bigger cities.

Increasingly, those who grew up here are returning, fixing up the old family house, or building a new one, or fixing up another old one, and joining retirees from colder and hotter more urban climates who thrive on the peace and quiet, and recreational opportunities out the front door, and the clean air and water are just what their hearts desire. The unspoiled beauty of the place draws artists and celebrations of the arts as well.

The simple, authentic delights of the small town abound here: the ease with which you can get around; the smiles, waves, and hellos you can count on when you go to the post office or the grocery store; the genuine sense of community, a community that still knows and cares about its neighbors; and the joyous, simple American traditions of high school football, the annual lighting of the Christmas tree, Fourth of July fireworks, the county fair, and the rodeo. And if you enjoy the flavor of historic hotels, with the resident ghost or two, northeast New Mexico can charm you with its legendary lodgings.

Yet these small towns are not immune from social problems. Unemployment, empty storefronts, domestic violence, drugs, degraded quality of education and health care, gangs, teen pregnancy, and poverty exist here alongside all that is desirable. And there is not much to do at night. But for all that, it is possible to live comfortably outside of the compulsion for conspicuous consumption, and thus to have a very relaxed visit. You will be judged on the reliability of your word, not on the model of your vehicle, and you will be respected according to your generosity to friends and the community, not according to the size of your house or the designer labels on your clothes.

Consequently, time takes on a different quality here. There is time to drop in and visit with a friend, to take a neighbor to the doctor, and the lake is close enough to take a child fishing. Hard work is valued, and there is a holdover from blue-collar days when people worked with their hands. It is a good place to kick back, whether for a weekend, a week, or who knows?

Much of this land, including Colfax County, Union County, and San Miguel County—once the hunting grounds and dwelling place of Ute, Apache, and Comanche—has seen mountain men, such as Kit Carson, and giants, such as Lucien B. Maxwell, whose Maxwell Land Grant, at 1.7 million acres, during the nineteenth century stood as the largest land holding in the hemisphere. It has seen the wagons of the military and merchants cross the Santa Fe Trail via the Mountain Route, over difficult Raton Pass, and the more dangerous Cimarron Cutoff—wagon traffic so heavy and frequent that the ruts those wagons left on the landscape are visible to this day. This route of commerce, over which merchants transported goods between Missouri and New Mexico, was used between 1821 and 1880 and died out with the coming of the railroad.

Approximately 19 miles north of Clayton, off NM 406, a portion of the Cimarron Route crosses the Kiowa National Grassland. It is a 2-mile section of trail, with an interpretive site. It has seen those who built the railroads and those who worked a living out of the land with every bit of their strength and ingenuity, and who built the towns and ranches that many of their families still inhabit, three and four generations down the line. The Grassland was planted following the Dustbowl, which took such a heavy toll in this area, as so brilliantly chronicled in Tim Eagan's book, *The Worst Hard Time*.

And it has seen the Colfax County War of the 1870s. There is much history to be learned here, and here it can be seen and felt and touched, because it is still remembered. The war pitted the settlers on the Maxwell Land Grant against the big company that claimed the land. And it tore the region apart.

At the Dawson Cemetery, the results of tragic early-twentieth-century coal mining accidents are visible in the hundreds of crosses marked with the same dates of death, plain crosses standing over the graves of dozens of nationalities.

From the mile Rim Walk around Capulin Volcano, it is still possible to see four states—New Mexico, Colorado, Texas, and Oklahoma. And in Las Vegas, you can visit the Montefiore Cemetery, where the German Jewish merchants of the 1800s lie and there is plenty of history not taught in schools.

This is where the Great Plains meets the Rockies. Beginning with the Homestead Act of 1862, settlers began to pour in. By the end of the 1870s, the Plains Indian tribes had lost their historic use of the lands. Cattle and sheep replaced the bison, and following their path came soldiers, prospectors, and railroad builders.

Las Vegas, New Mexico, has hundreds of buildings listed on the National Register of Historic Places, as well as nine historic districts, each worthy of a walking tour. Brochures are available at the Visitor Center. And preservationist Allan Affeldt has acquired the Harvey House Casteneda Hotel beside the railroad track, which is being refurbished with a restaurant and lodging to rival his La Posada in Winslow, Arizona. The restoration is stirring something of a revival of the town, as well as a new respect for its historic architecture.

By way of contrast, you can scuba dive in Santa Rosa's 67-foot-deep artesian Blue Hole as well as pet and feed the prize alpacas at the Victory Ranch outside Mora.

Colfax County is home to several hundred farms and ranches. A wonderful place to experience this traditional culture is at the annual Colfax County Fair, held the second weekend in August at the Springer Armory. Pie sale, junior livestock sale, steer show—all the treasured customs of rural Americana can be experienced here, and the annual cakewalk.

At the annual Fourth of July Santa Fe Trail Balloon Rally, brilliant hot-air balloons fly aloft over Raton.

So, if you like having the trail to yourself during an early-morning hike, the peace of a glass-smooth alpine lake with trout jumping a foot in the air, going eyeball to eyeball with deer and antelope, poking around and antiquing in little towns without stoplights, and historic hotels loaded with legend and lore aplenty, plus a few hardy ghosts—have we got the place for you!

SANTA FE TRAIL REGION

Capulin, Cimarron, Clayton, Des Moines,
Eagle Nest, Folsom, Raton, Roy, Springer,
Wagon Mound, Mosquero

The Old West is alive and well out here, where the code of the West still rules and the economy traditionally ran on ranching, railroading, and mining. It's pretty quiet, quiet enough to hear a meadowlark warbling. This is an excellent area to take your own wildlife photo safari. Springtime is windy, so you'll likely be dodging tumbleweeds, and there's a good chance you may get snowed in during winter. Not to worry; it can melt off pretty quick when the sun comes out. If you are sincere, and down to earth, Colfax County folk will befriend you; if you're not, don't expect them to be real sociable. Some of the oldest ranches in the country are located here, and many are run by the third and fourth, and even the fifth generation. The Santa Fe Trail winds through the country, and the ruts inscribed on the landscape by Conestoga wagons are still visible. Memories are long with history, and there's probably a cowboy with a good story sitting next to you at the St. James Hotel bar.

GETTING THERE *By car:* Private automobile is the only realistic way to travel and see the sights up here. From Albuquerque, drive north on I-25 for 123 miles to Las Vegas. Continue north on I-25 another 102 miles to Raton. Cimarron is 41 miles from Raton via I-25 south to US 64. Clayton is 90 miles east of Raton on US 64. Or, at Springer, exit I-25 and travel US 53 to Gladstone, then on to Clayton.

By train: Amtrak stops once daily, both north and southbound, in Raton and Las Vegas.

GUIDANCE Please be aware that in small towns, chambers of commerce are often staffed by volunteers and may be closed during posted hours of operation, which may also be irregular. Patience and some advance planning will help cut down on frustration. In general, they are open during the week—generally 10–2 is the safest times to find the staff in—and tend to be closed weekends in the smaller towns (or at best, open a half-day on Saturday). Some do not have a physical location, and others may just ask you to call back.

Cimarron Chamber of Commerce (575-376-2417), 104 N. Lincoln Avenue, Cimarron. A tiny wooden office in the town's central park off US 64 beside a statue of Lucien B. Maxwell is the place to find out about local happenings.

Clayton/Union County Chamber of Commerce (800-390-7858 or 575-374-9253), 1103 S. 1st Street, Clayton, is professional and will return phone calls in a timely manner. It's good to make contact here for specific directions and drive time to more remote locations.

Eagle Nest Chamber of Commerce (575-377-2420), 284 E. Therma Drive, Eagle Nest. Hours are catch as catch can.

Raton Chamber & Economic Development Council Inc. (575-445-3689), 100 Clayton Road, Raton.

Raton Visitor Information Center (575-445-2761), 100 Clayton Road, Raton, is a spacious, comfortable place offering an abundance of regional literature, weather information, and free Wi-Fi, staffed by friendly local volunteers

MEDICAL EMERGENCY **Miners' Colfax Medical Center** (575-445-3661), 203 Hospital Drive, Raton.
Union County General Hospital (575-374-2585), 300 Wilson Street, Clayton.
Alta Vista Regional Hospital (505-426-3500), Legion Drive, Las Vegas.

✳ To See

SANTA FE TRAIL COUNTRY TOWNS **Capulin.** A place name frequently encountered in New Mexico, the word is Spanish for "chokecherry," or "wild cherry." Here it refers to the hamlet 28 miles southeast of Raton on US 64/87 near the border of Colfax and Union counties. The main attraction is the dormant volcano that is the centerpiece of Mount Capulin National Monument. It was originally a settlement of Hispanic farmers founded sometime after the Civil War.

Cimarron. Four miles southwest of Raton. South on I-25 to exit 419, then US 64 west. Cimarron is located at the junction of US 64 and NM 58 and 21. While the exact meaning of this word is not certain, as it may refer either to wild Rocky Mountain bighorn sheep or the wild plum or wild rose that once grew here abundantly; the word *wild* is applied with accuracy to the town, which still exudes a Wild West flavor. Founded in 1841 as the headquarters for the Maxwell Land Grant and home of land baron *Lucien Bonaparte Maxwell*, it became known as a hideout for desperados as well as a gathering spot for traders, miners, and travelers on the Santa Fe Trail. The *Las Vegas Optic* once reported, "It was a quiet week in Cimarron. Only three shootings took place." Nearby are the Philmont Scout Ranch and the home of Kit Carson. Cimarron is a pleasant stop for exploring Santa Fe Trail history, browsing the unpretentious shops and galleries, and absorbing the energy of a place still inhabited largely by cowboys, ranchers, old-timers, and artists. The saloon of the St. James Hotel, with 27 bullet holes in the ceiling, is a good place to meet up with as many characters as you deserve to.

Clayton. Ninety miles east of Raton on US 64/87. Dating to 1888, Clayton was born with the arrival of the railroad, when it became a major cattle-shipping point. It remains to this day a center of ranching activity that pioneer descendants still call home. Among its historic treasures are WPA murals of the New Deal, the 1916 Luna Theater, the Herzstein Memorial Museum, and the recently restored 125-year-old Eklund Hotel. Nearby are Clayton Lake State Park and the Dinosaur Trackway, the second-largest preserved field of dinosaur tracks in the western hemisphere. The town was named for Sen. Stephen Dorsey's son, Clayton. Dorsey was a crony of Albert Fall, of Teapot Dome notoriety. Originally home to Indians, then a resting point for Santa Fe Trail settlers, Clayton grew from a campground for cattle drovers. The railroad came through in 1888, and the town subsequently became a prosperous shipping and supply station, as well as a target for Black Jack Ketchum, a notorious train robber. Clayton High School has a WPA museum, but appointments must be made in advance to see it. Check with the chamber of commerce.

Des Moines. Thirty-eight miles southeast of Raton on US 64/87 at the junction of US 64/87 and NM 325. Originally a village of homesteaders founded in 1887 when the railroad came through, Des Moines is named for the town of the same name in Iowa and pronounced with an audible *s* at the end of *Moines*. It supposedly got its name when two cowboys, wondering what to call the place, noticed a railroad car and saw the words *Des Moines* painted on the side. Today it remains a proud, small community of ranching folk and, if you are an artist or photographer, it's a gold mine of opportunities for making images of weathered barns, windmills, and tumbledown houses.

Eagle Nest. Sixty-four miles southwest of Raton, at the junction of US 64/87 and NM 38. The hamlet, in the shadow of 13,161-foot-high Wheeler Peak, the state's highest, is the gateway to Cimarron Canyon. Originally called Therma, for the daughter of the postal inspector, Eagle Nest is a lovely mountain village on the shore of Eagle Nest Lake State Park, a haven for fishermen, ice fishermen, and RV campers. Back in the day, Eagle Nest was known as a wide-open gambling town patronized by politicians traveling across the state. Now it is a quiet, restful place to kick back and enjoy the clear mountain air and excellent fly-fishing. Fourth of July is celebrated with a mighty fireworks display over Eagle Nest Lake; New Year's Day is celebrated with the Polar Bear Plunge.

Folsom. Across scenic Johnson Mesa, which may be closed in winter on account of snow, 38 miles east of Raton off NM 72, lies sleepy Folsom. When President Grover Cleveland's wife, Frances Folsom, came through on the train in 1888, the little railroad settlement known as Ragtown changed its name in her honor. Today the tiny town is known as the place where George McJunkin, the observant African American foreman for the Crowfoot Ranch, in 1926 made a remarkable discovery. He found large bones in an arroyo containing ancient Pleistocene bison skeletons and nineteen chipped stone spear points that revised estimates of how long man had inhabited this area—for at least 10,000 and as much as 15,000 years. The originals are housed in the Denver Museum of History and Science, and the Folsom site is designated a National Historic Landmark. Folsom was proclaimed a State Monument in 1951. It is also the site of Folsom Falls, a spring-fed waterfall on the Dry Cimarron River, 4 miles northeast of Folsom on NM 456. But beware of rattlesnakes if you go there! Folsom Museum is housed in the historic 1896 Doherty Building. The Folsom Hotel was built in 1888 and was originally the Drew & Phillips General Mercantile Store.

Raton is 225 miles north of Albuquerque on I-25. Originally called Willow Springs, this town on the edge of Raton Pass into Colorado was a watering stop for military and Santa Fe Trail travelers coming over the Mountain Route. The town came to life in 1880 as a support stop for the Santa Fe Railway roundhouse and shops. Yet earlier, following the Civil War, the government mail stage carrying passengers descended challenging Raton Pass and stopped at the Clifton House Stage Station below Red River Peak for dinner, then galloped into Cimarron on the way to Fort Union. Raton has vintage motels and eateries left over from the era of La Mesa Racetrack, a well-preserved historic walking district alongside the railroad tracks, and a museum packed with coal mining history, and it makes a good base for exploring the area. Locals appreciate the recent additions of downtown coffee shops, pizzeria, and brewpub.

Roy. Nine miles east of the Canadian River, Roy was originally a homesteading community that found its reason for existence when the railroad came through. Founded by Frank Roy and three brothers from Canada, it became a ranching center that was then decimated by the Dust Bowl. Today it is a sleepy village in the middle of Harding County, the biggest county in New Mexico by area, but with only 900 inhabitants.

Springer is 131 miles north of Santa Fe on I-25, at the junction of US 56. Formerly the capital of Colfax County, today Springer is the site of the Colfax County Fair and Rodeo held in early August, and the Santa Fe Trail Interpretive Center and Museum.

Wagon Mound. Twenty-five miles southwest of Springer on I-25, and a stop of the Santa Fe Trail, the town is named after the butte on its eastern edge that resembles a covered wagon, a Santa Fe Trail landmark. Its previous name was Santa Clara.

HISTORIC LANDMARKS, PLACES, AND SITES **Black Jack Ketchum's Grave** (575-374-0953), Clayton Cemetery, Princeton Avenue, Clayton. This is the final resting place of the notorious train robber who was hanged in 1901 at Union County Courthouse. His last words were reputedly, "I had breakfast in Clayton, but I'll have dinner in hell!" Free.

Dawson is a ghost town 5 miles northwest of Colfax, formerly a prosperous Phelps-Dodge mining town. In its heyday it was one of the liveliest towns in northeast New Mexico, known for its many winning teams, particularly baseball. Here miners of various ethnic backgrounds and their families lived, worked, and played together. While the town has been dismantled, the Dawson Cemetery, where hundreds of miners killed in tragic accidents in 1913 and 1923 are buried beneath simple white crosses, remains a moving sight and highlights an important, if often overlooked, chapter in the history of the West. Free.

Historic 1st Street, Raton. Paralleling the railroad tracks, this four-block historic district includes the Old Pass Gallery, occupying a former Wells Fargo freight office; the classic California Mission Atchison; Topeka & Santa Fe Railway station, antiques shops; and well-preserved late-nineteenth- to early-twentieth-century buildings.

Mandala Center (575-278-3012), 35 miles east of Raton on US 64/87, Des Moines. An ecumenical spiritual retreat center open to all, the Mandala Center on Sierra Grande Mountain offers workshops year-round, as well as opportunities for private retreats and workshops for leadership, spiritual development, writing skills, and health and wholeness, as well as personal renewal. Based on Christian religious principles, it is indeed welcoming to people of all faiths. And the food is wonderful!

Santa Fe Trail (SFT) sites: Point of Rocks, 23 miles east of Springer on US 56, north on County Road 52. Seven miles from rest area, 2 miles east, then 1 mile north, look for SFT sign-in box at ranch house, which is on the Santa Fe National Historic Trail.

DESERTED CALIFORNIA MISSION–STYLE RAILROAD STATIONS PUNCTUATE US 60

AT THE MANDALA CENTER, TIBETAN MONKS CREATE SAND PAINTINGS THEY WILL BEGIN TO DESTROY AS SOON AS THEY ARE FINISHED

Wagon ruts, graves, Indian campsites. **McNees Crossing** (575-374-9653), 25 miles north of Clayton on NM 402. Santa Fe Trail site named for trader killed there in 1828. Nearby are Santa Fe Trail wagon trail ruts.

Philmont Scout Ranch (575-376-2281), 137,000 acres 10 miles southwest of Cimarron on NM 21, Rayado. Oklahoma oilman Waite Phillips donated this lush property to the Boy Scouts of America. Each summer, it is used by scouts from all over the world for backcountry camping.

Shuler Theater (575-445-4746), 131 N. 2nd Street, Raton. Completed in 1915, this European Rococo jewel box of a theater, with WPA murals depicting the history of the area, continues to host a variety of outstanding theater and music productions year-round, from ballroom dance to mariachi, Neil Simon to Brazilian dance to Chinese acrobats. Tours by appointment.

MUSEUMS **Aztec Mill Museum** (575-376-2417), 220 W. 17th Street, Cimarron. In Memorial Day–Labor Day, 1–4. Originally known as the Aztec Mill, it was built by land baron Lucien Maxwell in 1864 to grind wheat and corn flour for nearby Apache and Ute, as well as Fort Union, with whom he had contracts to supply provisions. You can easily spend half a day wandering the three floors that tell the history of the Maxwell Land Grant, Native Americans, ranchers of the area, and scouting. $3 suggested donation. Call ahead to check hours, staffed by volunteers.

Folsom Museum (575-278-2122), junction NM 325 and NM 456, 101 Main Street, Folsom. Open daily 10–5 Memorial Day–Labor Day, weekends only May and September 10–5, winter by appointment only. Displays of Folsom Man, whose points (arrows) were first found in this area by African American cowboy George McJunkin. It has been a long time since this museum was updated, and the crowded walls recall a bygone, nostalgic perspective on the world. $1.50 adults, $.50 children ages 6–12, age 5 and under free.

Frank Brownell Museum of the Southwest (575-445-3615), NRA Whittington Center, 10 miles south of Raton on US 64. Open Mon.–Fri. 8–5, Sat.–Sun. 9–4. A celebration of firearms and the Second Amendment. There's much to learn about the region and the wars of the twentieth century here. Free.

Herzstein Memorial Museum (575-374-2977), corner 2nd and Walnut Street, 22 S. 2nd Street, Clayton. Open May–August Tues.–Sat. 10–5, September–April 10–4. The museum, donated by the pioneer Herzstein family, is home of the Union County Historical Society, which lovingly tends the collections housed in a former 1919 church. Collections include a wealth of homesteader artifacts, memorabilia, furniture, and art, and the museum makes for a surprisingly refreshing experience. Donation.

Kit Carson Museum (575-376-2281), Philmont Scout Ranch, Rayado. Eleven miles south of Cimarron on NM 21. Open June–August daily 8–5; September and May Mon.–Fri. 8–5. This hacienda, and home of Indian scout and mountain man Kit Carson, was actually the original Fort Union, protecting the frontier from Indian raids, built before the fort now bearing that name was constructed. As historically accurate as it can possibly be, down to the flour sacks in the storehouse, this living museum is an excellent way to get a true feel of the Santa Fe Trail day, the fur trade, and the early settlement of New Mexico. A really special experience is the Wednesday 7 PM candlelight and storytelling tour, June–August, $3. Reservations necessary. Free.

Philmont Museum and Seton Memorial Library (575-376-2281), 17 Deer Run Road, Cimarron. Open year-round. Ernest Thompson Seton, the father of scouting, is recognized here and will be hailed even more so in the future, as a multi-million dollar Boy Scout of America museum is planned for this site. Bookstore carries fine selection of western books and excellent Native American jewelry. Free.

Old Pass Arts Gallery (575-445-2052), 145 S. 1st Street, Raton. Open Tues.–Sat. 10–4. Closed major holidays. Here you will find exhibitions of local watercolorists and

WILD TURKEYS ROAM FREE AT THE PHILMONT SCOUT RANCH

photographers, as well as art of regional interest and a renovated Wells Fargo freight office. Free.

Raton Museum (575-445-8979), 108 S. 2nd Street, Raton. Open Wed.–Sat. 10–4. A collection of mining, railroad, Santa Fe Trail, and ranching artifacts that provides a history lesson for all who want to understand this place. Upstairs are changing exhibits of local contemporary artists. Free.

Santa Fe Trail Interpretive Center and Museum (575-483-5554), 606 Maxwell Avenue, Springer. Open Memorial Day–Labor Day 9–5; hours otherwise variable. This collection is housed in the 1882 former Colfax County Courthouse. Here you will find a tangled trove of Santa Fe Trail exhibits, historic photos, artifacts, old letters and maps, and information on the New Mexico Territorial period and pioneer life in northeast New Mexico. Free.

Villa Philmonte (575-376-1136), Philmont Scout Ranch, Rayado. Ten miles south of Cimarron on NM 21. Guided tours offered spring and summer. Please call for times and dates. This grand, elegant Mediterranean summer home of oilman Waite Phillips and his wife, Genevieve, is now the property of the Philmont Scout Ranch, of which Phillips is the benefactor. Built 1926–27; all art and furnishings remain intact, as does the splendid original tile work. Free.

NATURAL WONDERS **Capulin Volcano National Monument** (575-278-2201), Crater Rim Trail, Capulin. North of Capulin 5.5 miles on NM 456. Closed major holidays. Open Memorial Day–Labor Day 7:30–6:30, Labor Day–Memorial Day 8–4. This natural cone of a relatively young volcano, only 7,000 years old, is one of the few places in the world where you can hike inside a cinder cone. Visitors may walk 2 miles round-trip into the 415-foot-deep crater and hike along the 1-mile rim trail overlooking much of the Raton-Clayton volcanic fields. From the rim trail, you can see four states, and to the

SIGHTING THE TOOTH OF TIME MEANT ONLY SEVEN MORE DAYS TO SANTA FE FOR THE PIONEERS

west, view the snowcapped Sangre de Cristo Mountains. Watch for monthly summer star parties—the stars up here are amazing! Capulin recently received the Gold, or highest, International Dark Skies rating. $5 per vehicle.

Sierra Grande. Ten miles southeast of Folsom, off US 64/85, is the largest single mountain in the United States, measuring 40 miles around the base, covering 50 square miles, at an altitude of 8,720 feet.

Tooth of Time is a prominent, tooth-like rock formation visible from Cimarron that was significant to Santa Fe Trail travelers. When trail pioneers saw the Tooth of Time, they knew they only had seven more days to reach Santa Fe.

SCENIC DRIVES For information on New Mexico's Scenic Byways, visit www.new mexico.org/things-to-do/scenic-byways/.

Dry Cimarron Scenic Byway NM 406 north to NM 456, it extends 40 miles north of Clayton. The Dry Cimarron River ran mainly underground but would surface occasionally. This mostly deserted scenic road runs through Union and Colfax counties, and it has served as an alternate route between Clayton and Raton. There is much history in the way of Santa Fe Trail wagon ruts, old mining camps, and many landmark features. The drive brings the traveler through high prairie, national grasslands, nature preserves, volcanoes, mesas, and colorful geologic formations.

Johnson Mesa is 41 miles from Raton to Folsom along NM 72. Spectacular views of the Sangre de Cristo Mountains are yours here above Raton, and there is no better place for stargazing in the entire state. Settlers believed this was a paradise of rich grasslands. Many of the early settlers worked in the coal mines. When winter came, survival became difficult. The little stone church on the mesa is always open. This is truly a scenic byway, but it's not passable for much of the winter. Summertime, the mesa is covered with white flowers and herds of antelope gallop, while the land serves as summer pasture for local ranchers. Homesteader cabins and dugouts are visible still, and a few hardy souls continue to live up here.

Santa Fe Trail National Scenic Byway (www.newmexico.org/things-to-do/scenic -byways/santa-fe-trail-national/). Follow the actual path of the Santa Fe Trail wagons and see wagons and abandoned forts in the rugged landscape of mountain canyons. The byway extends 480 miles altogether. If you are following the route, you can go to Santa Fe via Clayton, Raton, Cimarron, and Springer, to Las Vegas. In New Mexico, highlights include Fort Union National Monument in Watrous, Kiowa National Grasslands in Clayton, Pecos National Historical Park, Pecos, and the Santa Fe National Forest.

✳ To Do

FISHING **Charette Lakes** (505-827-7882), 35 miles southwest of Springer. I-25 exit 404 and west on NM 569. Boating and fishing as well as primitive camping are yours on the shores of this deep natural volcanic lake, which can be windy in the evening.

Cimarron Canyon State Park (575-377-6271), 28869 Highway 64, Eagle Nest. One of the state's prime German brown trout fisheries, with 9 miles of fly-casting along the Cimarron River. Hiking, camping, picnicking. $5 day use; $10–18 camping.

Eagle Nest Lake State Park (575-377-1594), 42 Marina Way, NM 64 north of Eagle Nest. Boating, fishing, and ice fishing are popular on this 2,400-acre lake that yields some of the finest trout and Konkani salmon fishing in the state. The patient wildlife watcher will see elk, deer, bears, and eagles. This is a beloved lakeside summer picnic area. $5 per vehicle.

Springer Lake (no phone), 4 miles northwest of Springer on CR 17. Picnicking, camping, and fishing for northern pike and catfish make this small lake a favorite with locals. Free.

Lake Maloya. *See* **Sugarite Canyon State Park** under *Green Space, Route 66 Country.*

GOLFING **Raton Country Club and Municipal Golf Course** (575-445-8113), 510 Country Club Road, Raton. Voted "Best Nine Hole Course in New Mexico," this lovely 6,500-foot-high course, with plenty of hazards, was built in 1922 by a coal baron. Greens fee for nine holes: $16.

MOUNTAIN BIKING *See* **Sugarite Canyon State Park** under *Green Space, Route 66 Country.* You can just about choose your own level of terrain here, with this uncrowded, premium area that is pretty much an insider's secret. Here are challenging up-and-down trails and sweet flats packed with greenery, wildflowers, meadows, forests, and lake views. It's a fairly easy ride through ride former coal camp, around Lake Maloya, to the Colorado border. The visitor center provides trail maps. $5.

SNOW SPORTS **Enchanted Forest Cross-Country Ski Area** (575-754-6112). At the summit of Bobcat Pass, just north of Red River, the Enchanted Forest is the state's premier cross-country and snowshoeing venue, offering everything you could want or need, including rentals, yurt rentals, and lessons. There are almost 20 miles of groomed Nordic ski trails for varied skill levels, and close to 10 miles of snowshoe trails, plus designated dog trails, though you may use the trails if you are pet-free. Under $20. Warning: as of press time, there is talk this place may be closing.

✻ Lodging

BED & BREAKFASTS, INNS, AND MOTELS 🐾 ♿ **Best Western Kokopelli Lodge** (575-374-2589), 702 S. 1st Street, Clayton. Clean, light, spacious rooms with Southwest decor and all conveniences make this a most pleasant stop. A café serving a better-than-average complimentary hot buffet breakfast, swimming pool, and a swell gift shop are on the premises. $127.

🐾 **Budget Host Melody Lane** (575-445-3655), 136 Canyon Drive, Raton. My out-of-town guests rave about the in-room steam baths. Continental breakfast, pet-friendly (to small pets), friendly service, too. Although affiliated with a chain, this twenty-six-room lodging retains its local ambience. $51.

Raton Pass Motor Inn (575-445-3641), 308 Canyon Drive, Raton. "The home of vintage cool," with its remodel and new owners, this place has become a happening favorite of road-trippers

and motorcyclists. Many special events throughout the year. Definitely an experience. Try a stay in Bettie's Boudoir, the Wildlife Room, or the Man Cave. Lots of amenities. $60.

Casa Lemus Inn and Restaurant (575-445-2737), 350 Clayton Road, Raton. Well-managed, clean old-time motel with spacious rooms at inexpensive rates. Gets good marks from friends, and the on-site restaurant (B, L, D Sun.–Sat.) serves decent Mexican food, including good fajitas, American diner fare, and breakfast.

Heart's Desire (575-445-1000), 301 S. 3rd Street, Raton. This sweet three-story, 1885 Victorian home in comfortable walking distance of downtown, the historic district, and train station happens to be run by an antiques lover. This bed & breakfast reflects the charm and cozy clutter of her love. Plus, if you feel like doing a little shopping, many of the collectibles are for sale. You will feel cared for and catered to here, with evening snacks, chocolates, and egg puffs for breakfast. The third-floor Hunting and Fishing Room, with its views of nearby mountains, is truly a getaway, and the Blue Willow Room will romance the heart of any lady. An evening at this retreat into the past would make a darling Valentine's Day surprise. $69–$120.

🐾 **Oasis Motel** (575-445-2221), 1445 S. 2nd Street, Raton. With a popular café on the premises, and fourteen clean and serviceable rooms in classic motel decor, this locally owned and operated motel is a good choice. $75.

Express St. James Hotel (See "Historic Hotels," page 278).

🐾 **Plaza Hotel** (See "Historic Hotels," page 278).

LODGES AND RANCHES **Vermejo Park Ranch** (575-445-3097), 100 NM 555 Vermejo Road, Raton. Once part of the Maxwell Land Grant, later the private getaway of Mary Pickford and Douglas Fairbanks, this piece of grand history is today the property of media mogul Ted Turner. Former guests include presidents, industrialists, and celebrity movers and shakers from Hollywood to Washington, DC. An exclusive hunting and fishing lodge for the privileged, it is possible, for a price, to visit and enjoy the Vermejo, with its twenty-one stocked lakes, legendary trout streams, and abundant herds of elk and bison. Since Turner purchased the property in 1996, the Vermejo has actively sought to restore the ecology and bring back native animals, including black-footed ferrets and wild wolves. Two-night minimum required, guide services extra. Gourmet meals, served in the clubby dining room overlooking the Sangre de Cristo Mountains, are included. Fishing season is May–September. Starts at $1250 per double occupancy room per night and up, meals included; (non-peak season), children under 12 free with two adults. Winter season is divine.

CABINS AND CAMPING 🐾♿ **Summer-Land RV Park** (575-445-9536), 1900 Cedar Street, Raton. With forty-two full hookups, tent camping, cabins, a playground, laundry, store, free Wi-Fi, and even minor RV repairs available, this pet-friendly, handicapped-accessible park has a reputation for friendliness and service. It's at 7,000 feet, so nights can be chilly, but it's a great place for stargazing and wildlife watching. Located on a frontage road off I-25, it somehow manages to be a quiet spot. $28.50. Pet restrictions.

✳ Where to Eat

DINING OUT **Dining Room, St. James Hotel** (888-376-2664), 167 S. Collinson, Cimarron. D only. Steaks, Mexican food, and salad bar. Warmth emanates from the hearth-like fireplace in the center of this refurbished western saloon, and cowboy photos and memorabilia grace the walls. Originating in 1873 as a saloon operated by Lincoln's chef, Henri Lambert, this fine establishment offers a convivial full bar adjacent to the dining room. Today it is part of the Express Ranch empire. Moderate–Expensive.

Pappas' Sweet Shop Restaurant (575-445-9811), 1201 S. 2nd Street, Raton. Open daily, B, L, D. Sun. 8–2. A place for a nice lunch or dinner out, especially if there is business to be conducted, with decent prime rib, home-cooked stews, homemade soup daily, and dessert created by a respected local chef, plus a sense of itself as a bastion of gentility in a fast-food world. The new ice-cream parlor is pure nostalgia. It's still in the family, generations after the original Mr. Pappas started out selling candy to the coal miners. Wine and beer. Moderate.

Plaza Hotel Dining Room (See "Historic Hotels," page 278).

Eklund Hotel Dining Room (See "Historic Hotels," page 278).

EATING OUT **Colfax Tavern, Cold Beer, New Mexico** (575-376-2229), 11 miles east of Cimarron on US 64. You can see the tall white letters on the red-painted building from a mile out. The only establishment in the ghost town of Colfax, this bar has been here since Prohibition, so they say. Right up there with the best cowboy bars, with live music and lots of locals who'd never let the truth stand in the way of a good story. It's friendly and comfortable, with live music and dancing on weekends in summer on the outdoor dance floor. Burgers and pizza and pub food is what's on the menu. Just like an old-time roadhouse. Inexpensive.

Colfax Ale Cellar (575-445-9727), 215 S. 2nd Street, Raton. Grassroots microbrewery. Unpretentious, local hangout, very good seasonal brews, live music, food on the side, or order a pizza from Bruno's. Inexpensive.

Bruno's Pizza (575-445-9512), 133 Cook Avenue, Raton. Popular pizza spot beer and wine, vintage western building, convivial atmosphere, good service. Very tasty pie with a chewy crust.

Elida's Cafe (575-483-2985), 801 Railroad Avenue, Springer. With plastic tablecloths, fluorescent lighting, and a menu tilted south of the border, Elida's couldn't be a more real, down-to-earth stop for homemade, from scratch, every day, sopaipillas, Frito pie, or a torta—a "Mexican sub." Try the *gorditas,* a homey, hard-to-find specialty of fried masa (cornmeal) stuffed with ground beef and served with beans and rice. The service is caring and thorough. Inexpensive.

The Historic Ice House (575-445-0003), 945 S. 2nd Street, Raton. Open 11–8 daily, closed Sundays. Barbecue/smokehouse with brisket, chicken, salads, tacos, cobbler, and chocolate pudding pie. Desserts made fresh daily. Good family choice. Moderate.

✒ **The Art of Snacks** (575-707-8020), 1117 S. 2nd Street, Raton. Closed Sundays. Hawaiian shave ice, cinnamon rolls, doughnuts, Frito pie ... what's not to like? A snack for every appetite and time of day and season. Local art, too. Inexpensive.

Willie's Smokehouse (719-680-3607), 1005 S. 2nd Street, Raton. Willie's smoker is going from early in the morning, producing smoked barbecue pulled pork and chicken strips, hot dogs ... he's got a sign up telling passersby what's cooking. Drive-thru, inexpensive.

Enchanted Grounds Espresso Bar & Cafe (575-445-2219), 111 Park Avenue, Raton. Closed Sundays. 7–4 daily; may close earlier on Sat. Wi-Fi, fine lattes, wholesome soups and sandwiches, breakfast burritos, plus occasional live music and open mic on weekends, served in the old Silver Dollar bar. Read the paper, check your email, and catch up on the local gossip. Excellent coffee, house-baked pastries. Friday is Frito pie day, but you'd better get there early. Moderate.

Gladstone Mercantile (575-485-2467), 4618 US 56, Gladstone. Mon.–Fri. 8:30–5; Sat. 8:30–2. Just when you thought there was nothing out there but the high lonesome sky and the wind, along comes the quintessential stop in the road, where you can find a welcome with fresh hot coffee, hot soup, yummy barbecue brisket sandwiches, gifts to warm the heart of any cowgirl, and books by local authors. The place also doubles as a local grocery store. Serving a home cooked special every day. In-house baked goods, too. Mon.–Sat. Inexpensive.

✒ **Zayra's Cafe** (575-483-2813), 42 US 56, Springer. Mon.–Fri. 7–7. Wash down those cheeseburgers and fries with a chocolate malt or a thick, creamy milkshake at this old-fashioned, roadside stop. Tacos get raves. You'll have trouble spending more than $7 on lunch or dinner. Inexpensive.

Mulligan's Restaurant & Bar (575-445-8501), 473 Clayton Road, Raton. Soups, salads, pizza, pasta, appetizers, American fare, convivial bar. Since opening in the remodeled Best Western, spacious, comfortable Mulligan's has become the most popular local hangout in town. Moderate.

Rabbit Ears Cafe (575-374-3277), 1201 S. 1st Street, Clayton. The local favorite lunchtime destination in town. Hardly gourmet fare, but the lunch counter menu is filling and tasty. Standard burgers and Mexican fare. Inexpensive.

✱ Selective Shopping

Cimarron Art Gallery (575-376-2614), 337 9th Street, Cimarron. They've got it all! Strong coffee, hand-dipped ice cream treats at the old-fashioned counter, beautiful regional jewelry, hand-carved wooden wares, handmade pottery, and fine art. Best of all, they have the kind of friendly service that will keep you coming back.

Pack Rat (575-445-3242), 134 S. 1st Street, Raton. Lively collection of ceramics, regional books, gifts of all sorts, as well as ice cream and cold drinks. A good stop if you're waiting for the train.

Solano's Boot and Western Wear (575-445-2632), 101 S. 2nd Street, Raton. You'll look like a cowboy if you shop here, where all the most beloved brands are in stock—and in your size. Boots and jeans, belts and hats come in a wealth of styles and colors. They have vintage-look and retro fashion, too. Check out the collection of well-worn hats on the wall. Each has a story to tell. This family business has been around a long, long time, and does quite a bit of business online, too.

Patchwork Phoenix (575-445-8000), 228 S. 1st Street, Raton. So much more than a quilt shop, under the guidance of Hal and Laura Brewer, Patchwork Phoenix is something of a community center, with games, ice cream cones, a selection of fine tea, snacks, local art. Classes and workshops and always something fun going on!

LAND GRANT COUNTRY

Las Vegas, Maxwell, Mora, Ocate, Pecos

GUIDANCE **Las Vegas/San Miguel County Chamber of Commerce** (505-425-8631), 1224 Railroad Avenue, Las Vegas, housed in the renovated Santa Fe Railway Depot, is professionally staffed and well stocked with information about local attractions.

Mora Valley Chamber of Commerce (505-387-6072), NM 518, Mora, is the place to learn about the work of local artists and small-town festivals that feel like family gatherings.

MEDICAL EMERGENCY **Alta Vista Regional Hospital** (505-426-3500), 104 Legion Drive, Las Vegas.

✲ To See

TOWNS **Las Vegas.** Sixty-four miles northeast of Santa Fe on I-25. Named "the meadows," part of an original Spanish land grant, Las Vegas has 900 buildings listed on the National Register of Historic Places and a rough-and-tumble past. The historic structures may best be appreciated in individual self-guided walking tours described in chamber of commerce brochures. The "hanging tree" still stands on the Plaza, which is dominated by the 1880s Plaza Hotel, and a revived Bridge Street radiating out from that Plaza is a pleasure to stroll and browse, with bookshops, cafés, and antiques shops. Another interesting area surrounds the restored Santa Fe train depot, which houses the visitor center, next to the old Hotel Casteneda, an original Fred Harvey hotel. A major Santa Fe Trail stop, then railroad town, Las Vegas was once the dominant city in New Mexico. Now home of New Mexico Highlands University, the town is an interesting mixture of descendants of old families, college students, and recent retirees. There is much history, including that of the German Jewish merchant pioneers, and much of the outdoors to explore here. West Las Vegas, originally called Nuestra Señora de los Dolores de las Vegas Grandes, was begun in 1835 as a land grant community of Spanish sheepherders. After the Santa Fe Trail days, when it was an important trail destination 650 miles from Missouri, the Plaza area thrived. Later, as a result of the Atchison, Topeka, & Santa Fe Railroad line, Las Vegas split into a whole separate city to the east, and it remained so until the 1970s. Locals referred to these separate towns as Old Town and New Town. Most of the adobe structures, both residential and commercial, are west of the Gallinas River in Old Town. Plentiful lodging and a variety of restaurants make Las Vegas a reasonable travel base.

Maxwell, 30 miles south of Raton on I-25, is important chiefly as the site of the Maxwell National Wildlife Refuge, a superb birding locale. It was formerly the shipping center for the Maxwell Land and Irrigation Company, and a significant site for the Maxwell Land Grant.

Mora. Thirty-one miles north of Las Vegas on NM 518. A town remaining on the huge Mora Land Grant of 1835, located in the Mora Valley, that was inhabited since

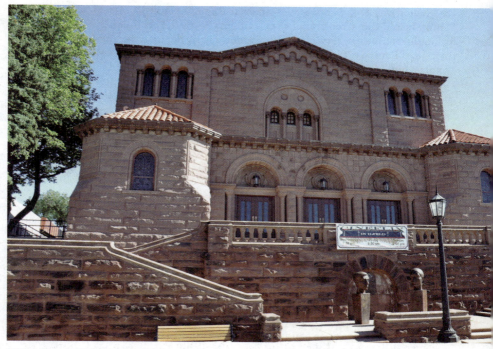

ADELE ILFELD AUDITORIUM IS THE PRIDE AND JOY OF THE NEW MEXICO HIGHLANDS CAMPUS

ancient times by Pueblo and Plains Indians, as well as the migrating Jicarilla Apache. Subsequently, Mora became rich territory of French Canadian mountain men and beaver trappers. Small farms and ranches populate the delightful valley, which offers excellent camping in lovely mountain campgrounds. Here may be found tiny, well-weathered Hispanic villages, churches, fishing, and wildflowers, and a feeling of the long ago as well as the faraway. The place and its people prefer their old ways and remain more or less isolated and somewhat off the grid. Expect to encounter the old wood carvers, *santeros*, weavers, farmers, and remnants of the Penitente brotherhood. This is not an easy area for an outsider to penetrate. Tread lightly.

Ocate. Twenty-three miles northwest of Wagon Mound on NM 120. A largely abandoned, scantly populated village that was home to Hispanic settlers about 150 years ago, and before that, was a hunting ground for Indians. Today, it makes appealing inspiration for photographers and artists.

Pecos. The gateway to the Pecos Wilderness, a popular fishing, hiking, and backpacking area, this little town on the Pecos River was once a mining center.

HISTORIC LANDMARKS, PLACES, AND SITES Bridge Street. The restored Plaza Hotel on the Las Vegas Plaza anchors Las Vegas, and this is a neighborhood of interesting cafés, bookstores, restaurants, and shops that appeal to locals and visitors alike. A stroll down the three-block area, with its imposing late-nineteenth-century architecture, suggests the powerful position Las Vegas once enjoyed as a major stop and trading center on the Santa Fe Trail and later on the Atchison, Topeka & Santa Fe Railway. Free.

Fort Union National Monument (505-425-8025), 3115 NM 61, Valmora. Take I-25 12 miles north of Las Vegas, exit 366, then 8 miles on NM 161. Open daily Memorial

Day–Labor Day 8–5, Labor Day–Memorial Day 8–4. Built in 1851 of adobe near the Mountain and Cimarron branches of the Santa Fe Trail, Fort Union became the largest fort in the Southwest, serving as defense and supply depot. It became a longed-for destination of Santa Fe Trail travelers. When they arrived here safely, they were as good as home. Living history programs, candlelight tours, and cultural demonstrations take place during summer months. An interpretive trail of 1.6 miles takes you through the ruins of the fort, and nearby, 1.1 miles east of the visitor center on Utah State Highway 24, are Native American petroglyphs. Free.

La Cueva National Historic Site and Salman Ranch (575-387-2900), NM 442 and NM 518; 25 miles north of Las Vegas via NM 518, Buena Vista. The mill, built by Vicente Romero, is the centerpiece of this historic site, along with the San Rafael Mission Church, known for its restored French Gothic windows and the mercantile, now the Salman Ranch Store. It is part of the Mora Land Grant of 1835, and Romero is believed to have been an original grantee. Much horse and ox wagon traffic between here and Fort Union took place, as La Cueva was a major shipping center for livestock and agricultural produce. Today, from Labor Day into the fall, depending on weather and harvest, visitors flock to pick raspberries and purchase fresh raspberries and raspberry sundaes sold in season on the **Salman Raspberry Ranch** located here (575-387-2900). Free.

Montezuma Castle (505-454-4200), 5 miles northwest of Las Vegas on NM 65, Montezuma. Originally known as the Montezuma Hotel, it was designed for the Atchison, Topeka, & Santa Fe Railroad in Queen Anne style. After a series of fires, in 1886, the final Montezuma Castle opened. In its heyday, it was a popular destination with casino, bowling alley, stage, dance floor, stained glass from Europe, and a staff from the finest hotels in New York, Chicago, and St. Louis. Guests included Theodore Roosevelt, Rutherford B. Hayes, Ulysses S. Grant, and Jesse James. Closed in 1903, it was from 1937 to 1972 a seminary for Mexican priests. In 2001, the landmark underwent a $10.5-million renovation, transforming it into an international center. Call for public tour information. Free.

FORT UNION, SANTA FE TRAIL DESTINATION

PECOS NATIONAL HISTORICAL PARK

Pecos National Historical Park (505-757-7241), 2 miles south of Pecos on NM 63. Closed Christmas Day. Open daily Memorial Day–Labor Day 8–5, Labor Day–Memorial Day 8–6. This abandoned site of pueblo ruins and eighteenth-century mission church ruins reveal 12,000 years of history. The ruins are all that remain of the ancient pueblo of Pecos. Additional historic and cultural layering is present in two Spanish colonial churches and plentiful Santa Fe Trail sites, while the museum in the visitor center tells of the history of the Forked Lightning Ranch (previously owned by actress Greer Garson, now the property of Jane Fonda) and the Civil War Battle of Glorieta Pass. A 1.25-mile self-guided trail through Pecos pueblo and mission ruins is the best way to see the park. Guided tours of the ruins and Glorieta Battlefield are available to groups booking in advance. The trails are 80 percent wheelchair-accessible. An essential stop. Free.

MUSEUMS **City of Las Vegas Museum/Rough Rider Memorial Collection** (575-426-3205), 727 N. Grand Avenue, Las Vegas. Open Tues.–Sat. (in summer also Sun.) 10–4. This museum houses extensive displays of city history, particularly around ranching and railroading, and Santa Fe Trail history, with maps, photos, ranching gear, household items, and Native American pottery. The distinctive feature is memorabilia of the Rough Riders who fought in the Spanish-American War, which was fought by the United States and Cuba in 1898, and who held their first reunion, led by Theodore Roosevelt, here. New Mexico contributed over one-quarter of the troops that fought. The Rough Rider Museum began as a private memorial. Between 1899 and 1968, reunions were held in Las Vegas. The museum is housed in a New Deal–era building. Free.

Cleveland Roller Mill Museum (575-387-2645), NM 518, Cleveland. Open weekends Memorial Day–Labor Day, 10–3. Two miles south of Mora in Cleveland, the 1901 mill operates only once a year, during the Cleveland Roller Mill Festival, Labor Day weekend. The Mora Valley was once a significant wheat-growing region, hence the need for the mill. This adobe mill was the last to be built in northern New Mexico and was one of the largest mills in the Southwest in its day. Significant photo exhibits celebrating local history. Free.

NATURAL WONDERS **Hermit's Peak** is a massive boulderlike butte of pink granite, north of Las Vegas and visible from I-25, that is believed by some local folk to have been the home of a hermit who would care for all who were lost by rescuing them, taking them to his cave, and feeding them bread.

✳ To Do

BIRDING **Las Vegas National Wildlife Refuge** (575-425-3581), NM 281, Las Vegas. Six miles southeast of Las Vegas off I-25. Providing wintering and migration habitat for ducks and geese of the Central Flyway, plus some 250 migratory bird species. With fourteen species of raptors inhabiting the area, this is a great place to see eagles. There is an 8-mile auto loop through the heart of the refuge with interpretive panels and observation decks. The Gallinas Nature Trail Walk is a half-mile round-trip into a beautiful canyon, but open only on weekdays. Free.

    Maxwell National Wildlife Refuge (575-375-2331), Maxwell, just off I-25. Winter wildlife viewing includes mule deer and much birdlife, with golden and bald eagles, owls, herons, cranes, and Canada geese. Established in 1966 at an altitude of 6,050 feet, the refuge includes over 3,000 acres of rolling prairie and prairie lakes and farmland. This untouristed refuge is capable of providing a truly thrilling birding experience, with numbers that can top 990,000 migratory birds, including snow geese and numerous varieties of ducks. Free.

FISHING **Pecos River**, Pecos Wilderness, Santa Fe National Forest (505-438-5600), Pecos. April–late September. To escape the crowds and find the native browns and Rio Grande cutthroats, it is necessary to hike into the high country of the wilderness area, a quarter-million acres of pristine beauty. If you want to cast your line without the effort required, seek the streams below Cowles.

HIKING **El Porvenir Canyon**, 17 miles northwest of Las Vegas on NM 65, past Montezuma. Take Hot Springs Boulevard northwest out of Las Vegas to where it dead-ends. The Skyline Trail, accessible out of El Porvenir Campground, is a 13-mile moderate hike with altitude that ranges from 7,520 to 11,280 feet. Wildflowers are abundant, particularly wild iris in late May–early June. Once the summer resort of Las Vegas families, this canyon is now a favorite locals' place to hunt and fish. There are two creekside campgrounds close to Hermit's Peak, in the Santa Fe National Forest. $2 hiking permit; $8 camping.

    Pecos Wilderness, Santa Fe National Forest (505-425-3534), Pecos. While there are dozens of trails through this stunning landscape, Jack's Creek and Baldy and Beatty's Trail among the most traveled, there are not any easy ones. Most are difficult or moderate to difficult. Be prepared for weather changes and afternoon rains, and remember, altitudes are from 9,000 to 12,000 feet. Tread carefully.

HORSEBACK RIDING **Circle S Riding Stables** (505-757-,8440 or 575-520-5775), Pecos Wilderness. Hunting, fishing, trail rides, aspen rides. Call for directions. Closed

November–April. Take one of their two-hour or overnight trips, or personalize your own journey for a half-day, a day, or longer. $200 per person two-hour ride.

HOT SPRINGS **Montezuma Hot Springs**, 5 miles west of Las Vegas on Hot Springs Boulevard at NM 65. Here find a very rustic, rather undeveloped hot natural spring in outdoor baths, adjacent to the Montezuma Castle. The setting is not secluded, and you need to bring your own towels. Some of the springs are scaldingly hot. Free.

GOLFING **Pendaries Village Golf & Country Club** (800-733-5267), Rociada. Open April 15–October 15. A stunning 18-hole mountain golf course perched at 7,500 feet, with, naturally mind-blowing mountain views. Greens fees for nine holes under $30.

SNOW SPORTS ✎ **Sipapu Ski & Summer Resort** (800-587-2240), 11 miles east of Peñasco on NM 75 and NM 518 at 5224 NM 518, Vadito, or 20 miles southeast of Taos on NM 518. With thirty-three trails, four chairlifts, snowboarding, a variety of trails, and terrain for all skill levels, with skilled, patient instructors, Sipapu has a well-earned reputation as a moderately priced family-friendly resort. This resort really tries to offer value, and consistently offers loads of specials and special activities. The base elevation is 8,200 feet. It has become over the years a year-round resort, with fly-fishing in a private pond and the rainbow-stocked Rio Pueblo River. Fall is a grand time for mountain biking on the over 300 miles of trails, and bike rentals are provided. Disc golf. You can kick back quite happily here, in the midst of the Carson National Forest. Café on the premises serves popular eats, such as burgers and fries. Tent campsites and RV hookups also available.

WINERIES **Madison Vineyards & Winery** (575-421-8028), 696 NM 3, Ribera. Twenty-six miles south of Las Vegas on I-25, exit on NM 3. Starting with eighty French hybrid vines in the village of El Barranca on the Pecos River, Bill and Elise Madison have been making wine here since 1980. They have kept their operation small and family-run, crafting only 5,000 gallons per year. Come enjoy a beautiful operation in an exquisite setting. Wines include European-style dry and semisweet. Tasting room open Mon.–Fri. noon–6; Sat. 10–5; Sun. noon–5. Closed Wednesdays. Irregular winter hours; call ahead.

✳ Lodging

BED & BREAKFASTS, INNS, AND MOTELS **Crow's Nest B&B** (505-425-2623), 524 Columbia Street, Las Vegas. Satisfy your appetite for Victoriana here, in this painted lady overlooking the dignified green square of the historic Carnegie Library district. Dream or daydream of bygone days, escape, and enjoy a generous breakfast of frittata, French toast, and another cup of coffee. Three rooms, one with Jacuzzi. $95–115.

    Wilderness Gateway Bed and Breakfast (505-757-2801), 2444 NM 63 at #1 Tree Farm Road, Cowles. Luxury in the wilderness of the Santa Fe National Forest; and, walking distance to Pecos River fly-fishing. Private cabin available. Gourmet breakfast, and lunch and dinner may be ordered separately. Two night minimum. $160.

RANCHES AND LODGES ✎ 🐾 **Cow Creek Ranch** (505-757-2107), 975 Forest Road 92, Pecos. If you choose to visit this well-weathered and well-loved mountain guest ranch in the Santa Fe National Forest, you will have a vacation to remember all year long. Cow Creek is an Orvis-approved historic fly-fishing guest ranch about 40 miles from Santa Fe off I-25. Open May 21–August 21. It

HISTORIC HOTELS

Plaza Hotel (800-328-1882 or 505-425-3591; www.plazahotel-nm.com), on the Old Town Plaza at 230 Plaza, Las Vegas. Built in 1882, when it was known as "The Belle of the Southwest," this is a great Victorian hotel renovated to preserve a clean, not fussy, nineteenth-century atmosphere. Now under new management, the Plaza has a swell new restaurant: The Range Café at the Plaza Hotel; with a lobby coffee bar, Byron T's Saloon (named for the resident ghost), high-speed Wi-Fi, room service, on-site masseur, and the fun of returning to those glorious days of yesteryear makes this an excellent choice for travelers. You can even stay in one of four suites overlooking the Plaza. Pet-friendly! $100–$149. ✆ 🐾

St James Hotel (866-472-5019 or 575-376-2664), 617 S. Collinson, Cimarron. Every outlaw who was any outlaw stayed at the St. James, as did Buffalo Bill Cody, Annie Oakley, Kit Carson, and Wyatt Earp. Photos of desperadoes and heroes line the downstairs hallway, decked with an antique roulette wheel. Mounted trophy heads adorn the period lobby. The beds are quilt-covered, the curtains draped in lace, and the rooms of the old hotel are not very soundproof. Twenty-seven bullet holes may be seen in the dining room. Fourteen restored rooms with nineteenth-century furnishings occupy the main hotel; a two-story annex adjacent provides an additional ten rooms. The St. James is located smack dab on the Old Sante Fe Trail. Begun as a saloon in 1873, established by Lincoln's chef, Henri Lambert, this place became a haven for Sante Fe Trail traders and mountain men. It has been featured on *Unsolved Mysteries* and is reportedly highly haunted. An elegant restaurant serves dinner, with a decent salad bar, and a comfortable café, plus a legendary bar provide venues for all sorts of social gatherings, though "dancing naked on the bar is no longer permitted." $80–$120.

🐾 **The Eklund Historic Hotel & Restaurant** (575-374-2551; 855-374-2551), 15 Main Street, Clayton. Pristine restoration of this twenty-four-room, 1894 railroad hotel is essential to the wild west experience. A cowboy is said to have ridden his horse into the lobby some time in the 1930s, the bar is iconic, and the dining room replete with tarnished grandeur. Excellent burgers and chile, too. Open mic Thurs. nights. Worth the trip to Clayton. Your hosts Jeanette and Keith Burras will do everything in their power to make your stay comfortable. Pet friendly. $100.

Casteñeda Hotel (505-425-8631), 524 Railroad Avenue, Las Vegas. Falling into increasing disrepair, the once-proud Casteñeda, an original Harvey House railroad hotel built in 1898, was closed for many years. Now in the hands of preservationist hotelier Allan Affeldt, the hotel is looking forward to great things. As of press time, restoration and installation of a fine restaurant are in process.

has twenty guest rooms, each with a kiva fireplace. The ranch bell chimes when it's time to dine. All meals are included, and there are enough outdoor activities to keep you busy all day, including riding, mountain biking, and children's programs, so you can enjoy a deeply restful slumber. Fishing trips offered beyond the full-service season. Minimum two-night stay weekdays. Minimum three-night stay weekends. $1,260; children over age four only.

🐾 **Los Pinos Guest Ranch** (505-757-6213), 20 Pecos Lane, Terrero; 45 miles from Santa Fe, 20 miles north of Pecos via NM 63. Since the 1920s, this small family-run guest ranch on the Pecos River in Cowles, with only 12 aspen log rooms, has been delighting guests with its superb birding, fly-fishing on the Upper Pecos River, hiking from trailheads right on the property, wildflowers, riding, and fine dining on home cooking prepared by dedicated owner Alice McSweeney. Breakfast and dinner are served in the lodge. The rooms have neither phones nor televisions. This is a perfect place to be cared for, and to renew and retreat. Guided horseback trail rides available. Rates include all meals. Open June 1–September 30. $145 per day; children over age five, $50–$80.

Pendaries Lodge (800-753-0447), Rociada. Go 12 miles north of Las Vegas on NM 518, then left at Sapello onto NM 94/105 for 12.5 miles. Go left into Pendaries Village and follow the signs. Justifiably well known for its golf course, Pendaries is a secluded, quiet, unpretentious lodge with eighteen rooms plus additional accommodations in summer homes. The restaurant serves dinner daily, and breakfast and lunch are available in the Club House. The Moosehead Saloon must be seen to be appreciated and is certainly the place for a drink. Golf packages are available at this challenging high mountain golf course tucked away in the Sangre de Cristo Mountains. $82–$99.

CABINS AND CAMPING **Pecos Cabins** (505-988-7517). Open May 1–October 30. Offering nine fully furnished, renovated log cabins overlooking the Pecos River a mile from Tererro, near Pecos, this is a place that can comfortably accommodate families and larger groups. Rustic comfort is the word. There is a three-night minimum, and reservations are required. $190.

Pendaries RV Resort (505-454-8304), 3 Park Place, NM 105, Rociada, 22 miles north of Las Vegas, NM 105, Rociada. Open May 1–November 1. With fifty RV units and six comfortable, two-bedroom, two-bath cottages. Jean Pendaries (Pan-da-rey) moved from France to build the Plaza Hotel in Las Vegas, then in 1875 moved to the Rociada area, still a gorgeous, quiet hideaway deep in the northern New Mexico mountains. There he built a sawmill and gristmill, which can still be seen near Pendaries Village. And today those visiting here can enjoy the high mountain golfing as well as serenity you dream about. Cottage $125; RV pad $32.

✱ Where to Eat

EATING OUT **Charlie's Bakery & Cafe** (505-426-1921), 715 Douglas Avenue. Open daily. B, L, D. Excellent green chile, tortillas so fresh you can watch them being made, a showcase of pastry delights, and Starbucks coffee. This is a local hangout for college students, professors, and old-timers, where everyone knows one another by their first name. Service is inconsistent; sometimes quicker than others. It is a clean, pleasant, spacious place that is a sentimental longtime favorite frequently referred to by its former name, the "Spic 'n Span." Charlie's is just about always open. Inexpensive.

Dick's Pub & Restaurant (505-425-8261), 705 Douglas Avenue, Las Vegas. Mon.–Sat. 11–9. Closed Sundays. One of the best sandwich shops in the state fronts the funky bar that is a favorite with college students and hard-cores. Order to go for a picnic. Ask about the imaginative daily specials, and anything with avocado. Everything is fresh, homemade, and fabulous. Love the cream of asparagus soup! Inexpensive.

Range Café at the Plaza Hotel. (575-425-3591). Local chain of Albuquerque-Bernalillo based eateries now offers casual-elegant dining at the Plaza. A good bet. Moderate.

Frankie's at the Casanova (505-757-3322), 12 S. Main, Pecos. Sun.–Thurs. 8–2. B, L. Fri.–Sat. 8–2, 5:30–8:15. B, L, D. Housed in the old Casanova Bar dating to the 1920s, Frankie's is an authentic Southwestern grill with a spiffy new outdoor patio bar serving a good selection of beer and wine. Go for the piñon pancakes for Sunday brunch. The chile, red or green, is hot and flavorful, and the fajitas practically sizzle off the plate. Live music Fri., Sat., and Sun. nights. Moderate.

🍽 **Kocina de Raphael** (505-454-1667), 610 Legion Drive, Las Vegas. B, L, D. Closed Sundays. Off the beaten path. A little tricky to find, but if you like humongous portions, worth the search. Packed with generations of families, who know a good deal. All traditional New Mexico fare served here. Inexpensive.

Teresa's Tamales (575-387-2754), 3296 NM 518, Cleveland. 8–5. Closed Sundays. You might have to search for a parking place between the big pickup trucks if you arrive during lunchtime. Excellent tamales, plus plates of traditional homemade New Mexico food. Consider calling your order in. Teresa makes everything to order in her closet-sized kitchen. Inexpensive.

Traveler's Café (505-426-8638), 1814 Plaza Street, Las Vegas. Excellent coffee, fresh-baked treats—cookies, croissants, scones—quiche, frittata, homemade soups, copies of the *New York Times*. A favorite stop of mine. Wi-Fi. While popular with college kids, this seems to be the adult café of choice.

✳ Selective Shopping

New Moon Fashions (505-454-0669), 132 Bridge Street, Las Vegas. Whether you're looking for a cut-velvet outfit for a wedding or a linen jacket, this boutique is fun to shop. Colorful, international-style travel clothing purchased here will set you apart at the party and bring compliments. One of my favorite shops. Reasonable.

Plaza Antiques (505-454-9447), 1805 Plaza Street, Las Vegas. The altar of the old Our Lady of Sorrows church stands as part of the back wall of this superb emporium. The best selection of Fred Harvey–era turquoise and silver bracelets I've seen, and the emporium is filled with alluring treasures from cowboy nostalgia to quilts.

Rough Rider Antiques (505-454-8063), 501 Railroad Avenue, Las Vegas, across the street from the restored Train Depot and Visitor Center. Walk in and surrender. This spacious, freshly restored historic building holds the premier collection of antiques, sold by assorted consigners, in a town jam-packed with antiques shops. Whatever your interest—vintage postcard collecting, finding that embroidered Mexican felt jacket from the 1950s, a fiesta skirt, or a Fiesta pitcher—your chances of finding it here are quite good. Prices are fair, and fun is guaranteed.

Tapetes de Lana (575-387-2247), NM 518 Junction 434, or Main Street, Mora. Check out the handmade rugs, table runners, and shawls, in beautiful, natural colors at reasonable prices. Factory direct yarn store. This is a wonderful place to find local craft gifts. Tours of the mill are available here during the week. This is a nonprofit organization that is an important local employer.

Tome on the Range (505-454-9944), 247 Plaza Street, Las Vegas. The only independent bookstore between Santa Fe and Colorado Springs. Regional literature, trendy reads, and kids' section, plus cute gifts and tchotchkes.

Gallery 140 (505-425-1085), 140 Bridge Street, Las Vegas. The gallery of the Las Vegas Arts Council showcases local artists and sponsors events of local interest.

El Zocalo Cooperative Art Gallery (505-454-9904), 1809 Plaza Street, Las Vegas. Well worth a visit. Pottery, jewelry, painting, cards, photography. Quality local work, always something interesting to look at.

Terrero General Store (505-431-1132), 14 miles north of Pecos via NM 63, 1911 NM 63, Terrero. Open May 31–September 30. Started in 1940, this remains a family-run business where you can outfit for an overnight camping trip at 10,500 feet in the Pecos Wilderness.

Paper Trail, 166 Bridge Street, Las Vegas. Whimsical assortment of cards, mugs, journals, wrappings, clever gift ideas, and much more.

Unikat Fine Jewelry (505-425-6113), 160 Bridge Street, Las Vegas. Handmade, contemporary unique designs sure to get noticed and enhance personal style.

ROUTE 66 COUNTRY

Santa Rosa, Tucumcari

etting your kicks is no problem out here. You'll find plenty of vintage neon and a culture that celebrates the Route 66 era and life on the Mother Road. In addition, Santa Rosa and Conchas Dam have swimming and boating and a way to stay cool. It's hundreds of miles of nostalgia.

GUIDANCE **Santa Rosa Visitor Information Center** (575-472-3763), 1085 Blue Hole Road, Santa Rosa, is a sophisticated stop with all the information and contacts you could want to experience the area fully.

Tucumcari/Quay County Chamber of Commerce (575-461-1694), 404 W. Route 66. Open Mon.–Sat. 9–5; closed Sundays. Tucumcari is a traveler-friendly, professional road stop.

MEDICAL EMERGENCY **Dr. Dan C. Trigg Memorial Hospital** (575-461-7000), 301 E. Miel de Luna, Tucumcari.

Guadalupe County Hospital (575-472-3246), 535 Lake Drive, Santa Rosa.

❊ To See

TOWNS **Santa Rosa**, 114 miles east of Albuquerque on I-40. This railroad-era Fourth Street Business District with its Ilfield Warehouse and many old storefronts has been known as a Route 66 stop since 1926, when the Mother Road first came through. Many landmarks are still visible in Santa Rosa, where part of the film *Grapes of Wrath* was shot. Plenty of colorful Route 66 establishments are still going strong in Santa Rosa, and it is, unexpectedly, known for its lakes and water sports, in particular, the Blue Hole of scuba diving fame.

Tucumcari, 173 miles east of Albuquerque on I-40. With probably the most and best-preserved vintage Route 66–era neon, including several installations that have recently been refurbished, Tucumcari is the largest town closest to the eastern border of the state. Nostalgia rules when the Blue Swallow Motel lights up at twilight. There is good access here to Conchas Lake State Park, Ute Lake State Park, and the Mesalands Scenic Byway, with plenty of wildlife viewing and excellent birding. Tucumcari has, in addition to marvelous Route 66–era architecture, with a restaurant shaped like a sombrero and a curio shop shaped like a teepee, plus the longest mural devoted to Route 66 in the United States at its convention center. Two museums of note are here—the Mesalands Dinosaur Museum and the Tucumcari Historical Museum. The name of the town is possibly derived from a Comanche term meaning "lookout point" or "signal peak." Tucumcari Mountain was, in fact, used as a lookout for Comanche war parties. The town's original name was "Six Shooter Siding."

MUSEUMS ⚲ **Mesalands Dinosaur Museum** (575-461-3466), 222 E. Laughlin Avenue, Tucumcari. Open Labor Day–February Tues.–Sat. 12–5; March–Labor Day 10–6. Closed

GOTTA LOVE THE CLASSIC NEON SIGNS OF TUCUMCARI

Sundays and Mondays. Who doesn't love a dinosaur? An in-depth collection of dinosaur skeletons, fossils, sculptures, and exhibits are shown at Mesalands College. $6.50 adults, $5.50 seniors age 65+, $4 children and teens, under age 5 free.

Route 66 Auto Museum and Malt Shop (575-472-1966), 2436 Will Rogers Drive, Santa Rosa. Sat.–Sun. 8–5. Winter hours December–February Tues.–Sun. 10–4. If you love vintage autos, this is the place for you. While dedicated to the preservation of Route 66 custom cars and memorabilia, this museum serves darn fine chocolate malts. $5.

Tucumcari Historical Museum (575-461-4201), 416 S. Adams Street, Tucumcari. Tues.–Sat. 9–3. Closed Sundays and Mondays. If you like looking into the way people lived in the past, from their parlors to their kitchens, you will enjoy this sentimental collection of treasures: furniture, farm and ranch exhibits, Indian artifacts, and early town memorabilia. Free.

SCENIC DRIVES **Mesalands Scenic Byway**, 320 miles total, in Quay and Guadalupe counties. *Mesa*, meaning "table" in Spanish, is the term used to describe high, flat plateaus. This is the country of high lonesome, a dry, dramatic, and evocative landscape. On the southern edge of this scenic byway is the El Llano Estacado, or the Staked Plains, a 32,000-mile mesa. *Estacado* refers to the cap rock, a geologic feature throughout this area. The habitat of pronghorn antelope and sandhill cranes, this byway encompasses Santa Rosa in Guadalupe County and Tucumcari in Quay County.

✳ To Do

BOATING See the state parks listed under *Green Space*.

Santa Rosa Park Lake Historic District (505-988-6701). Will Rogers and Lake Drive. Open for swimming Memorial Day–mid-September. Certified lifeguards are in attendance, and Park Lake is the Southwest's largest swimming pool featuring a free water slide. Kids and seniors can fish in two stocked ponds. You can rent a pedal boat for $1 each half-hour. No overnight camping. Free.

GOLFING **Tucumcari Municipal Golf Course** (575-461-1849), 4465 Route 66. Five miles west of Tucumcari. Closed Mondays. This pleasant, tree-lined nine-hole golf course with the greens located between high mesas will satisfy your need to putt while in town. Greens fees for nine holes $9–16.

❋ Green Space

MOUNTAINS **Sugarite Canyon State Park** (575-445-5607), northeast of Raton on NM 72 for 11 miles. 211 NM 526, Raton. Although the area endured the Track Fire the summer of 2011, the area is still popular for camping, fishing, and hiking. During the height of summer, this is a busy place, with coal camp tours, kids' programs, and occasional evening talks by local historians and naturalists. From the wild iris of late May to wild rose, bluebell, larkspur, scarlet penstemon, blue flax, and sunflowers and aster, Sugarite is unbeatable for wildflowers. Butterflies love it here, too.

There is year-round trout fishing on Lake Maloya, one of three alpine jewel lakes surrounded by an extended cliff of basaltic rock. Hikers and mountain bikers have access to more than 12 miles of trails. Motorless boats are OK. Kayaking is becoming more popular. This is the only place in New Mexico where you can explore the ruins of a coal mining camp. The former camp post office is the colorful visitor center, with vintage photo displays. The first mine in the canyon opened in 1901, with full-scale mining beginning in 1912 with the building of the Sugarite Coal Camp. In its prime, 500 people lived, worked, shopped, worshipped, and went to school here. It was a melting pot of Italians, Slavs, Japanese, Mexican, and British. The coal camp ended in 1941, when oil replaced coal. $5 day use per vehicle; $14–18 overnight camping.

Villanueva State Park (575-421-2957), Villanueva. Take I-25 exit 323, go south 23 miles, then 15 miles south on NM 3. Nestled between 400-foot-high red and gold sandstone bluffs along the Pecos River near the Spanish colonial village of Villanueva is a picturesque, remote campground shaded by giant cottonwoods along the Pecos River. This park is a nature-dominated haven with fishing, hiking trails within views of old ranching ruins, and one trail that leads to a prehistoric Indian ruin. The 2.5-mile Canyon Trail loops from the river to the top of the canyon and back. Kayaking and canoeing are enjoyed when the water level is high enough, from early May–mid-June, usually. $5 day use; $14–18 overnight camping.

RIVERS AND LAKES **Cimarron Canyon State Park** (575-377-6271), 3 miles east of Eagle Nest on US 64, 28869 NM 64, eagle Nest. Open year-round. The clear Cimarron River runs through the 8 miles of forested land on both sides of US 64, with abundant elk, deer, turkey, grouse, and bear for the sighting. Two billion years of complex geology are visible here, notably, the 400-foot-high crenellated granite Palisades. But the Cimarron is best known for its excellent fly-fishing for German brown and rainbow in a variety of waters: gravel pits, beaver ponds, and running streams. For peace, wildflower viewing, and getting away from it all, whether for a day or a longer stay, the Cimarron can't be beat. Many campers make long stays; make reservations early. The ninety-six sites in several campgrounds—Maverick and Tolby are favorites—offer good river access. The 2018 Ute Park Fire burned 37,000 acres in the area and has impacted the canyon and accommodations. $5 day use; $8–18 overnight camping.

UNIQUE ADVENTURES

Dinosaur Trackway (575-374-8808), Clayton Lake State Park. (See **Clayton Lake State Park** under *Green Space*.) More than 100 million years ago, this area was an inland sea extending from the Gulf of Mexico to Canada. The creatures that roamed here left their footprints, and at least eight different species have been identified among the 500 dinosaur tracks that have been preserved, including some of the winged pterodactyl. The tracks are located on the dam spillway, at the end of a gentle 0.25-mile trail. The best times to view the tracks, when they are most clearly visible, are in morning and late-afternoon light. 🐾 ♿

NRA Whittington Center (575-445-3615), 10 miles southwest of Raton on US 64. Shooting ranges and lessons in all sorts of weaponry are offered. Lodging, camping, and RV hookups are available, too. Many of the world's top competitions are played here. A variety of ranges available—skeet, sporting clays, black powder pistol, and more.

Santa Rosa Blue Hole (575-472-3763), Will Rogers Highway, Santa Rosa. A unique geological phenomenon—a natural bell-shaped artesian pool 82 feet deep with a constant water temperature of 62 degrees Fahrenheit year-round and visibility of 80 feet, making it ideal for training. Winter is most popular time. It is in the high desert at 4,600 feet above sea level, making the bottom equivalent to over 100 feet of ocean depth. Winter is actually the busiest season. The Santa Rosa Dive Center is open weekends to rent gear and fill tanks, and midweek by appointment. Go to the visitor center to purchase permits, 8–5 Mon.–Fri. Permits $50 weekly or $20 per day. To dive in the Blue Hole, you must have PADI or NAUI or other certification papers.

Clayton Lake State Park (575-374-8808; reservations 877-664-7787), 141 Clayton Lake Road, Clayton. Twelve miles northwest of Clayton on NM 370. Fishing and boating March–October; hiking, camping, Dinosaur Trackway. One-hundred-seventy-acre lake, a blue jewel in the desert. Boats are restricted to trolling speeds (no whitewater). During winter, the lake is a migration point for waterfowl. It's an excellent place to spot bald eagles. The Dinosaur Trackway and boardwalk along the gentle half-mile trail provide extensive information. Among rolling grasslands near Santa Fe Trail, the lake is a waterfowl resting area in winter. $5 day; $8–18 overnight camping.

Conchas Lake State Park (575-868-2270), 501 Bell Ranch Road, Conchas Dam. New Mexico State Park and Recreation Division, Conchas Dam. Thirty-two miles northeast of Tucumcari on NM 104. This is an outstanding getaway and prime recreation spot for fishing, boating, waterskiing, wind surfing, and swimming, with 60 miles of shoreline and plenty of coves, canyons, and sandy beaches to explore. Both north and south recreation areas have well-developed marinas, stores, cafés, camping, and picnic areas. South Conchas Lodge (505-868-2988) has cozy rooms as well, plus 110 RV units. Completed in 1939 by the Army Corps of Engineers, Conchas Dam rises 200 feet above the Canadian River. The lake covers about 15 square miles, extending 4 miles up the Canadian River and 11 miles up the Conchas River. Open year-round for fishing. Abundant walleye, catfish, and largemouth bass swim the waters. Have fun! $5 day use; $8–18 overnight camping.

Coyote Creek State Park (575-387-2328), NM 434, 17 miles north of Mora on NM 434. At 7,700 feet in the eastern foothills of the Sangre de Cristo Mountains, find in this off-the-beaten-path park mountain trout fishing in the most densely stocked fishing area of the state, lovely solitude, camping, picnicking, and a 1.5-mile, easy trail through ponderosa pine. $5 day use; $8–18 overnight camping.

Santa Rosa Lake State Park (575-472-3110), Santa Rosa. The lake is actually a high plains Pecos River reservoir 7 miles from Santa Rosa on NM 91, with waterskiing, wind surfing, and excellent fishing. Canoeing, too! Stay a while with seventy-six developed camping sites and twenty-five electric sites, restrooms, showers, and a visitor center. The easy to moderate hiking trails offer wildlife viewing through 500 acres of parkland. Here also is one of the state's few designated equestrian trails and all necessary accommodations for horses. There are two short paved wheelchair-accessible trails as well. $5 day use; $8-18 overnight camping.

Storrie Lake State Park (575-425-7278), north of Las Vegas on NM 518. Wind surfing, fishing, boating, waterskiing, picnicking. Camping and RVs. The park is open to all boating, with no horsepower restrictions, so it is geared for wind surfers and waterskiers. Kayaks and canoes are also popular here. There is year-round trout fishing as well. $5 day use; $8–18 overnight camping.

Ute Lake State Park (575-487-2284), 30 miles northeast of Tucumcari via US 54, then 3 miles west of Logan via NM 540; 1800 540 Loop, Logan. This 13-mile-long, narrow lake, producer of many state record fish, is a happy local camping destination with boating, welcome swimming in the summer heat, hiking, wildlife viewing, and fishing for walleye, bass, and catfish. $5 day use; $8–18 overnight camping.

WILDER PLACES **Canadian River Canyon** runs 13 miles through the Kiowa National Grasslands, approximately 10 miles northwest of Roy. The 800-foot canyon is a natural wildlife refuge in the prairie for mountain lion, wild turkey, eagles, and waterfowl. Mills Canyon Campground, offering primitive overnight camping, is located at the bottom of the gorge. A remnant herd of Barbary sheep roams through this stark, remote, and unforgettable place.

Kiowa and Rita Blanca National Grasslands (575-374-9652), 15 miles south of Clayton via NM 402 or east via US 87. Rita Blanca is 17 miles east of Clayton via US 64/56. For those who want to put their feet on the trail, here are 2 miles of Santa Fe Trail ruts, plus grasslands. In their entirety, these grasslands stretch through New Mexico, Texas, and Oklahoma. The New Mexico section of the Kiowa National Grassland

IT'S FUN TO COOL OFF IN THE CIMARRON RIVER

covers 136,562 acres near Roy and Clayton, with plenty of habitat for wildlife. This land was purchased by the federal government during the Great Depression following the Dust Bowl, removed from farm cultivation, planted, and maintained as grasslands.

WILDLIFE REFUGES AND AREAS **Colin Neblett Wildlife Area** (www.stateparks .com/colin_neblett_state_wildlife_area_in_new_mexico.html). These 36,000 acres between Eagle Nest and Cimarron along US 64 include Cimarron Canyon State Park, making it the largest state-run wildlife area for deer, elk, and other forest critters. The Cimarron River, a great German brown fishery, runs through it. Bring binoculars and cameras, and try your luck with a Rio Grande King.

Elliott S. Barker Wildlife Area (505-476-8000), 14 miles northwest of Cimarron. Here, in the heart of the northeast, find over 5,000 acres of hiking, hunting, wildlife viewing, and, should you choose, horseback riding. High-clearance vehicles are strongly recommended, as the roads can be rocky and the streams can swell in this pristine and primitive area. There's a good chance you'll spot bear up here. I have.

Valle Vidal (575-758-6200), 27 miles north of Cimarron off US 64. The name of this unit of the Carson National Forest means "valley of life." If you've ever longed to see herds of magnificent, noble elk in their natural setting, this is your best bet, particularly at twilight. The Valle Vidal is 100,000 acres of specially managed prime elk habitat, home to a herd of 1,700 elk, in the Carson National Forest. Also, in season, find fishing and backcountry camping. A word of warning: be sure your spare tire is in good working order. Perhaps it is our karma, perhaps it is the loose rocks in the road, but we get a flat every time we come up here. If you drive the entirety, from north of Cimarron across to Costilla, you'll put 64 miles on your vehicle.

❋ Lodging

BED & BREAKFASTS, INNS, AND MOTELS **Blue Swallow Motel** (575-461-9849), 815 E. Route 66, Tucumcari. Owned and operated by Lillian Redman, a former Harvey Girl, for over 40 years; current owners keep the tradition of this Route 66 beacon alive. With its classic Route 66 neon, the 1939 humble stucco motel, with eight rooms, preserves its comfy, vintage character. $75–129.

CABINS AND CAMPING **Santa Rosa Campground** (888-898-1999 or 575-472-3126), 2136 Route 66, Santa Rosa. Open year-round. With the extra added attractions of the Western Bar-B-Q (served each evening 5–8), homemade peach cobbler (in the restaurant with an outdoor patio), beer and wine, plus free Wi-Fi, you can enjoy all manner of camping. There are seventy pull-through RV sites, tent sites, and a cabin where you can get out of the camper and stretch out for a while. There's a gift shop, playground, heated swimming pool, laundry facilities and 50-amp services, groceries, and supplies here as well. $30.

❋ Where to Eat

EATING OUT ❧ **Del's Restaurant & Gift Shop** (575-461-1740), 1202 E. Route 66, Tucumcari. L, D. Closed Sundays. If you are actually eating a meal in Tucumcari, Del's is your best bet. This place, a standard roadside family diner that retains its original 1956 flavor (courtesy of the owners, sisters Yvonne and Yvette), serves reliably good homemade American cooking, the kind you long to find on a cross-country drive, as popular with locals as with travelers. The burgers are juicy, and the chicken-fried steak with mashed potatoes and cream gravy is a triumph, as good as the best on the road. Even liver is on the menu! Yummy beef taquitas, too. The salad bar is more than respectable, and two homemade soups are included. Inexpensive–Moderate.

Joseph's Bar & Grill (505-472-1234), 865 Will Rogers Drive, Santa Rosa. I usually eat here when I'm in town, and by now I can't tell if it's for the food or the nostalgia. This establishment is the offspring of the original Joseph's, and it does lean a bit on its reputation. You won't go wrong with the enchiladas, and don't pass up the gift shop. Expect a good helping of local friendliness. Inexpensive–Moderate.

La Cita (575-461-7866), 812 S. 1st Street, Tucumcari. L, D. You'll want to have your picture taken here, for sure, so you can show the world you actually dined in a sombrero. The Mexican food isn't the greatest, and some think the portions are too small for the price, but it's not bad, either, and you'll have so much fun you probably won't notice. The neon was part of the Route 66 sign restoration project. Inexpensive.

Pow Wow Restaurant & Lizard Lounge (575-461-2587), 801 Route 66, Tucumcari. L, D. This place is dark and would be smoky, if smoking were allowed. It is, and always has been, the premier town hangout, the place where visiting politicians rub elbows with the locals, the cowboys, the Indian traders, and the Route 66 tourists from Germany. It is also a good place to order a steak. Lunch buffet daily, more than decent New Mexico food. Mother Road art. Moderate.

Silver Moon Cafe (575-472-3162), 3501 Will Rogers Drive, Santa Rosa. Open daily. B, L, D. Serving travelers since 1959, with that cool Route 66 neon lighting up the night and home-cooked meals lighting up smiles. Spiffy gift shop. Tasty Mexican and American food served here.

❋ Entertainment

Aside from occasional live performance events at the **Shuler Theater** in Raton, the best we are likely to come up with

in the way of nightlife is a drink at the bar of the historic hotel or the chance to catch a movie at a vintage theater, such as the **El Raton**. The Shuler, too, has recently installed state-of-the art digital screening equipment, and is once again a movie palace. Mostly, folks go to bed early here, so it's a good place to catch up on your reading or do some stargazing. You can catch a first run, independent, or classic film at the **Indigo Theater** (505-434-4444); 146 Bridge Street, Las Vegas, a boutique theater that is an experience in itself.

❋ Selective Shopping

Tee Pee Curios (575-461-3773), 924 E. Route 66, Tucumcari. Not only is this a classic Route 66 photo op, with the front of the shop a white concrete teepee painted in bright turquoise lettering, but inside you can find every T-shirt, shot glass, key chain, and travel souvenir of your road trip that you could ever imagine. A highly amusing must-do. Its neon was one of the nine restored Route 66 signs.

❋ Special Events

January: **Ice Fishing Tournament and Chile Dinner** (575-377-2420), Eagle Nest. Look for this event midmonth, all you frozen fish lovers.

February: **Moonlight Ski Tours and Headlamp Snowshoe Tours** (575-754-2374), Enchanted Forest XC Ski and Snowshoe Area, Red River.

May: Guided ruins tours and cultural demonstrations, Pecos National Historical Park (505-757-7241), weekends, Memorial Day–Labor Day.

June: **Mule Days** (888-376-2417), Maverick Rodeo Grounds, Cimarron. **Raton Rodeo** (580-795-5703), York Canyon Rodeo Grounds, Raton. **Las Vegas Celebrates the Arts** (505-425-1085), Las Vegas, tours of artist studios. **Fort**

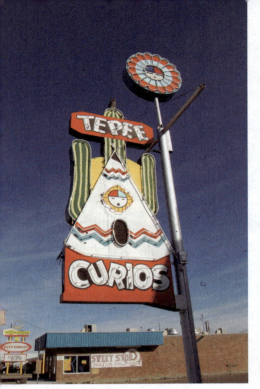

TEE PEE CURIOS IN TUCUMCARI IS WHERE TO GET YOUR SOUVENIRS OF THE MOTHER ROAD

Union Days (505-425-8025), Fort Union National Monument, Watrous. **Santa Fe Trail Rendezvous** (575-445-3615), Raton, mountain man gathering, NRA Whittington Center.

July: **Maverick Club Parade and Rodeo** (888-376-2417), Fourth of July, Maverick Arena, NM 64, Cimarron. Longest running open rodeo in the West. **Fourth of July Parade and Fireworks** (575-377-2420), Eagle Nest. **Route 66 Celebration** (877-795-2200), Convention Center, 1500 W. Route 66, Tucumcari.

August: **Las Vegas Places with a Past: Historic Home and Buildings Tour** (505-425-8803; www.lasvegasnm .org), Las Vegas, first Sat. **Colfax County Fair** (575-445-8071), Springer Armory, Springer. Cakewalk, parade, pie contest, barbecue dinner; second weekend. **Music From Angel Fire** (888-377-3300; www .musicfromangelfire.org). Outstanding

classical music performances throughout northern New Mexico in Raton, Las Vegas, Angel Fire, late August–early September.

September: **Cimarron Days Festival** (888-376-2417), Village Park, NM 64, Cimarron, Labor Day weekend. **Raspberry Roundup**, (575-387-2900) Salman Ranch, Labor Day weekend into September, generally the first three weeks of the month. Fresh raspberries and raspberry treats abound in country store at La Cueva Historic District. **Cleveland Roller Mill Festival** (575-387-2645), Cleveland, Labor Day weekend. This is the only weekend of the year when the creaky old mill operates, and it is a true festival of northern New Mexico dance, food, and crafts. **Wagon Mound Bean Days** (www .beanday100.com/), Wagon Mound, celebrates the days when Wagon Mound was the bean capital of the world, with barbecue worth waiting in line for, crafts, parade, and politicians aboard floats. **Nara Visa Cowboy Poetry Gathering** (505-633-2272) Nara Visa, third weekend. As much local color, with music and rhyme, as you can find anywhere. **Annual Route 66 Festival** (visitsantarosanm .com). Come on out and get your kicks here in Santa Rosa. **Shortgrass Music Festival,** (575-376-2417) Cimarron.

October: **Clayton Arts Festival** (575-374-9253), Clayton, first weekend. A long-established, much-anticipated, profuse display of western art. **Artesanos del Valle Tour**, Las Vegas area, first weekend. Diverse and wonderful artists' studio tour.

November–December: **City of Bethlehem** (575-445-3689), Raton. Thanksgiving weekend through Christmas holidays, enjoy a nostalgic tour of life-size cartoon characters that guide the way up into Climax Canyon, where the Christmas story is presented high in the rocky hills, accompanied by seasonal music. This free event is an annual family favorite. **Christmas on the Chicorica**—1,500 luminarias (575-445-5607).

INDEX

Italics indicate illustrations and maps